Software Design

INTERNATIONAL COMPUTER SCIENCE SERIES

Consulting Editor **A D McGettrick** University of Strathclyde

SELECTED TITLES IN THE SERIES

L

3703302734

Software Design

David Budgen

PEARSON
Addison
Wesley

Harlow, England • London • New York • Boston • San Francisco • Toronto
Sydney • Tokyo • Singapore • Hong Kong • Seoul • Taipei • New Delhi
Cape Town • Madrid • Mexico City • Amsterdam • Munich • Paris • Milan

Pearson Education Limited
Edinburgh Gate
Harlow
Essex CM20 2JE
England

and Associated Companies throughout the world

Visit us on the World Wide Web at:
www.pearsoned.co.uk

First published 1993
Second edition 2003

© Addison-Wesley Publishers Limited 1993
© Pearson Education Limited 2003

The programs in this book have been included for their instructional value. They have been
tested with care but are not guaranteed for any particular purpose. The publisher does not
offer any warranties or representations nor does it accept any liabilities with respect to the
programs.

All trademarks used herein are the property of their respective owners. The use of any
trademark in this text does not vest in the author or publisher any trademark ownership
rights in such trademarks, nor does the use of such trademarks imply any affiliation with
or endorsement of this book by such owners.

ISBN 0 201 72219 4

British Library Cataloguing-in-Publication Data
A catalogue record for this book is available from the British Library

Library of Congress Cataloging-in-Publication Data
Budgen, D. (David)
      Software design / David Budgen.—2nd ed.
          p. cm.
      Includes bibliographical references and index.
      ISBN 0–201–72219–4 (alk. paper)
      1. Computer software—Development.   I. Title.

   QA76.76.D47B83   2003
   005.1′2—dc21   2003041859

10   9   8   7   6   5   4   3   2   1
08   07   06   05   04   03

Typeset in 10/12pt Sabon by 35
Printed and bound in Great Britain by Biddles Ltd., Guildford and King's Lynn

The publisher's policy is to use paper manufactured from sustainable forests.

Contents

Preface to the Second Edition

'Science is built up of facts as a house is built of stones, but an accumulation of facts is no more a science than a heap of stones is a house.'

Jules Henri Poincaré (1854–1912)

At times, it is hard not to feel that our knowledge about designing software is rather too close to being a heap of stones. Indeed, a large element in the motivation for the first edition of this book was the desire to gather, classify, categorize, and interpret that knowledge, in the hope of providing a structure that would be of assistance to others. While the end result was certainly far from being a 'house', it did perhaps resemble a low wall or two!

Indeed, the production of this second edition (which I hope builds the walls a little higher at least), was motivated by the way that the first edition of this book has been generally well received by both teachers and students (a situation which is gratifying to any author!). In terms of its wider role, one of the more external signs of the recognition of its 'foundational' status is the extent to which it was cited in the Trial Version of the IEEE's SWEBOK (Software Engineering Body of Knowledge).

However, technology and design thinking march on, albeit not always at the same rate and, in preparing this second edition, the material from the first edition has been extensively revised and rewritten to reflect the many changes that have occurred since it was published. So what are the major changes? In brief, these are as follows.

- A much stronger recognition of the role played by the concept of *architectural style* in helping to structure our ideas about software design. This is used to provide an underpinning framework throughout this second edition.

- The inclusion of new forms of 'software' and of new approaches to design, ranging from *agile methods* and *design patterns* through to the component concept and the use of the *Unified Modeling Language*.

- An improved formalism to support the analysis of the processes embodied in design methods.

It would be nice if this list could also include the use of a suitably extensive body of empirical evidence about the effectiveness and limitations of the design approaches described. Indeed, where any such evidence is available, I have sought to give it due prominence. Unfortunately though, this particular field of research is one that remains only sparsely cultivated, not least because of the difficulties implicit in such research. Maybe in a future edition . . .

Obviously there has also had to be a degree of restructuring and reorganization of the existing material in order to accommodate the new. The number of design methods described has been slightly reduced, reflecting a more general reduction in the emphasis placed upon procedural methods by practitioners. The chapter on design representations has been restructured and also extended to include some new forms of notation. And the overall grouping of chapters has changed the book from a two-part structure to one of three parts. The bibliography has also been extensively updated, and, wherever possible, I have quoted from original source material in order to provide the supporting evidence for any assertions that might be made. Again, source material in a form readily accessible to the student, such as journals and textbooks, has been preferred where possible to less widely available forms such as conference proceedings.

What has *not* changed is what may be considered as the unique strength of this book, in that it seeks to describe the domain of software design in a scholarly and non-partisan manner. In an area that is so apt to be inundated with hype, and with advocacy so often replacing systematic evaluation, this role seems a particularly important one, as was indeed recognized by the authors of the design chapter of the SWEBOK (I should add here that this was a production in which I had no part!). Returning for a moment to the opening quotation, my aim for this book was at least to construct the foundational walls that would in time permit a more objective and systematic study of software design. Even if that goal has not been fully met in all aspects, at least the stones have been sorted into appropriate heaps!

However, I hope that the result is not a dry and dusty tome. Software design is a topic that readily begets enthusiasm among practitioners and students, not least because it is one of the most creative forms of activity possible in any technical sphere. It is certainly one that offers exciting opportunities to both the practitioner and the researcher, as should be evident in the pages that follow.

One last point, returning to the issue of source material, concerns the citation of websites, a vexed question for any author! During the development of this revised edition, I consulted a range of websites, some of which 'disappeared' during the process, while others ceased to be actively maintained. Also, of course, few websites contain material that has been reviewed through a peer process. So, where possible, I have cited only those sites which I consider to be relatively stable and which can also be regarded as authoritative in a technical sense.

Acknowledgements

The production of this second edition has been a rather lengthy process. So I should rightly begin by thanking my family and the staff of Pearson Education, especially Keith Mansfield, for their patience and tolerance, as well as a collective degree of ability to suspend too-evident disbelief at yet another claim of 'nearly completed'.

Thanks again to my many friends and colleagues for their support and encouragement. In addition to those listed in the original preface, many of whom have continued to provide help and ideas, I should recognise the support of my colleagues in the *Pennine Group*: especially Pearl Brereton, Keith Bennett and Paul Layzell. I should also acknowledge here the contribution made by the late Norm Gibbs when Director of the SEI's Education Program. Norm encouraged me to persist with my attempts to categorize and classify knowledge about software design, starting with my development of one of the SEI's first *curriculum modules*, and eventually resulting in the first edition of this book.

I should also express my thanks to those who patiently answered my queries about specific issues. In particular, I would like to acknowledge the help from Fred Brooks Jnr in explaining his ideas about 'shells of knowledge'; to Manny Lehman for helping me to pin down elusive references to his ideas about E-type software; and to Mary Shaw for discussion about pedagogical issues as well as checking my explanations of the concepts of software architectures. Also, Chapter 12 could not have been completed without the help that I received from the DSDM Consortium, and indeed from the wider DSDM community.

And as before, of course, any errors of fact and any omissions are entirely my own!

David Budgen
November 2002

Preface to the First Edition

Why you might benefit from reading this book

Why should software need to be designed at all? Well, you would not expect any other engineered artifacts such as bridges, cars or television sets to be built without someone first designing them and producing plans for their construction. And you certainly would not expect to modify them significantly without having some detailed documentation available either. Software is no different: throwing a few dozen programmers at a problem without having detailed plans is hardly likely to result in well-engineered software that actually works.

So, where does the design process fit in? It occurs somewhere between the optimistic phase where we decide what we would like our system to do (often termed 'Requirements Capture') and the increasingly pessimistic phase where we build it ('Implementation'), although it may appear in many different guises. Design is the highly creative stage in software development where someone (the *designer*) plans how the system or program should meet the customer's needs, be easy to implement, 'efficient' and easily extended to meet new needs.

If it's so creative a task, how will this book help? Mainly because any form of creativity is likely to be more effective when there are ways of learning from the experiences of others ('rules of form', design methods) and when there are well-developed notations that can be used for communicating the designer's ideas and plans to those whose task it is to implement them.

These are just the sort of issues that this book addresses: how to develop our ideas about a design, the criteria we might use to assess our ideas and the ways in which we might convey these ideas to programmers. This is a book about software design. It provides an analysis of a number of the currently-used approaches to the task of design, rather than being dedicated to describing just one representation or method.

OK, so who will benefit from reading it? Well, every author would like their work to be a best-seller that appears on every airport and railway station bookstall – but this one is perhaps a bit too specialist for that! It contains information and ideas that are relevant to anyone who is in the business of developing software (except, of course, those whom Tom De Marco has described as the 'Mugwump School, people who believe that design is for sissies'). However, it does assume a basic acquaintance with imperative programming languages (although it is certainly not language-specific) and with concepts such as abstract data types. It is suitable as a text for advanced undergraduate or postgraduate courses in software design or software engineering. Systems analysts/designers, programmers and project managers should benefit from the comparison of a broad spectrum of design methods.

Why software design is important

Writing a computer program is a challenging and creative experience, motivated by the desire to solve problems. The task of developing even a small computer program is not an easy one. Programmers are continually required to keep their attention focused upon many different aspects of both problems and solutions. Even when the static structure of a program is complete (that is, the program 'compiles' successfully), the correctness of its dynamic behaviour still needs to be confirmed. Indeed, it is this need to keep both static form and eventual dynamic behaviour continually in mind when developing a solution that forms a significant part of the challenge that programming provides.

During the 1970s a number of advances in software technology were designed to improve the task of developing computer programs: higher-level programming languages, more efficient compilers, structured programming practices and symbolic debugging facilities. All of these have assisted programmers with developing, controlling and visualizing their ideas about a program, mainly through increased use of the concept of **abstraction**.

Abstraction has played a central role in the development of better programming techniques, allowing the designer of a program to reason about its structure and behaviour without needing to address the detailed issues of determining implementation forms at the same time. While the benefits arising from these improved techniques were at first identified mainly in terms of programming activities, there was also growing realization of the need to develop better practices for programming-in-the-large, which is concerned with the design and development of 'systems' as a whole.

Programming-in-the-large

While the design of programs offers significant problems, the design of large systems provides a vastly increased degree of complexity. The increased levels of abstraction required for designing a large system make it more difficult for the designer to visualize and 'model' the behaviour of the eventual system. The greatly increased time interval that can occur between the origination of an idea and its actual realization leaves designers much more isolated from their actual creation, compounded by the likelihood that the task of implementation will be allocated to others. This means that designers also need to communicate their ideas to others in an unambiguous manner.

So the 1970s also saw the development of design representation forms, and the emergence of design methods intended to capture the experiences of other designers, and so to help designers describe their ideas and to control and structure their task. (Throughout this book the term design method has been used in preference to the much-abused design methodology when describing specific design techniques. According to the dictionary, *method* is 'a procedure for doing things', while *methodology* is the 'study of method'. What we will be doing in this book is methodological, as it involves the study of methods!) This process has continued, and many design methods have themselves been re-designed en route, and have gradually evolved far beyond their original forms. New ideas about design quality and new viewpoints describing the properties of software have emerged, and have in turn been incorporated into both new and existing design methods.

As software plays a central role in the operation of many systems, as varied as banking transactions, spreadsheet calculations, or aircraft control systems ('fly by wire'), it becomes increasingly important that such systems should be designed as well as possible. Faulty design can lead to disaster and can even be life-threatening.

It is increasingly accepted that the study of software based systems (whether we call it software engineering, computer science, information systems engineering, or even information technology) needs to involve some basic knowledge about the roles of design within the software development process. However, students of design are confronted with many of the same problems as the designer: the high level of abstraction required in the descriptive forms, and the resulting 'distance' from the eventual solution, can make it difficult to provide them with the necessary degree of 'feeling' for all the issues that are involved. As a further complication, the time required to develop a significant item of software from the abstract design to its final implementation usually makes it impractical for students to gain real feedback from carrying their designs through to fruition.

A field which provides a good (and partly comforting) analogy is that of the study of music. Musical composition is another highly creative task and, like software designers, composers need to use a complex static notation to describe the eventual dynamic performance of a piece of music. The student of music must become proficient in reading and interpreting musical scores, before ever attempting to master the rules of composition. In the case of software design the novice needs to learn to program effectively, and to be familiar with the manipulation of various forms of abstraction, before proceeding to design a system of any size or complexity.

The analogy should not be pushed too far (few symphonies have been produced by 'composition teams', organized by project managers), but we do need to realize that teaching design *methods* does not teach a student *about* design, or even necessarily how to *do* design. The would-be designer needs to study widely and to gain a thorough understanding of the many issues that influence the design process before taking on the role of a system designer, whether or not this involes the use of specific design methods.

How this book came about

I was fortunate enough to spend some time at Carnegie-Mellon's Software Engineering Institute (SEI) during 1986, during which an initial curriculum in software design was developed for the Graduate Curriculum Project. This was then extensively revised in 1988, taking on board subsequent thinking and experience. The aim of this work was to develop a 'road-map' for use by instructors which identified the principal issues in the teaching of design knowledge and suggested ways in which these might be introduced to the student, supported by a bibliographical survey.

In compiling the curriculum, one of the major problems that emerged was the lack of textbooks suitable for teaching *about* software systems design. There are relatively few books that address the subject of design in general (not just in terms of software), and nearly all textbooks about software design are centred on describing the use of one particular method. These can be considered as being books about how to *do* design, rather than what design *is*. While these books cater for a very important set of skill needs, teaching one approach does make it difficult for almost all authors to avoid some degree of proselytizing!

One of the aims of this book is therefore to redress the balance by providing a book that can act as a 'road-map' to the issues of software systems design, and survey the roles that design methods play in this. This book is therefore about design (with particular attention to software and its needs), rather than about method, although in the process of describing the one, we necessarily have to discuss the other. It is not meant to replace those books that teach specific design methods in detail, but rather to provide a broad intermediate level of understanding that might usefully precede any detailed study of one or more methods, or the selection of a design method to be used in a project.

Acknowledgements

Design in any sphere can be a pleasurable and creative act for those involved in it, whether it involves building simple sand-castles on the beach, engineering a complex structure such as the Thames Barrier, or writing a fugue. Writing books is a creative act, and can also give the writer pleasure (at times), especially so once the task is completed! Like so many creative tasks it also depends upon the help, advice and encouragement of many others, and I would like to thank the many people who have helped and sustained my efforts on this book from its original inception to the final product. These include: my friends and mentors at the SEI, especially Jim Tomayko, Mary Shaw, Carol Sledge and the other members of the Education Program; my friends and collaborators in industry, Mike Looney, Ken Jackson, Hugo Simpson, Ray Foulkes and Alastair O'Brien; my former colleagues at the University of Stirling, with special thanks to Chic Rattray and Maurice Naftalin for the many exchanges of ideas; and my present colleagues at the University of Keele, including Mike Brough and my other research collaborators, Mustafa Marashi, Andrew Reeves and Grant Friel, who have put in so much work on some of my ideas. All of them have had to labour long and hard to correct my misconceptions and to further my education on the subject of software design. The mistakes that remain are all my own.

I should also like to acknowledge the contribution of my various student classes, in the Universities of Stirling and of Keele, as well as in industry. It has been their unfortunate lot to provide some of the testing ground for the frameworks that have been used in this book, and their feedback has been invaluable for this.

Last (but certainly not least) grateful thanks to my family, who have put up with 'not another book' for so long; and to Simon Plumtree of Addison-Wesley for his encouragement, and amazing patience in waiting for the final manuscript!

David Budgen
November 1993

Publisher's Acknowledgements

We are grateful to the following for permission to reproduce copyright material:

Figure 2.6 from A field study of the software design process for large systems, *Comm. ACM*, **31**(11), (Curtis *et al.*, 1988); Figures 3.2 and 3.4 from A spiral model of software development and enhancement, *IEEE Computer*, **21**(5), (Boehm, B.W. 1988), Figure 3.3 from Open source software development: an overview, *IEEE Computer*, **34**(6), (Wu, M.-W. and Lin, Y.-D. 2001), Figure 9.4 from A generic model for representing design methods. In *Proceedings of the 11th International Conference on Software Engineering*, (Potts, C. 1989) and Figure 17.5 from What do you mean by COTS? Finally a useful answer, *IEEE Software*, **17**(2) (Carney, D. and Long, F. 2000) all with permission from the IEEE.

part 1

The Role of Software Design

The Nature of the Design Process

1.1 What is design?

1.2 The role of the design activity

1.3 Design as a problem-solving process

1.4 Design as a 'wicked' problem

This opening chapter is concerned with examining the role that design plays in a wide range of spheres. It looks at the ideas of design theorists and examines these in the light of some simple examples of design activity. In particular, it contrasts the use of design as a problem-solving technique with that of scientific method, and shows how these differ in a number of highly significant ways.

1.1 What is design?

While the subject matter of this book is concerned with exploring how we can make the most effective application of a technology which has a history of barely half a century – the ideas that it presents are rooted in one of the most distinctive of human characteristics. This characteristic is the making of, and the use of, *tools*. Tools are themselves artifacts, which are then in turn used to create further artifacts, whether the tool in question is a stone axe or a compiler – and producing any form of artifact is an act that implicitly incorporates some element of *design* activity, whether or not this is explicitly appreciated at the time.

A second distinguishing characteristic of human beings that provides an underpinning for any form of design activity is that of *communication*. Translating a 'design' into a 'product' almost always involves communicating the designer's ideas to the development team, whether it be for the purpose of building a megalithic barrow, or for creating an on-line banking system. Any discussion of design therefore requires due consideration of the means by which designers record their ideas and convey them to those who will be responsible for fabricating the final result.

Communication also plays another, rather different, role in design activities. This is to act as the vehicle by which experience and expertise are transferred from 'expert' to 'novice', as well as shared amongst a community of experts. Indeed, the ability to *reuse* ideas is a major element in the development of design expertise, and an important part of the transition from a *craft* to an *engineering* discipline also occurs when the scope of reuse is extended to include the process of fabrication.

All of these are core concepts that underpin the ideas presented in this book, and so it is appropriate to begin by looking at the first of them rather more closely. Indeed, various artifacts that are the outcome of many different applications of the design process extensively influence our lives. We ride in cars, trains, aeroplanes; we live in houses or flats; we use everyday domestic appliances such as washing-machines, television sets, vacuum cleaners; we sit on chairs, lie on beds, walk around in shoes; we play games, listen to music. All of these are artifacts because they have been devised and created by human beings, and all of them in some way are the products of some form of design process – whether a good one (shoes are comfortable, a washing-machine works reliably) or a poor one (the flat roof of a house leaks, or the chair collapses when the user leans back on two legs).

Our perception of the importance of the roles that design may play in producing these different artifacts will vary, although it may not always be correct. No-one is likely to deny the importance of using well-proven design practices for the design of motorway bridges, aeroplanes and buildings, not least because of the safety issues concerned with the use of such objects. Yet equally, good design is important for a wide range of less safety-critical objects – such as a domestic refrigerator: we do not want to have to de-ice it continually, nor to replace bottles that fall out when we open the door. Similarly, we also want to have well-designed footwear so that we do not find ourselves suffering from foot complaints.

Obviously design is not the only factor that matters in the production of artifacts. The fabrication process matters too, and a customer is unlikely to distinguish faulty design from faulty fabrication if shoes leak in the rain, or if the door falls off a car when it is opened. However, while good design may be marred by poor fabrication, usually no amount of constructional skill can disguise poor design.

Design is just as important with software systems also. Most people will readily accept that the software used in an aeroplane needs to be well designed and rigorously tested, not least because they might find themselves as passengers on that aircraft one day. Yet good design is equally desirable for smaller systems too, since the user still requires efficiency (if it can only be defined) and reliability (which suffers from a similar problem of being difficult to define in a precise manner). A word processor may not be a safety-critical item, but its user is unlikely to appreciate the occasional lost paragraph occurring at apparently random points in a document. It may not be appropriate or cost-effective to employ the same techniques for designing a word processor as for designing safety-critical avionics systems, but the need for a well-designed product is still there. The same parallel might apply to the design of major road-bridges and the design of seating in the dentist's waiting room: the structural complexities are very different, but both of them are expected to function well enough to meet our needs.

Despite extensive exposure to the products of the design process in general (with an associated awareness that good design practices cannot always ensure success in terms of design quality), people's awareness of how design is carried out is often rather unstructured and piecemeal. In the domain of computing science and software engineering, designing software is a major problem-solving technique, to be ranked alongside the concepts of theory and of abstraction (Denning *et al.*, 1989). Yet all too rarely do we have a clear idea of the nature and purpose of the design process, and our ideas about design are all too often muddled in with notions derived from the more specific practices of design methods. So this first chapter aims to explore some ideas about the design process and its nature, in order to provide a basic framework for an understanding of design issues that can then be used to explore the ideas and concepts introduced in the subsequent chapters.

Although this book is focused largely on the application of design ideas and methods to the production of software, the task of design involves the use of many ideas and concepts that can be applied more widely. To help reinforce this point, the examples used in these introductory chapters will be drawn from a wide range of fields, and not just from the field of software development.

So what is design exactly, what sort of activities does it involve, and what can we observe about the products of that process? Perhaps a good starting point is to consider the words of one of the pioneering design methodologists, J. Christopher Jones, taken from his classic work, *Design Methods: Seeds of Human Futures* (Jones, 1970).

> *'The fundamental problem is that designers are obliged to use current information to predict a future state that will not come about unless their predictions are correct. The final outcome of designing has to be assumed before the means of achieving it can be explored: the designers have to work backwards in time from an assumed effect upon the world to the beginning of a chain of events that will bring the effect about.'*

This concise description of the design process is more than sufficient to show that its form is very different from that of the scientific approach to problem-solving which will perhaps be more familiar to many readers. As shown in Figure 1.1, the interaction between mankind and the surrounding 'world' has historically taken two paths. The path of **science** has been concerned with studying things as they *are*, with observation and experimentation as its key activities. In its 'classical' form, the scientific approach

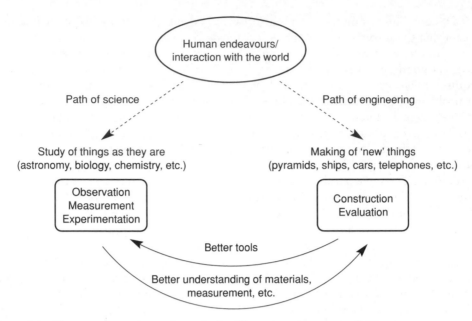

Figure 1.1 The complementary nature of scientific and engineering activities.

to problem-solving typically consists of observing the characteristics of some phenomenon, making measurements of these, building a theory to explain them (and preferably to predict additional characteristics), and then seeking to verify these predictions through further observation and measurements. In contrast, the path of what we can generally refer to as **engineering** has been much more concerned with creating *new* things, with the key activities involved being those of construction and evaluation. As Jones observes, these activities are directed much more towards achieving a goal (or 'effect') than conducting an investigation; hence they begin by assuming an end result and then go on to seek ways of bringing this about.

Of course, these two paths are not isolated from one another. Indeed, the interplay between them has always provided an important element for both. The products of 'engineering' have formed important tools for advancing scientific knowledge (from clocks to cyclotrons), while the observations and measurements of science have provided the understanding of their basic materials that engineers need in order to use them in new ways and to most effect. While the practices of both involve building 'models' of a problem, these are then used for very different purposes, as is shown in Figures 1.2 and 1.3, which summarize and contrast the forms of the scientific and engineering processes.

The descriptions of both of these processes provided in Figures 1.2 and 1.3 are of course relatively simplified. A rather more detailed and 'formal' description of the general design process is provided by the FBS framework (Function–Behaviour–Structure) described in Gero (1990).

The terms 'black box' and 'white box' used in Figure 1.3 merit a brief description here, and will be discussed more fully in Chapter 5. Briefly, a 'black box' model is one that describes the external functionality and behaviour of a system as a whole, without any reference to how this is to be achieved. In contrast, a 'white box' model is

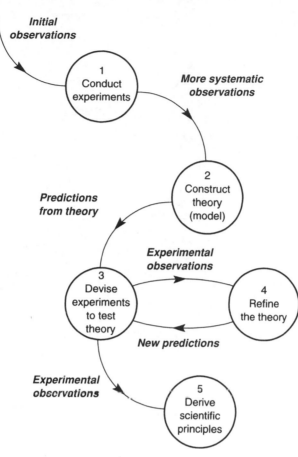

Figure 1.2 The nature of scientific analysis.

one in which the workings of the system are described. (The terms 'opaque' and 'transparent' would in many ways be better ones, but 'black box' and 'white box' are the ones most widely employed.)

Since software can be considered a prime example of an artifact, we can see why an understanding of the techniques of design are so important in its production. Indeed, this is true of the craft and engineering disciplines in general, in that they are usually concerned with the production of artifacts, whether these be bridges, buildings, statues, cars or space probes. The nature of software may make this design process more complex, not least because design and implementation may be less distinctly separated, but it does not alter its essential nature.

So if we examine the quotation from Jones a little more closely, and rephrase it a little, we can identify the set of actions that need to be performed by a designer in deriving and specifying a solution to a problem. (There may, of course, be more than one possible solution; indeed, this is generally so, and this is again where the process of design differs somewhat from the case of scientific investigation, since for the latter it is unusual for there to be more than one equivalent solution to a problem.) This set of actions can be summarized as:

The nature of the design process

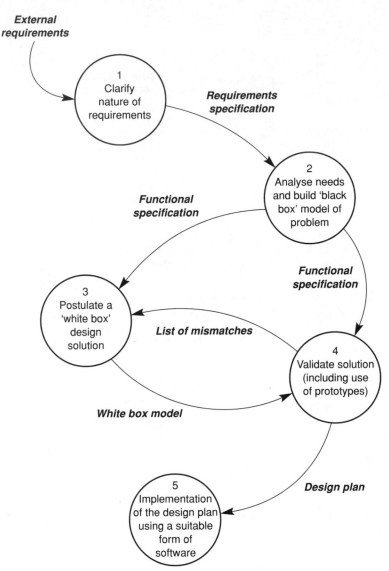

Figure 1.3   A model of the design process.

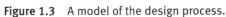

■ postulate a solution;

■ build a model of the solution;

■ evaluate the model against the original requirement;

■ elaborate the model to produce a detailed specification of the solution.

We will be using this very general 'process model' again at various points, and will make use of it to build up our own models of the various design processes used for software development. However, it should also be recognized that while there is an order to these actions, they are by no means performed in a single, precise sequence. It is usually necessary to perform many iterations between the different stages of the design process, as well as extensive backtracking that may be needed for the revision of design choices. Indeed, as Jones (1970) himself has recognized, the position may be even worse, since:

> 'If, as is likely, the act of tracing out the intermediate steps exposes unforeseen difficulties or suggests better objectives, the pattern of the original problem may change so drastically that the designers are thrown back to square one.'

In other words, the act of elaborating the original model might reveal its inadequacies or even its total unsuitability, so making the whole process of design essentially unstable.

At this point it may be useful to look at an example of a design process, and to use this to demonstrate how the practices of design may differ from those of scientific analysis.

CASE STUDY 1   Moving house

Moving to a new house is widely regarded as one of the major traumas in our lives. However, hidden within this operation lies a very good illustration of what designing can involve, and so for our case study we briefly examine some of the actions that might be involved when planning a move into a new house.

One practice widely recommended to the new owner is to begin by measuring the dimensions of the various rooms in the house, to obtain some squared paper and to use this for drawing up a scale plan showing all the rooms, doors, windows and so on. The next step is to measure the dimensions of various items of furniture and to cut out cardboard shapes to represent these on the chosen scale. Together these form a representation of the new house and its future contents that can be considered as forming the **initial model**. Figure 1.4 shows an example of such an outline plan for a small single-storey house.

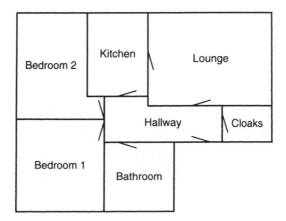

Figure 1.4   Outline plan of a single-storey house.

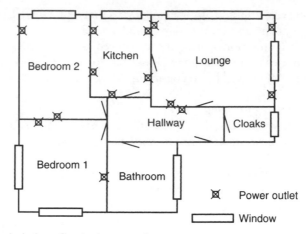

Figure 1.5 Expanded plan of a single-storey house.

The design process itself then involves trying to identify the 'best' positions for the pieces of card on the plan of the new house. There is really no analytical form that can be used to do this, since it is usually necessary to trade off different factors in making the choices. However, there are various **strategies** that can be adopted: for example, determine which rooms will take greatest priority, and then seek to find ways of producing a well-matched set of furniture for those rooms. This strategy may lead to greater mismatches in the remaining rooms than would occur if the owner tried for an overall best match.

Some of the **constraints** that apply to the various possible solutions will be more significant than others. Most people would not wish to place kitchen equipment in the living-room, for example, but might be prepared to position surplus fireside chairs in a bedroom. Other factors that might constrain the choice could be colour matches, style and so on. Equally, it is undesirable to obstruct power outlets – a point that leads on to our next issue.

The representation provided by the model as described above is somewhat incomplete, since it is only two-dimensional. On occasion it will be necessary to consider the vertical dimension too, in order to avoid blocking windows with tall furniture, or to ensure that a power outlet will still be accessible through the legs of an item of furniture. Again, it may be necessary to make some trade-offs between what is desirable and what is practicable. Figure 1.5 shows how the model used in Figure 1.4 can be extended to describe these factors.

The decisions that result from this process can then be regarded as providing a **plan** for use by the removal team on the removal day. Indeed, not only will it determine just where in the house the various items are to be placed when the removal van arrives, but it may also affect the way that the removal process is to be organized, since the removers might choose to pack their van in a particular way in order to make the unloading process easier.

From this relatively simple case study, we should be able to see some of the ways in which the process of design differs from that of scientific method. Rather than being able to identify a 'right' coordinate system that allows us to separate the variables and solve for each separately, we have to build a relatively complex model, and then make adjustments to this in order to produce a solution. There may be many possible 'solutions', and we may well have no very strong criteria that can be used to help us in choosing from a number of the better ones.

However, in some senses the problem that is presented in this case study provides a much simpler environment than is often available to the software designer. The form of the initial model used to describe the problem is directly related to that of the final plan used to describe the solution, in that both are scale drawings of the building. So there is no need to 'transform' between the representation used to describe the problem and that used to describe the solution, as is generally the case for software design. Similarly, the 'designer' is able to manipulate well-defined 'objects', in that each item of furniture already exists and its relevant properties (that is, its dimensions) are fixed, and can easily be measured. The equivalent properties for software objects will generally not be so easily quantifiable or even identifiable.

Before going any further, it may be useful to take a brief look at another example of a design problem. Again, it is taken from a more traditional field than that of software development, but this problem possesses a set of constraints that some readers will probably be more familiar with. In particular, it introduces the concept of *reuse*.

CASE STUDY 2   The garden shed

The Lotsalogs timber company is chiefly concerned with operating sawmills and with producing various standard sizes of timber. As a sideline, they are developing a new production unit that will use the timber to construct a small range of garden sheds. These sheds will all need to be constructed by using a set of prefabricated panels, so that they can be assembled at the customer's home with relative ease.

The manager of the shed production unit therefore needs to produce a set of designs for a number of different sheds. Much of the process for doing this is relatively direct, but this time there are some constraints upon the form of the end result that are rather different from those of the previous problem. These do not constrain the form of the design process directly, but they influence it indirectly in terms of their effect upon the design product.

Apart from the cost of the timber, the main cost to consider in developing a new shed is the cost of fabricating the parts. Since sawing timber is very time-consuming, the amount of sawing needs to be kept to a minimum. Consideration of this factor has therefore led to the following set of design constraints.

- A shed should be assembled from a set of prefabricated panels for the sides and roof.

- Assuming that the boarding on the sides runs horizontally, each panel should be of a height that allows it to be constructed from a whole number of boards.

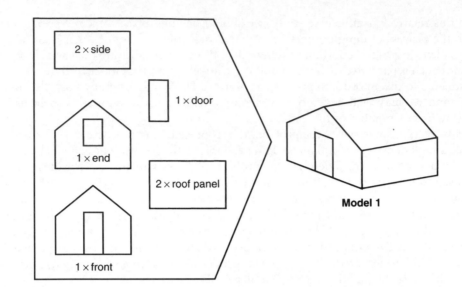

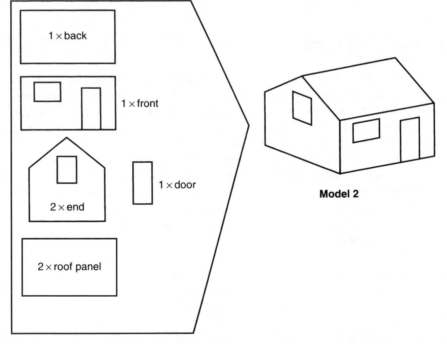

Figure 1.6 Assembling sheds from standard units.

- Where possible, the panels used in one shed should be of a size that allows them to be used in another: for example, the side panel for a small shed could also be used as the back panel for a larger model.

- Windows and doors should be of standard dimensions, and again the height of each should correspond to a whole number of boards, in order to reduce the time needed for cutting out special shapes.

These effectively form constraints upon the design process too, and the designer will also need to consider a number of practical issues about size and shape of the range of products.

As we observed for the previous case study on moving house, there is no evident prescription that can be used to produce a set of designs for garden sheds that will automatically meet all of the criteria, as well as being visually pleasing and practical to use. Given the nature of the problem, the process will certainly be more direct than for the previous case study, but it will still involve some feedback and iteration of ideas.

Given the original requirements that were identified by the company, and the constraints created by the nature of the material and the need for reuse of components, the outcome of the process will be a set of drawings showing the dimensions of each panel, the way that it should be assembled from the basic units of timber, and the ways that the panels can be assembled to create different sheds, as shown in Figure 1.6.

Obviously this problem could be explored further to provide more insight into the design process, but for the moment we can begin to see the importance of the basic idea of **modularity** and the way that it can be used in such a system. Modularity is an important tool in construction, and it is as important for constructing software as for constructing garden sheds, tower blocks and the like. However, it is not always quite so easy to see the most effective form it should take when we are designing software.

For both of the case studies introduced here, we can see how the concepts of design as described by Jones can be related to the processes involved in producing a solution, although the nature of the two problems is very different. In both cases the designer proceeds to build a model of what he or she wants to achieve – an organized house or a balanced range of products; modifies the model until satisfied that it can meet the particular constraints; and then elaborates it in order to specify clearly what needs to be done to turn the model into reality.

In one case the end product is an organizational plan for the removal men, in the other it is a set of plans and drawings that will be used by the joiners who produce the sheds. For both cases there are constraints operating upon the process, although these have very different forms, and in both cases the designer has some concept of **quality** to help with making choices. In the one case this may be the balance of style and colour for the furniture in a room, in the other it will be a matter of producing a shed that has the 'right' proportions and which is easily fabricated. Quality is an elusive concept, although an important one, and it is one that we will be returning to later.

The next section seeks to establish a clearer picture of the designer's goals, and to clarify how these can be described for software systems.

1.2 The role of the design activity

As we saw in the previous section, the principal task for the designer is to specify the best solution to a problem and produce a description of *how* this is to be organized. This description then forms a 'plan' that can be used by the eventual implementors of the system.

Just when this concept of the design task having a distinct role in the production of an artifact first began to emerge is likely to remain largely a matter for conjecture. It is unlikely that any of the major creations of ancient times, such as the pyramids, could have been achieved without a significant degree of 'design planning', and so it seems reasonable to identify *architecture* in its broadest sense as the most probable domain where this separation from the craft-level entwining of design and construction is likely to have begun.

The recognition of design as a distinct and identifiable task then introduces the question of how is a designer to learn their trade? For many centuries this was probably achieved primarily through some form of 'apprenticeship', whether formal or otherwise, and today there is still a strong element of this in many creative disciplines. Indeed, the concept of the 'design studio' is considered by some to be a very valuable and effective route for teaching about software design too (Tomayko, 1996). We might also note that great engineering designers have also maintained 'sketchbooks' (Leonardo da Vinci) or the engineer's 'commonplace book' (Isambard Kingdom Brunel) both to aid their own thinking and to provide a form of 'pattern book' for conveying these ideas to others.

The designers of pyramids and cathedrals will almost certainly have exchanged ideas with, and learned from, their peers. However, each of the resulting artifacts was a single unique creation, and only with the emergence of engineering practices were there significant new inputs to the designer's learning processes. Two of these are worth noting here, not least because of their longer-term implications for software design.

1. The first of these was the knowledge gained from scientific research. As the properties of materials became better understood, and the means of predicting their behaviour became more refined and dependable, so the designer could employ this knowledge in helping to create new structures. A good example is that of bridge building in the nineteenth century, when engineers such as I K Brunel were able to create structures that were radically different from their predecessors, while also proving to be remarkably durable.

2. The second was the concept of *reuse*. One consequence of the industrial revolution was the idea of 'standardizing' components.* The existence of such components extends a designer's repertoire – on the one hand offering speedier development of an idea ('improved time-to-market') with potentially lower costs, but also introducing new constraints and trade-offs into the design process.

---

* One of the very earliest examples of standardization of components was Sir Marc Brunel's block-making machinery, installed in the Portsmouth dockyard in the early 1800s. The intention here was to improve and standardize the production of the blocks that formed a major element in the rigging of a sailing vessel. While this might not have influenced the *design* of sailing ships, it certainly simplified their fitting out and reduced its cost (Rolt, 1970).

It might well be argued that while the first of these has had its most important impact in 'engineering design', the second has affected *all* domains – and has some important consequences for software design too. We will return to this as a topic in its own right in Chapters 16 and 17.

Returning briefly to the two case studies that were introduced above, we can see that the objectives for these are somewhat different in form. They can be described as aiming to produce respectively:

- a plan that informs the removal men where each major item of furniture is to be positioned;
- a set of plans that inform the joiner about the dimensions of the panels and how the panels are to be jointed and so on.

The first of these is largely approximate (the extent to which this is true is, of course, variable: repositioning a chair is a less daunting task than repositioning a piano). The second requires a greater degree of precision, and the degree of tolerance that is acceptable in the product may well need to be specified as a part of the plan. So the form of the output produced from the design process depends not only upon the nature of the problem, but also upon the nature of its eventual implementation.

In addition, the plans produced by the designer may need to indicate some information about the sequencing of operations in the eventual construction process. In the first example, some items of furniture may need to be positioned before or after others, perhaps because it will be difficult to move items past them; and in the second example, the directions for assembly may indicate any significant ordering that may be necessary. (We would generally expect to erect all of the walls before beginning to place the roof in position.)

From this, we can rightly conclude that *communication* with those responsible for fabricating the eventual solution is likely to be an important part of the designer's role, especially for larger-scale developments. However, an equally important channel of communication is with the source of the 'requirements' specification that a designer is being asked to address, whatever form this may take and however it may be obtained.

This specification is an important input to the design process and may address a wide range of factors. At the one extreme it may consist of a rather imprecise and general requirement for a solution in which the 'customer' trusts entirely to the designer to find the 'best' form (the medieval baron requires the craftsman to design a beechwood table for their great hall, large enough for 20 guests at a major feast). At the other it may provide details of very many constraining factors (a design for a table which is to be produced for use in village halls, needing to be cheap to fabricate, durable, easily cleaned, stackable, and light enough to be readily moved). However, what distinguishes all of the examples used so far is that we can assume that the designer is familiar with the context of the problem. Indeed, in this last example, we would not expect that the purpose of a table would need to be explained as part of the specification.

Here we begin to discern one of the more distinctive features of software design. In the nineteenth century, the great Victorian engineers were prepared to tackle a wide range of projects – for engineers such as I K Brunel, the designing of bridges, railways, station buildings and ships were all part of their portfolio. Later ages have opted for greater degrees of specialization, however, and we are unlikely to find an aeronautical engineer producing the design for a new oil tanker! This degree of specialization is less marked though in software development, which in some ways harks back to the more generalist practices witnessed in an earlier era – whilst being applied across what is in many ways a much wider range of domains. Admittedly a specialist in (say) database design might hesitate to design a real-time control system (or at least, *ought* to hesitate) but, in principle, one person could possess the necessary expertise to design both types of application.

One of the problems that this introduces, therefore, is that a software designer may need to acquire some degree of 'domain knowledge' as a routine part of the input needed for undertaking any particular design task. Some of this may be obtained from the specification (which may well run to hundreds of pages), but by no means all of the necessary knowledge is likely to be available in this way. So, as shown in Figure 1.7, the software designer may need to be responsive to many channels of communication. This is an aspect that will be addressed further in Chapter 3, while some of the ways of transferring the domain knowledge will also be examined more fully in later chapters.

To continue with the needs of software development: it is clear from the above that the main task of the design phase is to produce the plans necessary for software production to proceed. The form and extent of the plans will be determined by the design practices and means of implementation chosen, as well as by the size of the

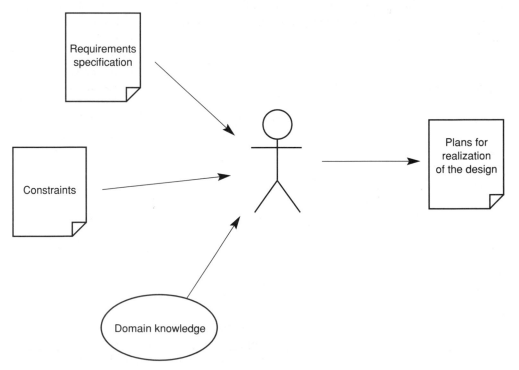

Figure 1.7   The designer's channels of communication.

system being developed. Clearly, in a large project employing many programmers the design plans will need to capture a much wider range of factors than will be needed by the one-person project, where the designer may well be the programmer too.

Typically, such plans will be concerned with describing:

- the static structure of the system, including any subprograms to be used and their hierarchy;

- any data objects to be used in the system;

- the algorithms to be used;

- the packaging of the system, in terms of how components are grouped in compilation units (assuming that implementation will use a conventional imperative programming language);

- interactions between components, including the form these should take, and the nature of any causal links.

These are all concerned with specifying the form of the design product itself. But as was observed above, the overall design task may also involve producing process-oriented plans too, concerned with such matters as the preferred order of development for subprograms/modules and so on, and the strategy for their eventual integration into the complete system. (These are rather like the assembly directions that are needed for construction of the garden shed.) However, for the moment we will chiefly concern ourselves with the needs of the design product.

As in many more 'classical' forms of engineering, software designers produce plans that specify how the final product is to be assembled in terms of the items listed above. This usually requires the use of a variety of forms of representation, since each of these provides a different 'view' of a system. In a way, the use of these multiple views corresponds to the use of plan, elevation and end views in technical drawing, as well as to the cross-sectional forms used to indicate assembly details. (The concept of tolerance is perhaps lacking though, since software components generally have to 'fit' rather precisely.)

For software systems, however, a further degree of complexity has to be considered. For designing software consists of designing a *process*; and so it becomes necessary to model and describe its *behaviour* as well as its structure, and also the *functions* that it will perform. So the designer's model will ideally include descriptions that also encompass these aspects of the eventual system.

To meet these needs, the designer will usually make use of a number of different forms of design representation to help with constructing the model, each representation providing a different **viewpoint** on the form of a design, as shown in Figure 1.8. The more complex the system, the more we need a full set of viewpoints to understand its behaviour, and to provide a specification that is sufficiently complete for it to be used as an aid in the construction of the system.

We will return later to consider more fully the ways in which the dynamic nature of a software system influences (and complicates) the process of design; for the moment we will continue to focus our attention upon the nature of the design process in general.

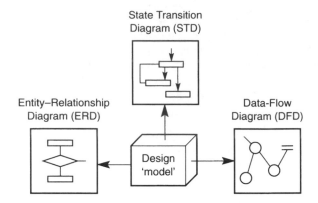

Figure 1.8 Examples of design viewpoints.

1.3 Design as a problem-solving process

Having considered the nature of the design process, and having examined its role and objectives in terms of software development, it is worth stepping back for a moment and reminding ourselves of the ultimate purpose of design.

The purpose of design is simply to produce a solution to a problem. The problem will typically be summarized by means of some form of requirements specification, and it is the designer's task to provide a description of how that requirement is to be met. Design is therefore essentially a problem-solving task, and the examples given show that it is not an analytical process. The process of design involves the designer in evaluating different options, and in making choices using decision criteria that may be complex and may involve trade-offs between factors such as size, speed and ease of adaptation, as well as other problem-specific factors.

Throughout all of this, the designer needs to keep in mind that the ultimate requirement is one of fitness for purpose. However elegant or efficient the final solution, the basic two needs are that it should work and that it should do the required job as well as possible. This is not to say that other factors and qualities are not important, but simply that they are subordinate to the need to produce a system that does the required job. However well structured, elegant or efficient a system may be, it will be assessed ultimately on how well it achieves its purpose.

The designer has a number of tools to help with the task of problem-solving. Design *methods* and *patterns* can provide strategies that will help to determine which choice may be most appropriate in a given situation. *Representations* can also help with the process of building models of the intended system and with evaluating its behaviour. In combination with these, *abstraction* plays a very important part, since to build manageable models of large and complex systems we need ways of abstracting their critical features for use in forming our models. Abstraction enables the designer to concentrate effort on building a logical model of a system, which is translated into a physical model at a relatively late stage in the design process.

The concept of abstraction is enormously important for all branches of engineering. Essentially, abstraction is concerned with the removal of detail from a description of a problem, while still retaining the essential properties of its structure. In our first case study, the outline plan on squared paper provided an abstraction of the idea of a house. It retained only those forms of information that were needed for solving the particular problem – namely two-dimensional areas – together with information about positioning of doors, windows, power outlets and so on. Clearly a house is a highly complex object, and the two-dimensional plan is the particular abstraction that is needed on this specific occasion. For the task of rewiring the house, a quite different abstraction would be needed, based on the use of some form of circuit diagram. Again, this would be a very incomplete description of the whole structure, but it would retain the basic information that was essential for the particular purpose.

This concept of abstraction is a very important one, and it is one that novice software designers are apt to find difficult to employ effectively (Adelson and Soloway, 1985). Programmers are accustomed to working with a wonderfully pliable medium, and so it is all too easy to be over-influenced by relatively detailed features of programming language structures when thinking about design. The designer needs to learn to think about a system in an abstract way – in terms of events, entities, objects, or whatever other key items are appropriate – and to leave questions of detail, such as the specific forms of loop construct to be used in a particular algorithm, until a relatively late stage in the design process.

Abstraction therefore plays a key role in this book, corresponding to its central role in design. In considering the forms of design representation that can be used for different purposes, we will be looking at ways of modelling a system using different abstract viewpoints. In looking at design methods, we will be seeing how the practices that they involve are intended to encourage the designer to think about a system in an abstract way. The effective use of abstraction is a key skill that any designer needs to learn and practise.

1.4 Design as a 'wicked' problem

Before concluding this general review of the nature of the design process, we should briefly consider some of the effects that the issues discussed in the previous sections have upon it. The major conclusion to draw is that the design process lacks any analytical form, with one important consequence being that there may well be a number of acceptable solutions to any given problem. Because of this, the process of design will rarely be 'convergent', in the sense of being able to direct the designer towards a single preferred solution. Indeed, the notion of the 'wicked' (as opposed to 'benign') problem, which is sometimes used to describe a process such as that of design, suggests that it is potentially unstable.

A 'wicked' problem demonstrates some interesting properties. It can be characterized as a problem whose form is such that a solution for one of its aspects simply changes the problem. The term was coined by Rittel and Webber (1984), and arose from their analysis of the nature of social planning problems and of the design issues that were involved in these.

Social planning has many examples of such 'wicked' problems. One of the better-known is evident in many large cities in the UK, where rehousing in tower blocks of people who previously lived in substandard housing may have improved living conditions, but at the cost of destroying communities and other social frameworks. In some cases, the living conditions may also be little better or even worse, owing to architectural design decisions to construct the tower blocks with relatively untried materials. So removing the original problem has revealed or created new ones that are even less tractable. There is sometimes a similar effect during maintenance of software systems; adding one relatively innocuous feature may subsequently require massive redesign of internal data structures and reorganization of subprograms.

Rittel and Webber identified ten distinguishing properties of wicked problems, most of which can be seen as applying equally well to software design (Peters and Tripp, 1976). The following properties, taken from their list, are particularly relevant.

- There is no definitive formulation of a wicked problem. The difficulties of specifying the needs of software-based systems are well known, and the tasks of specification and design are often difficult to separate clearly. Rittel and Webber also make the point that the specification and understanding of such a problem is bound up with the ideas that we may have about solving it – which is why the simple life-cycle model in which the task of specification is followed neatly by that of design is rarely a realistic description of actual practices.

- Wicked problems have no stopping rule. Essentially this property implies that there is a lack of any criteria that can be used to establish when *the* solution to a problem has been found, such that any further work will not be able to improve upon it. For software, this is demonstrated by our lack of any quality measures that can be used to establish that any one system design is the 'best' one possible.

- Solutions to wicked problems are not true or false, but good or bad. For many scientific and classical engineering problems, we may be able to identify whether a solution is correct or false. Software designs usually come in 'shades of grey', in that there are usually no right or wrong solutions or structures. (This point will be evident to anyone who has ever had cause to mark a set of student programming assignments.)

- There is no immediate and no ultimate test of a solution to a wicked problem. The difficulties inherent in any form of system evaluation process adequately demonstrate that this is very much a characteristic of software. Indeed, even an apparently simple exercise such as a comparison of the features of (say) a number of web browsers can demonstrate the multi-faceted way in which their features need to be classified and compared, and the lack of any one criterion that can be used to establish which one is 'best' in any sense.

- Every solution to a wicked problem is a 'one-shot operation', because there is no opportunity to learn by trial-and-error, every attempt counts significantly. This is particularly true for large-scale software systems such as those dealing with major national activities, for example paying pensions, collecting taxes, etc. The resources needed to explore different options are simply not available, and it is rarely possible to 'unpick' changes to operational practices once these have been implemented in order to meet the needs of such systems. Some good examples of the problems of creating and installing large public systems are illustrated in PAC (1999), although the conclusions there (that better project management is the answer) are simplistic, and, indeed, reflect a failure to really understand that the problems are wicked ones!

■ Wicked problems do not have an enumerable (or an exhaustively describable) set of potential solutions. We can readily recognize this as being true for software. Even where there is an agreed design plan, different programmers may implement this using quite widely differing structures. Indeed, this is one of the characteristics that strongly differentiates between 'design' solutions and the solutions to 'scientific' problems.

■ Every wicked problem is essentially unique. Of course, there are similarities between software systems, and in later chapters we look at ideas about reuse and about mechanisms such as *design patterns* which assist with exploiting similarities to aid reuse of design experience. However, all such techniques require some degree of *interpretation* by the designer in order to apply them to a given problem, which, of course, is precisely why design activities cannot be automated.

■ Every wicked problem can be considered to be a symptom of another problem. Resolving a discrepancy or inconsistency in a design may pose another problem in its turn. Again, in writing a computer program, a choice of data structure that helps with resolving one problem may in turn be the source of an entirely new difficulty later.

A slightly different but related view of design problems is that of Herbert Simon (1984). He has introduced the idea of well-structured and ill-structured problems (WSPs and ISPs). There is no space here to elaborate further on these ideas but, as one might expect, the task of software design emerges as having the properties of an ISP.

These ideas are somewhat at variance with the ideas that are generally encountered in the 'classical' or 'scientific' approach to problem-solving, where we might expect that some form of convergence will occur, leading us to a single solution to a problem. The use of 'scientific' methods typically aims to reduce a problem in such a way that each step in the process of developing a solution leads to a set of simpler problems. As an example, separating the description of the motion of a system into descriptions of motion in each of three coordinates may result in the formulation of three separate equations that can then be solved independently, or nearly so. And if this fails to work, we can always try another criterion for separation, such as using a different coordinate system (we might try adopting polar coordinates rather than cartesian coordinates).

Unfortunately the process of producing a design is not like that at all. In working back from the initial model, the designer makes various choices, and the consequences of any of these choices may well be such as to make further choices much more complicated to resolve. In the extreme, the overall design itself may be shown to be inadequate. An example of just such a 'wicked' problem feature is often encountered in designing real-time systems. It may be possible to organize the system so that it can produce a response to one type of event within some required interval, but the way that this is achieved may place such constraints upon the operation of the system that it will then be unable to meet some other demand in an adequate time. Worse still (since the new problem might well be overcome by increasing the computer power available), the need to handle one event adequately might lead to the occasional exclusion of knowledge about some other event that can occur independently.

Problems like these can be hard to resolve, since concentrating upon solving one aspect in isolation (such as handling the single event) may eventually result in an inability to produce a solution for the second at all. In such cases our problem becomes one of producing a solution to the combined needs, since separating them out is not a valid option.

Summary

This chapter has sought to examine the nature of the design process in fairly general terms. It has introduced a number of concepts, many of which will reappear later, and will be described in greater detail where appropriate. Some particularly important ideas presented in this chapter are:

■ the design process is concerned with describing *how* a requirement is to be met by the design product;

■ design *representation* forms provide means of modelling ideas about a design, and also of presenting the design plans to the programmer;

■ *abstraction* is used in problem-solving, and is used to help separate the *logical* and *physical* aspects of the design process;

■ the software design problem is a 'wicked' one and this imposes constraints upon the way in which the process of design can be organized and managed.

Further reading

Jones J. Christopher (1970). *Design Methods: Seeds of Human Futures*. Wiley International

The opening chapters of this book provide an excellent degree of insight into the nature of the design process. The later chapters are less directly relevant to the issues of software design.

Cross N. (ed.) (1984). *Developments in Design Methodology*. Wiley

This collected set of articles and papers contains some significant contributions from authors such as Horst Rittel and Herb Simon. There is a strong and valuable input from a number of authors who bring the ideas of cognitive science to the study of design and designing.

Design Studies. Butterworth

This journal of the Design Research Society provides an insight into design issues affecting a wide range of fields of application for design techniques.

Exercises

1.1 You are asked to plan a journey by air from Manchester in England to Pittsburgh in the USA. Airline A is cheap, but involves flying to Chicago, waiting there for three hours and then flying on to Pittsburgh. Airline B is the most expensive, but offers a direct flight. Airline C has a package that is cheaper than that of airline A, but which involves flying from Manchester to Gatwick Airport near London, and then on to Pittsburgh via yet another airport in the USA.

(a) What factors besides price might affect your choice of airline?

(b) How does the decision about which airline and route to choose meet the 'wicked' problem criteria?

1.2 Imagine that you live in a world in which the only available means for telling the time of day are sundials and large pendulum clocks. Given the following requirements specification, suggest how you might begin exploring the ways of meeting it by creating a suitable design solution:

> *The need is for a portable timepiece, to be carried in a pocket, or even (if possible) worn on one's wrist. It will have a circular dial, divided into twelve equal-sized portions, numbered 1 to 12. Two pointers will be fixed to a spindle in the centre of the dial: one (the longer one) will rotate once per hour, while the second (shorter) pointer will rotate once every 12 hours. The device should be capable of running unattended for at least 24 hours and should not need to be kept in a fixed position in order to work correctly.*

This problem is a good demonstration of why the simplistic approach sometimes advocated in favour of stepwise refinement of a formal requirements specification as a means of producing a design is unrealistic and impractical for most real systems.

1.3 Sketch out a design for one or more of the following:

(a) a rocking chair (to be made from timber)

(b) a wooden storage rack for audio cassettes

(c) a metal music stand that can be adjusted for height and taken apart for carrying and storage.

Then think about how you reached your design, and what changes you made to it as your thinking developed. What further changes do you think might occur if you had to produce detailed plans to help someone make this item?

1.4 Designing software is made more complex because we are designing for a sequence of actions. Sketch out a design for a set of instructions for making tea with a teapot and teabags. Try to consider the major problems that might arise (no water in the kettle, burst teabag, no kettle and so on). How would you organize the instructions for these exceptional situations so that they do not obscure the original design?

1.5 Planning a new garden is an example of design. Think about the abstractions that might arise in planning a new garden that is to have a lawn, patio, path and vegetable plot. Draw a diagram showing the different abstractions used as the plan develops.

chapter 2

The Software Design Process

This chapter begins by reviewing some ideas about what might constitute 'software' and then takes the ideas about design that were introduced in Chapter 1 and considers how they can be interpreted for the problem of designing software. It examines some of the conclusions that have been drawn from observation of software designers at work, and uses these to identify the forms of support that are required to help with transferring design experience and knowledge. Some of the other factors influencing software design are surveyed, and their influence upon the evolution of software design practices is considered.

2.1 What is software?

In the first chapter we examined the characteristics of the general process of design and identified those features of design that characterize it as being a creative task. In this chapter we will be concerned with examining the ways in which the design of *software* fits into this general pattern, and identifying any ways in which the task of designing software might differ from that of designing any other forms of artifact. So having begun the previous chapter by asking the question 'what is design?', it is appropriate to begin this chapter by considering the question 'what is software?'.

When people first began to develop computer-based applications that were recognized as being large enough to merit an explicit design phase, this question was one that was unlikely to have been asked by anyone. Until the mid-1970s at least, software was considered to encompass all of the forms that were concerned with generating 'executable binary code' that was intended for execution on a single machine. Indeed, this assumption was effectively implicit in all early thinking about software design. The structure of such systems was largely fixed when the code was compiled (which can be described as 'compile-time binding') and so the ideas of the designer(s) were directed towards producing a single monolithic unit of binary code. Indeed, while the term 'software' might be used at different times to describe both 'source code' and the resulting binary code, the close link between these generally rendered the distinction unimportant.

By the 1970s the idea that computing tasks could be distributed across multiple computers had been added, with the further possibility of changing the links between these at run-time. While this development could largely be considered to be a variation in the details of implementation, it did of course influence the thinking of the designers of such systems. Where the eventual system was to be implemented as a distributed one, the designers now had to incorporate additional factors into their decision-making, such as how functionality and data were to be partitioned or shared between machines, the form of communication mechanisms to employ, and the likely performance effects of these choices.

This process of variation in the forms of implementation has continued apace, and in the 1990s in particular, the development of the Internet has added many new parameters. Ideas about distribution have further extended the potential for employing run-time binding to determine the final structure of a system, as well as extending ideas about distribution (terms such as 'client–server' are now widespread, if not particularly well-defined). At the same time, the addition of 'scripting' forms to static description notations such as HTML and XML has further extended our ideas about the forms that 'software' might take.

In some ways, the effect of these developments upon design thinking has probably been less than might be expected (and arguably, somewhat less than might be desirable). At one level, such concepts as *architectural style* have helped with classifying the wealth of implementation forms. However, in some ways this is more a matter of having the question of implementation form considered earlier in the design process rather than being a radical change in the nature of the design process itself.

The one factor that these developments have particularly highlighted, and the one that existing design practices (including many described in this book) have been least successful in addressing, is the continuing demand for faster delivery of systems. While this has always been a problem, the concept of 'internet time' is one which probably conflicts most strongly with the need for a reflective design process. To a considerable extent this arises because we can much more quickly adapt and extend our ideas about what systems *should* do, than develop solutions that describe *how* they are to do it. One characteristic of good design is that, given due care to preserve its structure, a system can be extended and modified without harming such other characteristics as response time, dependability and consistency. However, this characteristic is one that is unlikely to be achieved without expenditure of considerable effort. Whether this will prove achievable for many 'web-based' systems is an open question (Brereton *et al.*, 1998).

One way of achieving faster delivery of systems to their users is to employ a higher level of abstraction in terms of what we think of as 'software'. In the 1970s such a step was achieved by moving from writing programs using machine-specific assembler code to writing them in 'high-order languages'. This freed them from dependence on one particular make and type of computer and also enabled faster production of code. An approach offering the potential for a similar step at the design stage is to place greater emphasis on manipulating existing 'objects' and 'components' rather than designing new ones. We will be discussing these ideas in our later chapters.

However, since the main theme of this book is one of 'software design', for much of the time we take a very general and abstract view of what might constitute 'software', although we do pay attention to the effects of choosing specific forms of implementation where this may significantly affect design decisions. Indeed, our thesis here is one of unification, in that it can be argued that whatever the form(s) of software that are used to implement a system, its design should still reflect a set of consistent concepts and principles.

2.2 Building models

The difficulties involved in creating software-based systems have long been recognized. While apparently-related technology such as hardware design and production has raced along gaining orders of magnitude in performance, and similarly reducing price and size, software development techniques seem to have inched along in a series of relatively small steps. Various reasons are cited for this, and in his widely acclaimed paper 'No silver bullet: Essence and accidents of software engineering', Fred Brooks has pointed out some of the principal causes of this relatively slow progress (Brooks, 1987). In particular, Brooks cites the following properties of software as major factors affecting its development.

- *Complexity*. This is seen as being an essential property of software, in which no two parts are alike and a system may possess very many states during execution. This complexity is also arbitrary, being dependent upon the designer rather than the problem.

- *Conformity*. Software, being 'pliable', is expected to conform to the standards imposed by other components, such as hardware, or by external bodies, or by existing software.

- *Changeability*. Software suffers constant need for change, partly because of the apparent ease of making changes (and relatively poor techniques for costing them).

- *Invisibility*. Because software is 'invisible', any forms of representation that are used to describe it will lack any form of *visual* link that can provide an easily grasped relationship between the representation and the system – unlike, for example, a building plan which can be easily linked to the visible features of the building. This not only constrains our ability to conceptualize the characteristics of software, it also hinders communication among those involved with its development.

For these reasons (and especially the last one), while the act of designing software usually shares the general characteristics identified for design activity in Chapter 1, it incorporates many additional problems for the designer. We therefore begin this chapter by considering the key design factor of model-building, used by a designer to posit a solution.

The idea of using some form of 'model' to help with exploring design ideas is hardly new. The seventeenth-century shipbuilders constructed magnificent scale models of sailing ships, both as an aid to their own planning and also (equally important) as a means of conveying those plans to the shipyard workers who were to be tasked with constructing the vessel. So what exactly is a model? A typical dictionary definition reads something like the following:

> '*A three-dimensional representation, usually in miniature, of a thing to be constructed.*' (Larousse)

However, this is a rather physical view, and models may well be more abstract and may be concerned with more than just construction. An example of such an abstract form is that of the mathematical model, which may be employed for such tasks as predicting the stress in the components of a metal bridge; describing the life expectancies of insurance policyholders; and describing traffic flow at road junctions. Models of this type can also be used to predict the *behaviour* of a system within a given context or scenario, a role which corresponds much more closely to the needs of the software designer.

In developing software, we need models that are often less precise than the mathematician's models, while also being more abstract than those used by the ship-builder, and that are certainly not three-dimensional in the physical sense! However, their role is still to provide some form of *representation* of the designer's intentions. Models of software will usually be *abstract* (reduced to only the properties of direct interest), which also helps to address the issues of how we handle *scale*. In later chapters we will be examining some of the forms that such a model can take.

Constructing a model for a proposed solution allows the designer to explore the potential limitations of the solution as well as to assess its behaviour and structure. However, the examples used in the first two case studies (Chapter 1) required the designer to construct only relatively simple models in order to explore the 'solution space'. Simple, that is, as compared with the models that are needed to assist with the process of software design. In this section we will try to identify some of the main features and characteristics of the models that are used in software design.

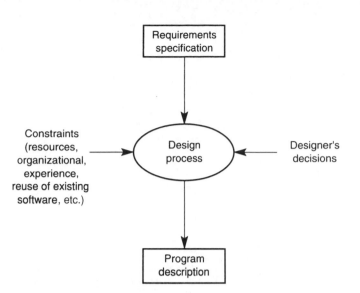

Figure 2.1   A general model of the software design process.

Figure 2.1 shows a (very general) 'model' of the software design process itself. The input to this process is provided by the Requirements Specification documents, while the outputs produced from it should consist of a set of detailed specifications that describe the form of the eventual program components. (Of course, we know from our discussion of the characteristics of wicked problems that this is a highly idealized account!)

In practice, and especially when developing larger systems, the process of design is apt to be divided into two distinct phases, as illustrated in Figure 2.2.

1. In the first phase, the designer develops a highly abstract model of a solution (the 'architectural' or 'logical' design) in which only the external properties of the model elements are included. This initial black-box partitioning of the problem is therefore largely concerned with the nature and form of the problem itself, and less strongly influenced by the eventual form that will be adopted for its solution.

2. In the second phase, the abstract 'chunks' of the problem that were identified in the first phase are mapped on to technologically-based units (the 'detailed' or 'phys-ical' design), hence turning the black box into a white box. Where design and implementation are separate responsibilities, it is the output from this phase that provides the specifications for the programmers.

Again, this is a rather idealistic description, but conceptually useful, even where it is not practical to keep the activities of the two phases separate (as, for example, when seeking to reuse existing components). So it is one that we will use when we come to review different approaches to software design in the later chapters. However, for the moment we will concentrate chiefly upon the general role of model-building during design, rather than upon the exact forms that the models and transformations will take for specific design strategies.

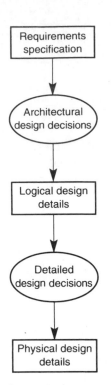

Figure 2.2 The major phases of the software design process.

The initial 'architectural model' that is used to describe the intended form that a system will take is generally highly abstract in its nature. The way that this is developed during the process of designing was examined in an interesting study of the ways that software designers work, made by Adelson and Soloway (1985). In their experiments, they studied the ways in which both experienced and inexperienced designers set about the task of forming their models when they were faced with a range of different problems. The experiments were based upon situations where a designer was posed:

- a familiar problem;
- a problem that was unfamiliar in detail, but taken from a familiar domain; and
- a problem that was unfamiliar in all senses.

The study was limited in scope, in that they looked at only a small number of subjects, and concentrated their study to a single specialized problem domain. Also, for practical reasons, the problems themselves were relatively small in scale. However, their findings do seem to reflect more general experience with the software design process. Some key observations that were produced from this research included:

- The use of abstract 'mental models' by the designer to simulate the dynamic behaviour of the eventual system that will be derived from the design.

- Expanding the detail of a model in a systematic manner by keeping all elements of the design at the same level of detail as they are developed. This then aids the task of simulation.

- The need to make any constraints affecting the design as explicit as possible when handling an unfamiliar problem.

- Reuse of previous design plans. This arises when part of a problem can be solved by using a previously developed design object or structure. Where this occurs, designers may use a 'label' to identify the plan, rather than describing it in detail at that point.

- Making notes about future (detailed) intentions, as an aid to systematic expansion of a design.

The last point is less directly concerned with the manner in which a model is developed and used, but it reflects the way in which an experienced designer avoids the pitfall of following one thread of a design in too much detail. (Fixing the details of one aspect of a design at too early a stage may severely, and inappropriately, later constrain the designer's choices for the other aspects.)

There have been relatively few empirical studies of software designers conducted within a controlled experimental environment that have examined the activities involved in software design from the viewpoint of the actions of the designer. However, others have conducted some similar studies of design activity in more 'normal' working situations (Curtis *et al.*, 1988; Visser and Hoc, 1990). While this work concentrated on studying the process of software *design*, rather than on *programming*, many programmers will recognize that some of the observed techniques are also used for the more detailed design tasks that they undertake when 'programming in the small'. For instance, many programmers probably perform simulations by executing mental models for sections of their programs when coding conditional loop structures: modelling the entry/exit conditions that occur when the loop is first executed, and checking to ensure that the loop will terminate in the intended manner. In that sense, the idea of simulation is a fairly familiar one, and it is clearly rather important at all levels of abstraction.

Returning to the large-scale issues of design (such as arise for the type of problem that we term 'programming in the large'), we will see when we come to examine different software design methods that many of these provide quite extensive forms of support for a designer in building initial abstract models in order to explore ideas. The forms used for the models may be graphical, as in the case of 'systematic' methods, or mathematically-based, in the case of the more 'formal' methods. In each case, the use of an abstract model generally allows the designer to predict the likely behaviour of a system for different scenarios. In addition, the models can be used to aid a systematic expansion of the initial ideas of the designer towards the production of a detailed design description.

The models formed during the early stages of design are mainly concerned with assisting either the analysis or the specification of the problem (or with both, since they are often entwined). If we return briefly to the more general view of the design process that was given on page 5, based upon the quotation from the work of J. Christopher Jones, we can see that this use of an initial abstract model corresponds with the idea that a designer needs to 'predict a future state' and so needs to assume the outcome of the design process in order to begin that process.

So in many ways, the various approaches to supporting and structuring the software design process that we will examine in this book are largely concerned with the different practices used for describing, constructing and elaborating models. Indeed, the knowledge that is needed to develop and assess such models can be considered as an important element in the designer's portfolio. In the next section, therefore, we examine this issue of knowledge transfer more fully and identify some of the other factors that may be involved in it.

2.3 Transferring design knowledge

Chapter 1 examined the nature of the general design process and showed that it is quite unlike the 'scientific' approach to problem-solving. The act of designing is not based upon an analytic strategy, aimed at identifying the one true solution to a problem, as determined by physical laws. Instead, it is a highly creative process, and certainly very unlikely to lead to the identification of a single solution to any given problem.

Experimental study of software designers and their practices suggests that, as might be expected, some people are better designers than others (Curtis *et al.*, 1988). However, since the number of truly great designers is very small, we need to seek ways of providing appropriate design skills to a wider group in as effective a manner as possible.

In Curtis *et al.*, (1988), the exceptional designers were observed to possess three significant characteristics. As illustrated in Figure 2.3, these are:

1. *Familiarity with the application domain*, enabling them to map between problem structures and solution structures with ease. (A domain in this sense may be one such as data processing, real-time, telecommunication systems, and so on.)

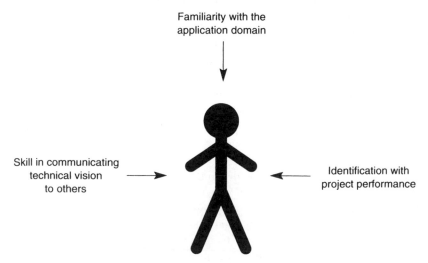

Figure 2.3 The characteristics of an exceptional designer.

2. *Skill in communicating technical vision to other project members.* This was observed to be so significant a factor that much of the design work was often accomplished while interacting with others.

3. *Identification with project performance*, to the extent that they could be found taking on significant management responsibilities for ensuring technical progress.

Interestingly, though, the exceptional designers studied often did not possess particularly good programming skills.

Others too have identified the importance of the domain knowledge of the designer for producing successful designs (Adelson and Soloway, 1985), and clearly this aspect can only come from the accumulation of experience in a particular problem domain. It may well be, though, that the process of acquiring such knowledge can be accelerated and improved.

When we look at how successful designers work, there are other factors to consider, apart from those that were outlined in the previous section. Visser and Hoc (1990) have used the term 'opportunistic' to describe observations of software design activity. Even where designers aim to follow a strategy such as 'top-down' (systematically refining the description of the solution into ever smaller actions), they may deviate from this plan, either:

■ to *postpone* a decision, if the information required is not yet available at this design level; or

■ to process information that is readily to hand, and which can be used for defining modules in *anticipation* of further developments in the design.

Such opportunistic design activity is not unstructured; instead, it is more likely to reflect the designer's experience and domain knowledge. One important consequence is that the developers of software design support tools should not give them an interface form that impedes this behaviour on the part of the designer.

Even if rigorous procedures for performing the transformations between the stages of a designer's model cannot be devised, there may still be benefits in seeking to codify design strategies in some way. Experienced designers can make use of opportunistic techniques precisely because they *are* experienced, and have extensive domain knowledge to guide their actions. However, such techniques are clearly inadequate where these characteristics are lacking, leaving the question of how are they to be acquired?

Domain knowledge can be acquired partly through experience, and also, to some degree, through learning a set of design practices that may be related to a particular domain. Such practices place emphasis upon making decisions that are based upon the key characteristics of the domain. One way of learning such practices is through the use of *design methods*. The idea of design methods emerged in the 1970s in order to meet this need for knowledge transfer, and in some ways their forms and use do seem to be something that is peculiar to software development. We can, therefore, regard the purpose of a software design method as being to provide the framework that will enable a designer to develop and elaborate a design in a systematic manner.

Design methods are not the only means of formalizing the transfer of domain knowledge, and more recently the idea of the *design pattern* is one that has offered a

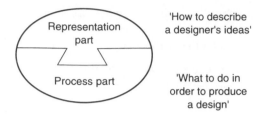

Figure 2.4 The two major components of a software design method.

less 'procedural' mechanism for this (Gamma *et al.*, 1995). However, since the use of design methods is deeply engrained in the software domain and hence in thinking about software design, we will focus here upon their role in knowledge transfer, returning to the concept of the pattern at a later point.

For our purposes, a software design method can be considered as providing a supportive framework that consists of two major components (shown schematically in Figure 2.4).

1. The *representation part* provides a set of descriptive forms that the designer can use for building both black box and white box models of the problem and their ideas for its solution, and for describing the structural features of the solution to the eventual implementors.

2. The *process part* is concerned with describing how the necessary transformations between the representation forms are to be organized, as well as with any elaboration of their detail that might be required.

A further component is provided in most design methods:

■ A set of *heuristics* that can be used to provide guidelines on the ways in which the activities defined in the process part can be organized for specific classes of problem. These are generally based upon experience of past use of the method within a particular domain or for a particular form of structure.

While these do not necessarily provide the domain knowledge that a designer needs, they may well aid in developing this knowledge.

The representation part of a design method will usually include forms that can be used for modelling the problem, as well as forms that reflect the significant structures of the implementation media. As an example of the latter form: in describing a garden shed, one would use drawings that described its plan, elevation and end view, and which showed how key joints were to be assembled. In describing software, one will typically use detailed design forms that describe the structures of the program sub-units, the relationships that these have with one another, and the relationships that they have with the other entities in the system.

So representation forms generally reflect the properties of the objects in the design. Those forms that describe the detailed design may be concerned with fairly concrete properties such as the calling hierarchy, complex data structures, number of parameters and so on. On the other hand, the forms that are used for problem modelling will be concerned with more abstract properties of the problem objects and any relationships that may exist between these. This model will usually be based upon relatively abstract concepts such as operations and information flow, and as such, comes closest to providing the 'domain knowledge' element needed by a designer by placing emphasis upon the domain features that are considered to be of the greatest significance.

The process part of design is rather more difficult to quantify and classify. Its structure may be derived from fairly general theory, from specific 'principles', or from heuristics ('it worked well when we did it this way before'). Most likely, it will reflect a mix of all three of these. In general there is a lack of strong theoretical underpinnings for existing design methods, and even the underlying principles may themselves be relatively empirical in nature. However, we can still identify some of the expectations that we have from the process part of a design method, which will include providing some degree of guidance for the following tasks:

- identification of the design actions to be performed;

- use of the representation forms;

- procedures for making transformations between representations;

- quality measures to aid in making choices;

- identification of particular constraints to be considered;

- verification/validation operations.

Most design methods provide strategic guidance for the designer, rather than detailed solutions to issues. To a large extent this is driven by the problem-oriented nature of many of the choices that a designer has to make: the role of the method is to help the designer to identify the choices available, and to evaluate these in terms of their likely consequences.

Akin (1990) has suggested that there are three 'classic' conditions that are observed in creative acts such as design. These are:

1. The *recognition step*, sometimes termed the 'Aha!' response. This is a skill in which the designer recognizes a solution that has been there all along. (This form of creative act is perhaps more typical of scientific progress than of design progress although when we later come to study the concept of the *design pattern*, we will see that effective use of patterns does depend upon a form of recognition step.)

2. The *problem restructuring* step, in which a change of viewpoint that is used to describe or model a problem leads to a major breakthrough in solving it. As an example, in solving a given problem, the designer may decide to store the data in an array. This choice may subsequently require a highly complex set of algorithms, and the designer may later realize that using a linked list in place of the array will result in much simpler algorithms.

3. The *development of procedural knowledge* about how such problems are best solved, allowing the designer to perform many creative acts within a domain. (Again, Akin notes that there are many fields of human endeavour where this can be seen to apply.)

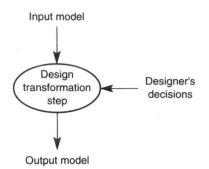

Figure 2.5 Transformation model of design activity.

A major component of the process part of a design method is the structuring of the design transformations. The sequence that is expressed in the 'process diagram' used in Figure 2.2 is, of course, still a fairly abstract one, and omits any detail about the iterations that will normally occur as a designer explores and evaluates the design options. Any 'formal' inclusion of the heuristics is also omitted, since the nature of these is too strongly method-specific.

If we explore further the transformation steps themselves, we find that for each step we can identify a general structure of the form shown in Figure 2.5. Each transformation involves:

- an *input model* that may be described by using a suitable 'representation' (which may be graphical, textual or mathematical);

- an *output model* that, again, can have any of these forms;

- *design inputs* through which the designer adds information to the model.

In addition, we can identify two principal forms of design transformation, which respectively involve:

- the *refinement* (or *elaboration*) of structures, in which the input and output forms of the model are the same, but extra detail is added;

- the *transformation of viewpoint*, which may involve a change of representation form or introduce a different interpretation of the representation form.

In general, the transformations that involve refinement are apt to preserve the representation form while adding more detail; while those that involve a change of viewpoint add both decisions and a change of the structure of the design model. In the former case, the designer is chiefly concerned with reducing the eventual 'solution space' by making additional choices and decisions; whereas in the latter he or she may be adding information about new relationships between design objects.

The view of design as being a series of transformations is one that has been explored and used in a number of ways (Lehman *et al.*, 1984; Friel and Budgen, 1997). As a general model it provides a useful summary of design method structuring, and it will be used for this purpose in the chapters that describe specific design methods.

As indicated earlier, design methods have formed part of the software designer's support base since the 1970s. However, in providing this support, their form and nature can also be a constraining influence upon creativity (Budgen, 1999) and there are aspects of 'conventional' design behaviour that they are ill-equipped to support, most notably the reuse of part-solutions that have previously been used successfully.

Partly through the need to address this problem, as well as for other reasons, two other approaches to assisting with the transfer of design and domain knowledge were developed in the 1990s. The concept of *software architecture* (Shaw and Garlan, 1996) can be considered as taking a more structural and less procedural approach to thinking about how a design can be developed. Similarly, the idea of the *design pattern* that was mentioned earlier (Gamma *et al.*, 1995) has focused upon categorizing solution structures that can be reused for different problems.

Of course, as always occurs when considering design issues, there are trade-offs involved in their application. While both of these approaches offer much better scope for reusing successful ideas than 'traditional' software design methods do, the lack of a procedural element can make them less readily accessible to the novice and, in the case of design patterns, there are questions about how well the concept will scale up (how many patterns are likely to be both useful and accessible in a given context?).

We will return to look at both of these approaches in later chapters. In many senses, their key contribution to the task of transferring design and domain knowledge is through providing strategies that are complementary to those employed in design methods. Unfortunately though, as so often occurs in software development, finding ways to combine the strengths of different approaches is apt to prove elusive.*

2.4 Constraints upon the design process and product

In practice, there are very few opportunities to design a system with a totally free hand, since each design task takes place within a particular context, and this will provide particular constraints upon the form of the design itself and possibly on the way that it is produced. We have already seen this in the case studies of developing designs for moving house and for a garden shed. In the example of moving house, the constraints were concerned both with functional issues (blocking power outlets or windows) and with aesthetic ones (clashes of style or colour, or putting a bed in the dining room etc.). These considerations largely act to constrain the form of the solution (or product in this case). For the example of designing garden sheds, the main constraints were again on the form of the product, and were driven by the need to provide a way of constructing sheds from easily prefabricated units.

Similarly, for the case of software design, we can readily identify many of the constraints imposed upon the form of the product. Some may be determined by the eventual run-time environment (organization of file structures; the 'look and feel' of the user interface), while others may relate to the need to conform to the conventions required by a chosen architectural style (JavaBeans; forms of remote access; choice between

---

* Software often seems to possess characteristics that resemble the physicists' dilemma with the *particle-wave duality* exhibited by light, in which it can have the characteristics of one form or the other in any given situation, but not both.

processes or objects; etc.). Where it is also intended that the eventual system will be constructed by reusing existing software components, this may lead to further constraints upon the 'acceptable' architectural styles that the components may possess (Garlan *et al.*, 1995) as well as upon the task of allocating functionality between components.

Perhaps one of the most important constraints on the design task and the form of the design itself is that of the eventual form of implementation. For many years the approach used by most software development projects has been to purchase the hardware and select the major software facilities (operating system, programming language) before even beginning on the design task itself. While enlightenment may be (very slowly) dawning, the choice of the programming language is still more likely to be determined by external factors such as programmer skills and knowledge than by the features of the problem itself.

The imperative forms of programming language (COBOL, ALGOL, FORTRAN, Ada, C, C++, Modula-2, Java and scripting languages such as Javascript etc.) have remained the dominant tool in software production. Indeed, the use of imperative language constructs is implicit in almost all design methods currently available, and so will be assumed throughout this book. However, the use of imperative forms is not essential to the design process, and the principles of design studied here are certainly not restricted to the imperative paradigm alone.

Constraints on the process of design are more difficult to identify. They may be concerned with designer skills and knowledge (experience with a particular method), or with a need to conform to a particular 'architectural style' of design, in order to aid future maintenance. In some cases, a constraint upon the product leads to a constraint upon the process – where, say, the output form needs to be consistent with that generally produced from a particular design strategy.

Whatever form they take, constraints can be considered as forming a set of bounds upon the 'solution space'. Even if the process of design will not necessarily converge upon one solution for a given problem, the effects of the constraints may be to limit the amount of possible divergence that will be acceptable in particular circumstances.

Many constraints will be identified in the initial specification documents (or at least, they *should* appear here), although this will not necessarily be true for those that are related to any expectations of reuse. Whatever their source, constraints effectively limit the overall solution space by limiting the range of choices available to the designer. (There is also the risk, of course, that inconsistencies in specification may actually make it impossible to find a solution!) Some constraints are problem-specific (such as the level of user skills that should be assumed for a new application), while others are more solution-specific (such as architectural style). While problem-specific constraints cannot readily be incorporated into any formal design process (such as a design method), their influence does need to be considered at every step. One way to identify and track constraints is through the use of regular *design reviews*, which can be given the role of ensuring that an audit trail is maintained.

2.5 Recording design decisions

The need to record the decisions of the designer (or, for larger projects, of the design team) is important, from the viewpoint of the design task itself, and even more so from the viewpoint of the maintenance team who may later need to extend and modify the design. Unfortunately, while designers may diligently record the actual decisions, it is much rarer to record the rationale that forms the basis for the final choice. (Experience suggests that this is not a problem that is confined to software engineering alone: it seems to occur in many other branches of engineering practice too.)

Beginning with the original task of design, the recording of rationale is likely to be encouraged if the design process includes any form of **design audit**. Such an audit may consist of peer review of the designer's ideas, or may be something more formal that is conducted by the project manager. Whatever the form, if audits are held, they will be more systematically and usefully performed if the reasons for decisions are recorded.

There is an even stronger need on the part of the system maintenance task (which is thought to involve around 50–80 per cent of programmer and designer effort). In order to modify or extend a design, the maintenance designers need to be able to recapture the original models that were used by the designers of a system. Only when they have a reasonably complete model can they reliably decide how to implement their changes in the most effective manner (Littman *et al.*, 1987). Possessing some record of the reasons for the existing structure can help both with recreating this model and with evaluating the effects of any changes. In turn, the reasons for the change need to be added to the records kept by the maintainers, in order to maintain a consistent and complete history of the system design.

So a major motivation for recording the reasoning behind any design decisions is one of quality control, both at the design stage and also much later, during maintenance. Only if we have a complete picture can we hope to fully understand a design, and this is an essential factor in producing a good, reliable design.

Unfortunately, while software design methods generally provide good forms of support for recording decisions about product issues, usually through diagrams or other notation, they are generally weaker on process matters, such as recording the reasons for the decision. While the recording of decisions and their reasons can fairly easily be made a part of design practice, it is relatively hard to enforce it unless there is a strong quality control system in operation.

The way in which design decisions are recorded is obviously somewhat dependent upon the design process adopted. Some work has been performed to look at ways of modelling this process of design deliberation – the 'Potts and Bruns model' (Potts and Bruns, 1988; Lee, 1991) – and it has been demonstrated for the JSD method. As yet, though, there is little or no general tool support that can be used for this task.

An important issue in terms of recording decisions about a design has been raised by Parnas and Clements (1986). They have observed that, even if the design process actually used to produce a design is not a rational one, the documentation that is finally produced should still make it appear as though it were. In other words, the documentation should be written as though the 'ideal' design process was the one that was followed. Indeed, they argue that since design will never be a rational process (as we have been observing throughout this and the preceding chapter), any documentation produced will always need to 'fake' this appearance of rationality.

The principal benefits of such an approach are that new members of a design team should be able to absorb knowledge about the project much more easily, and also that the eventual task of maintaining the system will also be made easier. Parnas and Clements observe that even for a scientific document such as a mathematical proof, the form published is rarely the form of the initial derivation, since, as understanding grows, simplifications can usually be found. Readers need the simpler proof, since they are interested in the truth of the theorem, not the process of its discovery. In the same way, it is the structure of a design that matters to the new team member or the maintainer, and not the way it was developed.

Before concluding this section, we should also briefly refer to one of the more interesting social and technical developments of the 1980s and 1990s, namely the emergence of *open source software*. Such software is made freely available and is usually the work of many developers, contributed on a voluntary basis. While there are many examples of this type of software product, the *Linux* operating system is probably the best known (and has been used as the platform for preparing this revised edition). We will be returning to look at how the development of such software is organized in the next chapter, but in the context of this section we should note that both version control and documentation are essential elements in managing the efforts of so many volunteers (Wu and Lin, 2001). Curiously though, at time of writing, there has been little academic study into how the processes that are involved in developing open source software differ from those employed in the more 'traditional' forms of development described in the preceding paragraphs.

We will return to the issue of design documentation in later chapters. It is certainly one where software's characteristic of 'invisibility', and the complexity of its nature, are made very evident!

2.6 Designing with others

While the development of a sound design is important for software development tasks of any scale, it is essential for any form of programming in the large, where a project is likely to involve a design team rather than a single designer. Given the nature of the design process, it is hardly surprising that designing as a team adds further complications, many of them in the form of added constraints upon the process, and hence upon the form of the product. (For medium-sized systems it sometimes appears as though there were an invariant 'law' of design that specified that the number of design modules should be equal to the number of members of the design team!)

Many of the very successful and 'exciting' software systems have been the work of one or a few 'great designers'. Brooks (1987) contrasts the 'excitement' of Unix, Pascal, Modula, SmallTalk and similar systems with the 'blandness' of COBOL, PL/1, MVS/370 and MS-DOS as examples that support this point. (A more recent contrast might be Linux versus Windows XX!)

In the absence of any great designers, designing a system through the use of a team brings two major additional issues that need to be handled within the chosen design strategy. These are:

■ how to split the design task among the team, and to determine the interfaces between the parts;

■ how to integrate the individual contributions to the design, which may well involve a process of negotiation between the members of the team.

The first of these problems is at least partly aided by the increasing trend towards modular designs, an issue that will be examined at a later point. For the moment, it is sufficient to note that this strategy does help with the problem of subdividing the design operations among a team, although it is still necessary to ensure a fair balance of effort, where appropriate.

Bringing the elements of a design together, along with the accompanying negotiations, is again a mix of technical and managerial issues. While a process of negotiation may be right and necessary, it should not be allowed to reduce the integrity of the overall design.

Some of the original research studying how programming (and hence designing) is performed by teams was described in Gerald Weinberg's classic book *The Psychology of Computer Programming* (Weinberg, 1971). In this he observed the effects of different forms of group organization, ranging from groups that worked as an 'egoless' set of peers (in which different members of the group might take the lead for specific tasks), to those that had a highly hierarchical form.

The more hierarchical approach was at one time advocated by the exponents of the 'chief programmer' school (Baker, 1972; Brooks, 1975). Set in the design context, the chief programmer functions as a chief designer, acting in a highly centralized role, with the other members of the team performing functions that are solely intended to support his or her activity. The parallel usually drawn has been with the surgical team – which rather begs the question of the very different purpose of the latter. Members of the team might have specialized roles themselves, such as librarian, administrator or documentation expert, and there is a back-up who acts as the technical deputy to the chief programmer.

In practice, few design teams seem to act along such lines, perhaps because there are few great designers who can take on the very exacting central role it demands.

Researchers have also sought to understand and model the psychological factors that influence team behaviour in designing (Curtis *et al.*, 1988; Curtis and Walz, 1990). The factors discussed in these references include:

- the size of a team (there seem to be pointers that a size of 10–12 members is probably an upper limit for productive working);
- the large impact that may be exerted by a small subset of the members of the team who possess superior application domain knowledge;
- the influence of organizational issues within a company (and particularly the need to maintain a bridge between the developers and the customer).

This last point raises an important issue in that:

> 'Designers needed operational scenarios of system use to understand the application's behaviour and its environment. Unfortunately, these scenarios were too seldom passed from the customer to the developer. Customers often generated many such scenarios in determining their requirements, but did not record them and abstracted them out of the requirements document.' (Curtis *et al.*, 1988)

This point is an interesting one, for it is relevant not only to the use of design teams, but addresses a much wider organizational issue in itself. (Figure 2.6 shows the full set

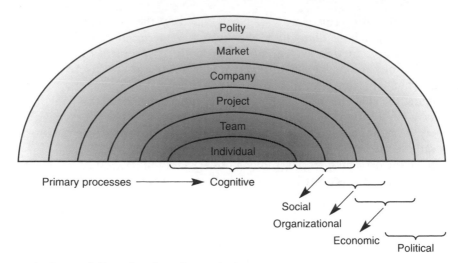

Figure 2.6 Factors influencing the software design process.

(After Curtis *et al.*, (1988))

of factors identified in Curtis *et al.*, 1988.) We will return later to examine more recent thinking about the roles of scenarios and 'use cases' in software development.

For the present, however, the key issues of design team operation seem to lie more in the domain of group psychology than in that of design technology. Certainly few, if any, of the more widely used design methods offer any significant guidance on how they should be adapted for use by a team as opposed to an individual, and it would seem that they are probably correct to avoid doing so. To quote from Curtis and Walz (1990):

> '*Programming in the large is, in part, a learning, negotiation, and communication process.*'

Unfortunately, to date far more effort has gone into technical research than into investigating team and organizational factors.

Summary

This chapter has enlarged upon the issues that were raised in Chapter 1 by considering how they apply to the particular domain of software design. Major points from this chapter are:

■ the widening interpretation of what consists 'software';

■ the complexity of the model-building processes for software systems, with their need to consider static forms as well as the dynamic behaviour of the eventual system;

■ the influence of the invisible nature of software upon any attempts to describe it;

■ the need for domain knowledge on the part of the designer;

- how the observed practices of software designers relate to the model of the general design process that was presented, and in particular, the use of opportunistic design practices by designers;

- the general form of a design method, and its three major components: the representation part, the process part, and the heuristics;

- how to go about recording the results of the design process, presenting an ideal view of design development by 'faking' an ideal development process;

- some of the factors that affect the operation of design teams, and how this differs from individual design practices.

Further reading

Brooks F.P. Jr (1987). No silver bullet: Essence and accidents of software engineering. *IEEE Computer*, 10–19

This paper brings together the many years of experience gained by Professor Brooks, and comments upon the prospects for improving the development processes for software that are offered by a number of emerging technologies. A good summary of the issues that make progress with software development so difficult.

Curtis B., Krasner H. and Iscoe N. (1988). A field study of the software design process for large systems. *Comm. ACM*, **31**(11), 1268–87

This paper describes an analysis performed on data gathered by interviewing personnel from 17 large projects. A particular feature is the consideration of the influence of various factors within the organization.

Détienne F. (2002). *Software Design – Cognitive Aspects*. Springer Practitioner Series ISBN 1-85233-253-0

A very scholarly text which takes a psychological view of software design, reviewing both theoretical ideas and also empirical studies. Useful reading for anyone wanting a more cognitively-oriented view of software design issues.

Exercises

2.1 Consider a recent item of software that you may have written. Thinking about how you developed it, are you aware of any way in which you might have reused experience from previous programs in deciding upon particular structures or algorithms?

2.2 The reuse of domain knowledge is clearly a feature that will take different forms in particular domains. Consider what particular forms of experience might be useful in the domains of

(a) processing financial transactions
(b) real-time process control for chemical plants
(c) writing compilers for imperative programming languages.

2.3 Design documentation, if available at all, often merely details the final structure of a system. Write down a list of the information about the development of a system that would be useful to you if you had to undertake a major revision of it in order to add new features.

2.4 Committees are a form of design team in some circumstances. Think back to when you were last a member of a committee that successfully produced a 'design' as a collective exercise, and identify the factors that made this possible.

chapter 3

Design in the Software Development Process

The development of any large computer-based system (sometimes referred to as 'programming in the large') is one that involves many activities – of which software design is but one – even if a very central one. In this chapter we examine some of the ways in which systems are developed, and consider how the organization of the development process can influence the design task. We conclude by considering a longer-term view of systems and their evolution and maintenance, and consider what effect this might have upon design choices.

3.1 A context for design

The discussion of the preceding two chapters has been very much for the purpose of clarifying our views of what constitutes the subject matter of the book, in terms of both the design process in general, and the ways in which this is influenced by the characteristics of software. However, the task of design is not something that takes place in isolation, and in this chapter we examine some of the other factors that can influence the design process, by virtue of its context within the overall task of software development.

There are many ways in which a 'large software system' can be developed to meet particular needs or perceived markets. While each of these generally involves performing largely the same set of activities, the emphasis put upon each one, and the ways in which they are ordered and interwoven, will be very different. Table 3.1 provides a brief overview of some of the forms of development that are commonly adopted, the reasons why a particular form might be used, and some examples of the domains where its use might be most appropriate.

For many years, almost all systems were of course 'made to measure', and the concept of the *software life-cycle* which emerged as a description of how the necessary development activities were usually organized has been widely recognized to be very valuable – provided we accept that it encompasses many forms and variations (Royce, 1970; Boehm 1988; Davis *et al.*, 1988). It is also important to recognize that one of the risks involved in employing such a useful concept is that its very usefulness might result in it becoming institutionalized, and then used to *constrain* creativity rather than to support it (McCracken and Jackson, 1982; Gladden, 1982).

Ideas about how the software development process might be best organized have undergone a process of evolution that is similar to the way in which ideas about design have evolved. (A good overview of this evolution of thinking about life-cycle models is

Table 3.1 Some examples of software development processes

Development process	Reasons for adoption	Typical domains
Linear (e.g. 'waterfall')	Where the needs are reasonably well determined and a 'longer' delivery time is acceptable.	Many 'made to measure' systems are developed in this way. This approach is one that has been used very widely and is still appropriate for systems that need to demonstrate any form of high integrity.
Incremental	Where there may be a need to demonstrate feasibility of an idea; establish a market position rapidly; or explore whether a market might exist. Providing a rapid time to market is often an important factor for adopting such an approach.	Widely used for 'shrink wrap' software of all sorts, such as office packages, games, operating systems. Also, where there is a need to interact closely with the end-users during development.
Reactive	Where evolution of a system is largely in response to what the developers perceive as being needed.	Open source software of all kinds is generally developed in this way, as are many websites.

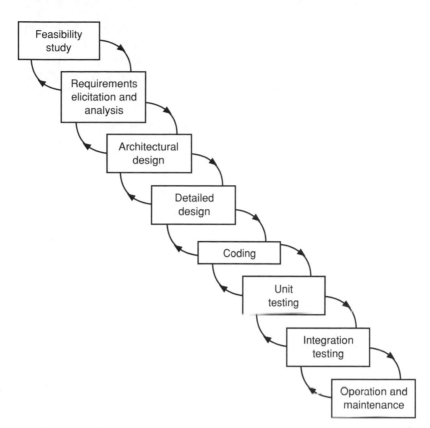

Figure 3.1 The waterfall model of the software life-cycle.

given in Boehm (1988).) Royce's formulation of the **waterfall model** (Royce, 1970), a version of which is shown in Figure 3.1, was a particularly influential refinement of earlier thinking that explicitly recognized the presence of 'feedback loops' between the various stages of development. (In many ways, this corresponds to recognizing that the task of development is yet another example of a 'wicked problem'.)

Boehm (1988) has pointed out that a software process model of this form addresses the following software project questions.

1. What should we do next?

2. How long should we continue to do it?

However, as we will see with the case of design methods in later chapters, its role is much more concerned with identifying where these questions should be asked than with answering them!

However formulated, most development processes tend to be couched in terms of the phases identified in the original waterfall structure shown in Figure 3.1, and one might well argue that these encompass a set of tasks that always need to be addressed in some way, regardless of their sequencing. The specific processes described in Table 3.1 are discussed more fully in the following two sections, and in the rest of this section we briefly review the roles of the different development phases. In keeping with the spirit of our main theme, however, our discussion will be mainly in terms of how these tasks relate to the design phases; for a fuller discussion of process models and development tasks the reader should consult a more general text on Software Engineering such as Pfleeger (2001), Pressman (2000), Sommerville (2001) and Van Vliet (2000). Although terminology differs slightly between these sources, all discuss the main two forms, namely the waterfall model and the prototyping approach.

As with processes, so it is with tasks. While the terminology used in different sources may differ a little, the following are a practical set for our purposes:

- *Feasibility study*. The role of such a study (where performed) is essentially to explore whether a solution is attainable within the given set of constraints. So such a study will at least give some preliminary thought to design issues, even if only at the architectural level (what form of solution might be most practical).

- *Requirements elicitation*. Here the objective is to identify what 'end-user' needs the intended system is required to meet. It is sometimes suggested that an ideal approach to this task is for it to be completely independent of any considerations of eventual design and implementation. However, this is increasingly less appropriate, especially where one system will need to interact with others, and also where the reuse of existing software is encouraged.

- *Analysis*. Traditionally this is usually seen as a more formal modelling of the *problem* (that is, of the needs identified in the documents produced from the requirements elicitation stage). Obviously this forms a major input to the design process, and can very easily drift into making solution-based assumptions.

- *Architectural design*. Concerned with the overall form of solution to be adopted (for example, whether to use a distributed system, what the major elements will be and how they will interact).

- *Detailed design*. Developing descriptions of the elements identified in the previous phase, and obviously involving interaction with this. There are also clear feedback loops to earlier phases if the designers are to ensure that the behaviour of their solution is to meet the requirements.

- *Coding (implementation)*. This may involve devising data and communication structures and writing large amounts of code or, increasingly, involve writing 'glue' code to join existing components together. Effectively, though, it involves 'translating' the abstract design plans into some form of realised system and therefore takes its inputs from the design phase.

- *Unit and integration testing*. Essentially these phases involve validating the implemented system against the original requirements, the specification produced from the Analysis phase, and the design itself.

- *Operation and maintenance*. Operation can sometimes resemble an extended testing phase, providing feedback from users in many ways. Maintenance is a rather different issue – it may involve repeating all the tasks of the preceding phases and, indeed, preserving the integrity of the system (in other words, the consistency of its design plan) could well be an important constraint upon the task of maintenance. The timescale for these last two phases can also be very long.

The proportion of effort allocated to these tasks is one that depends upon many factors. However, a study of the practices of software developers that drew upon a global set of data suggests that the variations are not as great as might be expected (Blackburn *et al.*, 1996). The task classified in the study as 'detailed design' was particularly stable, taking around 20 per cent of total effort and 20 per cent of total time. Interestingly, this seemed to be true regardless of whether the organizations were classified as being 'fast' (showing improvements in development speed of over 25 per cent during the previous five years) or 'slow' (improvement of 25 per cent or less).

As might be expected, regardless of how these tasks are organized, the design task is strongly linked to the tasks that precede it in the above list. To clarify their roles a little more, therefore, we shall examine the simple example of a computer system that is to support the issue, reservation and recall of books, CDs and videos for a local library branch. Very briefly, these are as follows.

Requirements elicitation will be concerned with identifying the needs of the library staff and users, in terms of the purposes of the library. An example of such a need might be the facility for identifying those books that have particularly long reservation lists, so that the library staff can consider whether to order additional copies. Such an analysis will usually also consider the interactions and organizational relationships that may exist between the various needs of the users of the system.

Analysis will create a model of how the library works and hence produce a list of functions that the system will need to provide, and the behaviour it should exhibit when performing these functions under given conditions. As an example, the book reservation function should specify the effects of adding a request when the maximum number of books that a borrower has on loan or requested is exceeded – and even what is to happen when the borrower already has the book being requested! (One problem for analysis is that it may not be appropriate to 'freeze' particular organizational models of practice without considering the likely effects of introducing the new system. It may well be that in our example the library might be better advised also to change some of the practices or rules that were originally formulated for the purpose of handling paper-based records. One of the roles of the analysis task should, therefore, be to identify where such changes might be appropriate.)

The specification for this system may also need to describe the way in which the users' interactions with the final system are to be organized (the 'look and feel' aspects). The design of human–computer interfaces is still a relatively specialized and difficult art, with a strong multi-disciplinary flavour. In this example it will be a very important element, since the efficiency with which the librarians will be able to perform their tasks will be strongly affected by the ease with which they can interact with the information presented to them. (In some ways, this relates to the designer's own use of 'mental models', since the interface should provide the librarians with a structure that matches their own mental models of the processes that are involved. We might reasonably also expect that this will be expressed in terms of 'library objects' rather than 'computing objects'.)

So the output from requirements elicitation is *user*-oriented, while that from analysis is *solution*-oriented. Indeed, the role of analysis is an important one, since it forms the 'watershed' at which thinking moves from stating the problem or need, to beginning to think about how it can be met.

As the discussion of the following sections will show, the processes involved are rarely as sequential as might have been implied in the preceding paragraphs. Even where a sequential process of development is pursued, some backtracking and revision to the outputs from earlier phases will be needed each time some inconsistency or omission is revealed while performing the later tasks. Also, as we will see later, eliciting the 'real' needs of the user may involve some development of prototypes in order to help them see new and better ways of organizing their work to take advantage of what a computer-based system can do for them.

This last point is particularly true where there is no established 'market' for a new application. In that case, the usefulness of the application needs to be demonstrated at an early stage of development, and user feedback may well be essential for it to fully develop its potential. One of the characteristics of developing software artifacts (indeed, many other forms of artifact too), is that users may well devise new and imaginative applications for an item of software that are very different from those that the original developers had envisaged!

3.2 Linear development processes

The most familiar form of linear development process is that based upon the waterfall model shown in Figure 3.1. As indicated in Table 3.1, this has traditionally been the development process used to create 'made to measure' systems.

One of the attractions in such a form (and, indeed, one of the motivations for developing life-cycle models) is that it provides a strong management framework for planning developments as well as for monitoring and controlling them. Within such a form, the planning can identify 'milestones' that can be used to record progress against some general plan of production. However, as already observed, such an approach can easily result in the framework becoming a straitjacket (Gladden, 1982; McCracken and Jackson, 1982), and it is far better employed for providing a description of what *has* been done than for assisting in the planning of what *is* to be done.

Such a form is, therefore, also attractive to the purchasers of such systems, since it allows for long-term budgetary planning, as well as providing the basis for legal contracts. The fact that this is almost certainly inappropriate for a creative process may well explain why the history of procurement of software by government agencies has tended to form something of a dismal catalogue!

One thing we can conclude is that the main effect of production models of any form is to influence the *organization* (and hence the form) of the software design process itself. Since linear forms usually provide a stronger framework for management, it will not, therefore, be surprising when we come to look at design methods to find that these largely assume the use of a linear life-cycle, and of the waterfall model in particular.

While process models are an important element in Software Engineering as a whole, it is inappropriate to pursue the topic too deeply in this book, since our only real concern here is how they affect the process of design. However, before moving on to look at other, non-linear, forms of model, we should very briefly mention one other linear form.

The *transform model* is one that periodically attracts attention. In many ways, the aim is to extend the idea of the compiler (which automatically generates machine-specific code) to a higher level of abstraction (Lehman *et al.*, 1984). The goal, therefore, is to achieve automatic conversion of a formal specification of a system into a program that satisfies that specification. Little practical progress has been made in this area, and the arguments of the preceding two chapters suggest some good reasons why this might be so. However, more limited versions of the model do seem to offer more scope for progress (Friel and Budgen, 1997).

3.3 Incremental development processes

A major limitation of a linear development process is that the need to identify exactly what is required of the eventual system has to be addressed right from the start. In some cases this is effectively impractical, and there are many more where, despite considerable advances in techniques for determining the eventual requirements, there may be many uncertainties and possible omissions.

In other engineering domains, such a situation is often resolved by the construction of some form of **prototype** which can be used to investigate both problem and solution. However, where software is concerned, the concept of the 'prototype' is a bit harder to define with any exactitude. For more traditional forms of engineering, a prototype is generally regarded as being a 'first of its kind', or some form of model that is produced to scale. We are all familiar with the idea of a prototype of a new model of a car, and with scale models of buildings or ships. (On a somewhat larger scale, the civil engineers constructing the Thames Barrage down-river from London built a scale model of it in the nearby marshes.)

In the case of software, where manufacturing the end product is simply a matter of making copies, these analogies do not really apply. In software production it is quite possible that the prototype will actually *be* the product in due course, and there is really no concept equivalent to that of the scale model. (In that sense, there are really no short-cuts to writing software, although sometimes more abstract toolkits can help.) However, while the *form* of a prototype might be different for the case of software, the basic *reasons* for building prototypes remain much the same as in other forms of engineering: prototypes are constructed in order to explore an idea more completely than would be possible by other means.

A useful categorization of the different roles that prototyping can play in software development has been produced by Floyd (1984). Her analysis recognizes three principal roles for software prototypes.

1. *Evolutionary.* This is the form that is closest to the idea of the 'incremental development' of a solution. The software for a system is adapted gradually, by changing the requirements step by step as these become clearer with use, and changing the system to fit these. In this form, prototyping is used to develop a product and the prototype gradually evolves into the end product.

   One benefit of this strategy is that it may be possible to issue a release of the product while it is still technically incomplete, although usable. (Of course, many software products such as word processors, operating systems, etc. are really never complete, since their roles are effectively unbounded.) Later releases can then provide the users with a gradual increase in product functionality. While this approach to development may not be appropriate for all purposes, it does have some attractions in areas that involve a degree of 'pioneering', and also where it is important to get an early release of a system into the marketplace (Cusumano and Selby, 1997).

2. *Experimental.* This role is distinguished by the use of the prototype for evaluating a possible *solution* to a problem, by developing it in advance of large-scale implementation. The reasons for doing this may be manifold, including the assessment of performance and resource needs, evaluation of the effectiveness of a particular form of user interface, assessment of an algorithm and so on. This form of prototype is essentially intended to be a 'throw-away' item, and might well be implemented in a form quite different to that which will be used for the final system itself.

3. *Exploratory.* In this role a prototype is used to help with clarifying user *requirements* and possibly with identifying how the introduction of the system might lead to the need to modify the wider work practices of an organization. One purpose might be to help with developing an analysis of users' needs by providing a set of possible models for them to use and assess. Essentially this form of prototype is also likely to be a 'throw-away' item, and it can be considered as enhancing the information that is provided from the requirements analysis and the functional specification activities.

   Used in this role, the prototype provides something in the nature of a feasibility study. Much of it may be incomplete, since the purpose may be focused on resolving only limited aspects of system functionality. Some form of monitoring facility is likely to be a useful feature in this kind of prototype, its aim being to use the data collected to help with making a final evaluation.

Of course, any actual use of a prototyping approach may span these forms, since there may be many different reasons for developing a prototype. However, going back to the theme of this chapter, regardless of purpose, the processes of prototyping are (not surprisingly) relatively difficult to describe within a process model.

Boehm's **spiral model,** while in many ways a rather 'visionary' one when published, is probably the most effective approach to combining experience in using the waterfall model with greater knowledge of how software projects have actually been developed (Boehm, 1988). As such, it explicitly assumes the use of prototyping (although not of a particular form or purpose). An outline of this is shown in Figure 3.2, and at each stage of the spiral the following activities should occur:

■ the *objectives* of the stage are identified;

■ the *options* and *constraints* are listed and explored;

■ the *risks* involved in choosing between options are evaluated;

■ a *plan* for how to proceed to the next stage is determined, which may require the development of a prototype, or may more closely approximate to a traditional waterfall step, according to the conclusions of the risk analysis.

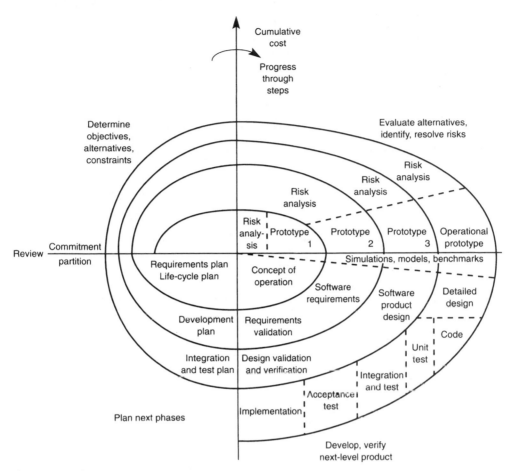

Figure 3.2 The spiral model of the software life-cycle.

(After Boehm (1981) © 1981 IEEE)

Within the context of a prototyping strategy, perhaps the most important element to highlight from this list is that of *risk evaluation*, since this links back to the very reasons why such an approach might need to be adopted. In particular, given that one of the risks implicit in the use of prototyping itself is that the sense of 'direction' may become lost, the spiral model offers a particularly valuable means of monitoring and controlling the development process.

The third form of development cycle that was identified in Table 3.1, the *reactive*, is one that it is also appropriate to consider in this section, since it can be seen as a variation upon the incremental approach. Since the development of **open source** software is probably the best-known example of this approach, we will discuss it largely in this context.

While the roots of the open source movement lie back in the pioneering work of Richard Stallman's *Free Software Foundation* (http://www.fsf.org/fsf/fsf.html) and the GNU project (a recursive definition of GNU is 'GNU's Not Unix'!), wider awareness of the concept did not emerge until the 1990s, when the Linux operating system kernel came together with GNU to provide a widely distributed free operating system for PCs.

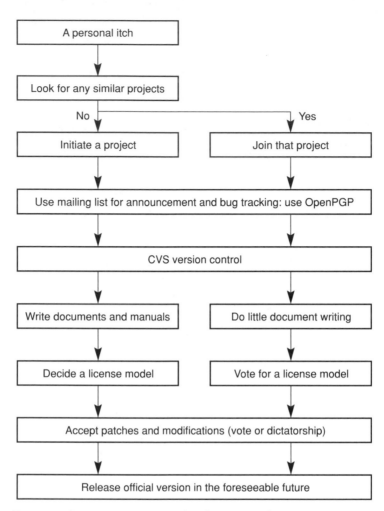

Figure 3.3 The general open source system development cycle.

(Taken from Wu and Lin (2001) © 2001 IEEE)

In many ways the development life-cycle of open source software is totally different to those considered so far, even though it is incremental in form (Wu and Lin, 2001). The key difference lies in its organization, rather than in the steps themselves. Instead of the ideas from a small number of decision-makers (designers) directing the efforts of many developers, the open source model involves a small number of co-ordinators drawing together the ideas of many participants. Figure 3.3 shows a model of this process, taken from Wu and Lin (2001). However, even this model is not wholly consistent. Many projects have begun with a single developer (as did Linux), and it is the extension and evolution that is then influenced by the many. (We will return to this issue of evolution in Section 3.5.)

The open source movement provides an interesting (and increasingly important) context for design activity. However, in terms of the subject matter of this book, it does not actually introduce many new issues of a technical nature, and so can largely be regarded as an example of a particular form of prototyping.

The second example of reactive development is that of the 'website'. Responsibility for the development and maintenance of the elements of these is often widely devolved within an organization, with the 'site manager' being much more concerned with co-ordination of style than with management of content. The growing use of 'active' site elements, such as scripts, also means that site development increasingly comes to resemble evolutionary prototyping, although not necessarily of a co-ordinated form. In recognition of this, a discipline of *Web Engineering* is struggling to emerge in order to address the challenges presented by both the rapid rate of technological change and also the devolved nature of development.

Again, from the viewpoint of this book, while interesting in itself, this domain does not (so far) provide any particular example of design technology for us to study, although arguably, this may be one of its most urgent needs.

3.4 Economic factors

When the nature of the design process was examined in Chapter 1, a key point that emerged was that it is not *analytic* in any sense, and that it involves navigating through a 'solution space' that may be very – indeed, extremely – large. This is partly because of the abstract nature of software, which makes it difficult to identify and specify all needs, and also because the medium makes it possible to identify many solutions to a given problem.

A consequence of this is that, with so large and ill-defined a solution space, the design process can easily lead to a design that contains 'errors'. These might be of many kinds, but some particularly significant ones are:

■ the design is not self-consistent, so that it cannot be successfully or efficiently implemented as it stands;

■ the design and the specification are not consistent;

■ the design and the requirements are not consistent.

Inconsistency in the form of the design itself may be revealed at various stages in its development. It may appear:

■ when the design is being refined, perhaps arising from structural inconsistencies that emerge when comparing information that is obtained from different viewpoints – a widely used technique for seeking out such errors is that of the design review (Yourdon, 1979; Parnas and Weiss, 1987);

■ while the design is being implemented (transformed into programming structures);

■ while the implementation of the system is being tested, since this may reveal logical inconsistencies in its behaviour.

The degree to which the design will need to be changed depends solely on the particular form and type of error.

Inconsistency between the design and the specification is more likely to be detected during testing (although if prototypes are constructed during development, it may well

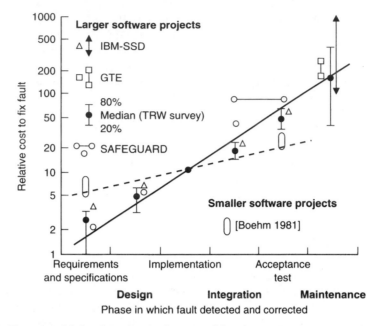

Figure 3.4 The cost of fixing 'bugs' at each stage of development.

(After Boehm (1981) © 1981 IEEE)

be detected earlier). The term 'verification' is usually used for this task of checking a design against the specification for the system.

Inconsistency between the design and the actual needs of the user (the requirements) is a much more difficult issue, although again it may be assisted by the use of prototypes. The procedure of checking for such inconsistencies is normally termed 'validation'.

Boehm has provided a very useful way to distinguish clearly between the actions of verification and validation (often combined together and referred to as 'V & V' – possibly to duck the question of making the distinction!):

Verification: are we building the product right?
Validation: are we building the right product?

Any inconsistencies in a design, whatever their form, need to be detected and identified at as early a stage as possible, so that a decision can be made about what to do. The later in development they are detected, the larger a task it will be to put them right. The results of a study by Boehm, shown in Figure 3.4, suggest that the cost of error detection and correction goes up by an order of magnitude at each stage in development (Boehm, 1981), a ratio still widely considered to be the case. That is, an error in the design costs ten times as much to fix if it is detected during the testing phase as it would if it were detected during the implementation phase.

Unfortunately, since the main error-detecting tasks are performed later on in the life-cycle, errors in specification and design can prove costly to fix when compared with errors in coding. Ideally, therefore, we need to find ways of evaluating designs and finding errors *before* proceeding to implement them. Prototyping offers one such approach, although there are some possible side-effects to this approach that can reduce its cost-effectiveness.

Another economic issue that needs to be considered is the cost of making *changes* to a system. Most software-based systems evolve with time, undergoing enhancements and changes as the needs of the users alter, the environment alters, and faults in performance are identified. Lientz and Swanson (1980) studied the types of software maintenance activity that occur in practice, and identified three main forms.

1. *Perfective* maintenance is concerned with extending and improving a system once it is operational, typically by providing new forms of functionality requested by users.

2. *Adaptive* maintenance is performed in order to meet needs for change that are imposed from outside (examples of these might be changes in legislation affecting a financial package, change of operating systems, or any similar type of change that arises from external factors).

3. *Corrective* maintenance is performed to fix any 'bugs' that may be detected in the operational system.

In practice, the first of these is generally dominant, and it has been estimated that around 65 per cent of all maintenance work falls into this category.

This reinforces the earlier point that the structure of a system should allow it to be modified fairly easily, so that it can be adapted to cope with likely changes (or, at least, with perfective and adaptive changes; it would be difficult to make much useful allowance for likely corrective changes!). This is a principle that has been common in many other branches of engineering for a long time. (Examples of the design of components undergoing frequent revision can often be found in the design of cars and electronic goods.) As already observed, such practices may create constraints that limit the 'solution space' available to the designer, so increasing the initial cost while decreasing the long-term cost. Unfortunately, the way in which most organizations budget for software production is too short term for such practices to be adopted as effectively as might be desired.

3.5 The longer term

Most of our discussion so far has been centred upon the notion that the design process is completed once it has delivered some form of plan that can be used for developing a product. However, as the preceding sections of this chapter have indicated, once created, the form of the product may itself then need to evolve and change over time.

Of course, this concept is familiar enough when applied to manufactured items such as motor cars, washing-machines, cameras, etc. For a given model of car, the general characteristics might not change greatly from year to year, but the manufacturer will almost certainly introduce annual changes to styling, features, choices. As these accumulate over a number of years, the result is that the appearance and form of the current version of a given model may be very different to those of the same model when it was first launched on to the market.

For software, the equivalent to this process is the concept of *perfective mainten-ance* that was described in the last section (Lientz and Swanson, 1980). While strictly, this is not 'maintenance' as the term would be used with a physical product in a domain such as motor car engineering, as a process of *evolution* it is essentially identical.

When designers have failed or been unable to anticipate future needs for change, and when maintenance teams have failed to preserve design structures, there is ample scope for problems to arise within this process of evolution. Probably the best known example of this was the need that arose to extensively revise many systems at the start of the year 2000 (the Y2K problem) in order to be able to handle dates that began with a '2' rather than a '1'. In many cases, this was simply because the original developers had not expected that their software would be used for such a long period of time. Indeed, in many cases this was probably a reasonable expectation, in that the original system may well not have lasted so long; however, the failure lay in not anticipating that it would survive, at least in part, in systems that evolved from the original one.

There are of course many reasons why designers might fail to anticipate the future adequately. A very common one arises from the practice of regarding system develop-ment and maintenance as coming under quite different budget headings, which can easily lead to a situation where developers have no incentive to consider future changes. Another is that designers themselves may also lack vision about the future, especially where they lack any very deep knowledge about the domain in which the system is to operate. Similarly, maintainers may find themselves with inadequate or inaccurate documentation, making it hard to ensure that their changes are consistent with the original plans.

A useful distinction between systems that do evolve and those that are essentially 'static' has been made by Lehman (Lehman and Ramil, 2002). Very simply, an **E-type** system is one that is used to 'mechanise a human or societal activity', and so it must evolve and change with its context in order to remain satisfactory. There are many examples of such systems: operating systems need to support new activities and to make use of new devices; office packages need to support new tasks or new ways of doing business; pay-roll packages may need to incorporate legislative changes, and so on. In contrast to this, an **S-type** program or system is one which is only required to meet a 'formal' specification. One example of such a program might be the cp utility used in the Unix and Linux operating systems. The specification for this is simply that it should make a copy of a file. This specification, and hence the program, is something which does not really change over time, and such changes as might occur, such as (say) extending it to handle distributed filestores, are ones that will not change its basic functionality.

The evolution of E-type systems through a series of *releases* usually exhibits certain characteristics when viewed over a period of time, requiring both anticipation and planning for change. The nature of this process of evolution is not something that we have space to discuss here but, for those interested, a very comprehensive review of the issues involved is provided in Lehman and Ramil (2002).

If we continue to concentrate on E-type systems, then for our purposes this concept of system evolution introduces two questions. The first is how the overall development process needs to be modified to describe its effects, while the second is how is the design process itself affected?

At its most simple, the effect upon the life-cycle is to extend it to recognize the process of evolution right through to the eventual 'retirement' of a system (Rajlich and Bennett, 2000). Indeed for more evolutionary development forms that more closely resemble Boehm's spiral model, this is a fairly natural step, at least from a technical viewpoint. Rather than seeing development and maintenance as totally different processes, this view argues that the former is simply the initial step in the evolutionary process and that it should be planned and financed on this basis.

The effect upon the design process is less readily characterized. The need to address this problem of evolution was recognized by David Parnas in 1979 (Parnas, 1979), who argued that 'flexibility cannot be an afterthought' and identified the need to plan for extensions when formulating the requirements for a system. Parnas also argued for making conscious design decisions about generality and flexibility, where the design of software could be considered as being **general** if 'it can be used, *without change*, in a variety of situations', and **flexible** 'if it is *easily changed* to be used in a variety of situations'.

Software development technology has been extensively influenced by this and by other ideas of David Parnas, and in some ways these goals are more readily achievable than they were when he first stated them. However, while they may be technically realizable, achieving this still requires the design process to encourage the designer to seek opportunities to reuse design ideas or structures.

Planning for reuse in this way has not generally been one of the more effective elements of software design methods, which have generally been formulated on the basis of treating each design problem as a new and unique one. Indeed, as we will see later, their *procedural* forms tend to be unsuited to encouraging reuse, other than in a fairly general way.

In contrast, the concept of the *design pattern* (Gamma *et al.*, 1995) is much more readily related to the ideas about generality and flexibility that Parnas put forward, largely because the idea of reuse is encouraged. However, the pattern concept is more strongly oriented towards recording instances of such ideas, or identifying how they might be organized, than to finding ways to create the opportunity. In that sense, although they extend the ideas of Parnas, the basic problem remains.

Following from the discussion of the two preceding chapters, this should perhaps come as no surprise. If the act of designing is essentially a process of postulating solutions to a problem, then adding the need for postulating how the problem itself might change over time is hardly likely to simplify that process! However, it is a very real need, and one that we will return to later.

Summary

An understanding of software design requires an appreciation of its role in the software development process, since the context that this provides influences the form of design approach needed. In this chapter we have examined:

- design in the context of particular life-cycle models, most notably the linear (waterfall) and incremental models;

■ the associated role of requirements elicitation in setting the context for the various design activities;

■ the roles that software *prototyping* can play in supporting aspects of the design process;

■ the question of how well a design meets the users' needs, and the roles of:

> *verification*: are we building the product right?
> *validation*: are we building the right product?

■ the cost of fixing errors in design at a later stage of development;

■ the influence of the *maintenance* phase, and upon the design of E-type systems in particular.

Further reading

Boehm B.W. (1988). A spiral model of software development and enhancement. *IEEE Computer*, **21**(5), 61–72

This is a very clear exposition of the forms and roles of software life-cycle models from the pen of the guru himself. It provides a historical introduction and then the rationale for the form adopted for the spiral model.

Lehman M.M. and Ramil J.F. (2002). Rules and tools for software evolution planning and management. *Annals of Software Eng.*, **11**(1), 15–44

A comprehensive review of the laws of software evolution that considers the ways in which software elements and systems evolve over time. Includes a useful discussion of the characteristics of E-type systems.

Exercises

3.1 How do your techniques for testing an item of software conform to the objectives of

(a) verification
(b) validation

and how might they be improved for these purposes?

3.2 Consider the roles that different forms of prototype could perform (if any) in the development of the following software systems:

(a) an interactive word processor;
(b) a web-based e-commerce site dedicated to selling sheet music of all types;
(c) a bank auto-teller network for dispensing cash and providing receipts.

In each case, which group of people would be involved with reviewing any prototypes that were produced, and what forms might a prototype usefully take?

3.3 List reasons why each of the following systems may require 'maintenance' in the future and, as such, whether they might be classified as being E-type or S-type. Identify the relevant form of maintenance likely to be employed for each case:

(a) a spell-checking program used with a word processor that supports multiple languages;

(b) a program used to list the contents of a directory (folder) used in an operating system;

(c) a system used to display information about the position of aircraft in an air traffic control system that is used to manage the airspace for a number of busy airports.

Design Qualities

Since one of the objectives of the software design process is to produce as 'good' a design as possible, this chapter is concerned with examining some of the ideas about what exactly constitutes a 'good' software design. It begins by examining some ideas about the properties associated with good quality in software, and then proceeds to consider how it is possible to make measurements at the design stage that might identify these properties and how the design process can be involved in meeting quality objectives.

4.1 The quality concept

The concept of quality is a familar one, although we tend to associate it with properties that arise from the tasks of construction rather than with those of design. Asked for examples of 'good' quality, many people are likely to identify such examples as well-made joints on an item of furniture, the quality of the paintwork on an expensive car, or the texture of a woven fabric. All these are examples of quality of construction rather than of design, yet quality in construction depends upon good design: to achieve a high-quality product high standards are needed in both, and in order to achieve high standards of quality in design *products*, one needs to seek high standards of quality in the design *process*.

Unfortunately, quality is a concept that can rarely be related to any absolutes, and even for manufactured items ideas about quality usually cannot be usefully measured on any absolute scale. The best that we can usually do is to rank items on an ordinal scale, as when we say that we believe the construction of this coffee table is better than that of another, in terms of materials used and the workmanship it exhibits. However, we lack any means of defining *how much* better the one is than the other.

When it comes to assessing design, rather than construction, the problem is, if anything, worse. Quality in design is often associated with visual properties, as when we appraise the quality of typefaces, furniture and clothes. We associate elegance with good design, yet it offers no help in quantifying our thinking and, even worse, is likely to have ephemeral aspects: it may be strongly influenced by our ideas about fashion – so creating a context for quality. (As an example, a 1930s radio set might look quite in place in a room that is furnished in 1930s style, but would be most unsuited to a room that was furnished in the style of the 1980s.)

Since software is such an abstract product, it is perhaps less apt to be influenced by fashion (a debatable point, perhaps, especially in relation to user interface design), but it is hardly surprising that the concept of quality is equally difficult to define for software. Few quality attributes can be quantified in any way, and those measures that we do possess are of uneven value. Furthermore, the idea of quality as applied to software is at least partly problem-related in nature, so it is certainly not guaranteed by the use of some particular form for the design process.

For software, as for other artifacts, it is also difficult to separate ideas about design quality from one's thinking about implementation quality. To return for a moment to the example of the garden shed that was introduced in Chapter 1: no matter how good the design is, in terms of proportions, efficient use of materials and ease of construction and modification, our ideas about its quality will still be very largely influenced by the actual construction. If it is badly assembled, then, regardless of how good its design may be, we will not consider it to be of good quality. Equally, if the design is poor, no amount of good craftsmanship applied to its construction will be able to disguise its fundamental failings. (The door may be well made and may close well, but if it is positioned so that we graze our knuckles each time it is opened, then we will still find it inconvenient to use.)

We also encounter once again the dual nature of software in thinking about how we can identify its quality. Software has both static and dynamic attributes, and so any set of measures that we can develop should seek to assess both of these, and should recognize the potential for conflict between them. (A program may meet the specified real-time needs very well, but its internal structure may be so poorly organized that it is virtually impossible to modify it in any way. Equally, the structure of a program may be very good, while its run-time performance is awful!)

While our ideas of quality measures are perhaps essentially determined by the nature of the design object itself, it is still possible to find some very general measures of quality that are fairly universal, and which can be applied to software. In terms of the objectives for these, for any system the ultimate measure of quality should normally be that of *fitness for purpose*, since the end product must be capable of performing the task assigned to it. As an example, however elegant the design of a chair may be, it must still meet the basic requirement that we should be able to sit on it, and preferably in comfort. Therefore the quality factors to be used for assessing this will be selected and weighted by considering the role (purpose) of the system that is being designed.

This acts as a reminder that we should not seek to achieve elegance of form at the expense of function. So for software systems, we can reasonably expect to find that the final implemented system works, and works correctly in all the required situations. That is, it should perform the required tasks in the specified manner, and within the constraints of the specified resources. (Once again, we can only measure the ultimate success of a design through its implementation.)

This concept is related to the ideas of verification and validation that were introduced in the last chapter, since comparisons are being made with expectations as expressed in the requirements specification. As a measure for practical use, however, it can be assessed only by indirect means. So it may be better to consider fitness for purpose as an ultimate goal, and to look for ways of assessing it by finding a set of associated properties and then some system attributes that provide measures of these.

The next section begins by looking at a framework that enables us to identify some of the system properties that reflect our general ideas about quality. Section 4.3 examines some of the system attributes that relate to these properties, and briefly considers how these might be assessed. Finally, the influence of the design process itself in helping to produce the desired design properties is considered.

4.2 Assessing design quality

'When you can measure what you are speaking about, and express it in numbers, you know something about it, but when you cannot measure it, when you cannot express it in numbers, your knowledge is of a meagre and unsatisfactory kind.' (Lord Kelvin.)

4.2.1 A framework for assessment

While Lord Kelvin's dictum is widely quoted, it is easy to overlook the context within which it was made. Ideas about measurement originally emerged largely within a community of scientists and engineers who were seeking to capture ideas about *physical* properties such as mass, length, velocity, etc., where measurement scales could be more readily developed and shared. The scales used for such properties are **ratio** scales (they possess well-defined intervals and a zero point), so we can be sure that when measuring the property of length in units of centimetres, something which has a length value of 8 will be twice as long as something with a length value of 4.

Once we move away from this context, while the idea of measurement is still a valuable one, we often have to accept a more limited type of knowledge than that which Lord Kelvin aspired to. Many of the properties of interest to us are more likely to be 'measured' using an **ordinal** scale (where elements can be ranked, but where the sizes of the intervals between the elements cannot be specified), and this is particularly true when we come to consider the problem of making an assessment of design qualities. (Even when we do obtain numerical values for properties that relate to ideas about design quality, we will need to treat them with care. The act of assigning a numerical value to a property does not necessarily mean that it has been measured using a ratio scale.)

Fenton and Pfleeger (1997) have observed that 'measurement is concerned with capturing information about *attributes of entities*', so at this point it is useful to identify more carefully how our ideas about quality can be tied to ideas about measurement.

Figure 4.1 shows an initial set of mappings that can be constructed to link these ideas. The key terms used in the figure can be interpreted as follows.

- **Quality concepts** are the abstract ideas that we have about what constitutes 'good' and 'bad' properties of a system, and which will need to be assessed by the designer when making decisions about design choices.

- **Design attributes** provide a set of measurable (or at least, identifiable) characteristics of the design entities and so provide mappings between the abstract idea of a property and the countable features of an actual design (and therefore effectively correspond to the general concept of a *metric*).

- **Counts** are concerned with realizing the design attributes, and so involve identifying the lexical features of a representation that will need to be counted in order to obtain some form of values for the metrics.

As an example of a widely used metric that fits into this framework, the quality of program code is often considered to be related to its structural complexity. One

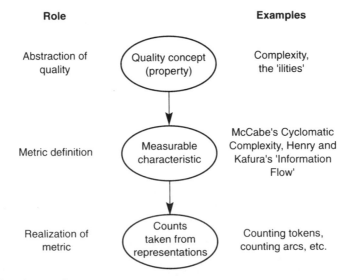

Figure 4.1 Mapping quality concepts to measurements.

measurable characteristic that can be used to assess this complexity is the number of possible control paths that exist within a program unit, as measured by McCabe's Cyclomatic Complexity measure (McCabe, 1976). This is derived by counting lexical tokens such as IF and WHILE in the source code, with the set of tokens used being specific to a particular implementation language.

The mapping from a measurable characteristic to a set of good and unambiguous counting rules to be used with a particular implementation language is essentially one of transformation. However, the mapping from a quality concept to a set of measurable characteristics is much more a case of making an *interpretation*. (This point tends to be glossed over in much of the literature on code metrics! McCabe's metric is also a good illustration of the point made above that a numerical value does not necessarily imply a ratio scale. Few would be likely to argue that an item with a Cyclomatic Complexity value of six was exactly twice the complexity of an item with a value of three.) To help with this interpretation, we need a fuller model to help identify the mappings required. An expanded form of the framework provided in Figure 4.1 is shown in Figure 4.2: here the idea of a quality concept has been expanded into three further levels in which:

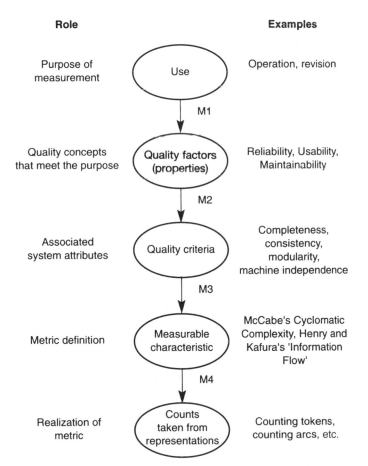

Figure 4.2 A fuller mapping from concepts of quality to countable attributes of a design/implementation.

■ *use* identifies the purpose of making measurements (and hence strongly differentiates between measuring static properties of a design and measuring dynamic behavioural qualities);

■ *quality factors* determine the quality concepts that are associated with the purpose (these items are often referred to as the 'ilities');

■ *quality criteria* relate the requirements-oriented properties of the intended system (the 'ilities') to the solution-oriented properties of the design itself, and these are then mapped onto a chosen set of metrics.

While this does not reduce the degree of interpretation involved, it does provide a clearer path between the need for quality assessments and the forms used.

An example of the mappings M1 and M2 from Figure 4.2 is shown in Figure 4.3, and is based on an example of the needs identified as being significant for a real-time system, and, for comparison, those that are considered as significant for a compiler.

In the previous section it was observed that any assessment incorporating the ultimate goal of fitness for purpose needed to recognize the nature of the problem and its domain. This balance is reflected in the weightings that we give to the uses, and hence the choice of weightings for the 'ilities' is strongly related to both the problem itself and its domain. For example, efficiency may be of greater importance for an embedded control system than usability, while for an aircraft autopilot reliability might reasonably be regarded as by far the most important factor.

When we come to make use of these ideas, we find that the needs of the designer and the needs of any system of measurement unfortunately tend to create forces that pull in opposing directions. As was observed in Chapter 2, experienced designers will frequently seek to maintain a reasonably consistent level of abstraction in their reasoning at any given stage in the design process, and will avoid descending into detail at too early a stage in the development of this reasoning. However, it is difficult to measure abstractions, and so metrics analysis schemes seek to have available to them as much detail as possible about a design.

Even for program code, which at least possesses well-defined syntax and semantics, the process of defining attributes and making measurements of these can be a difficult exercise requiring the careful specification of any counting rules to be used (Conte *et al.*, 1986; Fenton and Pfleeger, 1997). For design description forms, the problem is compounded by the relatively poor syntax of most abstract design notations. (There are very few design notations that are unambiguous, and almost all graphical forms require careful use of the free-text component to make their purpose clear.)

So the automatic processing of design notations in order to extract measurements of particular attributes has not made a very significant impact to date, although a number of experiments have been conducted to extract various counts from systematic design notations (Troy and Zweben, 1981; Hall and Preiser, 1984; Budgen and Marashi, 1988). The use of CASE (Computer-Aided Software Engineering) tools as an aid to documenting designs and, in some cases, assisting with code generation, offers a useful means for gathering such data, but weak syntax and semantics, needing careful interpretation of any textual components, remain problems for most notations.

| Use | Quality factors | Quality criteria |

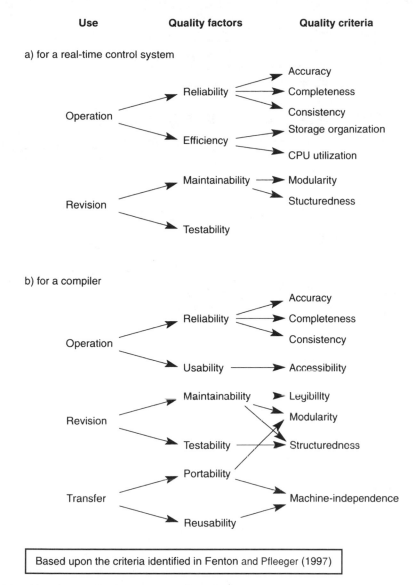

Figure 4.3 Mapping quality factors to quality criteria.

A further problem with metrics analysis procedures is that they have so far been almost entirely concerned with assessing static attributes of a design, since these can at least be directly extracted from any forms of notation through some form of property counting. Attempts to extract information about the dynamic attributes require making some behavioural interpretations from the static information provided (Friel and Budgen, 1997), as well as making assumptions about the performance characteristics of any eventual implementation.

Unfortunately, as Figure 4.3 demonstrates, the factors that the designer considers to be particularly important may well relate most closely to dynamic attributes, and so

Figure 4.4 Example of musical score notation.

assessing the static attributes is insufficient when seeking to assess the ultimate criteria of fitness for purpose. We can demonstrate why this is so by using an analogy with musical notation. Music has some similar properties to software, in that a static notation is used to describe something that needs to be 'executed', and which therefore possesses a similar mix of static and dynamic attributes. (Again, it is relatively easy to make a broad distinction between good and poor quality in music, but very hard to quantify that distinction.)

The section of a musical score in Figure 4.4 shows that it should be possible to specify some form of analysis rules for checking basic properties such as the number of beats in a bar. We might also devise rules to check chords and sequences, to identify the intervals between the notes and hence to check for particular dissonances. Given enough musical knowledge, this might then tell us quite a lot about the piece of music it represents – but of course, the ultimate test is to hear it played. Only then can we be sure whether or not we like it, and whether it will be suitable for some particular purpose. (The 'mental' model applies here, too, as anyone with sufficient knowledge is likely to 'play' the score in his or her head in order to assess its qualities!)

4.2.2 The 'ilities'

The 'ilities' form a group of quality factors that need to be considered when making any attempt to assess design quality. Since there are many ilities, our discussion in this section is limited to the group that can be considered as being the most widely applicable, namely:

- reliability
- efficiency
- maintainability
- usability

(The other ilities, such as testability, portability, reusability and so on are rather more specialized in purpose.)

Reliability

This factor is essentially concerned with the dynamic characteristics of the eventual system, and so involves the designer in making predictions about behavioural issues. In particular, for the purpose of design we are concerned with ways of determining whether the eventual system will be:

- *complete*, in the sense of being able to handle all combinations of events and system states;
- *consistent*, in that its behaviour will be as expected, and will be repeatable, regardless of the overall system loading at any time;
- *robust* when faced with component failure or some similar conflict (for example, if the printer used for logging data in a chemical process-control plant fails for some reason, this should not be able to 'hang' the whole system, but should be handled according to the philosophy summed up in the term 'graceful degradation').

As systems get larger and more complex, so the problems of ensuring reliability will also escalate.

For safety-critical systems, where this factor is paramount, various techniques have been developed to help overcome limitations in design and implementation techniques. For example, in a system used in a 'fly-by-wire' aircraft, in which the control surfaces are managed by computer links rather than direct hydraulic controls, the implementation will be by means of multiple computers, each programmed by a separate development team and tested independently. Any operational request to the control system is then processed in parallel by all the computers, and only if they concur will the requested operation be performed.

Efficiency

The efficiency of a system can be measured through its use of resources such as processor time, memory, network access, system facilities, disk space and so on. It is a relative and multi-variate concept, in that one system can be identified as more efficient than another in terms of some parameter such as processor use, but there is no single scale on which to specify an optimum efficiency.

In the early days of computers, when programs were small and computer time was relatively expensive, efficiency was considered a prime criterion, and was measured chiefly in terms of memory use and processor use. So systems that were implemented in machine code or assembler were generally considered to be highly efficient, but of course would rank very low on maintainability and portability.

As a design factor, efficiency is a difficult property to handle, since it involves making projections from the design in order to estimate the effects of choices upon eventual resource needs. However, as these are of considerable importance in terms of the implementation of the eventual system, it is often necessary to make at least crude predictions of needs.

Maintainability

As systems get larger and more costly, the need to offset this by ensuring a long life-time in service increases in parallel. To help to achieve this, designs must allow for future modification. To some extent, this also relates back to the idea of incremental development and evolution discussed in Chapter 3.

Many of the factors that affect maintainability are related to implementation factors or, at least, to very detailed design issues. Examples of these are the choice of identifiers, comment structuring practices, and documentation standards. However, design is also an important factor since, by careful separation of concerns, the designers can help the future maintainers to gain a clear understanding of their original 'mental models' (Littman *et al.*, 1987). Some of the factors that affect this in terms of design structure will be discussed in the next section.

Usability

There are many issues that can affect usability, but for many systems the design of the user interface (usually termed the Human–Computer Interaction, or HCI) will form an important component, and will influence other design decisions about such features as module boundaries and data structures.

A useful review of the issues that need to be considered in designing for 'ease of use' is provided in Branscomb and Thomas (1984), where the authors observe that the use of the term HCI is perhaps misleading, since 'people communicate via, not with, computer systems'. There is a strong cognitive element involved in this task, and a need for the designer to provide the user with a consistent 'mental model' of system behaviour. The techniques affecting the design choices are fairly specialized and largely outside the scope of this book. Preece *et al.* (2002) provides a good introduction to the wider aspects of this field of design.

4.2.3 Cognitive dimensions

The 'ilities' are by no means the only framework that we can employ for thinking about system properties within a quality context. A useful set of concepts that originated in the field of HCI is provided by Green's **Cognitive Dimensions** framework (Green, 1989; Green and Petre, 1996). The focus of this is upon 'information representation' (which can of course include the description of a design solution), and the purpose of the dimensions is to provide a set of 'discussion tools', which is just the sort of thing that is needed for evaluating quality concepts which are themselves often ill-formed and imprecise.

Table 4.1 The cognitive dimensions

73

Assessing design quality

Dimension	Interpretation
Abstraction	Types and availability of abstraction mechanisms
Hidden dependencies	Important links between entities are not visible
Premature commitment	Constraints on the order of doing things
Secondary notation	Extra information provided via means other than formal syntax
Viscosity	Resistance to change
Visibility	Ability to view components easily
Closeness of mapping	Closeness of representation to domain
Consistency	Similar semantics are expressed in similar syntactic forms
Diffuseness	Verbosity of language
Error-proneness	Notation invites mistakes
Hard mental operations	High demand on cognitive resources
Progressive evaluation	Work-to-date can be checked at any time
Provisionality	Degree of commitment to actions or marks
Role-expressiveness	The purpose of a component is readily inferred

While the ideas concerned have been couched largely in the terminology of HCI and of the more visual aspects of systems, they have nevertheless something useful to offer to the more general process of design. In this section, therefore, we briefly review some of the more directly relevant dimensions and suggest where they may be able to offer some particularly useful insight.

Table 4.1 summarizes the cognitive dimensions and their meanings. (For a fuller discussion of the complete framework, readers should consult the above references and also the website at http://www.cl.cam.ac.uk/~afb21/CognitiveDimensions/.)

As concepts, many of these provide a rather different insight into the issue of how we might think about and assess a design, although clearly not all are directly relevant to the current discussion. To explain how these might help with thinking about design quality and attributes, it may be useful to consider some small examples that illustrate some of the more relevant dimensions.

Premature commitment (and enforced lookahead)

This arises when an early design decision which was made before proper information was available has the effect of constraining later ones. It may be unavoidable (information may not be available within a practical timescale), but it may also arise through the use of procedural design practices such as design methods that encourage a particular ordering in the decision-making process. (As a simple example, a spoken telephone menu system, especially one using a hierarchy of menus, tends to encourage this characteristic. Each set of choices is presented in turn and the user must make a decision while lacking a full knowledge of what other choices will be available later.)

Although intended as a 'measure' that can be applied to HCI designs, for our purposes, this concept can provide a 'measure' of the quality of the design *process*, rather than of the design *product*, although obviously the consequences are likely to be exhibited in the latter. A life-cycle which allows design decisions to be revisited may help, as will a design process which recognizes the need to make several iterations through the decision-making steps.

Hidden dependencies

This concept describes a relationship between two components, such that while one is dependent upon the other the relationship is not fully visible. From a design standpoint, this touches upon one of the problems that we will be addressing later when examining design notations. Notations often capture one type of dependency (for example, that component A invokes component B) but say nothing about other dependencies that exist between them (A and B share knowledge about certain data types and structures). However, in thinking about their solution, the designer will need to consider all of these relationships. Indeed, the problem becomes potentially much more significant when a design is being modified during maintenance: changing a design is likely to be much more difficult if the designer has only a part of the necessary knowledge about dependencies directly available to them, a point that is illustrated particularly effectively in the study reported in Littman *et al.* (1987). (This dimension is also one that is particularly relevant for websites and their maintenance.)

Secondary notation

This dimension describes additional information that is conveyed by means other than the 'official syntax'. We will only touch on it briefly here, as we will return to this issue in the following chapters but, in brief, a good example of this problem is where designers make use of local layout conventions when using particular design notations. While these may be familiar to the originators of the design, they may not be so evident to others who join the team, or to those who later need to maintain the resulting system.

Viscosity

This describes the concept of 'resistance to change'. During design development, this may well arise as a consequence of premature commitment, and during maintenance it may be a significant reflection of the resulting design 'quality'. Both conventional software and websites have many mechanisms that can easily result in high viscosity, especially at the more detailed levels of implementation. (As an example of this dimension within the context of program code, we can consider the practice of using embedded numerical constants rather than declaring symbolic forms. Using the specific value 17.5 at various points in the code, rather than declaring a constant value such as VatRate = 17.5; at the start of the program, is only too typical an illustration of this practice. When it becomes necessary later to adjust the value of the VAT rate, then each instance has to be located and modified, rather than simply changing the value defined for the constant. Even worse, since 17.5 might occur within a program for other reasons (for example, within 217.53), some values may even get changed in error!)

Viscosity is a readily recognizable property at many levels of abstraction, even if it is not one that is easily quantified in design terms. For a design it may represent the extent to which modules are interdependent, and the differences that exist between the 'conceptual' form of a solution and the one that actually emerges from the design process. (An interesting illustration of this is provided in Bowman *et al.* (1999), which analyses the 'architectural structure' of the software making up the Linux operating system. The results of this study undoubtedly provide illustrations of several of the cognitive dimensions!)

The cognitive dimensions offer some interesting ideas to employ in thinking about design quality and what it can mean for software. We will be returning later to make further use of some of the ideas that they embody. However, having examined some of the quality factors that designers would *like* to be able to assess in making their decisions, we now go on to consider what measures of quality we actually have available to us at the design stage. We can then consider how well these are able to provide help with assessing the extent to which a design meets the factors that have been described above.

4.3 Quality attributes of the design product

Now that a number of ideas about design quality concepts have been examined, it is clear that the two principal problems that they present for measurement are:

■ to identify a set of design attributes that are related to these properties;

■ to find ways of extracting information about these attributes from the available forms of design document.

In the first part of this section some of the attributes and criteria that are widely used for design assessment are described, and this is followed by a brief discussion of one of the ways in which these might be extracted.

4.3.1 Some design attributes

Simplicity

Characteristic of almost all good designs, in whatever sphere of activity they are produced, is a basic simplicity. A good design meets its objectives and has no additional embellishments that detract from its main purpose. (Perhaps this is why so many dual-purpose artifacts fail to achieve either of their objectives clearly and well. One example that comes to mind is a rucksack that expanded to become a tent, but was unsuccessful because it was much more convenient to have a good rucksack and a good tent as separate items. Most of us can probably think of similar examples of misplaced ingenuity.)

The often-quoted saying 'a solution should be as simple as possible, but no simpler', which is usually attributed to Albert Einstein, is more profound than it might seem at first. This is the opposite of the argument against unnecessary embellishment: it argues against attempting to oversimplify, since the result will be a product that will not be able to do its job. One important aid to achieving simplification is abstraction, but it is necessary to use an abstraction that preserves the relevant attributes if it is to be of any help in solving the problem.

While simplicity cannot easily be assessed, one can at least seek measures for its converse characteristic of *complexity*. A number of these, which measure different forms of complexity, have been developed for use with software, including:

- complexity of control flow (McCabe, 1976), concerned with the number of possible paths of control during execution of a program unit;

- complexity of structure in terms of information flow around the system (Henry and Kafura, 1984; Kitchenham *et al.*, 1990; Shepperd and Ince, 1993);

- complexity of comprehension, as measured by the number of different identifiers and operators (Halstead, 1977);

- complexity of structure in terms of relationships between system elements (primarily object-oriented forms), with the measures proposed in Chidamber and Kemerer (1994) being particularly widely cited, although by no means the only candidates (Briand *et al.*, 2000).

Unfortunately only the last of these readily scales up for use in design, although all could possibly be applied to detailed design documentation forms. There are no ready measures that can currently be used to help assess the architectural complexity of a design other than for object-oriented forms (although tools can help – see Bowman *et al.* (1999) for an illustration of this).

In terms of the design quality concepts, simplicity is clearly related to maintainability and testability as well as reliability and possibly efficiency.

Modularity

The use of an appropriate form of modular structuring makes it possible for a given problem to be considered in terms of a set of smaller components. Once again, modularity is not a concept that relates only to software: this principle has long been established in other forms of engineering. In electronics in particular, the idea of replacing one unit with another simply by unplugging one and plugging in the other has made the maintenance and upgrading of electrical and electronic equipment into a relatively straightforward task.

This is generally only possible where a well-defined set of interface standards is in existence. For electronic components this is generally achieved with some form of 'backplane' providing a data highway, together with the necessary signal lines. While this form of module connectivity is also possible with software (as is evident from the existence of libraries of subprograms), the standardization of the interfaces involved is much more limited. Despite this, however, the concept of the software component is an important one, and we will review this more fully in Chapter 17.

To make good use of a modular structure, one needs to adopt a design practice based on a **separation of concerns**. Simply defining interfaces is not enough: a designer needs to group functions within modules in such a way that their interdependence is minimized. Such a grouping results in a less complex interface to the module: in the case of hardware, it may simply be that fewer interconnections are required; for software, we need to find other criteria in order to measure this factor.

Viewed generally, and also from a software perspective, finding a suitable scheme of modularity to apply in solving a given problem provides at least the following benefits:

- modules are easy to replace;

- each module captures one feature of a problem, so aiding comprehension (and hence maintenance), as well as providing a framework for designing as a team;

- a well-structured module can easily be reused for another problem.

So in terms of the design properties that we are seeking, the successful use of modularity should be related to such quality concepts as maintainability, testability and (possibly) to usability and reliability too.

Two useful quality measures that have long been used for the purpose of assessing the extent of modular structuring in software are 'coupling' and 'cohesion'. These terms were defined in the early 1970s (Stevens *et al.*, 1974; Yourdon and Constantine, 1979), based upon observations of the problems arising when developing large systems, and were used to identify the complexity of a system in terms of the form and interdependence of the component modules. In the original work, the basic unit of modularity was assumed to be the subprogram unit, but the concepts are still valid for such modular forms as the Ada 'package', the Modula-2 'module' and the Java 'class'.

Coupling is a measure of intermodule connectivity, and is concerned with identifying the forms of connection that exist between modules and the 'strength' of these connections. Table 4.2 summarizes the principal forms of coupling that are generally regarded as being significant in terms of design features.

In general, the forms of coupling listed are somewhat biased towards modules based on the procedure, or subprogram, rather than on such forms as the class. The measures of coupling are generally related to the different ways of invoking procedures,

Table 4.2 Forms of module coupling.

Form	Features	Desirability
Data coupling	Modules A and B communicate by parameters or data items that have no control element	High
Stamp coupling	Modules A and B make use of some common data type (although they might perform very different functions and have no other connections)	Moderate
Control coupling (i) Activating	A transfers control to B in a structured manner such as by means of a procedure call	Necessary
(ii) Coordinating	A passes a parameter to B that is used in B to determine the actions of B (typically a boolean 'flag')	Undesirable
Common-environment coupling	A and B contain references to some shared data area that incorporate knowledge about its structure and organization. Any change to the format of the block requires that all of the modules using it must also be modified	Undesirable

Note: The forms of coupling that can exist between modules A and B have been ranked in decreasing order of desirability.

and to the use of different parameter-passing mechanisms. However, the concept can also be applied to the 'uses' hierarchy (Parnas, 1979), concerned with the packaging of information, and so can be used as a guide in making design decisions at a number of different levels of abstraction.

A problem with the basic concepts involved in coupling and cohesion is the difficulty of quantifying these measures systematically. However, this is less of an issue for the design process than for assessing program structures, since there is only really scope to identify their *presence* during design, and determining their *extent* is rarely practicable. With coupling, there is at least the possibility of performing such operations as counting links, using sizes of data structures exchanged and so on, but even then the value of any such measures is somewhat limited.

As an example of the point about the extent of coupling being less critical in design assessment than the presence of particular forms, we can consider the case of co-ordinating control coupling, sometimes termed 'switch coupling'.

This form typically arises when one of the parameters of a procedure is used to determine the way that the procedure is to perform its task. This in turn may arise where a procedure is invoked from a number of different sections of a program, and where, at a fairly late stage, it may be realized that the task it performs may differ slightly according to section. The 'switch' parameter is then added to enable the invoking routine to indicate which variant of the task needs to be performed. In other words, it acts as a 'fix' for a design error! (A classic example of a situation in which this may occur is in writing any form of multi-pass program, such as an assembler, compiler or link-editor. These all have a number of fairly low-level tasks that need to be repeated, but which on inspection are seen to differ slightly on each pass.)

This form of coupling is therefore likely to arise from a failure to perform the detailed design tasks adequately. In making any form of design assessment the need is therefore to identify its presence. Any notion of its 'extent' is harder to determine, and of doubtful value if achieved.

Cohesion, in its turn, provides a measure of the extent to which the components of a module can be considered to be 'functionally related'. The ideal module is one in which all the components can be considered as being solely present for one purpose. Where the Java *class* is the basis of modular structuring, an example of functional relatedness might be a stack class that contains only a set of public methods for accessing the stack, together with the data structure for the stack itself. Such a class can be considered as exhibiting functional cohesion, since all its components are present solely for the purpose of providing a stack facility.

Table 4.3 lists the main forms of cohesion (sometimes termed 'associations') that are generally recognized. As can be seen, cohesion is quite easily related to packaging forms of modular structure, as well as to procedural units. Perhaps the main exception to this is procedural association, which is very much concerned with sequencing of operations, and hence fits less easily with the packaging concept. (This form was not included in the original list (Stevens *et al.*, 1974) and was added later in Yourdon and Constantine (1979).) However, one consequence of re-interpreting these within a context of packaging units such as the *class*, rather than procedural ones, such as the sub-program or *method*, is that our ideas about the ranking order of the more desirable forms may then need some revision. (The overall distinction between desirable and undesirable is unaltered though.) The main issue is whether we should now consider

Table 4.3 The principal forms of cohesion.

79

Form	Features	Desirability
Functional	All the elements contribute to the execution of a single problem-related task	High
Sequential	The outputs from one element of the module form the inputs to another element	Quite high
Communicational	All elements are concerned with operations that use the same input or output data	Fairly
Procedural	The elements of the module are related by the order in which their operations must occur	Not very
Temporal	The elements involve operations that are related by the time at which they occur, usually being linked to some event such as 'system initialization'	Not very
Logical	The elements perform operations that are logically similar, but which involve very different actions internally	Definitely not
Coincidental	The elements are not linked by any conceptual link (such modules may be created to avoid having to repeat coding tasks)	Definitely not

communicational association to be ranked higher than *sequential* association since it more fully exploits the facilities of the *class* mechanism. The point is relatively minor, but it does illustrate how our ideas about quality may change with the evolution of implementational forms.

Cohesion is probably even more difficult to quantify than coupling; however, it does provide a measure that can be used to help the designer with assessing the relative merits of possible options. The challenge of finding ways of measuring its presence in an acceptably objective way has therefore been one of considerable interest to metrics researchers (Bieman and Kang, 1998).

While almost any general textbook on software engineering will contain a discussion of coupling and cohesion, more detailed discussions are usually to be found in the 'structured design' school of textbooks. Probably two of the most thorough ones are those provided in Yourdon and Constantine (1979) and Page-Jones (1988).

Information-hiding

This concept is related to that of modularity, but it also incorporates additional notions about managing information in a system. The basic concept encourages the designer to keep information about the detailed forms of such objects as data structures and device interfaces local to a module, or unit, and to ensure that such information should not be made 'visible' outside that unit (Parnas, 1972). Again, like the preceding concepts, it was first recognized through a process of observation (Parnas, 1999).

Where this principle is applied, knowledge about the detailed form of any data structures within a module is kept concealed from any other software components that may use the module. In many cases, a number of 'access procedures' may be provided

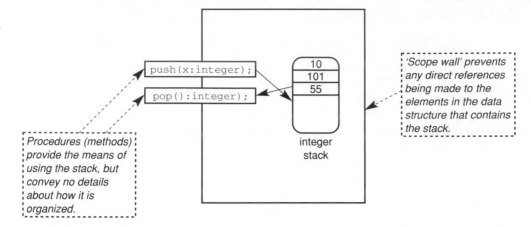

‘Scope wall’ prevents
any direct references
being made to the
elements in the data
structure that contains
the stack.

Procedures (methods)
provide the means of
using the stack, but
convey no details
about how it is
organized.

integer
stack

push(x:integer);

pop():integer);

10
101
55

Figure 4.5 Example of information-hiding used with a module that provides an integer stack.

to give controlled forms of access to the 'clients' of the module. The effect is to provide a 'scope wall' around information, preventing direct access to it.

As an example, this principle might be used in designing a module to provide an integer stack facility to support a set of reverse Polish calculations using integers. Using the principle of information-hiding, one would seek to conceal the form adopted for implementing the stack, and provide a set of procedures for accessing it, such as:

> push an integer onto the stack
> pop an integer from the stack
> test for an empty stack

as is shown schematically in Figure 4.5.

This interface then conceals the detailed design decisions about how the stack is to be implemented, which helps to ensure its integrity by preventing 'short-cut' access directly from other program units. It also makes it possible to change the detailed form of implementation without requiring changes in any of the units that make use of this stack.

Powerful though the concept is, it is difficult to make use of it in any procedural practices for design, and equally difficult to devise a set of tests to identify its use. In terms of system quality factors it is clearly related to both reliability and maintainability. In terms of processor time and memory use, it is apt to conflict with ideas of efficiency on occasion, since the use of a hierarchy of access procedures may lead to reduced run-time performance.

The detailed forms in which these attributes manifest themselves in software systems are somewhat elusive, although the concepts involved are generally quite tractable. A useful aid to considering the extent of their presence in a design is to examine it for signs of those features that indicate that a design may lack these qualities. This involves identifying a suitable set of features corresponding to attributes that are the inverse of those mentioned above. The presence of any of these features can be expected to make it difficult to read and understand the designer's intentions and to make the resulting system difficult to modify.

Identifying attributes that are the direct inverses of those described above is a significant problem. However, the following undesirable characteristics of a design can be considered to stem from the presence of the inverse properties.

- Having many copies of 'state' information spread around the system. This complicates the updating of information, and may lead to inconsistencies in system behaviour.

- Using interfaces that are too complex. In programming terms these are usually characterized by procedures that have too many parameters, some of which may not even be necessary. In design terms, they are more likely to be identified by the degree of information flow associated with them.

- The use of excessively complex control structures. This may indicate design modules where the designer has chosen unsuitable interfaces and data structures.

- Needless replication of information. This can also be reflected in module interfaces: for example, procedures may pass a complete record as a parameter, when only one field of the record is relevant to their operation.

- Using modules that lack 'functional strength'. Program units of this type are not well focused in terms of their purpose, and may well be parametrized for use on different tasks.

These characteristics have been expressed largely in terms of implementation features, since these are more familiar and are more readily quantified. However, they can equally well be assessed for design descriptions, although extracting the information is less easily achieved through any form of automatic analysis (Rising and Callis, 1994).

4.3.2 Assessing design quality

A technique that has proved itself useful in assessing design structure and likely behaviour is the review, or walkthrough (also sometimes termed an inspection). The use of reviews for this purpose is quite well established, and a set of basic rules has been assembled from experience (Yourdon, 1979; Weinberg and Freedman, 1984; Parnas and Weiss, 1987). In using such a technique, though, it is essential to distinguish between the **technical review**, which is concerned with assessing the quality of a design, and the **management review**, which is concerned with issues such as project deadlines and schedule. This section and the next are concerned only with the role performed by the first of these forms of review.

Technical reviews can include the use of forms of 'mental execution' of the design model, and so can help with assessing dynamic attributes as well as static ones. The references cited above provide some valuable guidelines on how such reviews need to be conducted in order to meet their aims and not to become diverted to issues that are more properly the province of the management review. It is also essential that the review does not become an assessment of the design team, rather than of the design itself.

While a design review cannot provide any well-quantified measures of 'quality' (if such a thing is even possible), it can help to identify weaknesses in a design, or potential weaknesses that might arise as details are elaborated. It therefore provides a means

of answering the second question posed at the start of this section: 'How can information about these attributes be extracted from design documents?' In the present state
of the art, the technical design review probably offers the best means of both extracting and assessing information relating to the quality of a design. In particular, if carefully planned and organized, it brings together those people who have both the domain
knowledge and the technical knowledge that is needed to make realistic projections
from the available design information.

Reviews and inspections have undoubtedly proved to be a successful mechanism,
although as Glass (1999) paraphrases rather neatly: 'inspection is a very bad form of
error removal – but all the others are much worse'. However, as Glass has also
observed, an examination of research on *code* inspections does not necessarily support
the use of 'traditional' review meetings, and certainly not of meetings with more than
two or three participants. Whether the same conditions apply to *design* reviews is
unclear, but certainly the size of these is an issue to consider with care.

This section ends with a summary of those properties of a design that Parnas and
Weiss (1987) believe should be the designer's goals and hence should be studied in a
technical design review. Most of them are properties that we have met already in this
book, but they bear repeating at this point.

The eight requirements that they identify for a good design are that it should be:

- well structured: consistent with chosen properties such as information-hiding;

- simple: to the extent of being 'as simple as possible, but no simpler';

- efficient: providing functions that can be computed using the available resources;

- adequate: meeting the stated requirements;

- flexible: able to accommodate likely changes in the requirements, however these
  might arise;

- practical: module interfaces should provide the required facilities, neither more nor
  less;

- implementable: using current and available software and hardware technology;

- standardized: using well-defined and familiar notation for any documentation.

The last point obviously has special significance in the context of a review, since the
reviewers must be able to capture and comprehend the 'mental models' developed by
the designers. They are likely to find this much harder if the notation used is unfamiliar and itself undocumented.

4.4 Assessing the design process

Any design product emerges as a result of some form of design process, however structured or unstructured this might be. So while no degree of quality in the process can
actually ensure some particular degree of quality in the product, the quality of the
design process is obviously an important factor that needs to be considered when seeking to understand design quality issues.

Our study of the nature of the design process so far has shown that it typically involves the designer in building a 'model' of the end system, and then exploring ways of realizing that model (Jones, 1970). We have also seen that opportunistic design techniques are widely used for these tasks (Visser and Hoc, 1990), even where structured design practices are also in use. So we might reasonably expect that the creative nature of this phase in the process of software development does not readily lend itself to any rigorous measures of quality.

Experience seems to suggest that this is so, and that even for the more quantifiable tasks involved in software development, such as coding and testing, the existing measures of productivity and of quality are rather limited. In his book *Managing the Software Process* (Humphrey, 1991), Watts Humphrey has drawn together a valuable survey of quality issues applied to software development processes. In particular, within his 'Software Process Maturity Model', he identifies five levels of maturity that occur in the processes that an organization uses for producing software systems.

■ *Initial.* The software process is characterized as *ad hoc*, and occasionally even chaotic. Few processes are defined, and success in a project depends upon individual effort.

■ *Repeatable.* Basic project management processes are established and used to track cost, schedule and functionality. The necessary process discipline is in place to repeat earlier successes on projects with similar applications.

■ *Defined.* The software process for both management and engineering activities is documented, standardized and integrated into an organization-wide software process. All projects use a documented and approved version of the organization's process for developing and maintaining software.

■ *Managed.* Detailed measures of the software process and product quality are collected. Both the software process and the products are quantitatively understood and controlled using detailed measures.

■ *Optimizing.* Continuous process improvement is enabled by quantitative feedback from the process and from testing innovative ideas and technologies.

The material of the preceding sections and chapters will have made it clear why the design solution developed for a system will be much more strongly problem-oriented than (say) the structuring practices that might be adopted for coding, or the testing strategies that might be used. This is most certainly not an argument against seeking to find quality measures for the design process, but it does indicate why, regardless of the levels that may be achieved by the overall development process, it is hard to get the design phase even to the point of being repeatable.

To improve the quality of the design process it is particularly necessary to find ways of including input to design activities that can provide:

■ domain knowledge about the type of problem involved, and about important aspects of any implementation features;

■ method knowledge that helps with understanding any design techniques being used;

■ experience from similar projects, wherever available.

There are three widely adopted ways of providing these inputs to the design process.

1. **Technical reviews** were outlined in the previous section; their use allows the design team to gain knowledge from the experiences of others, and particularly from any domain and method knowledge that they might possess. While this form of input is largely aimed at improving the design product, it can also have a significant impact upon the design process by identifying useful techniques or notations that might be applicable to a particular problem.

2. **Management reviews** are primarily concerned with developing and refining estimates of effort and deadlines for the project as a whole, and with gathering any data that might be needed for such estimates. The task of estimation is one that draws heavily upon both domain knowledge and experience, since it requires the use of these to make the projections needed.

3. **Prototyping provides** the means of gaining both domain knowledge and some forms of experience about a particular problem. (In this context, prototyping may be considered to play what Floyd (1984) has termed the 'exploratory' or 'experimental' role.) By constructing suitable prototypes, it may therefore be possible to supplement the knowledge and experience available to both management and the design team.

Of these three, it is the management review that is most likely to involve making some form of assessment of the way that a design is being developed, and which may provide a framework for using the other two forms. The use of reporting and tracking mechanisms will play an important role in monitoring quality issues, and with ensuring that these issues are actually addressed during a review.

Once again the quality of design documentation (and in larger projects the quality of any configuration and control procedures used for organizing this documentation) plays an important role in establishing a high-quality process by reusing experience.

While the use of standard notations for design, and of specific forms of design practice, cannot *ensure* quality in either the design product or the design process, it should be clear by now that their use is likely to be highly influential. We are therefore now in a good position, in the next chapter, to begin examining their roles in terms of the more technical issues affecting software design.

Summary

In examining ideas about 'good' design, the following points are particularly significant.

■ Software quality concepts are concerned with assessing both the static structure and the dynamic behaviour of the eventual system.

■ The ultimate goal of quality must be that of fitness for purpose, although the criteria for determining whether this is achieved will be both problem-dependent and domain-dependent.

■ While the use of abstraction is an important tool for the designer, it makes it difficult to make any direct product measurements during the design process.

■ Technical design reviews can provide a valuable means of obtaining and using domain knowledge to aid with assessing the design product as well as method knowledge to aid with assessing the design process.

Further reading

Parnas D.L. and Weiss D.M. (1987). Active design reviews: Principles and practices. *J. Systems & Software*, 7, 259–65

A short paper that focuses on the use of reviews in the design process and identifies (from experience) some rules to assist with making design reviews as effective as possible.

Humphrey W.S. (1989). *Managing the Software Process*. Addison-Wesley

One of the very few books to examine the context within which software is produced, and to study the nature of the development process.

Green T.R.G. and Blackwell A.F. (1998). Cognitive Dimensions of Information Artefacts: a tutorial. Posted at www.cl.cam.ac.uk/~afb21/CognitiveDimensions

A tutorial document that provides a comprehensive survey of the concepts involved in cognitive dimensions, supported by some illuminating illustrations.

Exercises

4.1 Given the four 'ilities' *reliability, usability, maintainability, reusability,* consider how you would rank them in order of importance for each of the following systems:

(a) a process control system for a chemical plant that produces toxic insecticides;
(b) a bank autoteller network used to issue cash and short statements describing accounts;
(c) an interactive database used for stock control at each branch of a chain of stores that sells electrical goods.

4.2 A computer program uses a number of resources, including processor time, memory, devices and system facilities (such as windows). Consider how you would measure *efficiency* in terms of these and identify your priorities for the two programs that you have written most recently.

4.3 List the criteria that you would expect to be used in planning a design review in your own organization and suggest some basic rules that might help to ensure that these are met.

4.4 For a (relatively simple) website, consider how the ideas in Table 4.2 would need to be interpreted and applied. Do they help with identifying any changes that would be desirable?

part 2

Transferring Design Knowledge

Describing a Design Solution

5.1 Representing abstract ideas

5.2 Design viewpoints for software

5.3 Forms of notation

Much of the discussion of the book has so far concentrated on examining the actions that are involved in the process of design, and the constraints that affect these. The preceding chapter began to consider the attributes possessed by the particular design medium of software; now this chapter starts to examine some of the ways in which these different attributes can be described and modelled by the designer.

5.1 Representing abstract ideas

Abstraction performs an essential role in the design process, by allowing the designer to concentrate on those features of a problem or its solution that are the most important at any particular stage in the development of the design. Therefore the designer needs ways to represent abstract ideas about problem and design objects, and about the various relationships that will exist between these. While this is a general design requirement, and not specific to software design, the 'invisible' nature of software adds some problems of its own.

A **representation** is used to provide a particular abstraction of the characteristics of a system, and is typically needed for such purposes as:

■ capturing the designer's ideas for a solution;

■ explaining the designer's ideas to others (such as customers, fellow designers, implementors, managers);

■ checking for consistency and completeness in a solution.

A representation, whatever its form, can help the designer to concentrate his or her attention upon the issue that is most important to them at any particular stage of the design process.* In particular, it aids the designer by providing a mechanism for reducing the problem of 'information overload'. Indeed, as Vessey and Conger (1994) have observed: 'human problem-solvers resort to various ways of effectively increasing the capacity of short-term memory as well as using external memory devices and/or techniques to support working memory'. In this context, therefore, a representation can also be considered as providing an 'external memory device'.

Representations can also be employed across a wide range of levels of abstraction. For example, in Figure 5.1 we provide a 'sketch' of a building, which might be considered to provide a good example of a 'black box' description, providing only a (partial) description of the external appearance of the building. Figure 5.2 provides a very different representation of a specific property of the same building, in the form of a description of a small part of the internal electrical circuitry. While this is clearly a 'white box' description, it is still an abstraction from the final physical realization of the cables, switches and sockets which will be used in the circuits.

Software designers similarly use a range of levels of abstraction, although the invisible nature of software provides a particular problem in terms of how to describe the properties involved. Whereas the representation used in Figure 5.1 is fairly self-explanatory, and even that used in Figure 5.2 has a fairly distinct link to the physical realization, the lack of any 'visual' properties for software does create a conceptual gap between representation and implementation. We will examine this further in Section 5.3. For the moment, we should simply note that software design techniques tend to make extensive use of various forms of **box and line** notations to provide visual descriptions that are intended to represent the various properties of software.

---

* Of course, the design process can itself be represented by the use of abstract notations, as we will see in later chapters.

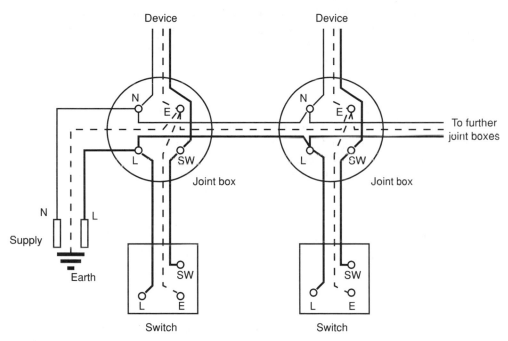

Figure 5.1 Example of a 'physical' description of a building.

Figure 5.2 Example of a part-description of the electrical distribution for the building.

Historically, a major use for representations has been to provide support for particular steps in a design method: each design method makes use of a particular set of representations to form the inputs and outputs for the various transformations it uses.

However, this should not constrain one's thinking about how design representations should be used. Although design methods use representations, so can any form of design activity, whether it be graced with the name of a 'method' or not. Indeed, it is likely that most software is designed without the use of a particular defined 'method', but that is not to imply that designers do not use any form of representation to describe their ideas. Representations can be associated with problem models and solution (program) forms, quite independently of any particular form of design process.

Nor should the association between methods and representations be regarded as particularly rigid, so that the adoption of a method precludes in some way the use of any representation that is not normally associated with it. The objective of design is to solve problems, not to be 'politically correct' in its use of a form! (To some extent this association of method with representation forms is a natural enough consequence of using a design method, since the method guides the designer into considering particular issues in sequence, and so into using specific notations to support these.) For that reason the discussions of representations and methods have been separated in this book, so that the power of abstraction provided by different representations can be seen in a wider context than that of a particular method.

Because representations provide particular abstractions of a system, they are closely linked to the concept of a **viewpoint**. Many of us are familiar with the type of plan drawing that is used for describing buildings and other physical objects. Such a drawing can be considered as describing the 'physical' appearance of the object. However, as demonstrated in Figure 5.2, the wiring plan will also provide an abstract representation of the building, although it may look very different from the physical plan. While these viewpoints are very different in many ways, they need to be kept consistent at the points where they 'intersect' through references to common attributes of design objects.

The notion of a viewpoint puts a particular emphasis upon the role of a representation. A representation is the means that we use to capture certain properties of a design, and it should not be regarded as being the design itself. This concept of the viewpoint as a projection of a design model is illustrated in Figure 5.3. When using this conceptual framework, we can regard the different viewpoints as encompassing particular sets of properties of the design model, and the representations are then the means that are used to describe the corresponding attributes or characteristics (Brough, 1992). (There may, of course, be more than one representation that can be used to describe the properties corresponding to a particular viewpoint, a point that will be examined further later in this chapter.)

We should note here that the use of the term 'viewpoint' in this book does differ somewhat from the way that it is apt to be used in requirements engineering, where the

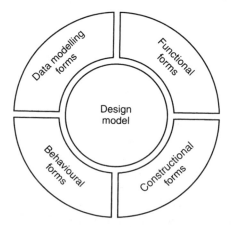

Figure 5.3 The four principal viewpoints as projections from the design model.

term is used to describe 'stakeholder' views of the model (Finkelstein *et al.*, 1992). So, whereas its use in this book is much more focused upon the model-centred idea of providing *projections* of the properties of the model outwards to the users, its use in the requirements context is much more inward-facing, being concerned with the users' particular *perceptions* of the model. Conceptually the two are not very different, in that both are concerned with the interface between the user and the model, but whereas one begins from the model, the other begins from the user.

Returning for a moment to the description of a building that was used in the earlier example, we can now see that:

- 'plan' diagrams capture the attributes that are concerned with spatial dimensions, accessibility, and the like;

- a wiring diagram captures the attributes that are concerned with the logical organization of the distribution of electrical power and its control.

However, both are particular projections of the architect's (mental) design model for the building. Indeed, such representations are the only real means that the architect can use to convey ideas about the design to others. Even so, the representations are not the design model, they are only projections from it, as is illustrated in Figure 5.4.

Of course, these projections need to be kept consistent with one another, in order to maintain a consistent design model. Since each representation describes a set of design properties, there is frequently some intersection between the different sets of properties, and hence some means of checking for consistency between the corresponding forms of representation. Figure 5.5 shows this concept in a symbolic manner. Unfortunately, since the design model is captured only through the representations, we can only check for consistency between forms, and so cannot use the model itself to check that the representations are 'correct' in any absolute sense.

The next section examines more closely the ways in which these concepts can be used in the domain of software design. In particular, it considers the principal features

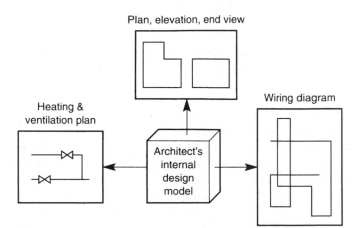

Figure 5.4   Examples of representations as realizations of viewpoints.

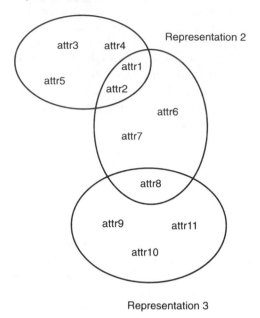

Figure 5.5 Intersecting attributes for different representations.

that distinguish software systems, and the ways in which design representations can be used to describe the characteristics that reflect these features.

5.2 Design viewpoints for software

Perhaps the most distinctive property of software is its dynamic nature. Software is not only an abstraction (which adds to the complications of describing it with abstract forms), it is also the description of a process. So in order to formulate and explore the design model, a designer needs to use a set of description forms that are able to describe both the static and the dynamic properties of a system.

In order to describe *system-oriented* properties, the designer usually needs forms that describe the dynamic behaviour of the system. Such forms tend to emphasize features such as the flow of data or information around a system, or the sequencing of operations. For more detailed *solution-oriented* design needs, which are often concerned with describing 'constructional' issues such as packaging, procedure hierarchy, and data organization, the chosen forms will generally focus on static design attributes. This change of emphasis during design is illustrated in Figure 5.6.

The nature of software and the many paradigms that exist for developing software systems, based on different structuring criteria, has led to the use of a large number of design representations (Webster, 1988; Harel, 1992; Wieringa, 1998). These can be broadly classified as follows:

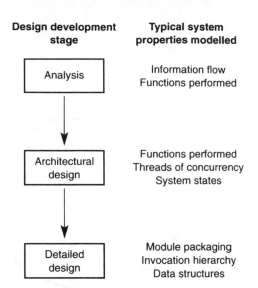

Design development stage	Typical system properties modelled
Analysis	Information flow Functions performed
Architectural design	Functions performed Threads of concurrency System states
Detailed design	Module packaging Invocation hierarchy Data structures

Figure 5.6 Changes of viewpoint with evolution of the overall design model.

- constructional* forms, in which the viewpoint is concerned with essentially static aspects of the system;

- behavioural forms, a set of viewpoints that seek to describe the causal links between events and system responses during execution;

- functional forms, viewpoints that seek to describe what the system does in terms of its tasks;

- data-modelling forms, concerned with the data objects used within the system, and the relationships between these.

Within each of these broad classes, there are a number of forms in general use, partly because the many possible relationships require different sets of attributes for their description, and partly because no representation ever quite captures all of the properties that a designer needs to consider.

These representations can all be classified as 'direct' viewpoints, in that they are created directly by the designer. A further class of viewpoints can be described as 'derived' viewpoints (Budgen and Friel, 1992), shown in Figure 5.7; in these some transformation is applied to the design model in order to generate a 'new' representation form. An example of such a derived viewpoint is that produced by the use of some form of interpreter in order to 'execute' a design (Harel, 1992; Friel and Budgen, 1997); here the output from the interpreter forms the derived viewpoint in terms of some sequence of states or diagrams. (This particular example is based on the

---

* In the first edition we used the term 'structural' for these forms, on the basis that they described the structure of a solution. However, this unintentionally introduced a note of ambiguity, in that all of the viewpoint descriptions can themselves be 'structured'. Hence for this edition we have preferred the use of 'constructional' to make the emphasis clear.

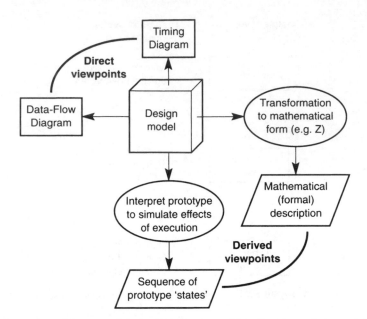

Figure 5.7 Examples of the use of derived viewpoints within the viewpoints model.

observed behaviour of designers in 'mentally executing' a design in order to assess its behavioural aspects (Adelson and Soloway, 1985).) While observation suggests that designers make use of a number of such viewpoints in an informal way, they do not form part of any currently formalized design practices and they will not be explored further in this book.

While the above classification of viewpoints is a useful and practical one, it is by no means the only way that we can classify software design descriptions. As an example, Kruchten's (1994) **'4+1 View'**, provides an object-oriented classification (logical, process, development, physical + scenarios). While it is less general-purpose than the form adopted here, there are some similarities, including the shared recognition that attributes are not necessarily uniquely confined to one viewpoint.

The rest of this section looks briefly at some of the characteristics of the four classes of direct viewpoints. The following section then considers how these can best be described in terms of the use of text, diagrams and mathematical forms.

5.2.1 Constructional forms

As the name implies, these are primarily concerned with describing how the various software-structuring forms provided in programming languages, mark-up languages, etc. are to be used in the final system. A characteristic role for this viewpoint is therefore that of describing the outcome of using a design practice such as a method. Some of the constructional forms described by this viewpoint include:

- *data specification*, which may include files of data, files containing information about the organization of a program (such as a *.h* header file), and data in the form

of mark-up languages such as HTML (HyperText Markup Language) and XML
(Extended Markup Language);

- *threads of execution*, usually in the form of sub-program organization, but also including constructs for handling parallel threads of execution;

- *packaging constructs*, such as the Java *class* or the Ada **package**, where such constructs may be used to construct some form of 'scope wall' around sections of the system, or to create inheritance hierarchies.

An important part of the description involves specifying the relationships and dependencies that will exist between the elements of the system. Typically, these are such forms as:

- *data flow*, concerning the sources and forms of data;

- *invocation*, describing how the 'flow of control' is managed between program elements;

- *uses hierarchy*, describing the dependencies that exist between classes (Parnas, 1979).

Generally, this viewpoint is concerned with modelling static structures rather than with any form of run-time behaviour. (An attempt was made to combine constructional information and behavioural features in a development of the Structure Chart notation that was proposed in Yourdon and Constantine (1979), but this does not appear to have been used to any significant degree.)

While this viewpoint is largely used to describe the outcomes of the design process, it can also be used at a more abstract level when considering major units that might be used in some overall design plan. However, this role is more likely to be one of partitioning major elements of functionality rather than being constructional in nature.

We should also note that, partly because this form describes the designer's ideas at relatively low levels of abstraction, the detailed notations used are usually very dependent upon the 'architectural' form of the eventual system. We will discuss this point in rather more detail in Chapter 6.

5.2.2 Behavioural forms

These are essentially concerned with causal issues, connecting an 'event' to a 'response' via any necessary conditions. These forms tend to be far more abstract than the previous class, which are usually concerned with compilable entities that have definite syntax and semantics. In contrast, behavioural forms are more likely to be concerned with operations that may actually be spread across a number of the physical elements in a system.

Most of these forms can be considered as examples of *finite-state machines*, being concerned with the transitions that occur between different states of a system (waiting, processing, output and so on), and the conditions (events) that are required to make them occur. Being concerned with dynamic relationships (causality), these forms are required to handle some of the design properties that are concerned with time. Our ability to represent the varied influences of time is rather uneven, as the examples of Chapter 7 will show, and can be summarized thus:

- *sequencing* aspects can be described fairly well;

- *fixed-interval* descriptions are also fairly tractable, although their use is mainly restricted to particular features of real-time systems;

- *constraint* effects are very difficult to capture and describe using existing forms of description.

Behavioural descriptions can be used for both black box modelling roles (considering how the system as a whole will respond to specific events) and white box modelling (describing how the system elements will interact in terms of 'chains' of events and actions). Overall, their importance and use has probably become much more pervasive as systems have become larger and also as constructional forms such as classes and objects have come into more widespread use.

5.2.3 Functional forms

One of the hardest tasks for the designer is to describe exactly what it is that a system does. This is essentially a problem-driven issue and hence is difficult to describe in any general form. However, in exchange, this may well be one of the better-defined aspects of the initial problem specification, and the algorithmic aspects in particular may be better specified than other features.

At the detailed design level such forms are generally needed to describe the run-time behaviour of program elements such as subprograms.

5.2.4 Data-modelling forms

While the description of data structures need not be a very significant issue in architectural design terms, it is often a critical aspect of a detailed design. Again, there are a number of relationships that may need to be captured. These include such dependencies as: *type* (both in compounding types to create new ones, and in such mechanisms as inheritance, used to create new 'classes'); *sequence* (in terms of structures such as trees and lists); and *form*.

For some classes of problem, the choice of data structures is a central one, and cannot easily be divorced from the functional issues. Because the viewpoints describing data structures are essentially static in nature, and hence more easily handled, there are a number of well-established representations that are widely used for modelling these forms.

Modelling of data structures, which themselves may well be imposed by external factors, is often seen as being more a task for *analysis* than design, for this very reason. Whatever the role, the data-modelling notations do tend to be used primarily in white box roles, due to the relatively detailed nature of the information involved.

5.3 Forms of notation

This section examines how the different forms of notation for constructing representations are used. The three basic components that can be used in a representation are:

- text
- diagrams
- mathematical expressions

Of course, these are not mutually exclusive in any sense: indeed, neither of the latter two forms is likely to be of very much use without a textual component (try removing all of the text from *any* diagram and see what sense it makes!). Their use during the design process also need not be mutually exclusive.

5.3.1 Textual description forms

Text is very widely used as a means of summarizing information, not just for design. In particular, 'structured' forms such as ordered lists and tables provide a ready means of referring to information – many examples of 'bullet' lists and numbered lists appear in this book. Since a summary is a form of abstraction, such mechanisms are therefore useful to the designer too.

The main problems with using text alone are that:

- any structure that is implicit in the information can easily be obscured, unless it is in a form that maps easily onto lists and tables. Indentation can help with providing structure, but its usefulness is limited, owing to the difficulty of recognizing alignments over long blocks of text;

- natural-language forms are prone to ambiguity, and resolving this can lead to the use of long and complex sequences of text.

This shows that text is often most effective in conveying information when it is used in small blocks or tables. The use of **bold** or *italic* fonts (when available) can help to highlight items, but the effect of this is rapidly lost if used to excess. (In handwritten material, underlining acts as an adequate substitute.)

So textual forms are rarely used as the sole means of providing information about design ideas, although they can play a supplementary role. A good example of text in this role is the use of standard 'pro-formas' in the SSADM method (Longworth, 1992) in order to capture information about certain design decisions. The use of a standard form provides the structure needed to overcome the problems of producing and reading free text.

5.3.2 Diagrammatical description forms

Diagrams have been extensively used in the first four chapters of this book to illustrate concepts about hierarchy, position, flow of information and other forms of relationship between abstract objects. As with text, diagrams also benefit from simplicity of form, and there is probably a 'natural limit' to the number of items of information that can be easily assimilated when reading a diagram. (Miller's 'magic number', 7 plus or minus 2, is much quoted in this context of handling information within the human brain (Miller, 1957); but it may be somewhat misused here, since it referred to handling 'events' rather than abstractions.)

Diagrammatical notations are very widely used in software design, as in many forms of design activity. Indeed, most of the forms that will be discussed in this book are diagrammatical, and so their properties will be discussed only very briefly at this point.

For largely pragmatic reasons, all of them are also what we have already referred to as 'box and line' forms. Such diagrams are easily produced with a pencil, or sketched on a whiteboard and, in the absence of any visible characteristics of software, they are as representative as any other visual form might be. Curiously, given their long history of use and variety of form, there appears to have been little research into the cognitive aspects of using such notations to describe software properties.

Historically, the earliest form of diagram associated with software design is probably the flowchart. Figure 5.8 shows some of the main symbols that are used in drawing flowcharts, together with a very simple example of the form. As sometimes

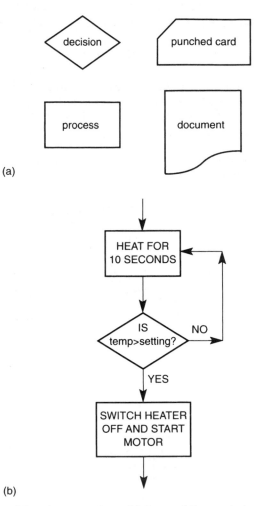

Figure 5.8   The traditional flowchart notations: (a) Some of the symbols used; (b) A simple example of a flowchart.

happens with pioneering ideas, it has not stood the test of time very well and is now used only for specialist purposes.

A major criticism of the flowchart is that it chiefly describes a solution in terms of the operations of the underlying machine, rather than in terms of the problem and its structures. As a part of this, it also places great emphasis upon forms for sequencing operations, a feature of detailed design that is now made much more explicit by modern programming structures. Perhaps the most significant reason is that the flowchart describes structural forms that are not much more abstract than the final program code, and so offers little benefit. (Some years ago now, we experimented in a small way with documenting the development of a system by using both flowcharts and pseudocode. After a few months, we decided to drop the flowcharts as we found that our information was always extracted from the pseudocode.)

The use of flowcharts for general software development is certainly not recommended, and they are now rarely taught or used except for specialist purposes. However, very many other forms of diagram are now used in software design, with properties that more closely reflect the forms of abstraction required in the design process.

It is interesting to look at the number of symbols that are used in the more successful diagrammatical forms. (By 'successful' is meant those that continue to be used over a period.) Many of them have no more than four or five symbols, which in itself is a measure of the degree of abstraction involved in their use. As a general rule, the forms with the larger numbers of symbols tend to be at lower levels of abstraction (the flowchart is a good example), and one problem with their use is that of remembering all the nuances of the notation.

For most users, diagrams are usually the most effective way of providing a clear summary of abstract concepts and relationships. However, this is not guaranteed, and a poor diagram is no more helpful than a heap of unstructured and ungrammatical text. Like text, diagrams have both a syntax ('how we say it') and a semantics ('what it means'), and these need to be used correctly to ensure that the diagram meets its purpose.

As mentioned earlier, a desirable quality in any diagrammatical form of representation is that it should be easily produced using only a pencil and paper (or pen and whiteboard, and so on). This is an essential criterion to meet if diagrams are to be easily and rapidly sketched out as a means of exploring ideas about a design and communicating those ideas to others. Such conventions as the use of thick and thin lines to distinguish between attributes are ruled out by this criterion, as are the use of complex icons or symbols. (Unfortunately some object-oriented design forms fail this test, and when they are combined with the widely available powerful diagramming tools on work-stations, their adoption can have the effect of binding a designer into the use of these tools even for early architectural design tasks.)

A further useful property of many forms of diagram is that of *hierarchical organization*. This occurs where one or more forms of 'diagram element' can themselves be described using a diagram of that form. Hierarchical organization offers the advantage that diagrams can then be 'layered' into levels of abstraction, avoiding large and complex diagrams and so aiding comprehension.

As a footnote to this discussion: the use of colour is probably best restricted to presentations, where it can be used to highlight features of a diagram. However, even then, do remember that a substantial percentage of the average audience may have problems in distinguishing between many of the colours that you use.

5.3.3 Mathematical notations

In recent years there has been an increased interest in using mathematical forms to provide abstract descriptions of software designs (Fraser *et al.*, 1994), and we will look briefly at some examples of this in Chapter 18. Much of this interest stems from the great advantage that mathematical forms have in being able to combine abstraction with a lack of ambiguity.

Since computers are discrete machines, with finite word size and many states, the form of mathematics most appropriate for the needs of software design is that which describes discrete structures. Unfortunately, discrete mathematics is still less likely to be part of the engineer's armoury than more classical forms, and so one of the disadvantages of using mathematical forms is the need for additional staff training and education, often at quite advanced levels. However, this problem should not be exaggerated, since the concepts involved are frequently familiar enough to programmers.

Mathematical forms have particular strengths in describing system behaviour, and in handling some of the issues of time dependency. Major limitations include the complexity of the notation in terms of using a range of unfamiliar symbols (together with a certain lack of standards for these on occasion) and difficulties with handling descriptions of large-scale systems.

Summary

This chapter has examined the issues involved in providing descriptions of a designer's ideas. Some key points and terms that were identified in this were:

- the roles of representations in capturing, explaining, and checking design information;

- the concept of a viewpoint of a design model, as a means of capturing a particular set of design properties, and as projected through the use of a representation;

- the principal classes of direct design viewpoint – the constructional, behavioural, functional, and data-modelling forms;

- the use of text, diagrams, and mathematical expressions as the three basic forms in constructing design representations.

Further reading

Wieringa R. (1998). A survey of structured and object-oriented specification methods and techniques. *ACM Computing Surveys*, **30**(4), 459–527

A comprehensive analysis of a wide range of design methods, together with an analysis of their use of notations, which is of particular relevance here.

Harel D. (1992). Biting the silver bullet. *IEEE Computer*, **25**(1), 8–20

This paper was written in answer to an earlier paper by Fred Brooks Jr (Brooks, 1987). It is mainly concerned with the problems of describing reactive systems and discusses the use of what

I have termed 'derived viewpoints' for design model execution as well as representation forms in general.

Exercises

5.1 For the example of building design that was used in this chapter, suggest any other viewpoints that might be needed in order to provide a full design description, and the representations that could be used for these.

5.2 Write down:

(a) a list of reasons *in favour* of standardizing any particular form of design description;

(b) a list of reasons *against* standardizing the same form of description.

5.3 Consider the (much-maligned) example of the flowchart. What design attributes does it capture, and hence what viewpoint on the design model does it provide?

5.4 Suggest how you might represent the following viewpoints using in turn: text on its own; a diagram; a mathematical form:

(a) the hierarchy of pages in a website;

(b) the program units (procedures) that make use of a particular data type in a program.

chapter 6

Transferring Design Knowledge

6.1 The need to share knowledge

6.2 The architecture concept

6.3 Design methods

6.4 Design patterns

6.5 A unified interpretation?

Codifying and exchanging experiences about both the processes involved in designing and the resulting design features that have proved effective, are essential activities (indeed, they form the core theme of this book!). One role for these activities is the promulgation of new knowledge to existing practitioners. A second is to provide the means of conveying the 'body of knowledge' about software design issues to new or would-be designers. In this pivotal chapter, we examine the forms that are most widely employed for these purposes, and conclude by providing a simple framework that shows how their roles can be related to each other.

6.1 The need to share knowledge

Since the theme of this chapter is the various forms employed to convey 'knowledge' about software design (both process and product), this opening section examines both some of the motivations for transferring knowledge and the factors that are apt to impede this.

6.1.1 Why share?

Wherever a body of practitioners need to employ specialized knowledge, it is customary to find that the ways in which that knowledge is transferred between them become codified in some appropriate forms, in order to provide for:

- *peer to peer exchange*, so that new knowledge can be promulgated throughout the body of practitioners;

- *teacher to pupil instruction*, so that the accumulated experiences of the practitioner group can be conveyed to new members or to those aspiring to join the group.

The craft guilds of the Middle Ages provided classical examples of a structure organized for this purpose, acting to preserve and exchange (and, possibly, protect) the knowledge of how to pursue a given craft, together with an apprentice–master structure used to add new members to the group. A more modern example is the way in which aspiring London cab-drivers are required to acquire and be tested on 'The Knowledge' about routes around the city in order to be licensed. In the context of more creative activities, while we might now use terms such as 'Continual Professional Development' (CPD), and employ mechanisms such as the 'pattern book' (in a very general sense) and interactive on-line instruction, the basic purposes behind their use are largely the same as they were for the craft guilds.

The type of knowledge that needs to be transferred will obviously vary. For scientists, the relevant knowledge may include models of how their particular aspect of the world works, of the techniques considered to be suitable for conducting experimental studies, and of the results from particularly significant experiments. Between peers, knowledge of new work and new results may be transferred by means of personal links, as well as through books, papers, the web and conferences. For their pupils, there is the need to learn about the 'classical' experiments, models and practices, largely through various forms of classroom study. Within those domains that are centred around more 'creative' activities, including both craft and engineering disciplines, while the mechanisms used to transfer knowledge may not be very different, the 'knowledge' involved may also include experience of when particular forms of solution may work well or otherwise and, if possible, the reasons for this.

The last point is significant. An expert practitioner may well be unable to explain *why* they know how to do something, while manifestly being able to demonstrate their knowledge in practice. For example, an expert in graphic design may 'know' which typefaces are most effectively used together for particular styles of document, but may have no rationalized explanation as to why this is so. Such 'heuristics' or 'rules of thumb' are no less valid for the lack of an explanation. Indeed, they may be based upon such deep and complex cognitive issues that any explanation will be of limited general usefulness. (In Vessey and Conger (1994), the authors make this very point when considering software design: 'examining expert problem solving can be quite difficult, since experts automate their problem-solving processes to the point at which they are no longer able to articulate what they are doing'.) Unfortunately though, without some knowledge of 'why' particular solutions work – one of the issues that helps to distinguish an engineering discipline from a craft – a heuristic may be limited in its scope, and it may be difficult to apply it outside of a limited set of problems. In a domain where the problems are relatively repetitive (which characterizes many crafts), this may not be too critical an issue. However, software development (and hence software design) certainly does not constitute a domain where that is true.

Not only is the transferability of knowledge a problem, the quality of that knowledge may also be rather mixed. Indeed, Brooks has suggested that it is useful to differentiate between the following three kinds of results ('shells of knowledge') when considering computing issues (Brooks, 1988).

1. *Findings*, or well-established scientific truths, with their value being measured in forms that correspond to the rigour with which they have been established.

2. *Observations*, which report on actual phenomena, and for which the value is determined by the degree of 'interestingness' that they possess for us.

3. *Rules of thumb*, which are generalizations that are 'signed' by the author, but which are not necessarily supported by data, and where the value is determined by their usefulness.

Unfortunately these distinctions are not always recognized! Certainly though, where design issues are concerned, much of our knowledge is likely to be of the second and third kinds, with correspondingly greater problems in terms of codifying it.

Both of the reasons for transferring knowledge that were identified at the beginning of this section are as relevant for software design as for any other form of design. Indeed, the instruction of pupils (novices) is necessary in any domain and so needs little further discussion at this point. In addition, even expert software designers cannot be expected to possess the knowledge needed to produce creative solutions across the wide range of problem domains and solution forms that we encounter. Other disciplines may address this problem through specialization: a specialist in ear, nose and throat surgery would not normally attempt to remove an appendix; nor would a shipbuilding firm be likely to attempt to enter the luxury car market. However, the distinctions and specializations in software systems are less clear-cut. Even where software producers do specialize to some degree, such as in the development of real-time systems, databases, games, etc., the designer is still likely to be expected to tackle all aspects of software development that might arise.

Our ability to transfer knowledge about how to design software is also constrained and limited by a number of factors, some of which have already been mentioned in the preceding chapters. In the rest of this section we briefly remind ourselves of some of these, and then review some of the mechanisms by which we seek to codify and transfer knowledge. The remaining sections then examine the nature of these mechanisms in rather more detail.

6.1.2 Factors that constrain codification and transfer of design knowledge

For software design the constraints we encounter are a mix of those that arise from the nature of the medium itself and those that arise from the limitations of our knowledge about the wider issues of design.

- *Invisibility of the medium.* One major consequence of this was discussed in the previous chapter, namely the difficulty of linking 'box and line' representations to both abstract concepts and to their eventual implementation in any consistent manner. Indeed, the variety of notations available is apt to create our own version of the 'Tower of Babel' when we are faced with the need to communicate design ideas. While some standardization of notation is helpful, the conceptual barrier is still present.

- *Influence of implementation.* Our assessment of the degree of success or failure of particular design solutions is apt to be entangled with the success or failure of their implementation. This is particularly true of failure, where poor programming or the lack of computing power can completely nullify any good qualities of the design itself. While it can be argued that the influence of implementation issues is equally significant when assessing any other form of artifact, the distinction is much more blurred for software, where the 'construction' element is so directly linked to the design element and no separate manufacturing phase exists.

- *Domain factors.* Design solutions are inextricably interwoven with domain knowledge. One role for domain knowledge is to 'bound' the set of acceptable solutions to a given problem. The knowledge involved in this role may be *direct* in nature: for example, a real-time solution is highly likely to require the designer to make decisions about priorities for the elements of that solution, to ensure that the key elements are able to meet the required response time. It may also be more *indirect*, perhaps involving knowledge about the properties that can be considered when making design trade-offs in a particular domain, and how these can be prioritized. Failure to fully understand the implications of the domain context may be a significant factor in failed solutions. A good example of this issue is provided by the experiences of the Denver Airport automated baggage handling system, which achieved some degree of notoriety in the mid 1990s (Swartz, 1996).

- *Process versus product.* The act of designing involves employing knowledge about *products* (reusable elements, materials used in implementation, etc.) and about *processes* (how to go about solving a particular type of problem). Transferring knowledge about products is usually well understood as a problem, and a mechanism such as the 'catalogue' is generally employed. However, as we will see when we come to consider reuse in Chapter 17, because software is really a process, such tried and tested forms are less effective. Transferring knowledge about a creative process such as designing is more problematical. Mechanisms such as case studies and stylized design processes both have useful roles to play but, by the nature of the problem, they also have quite significant limitations. This issue is one that is explored more fully in the next sub-section.

From the above, we can see that transferring knowledge about a creative process such as design is by no means a simple task, or one that is easily automated.

6.1.3 Mechanisms for codifying and transferring design knowledge

Here we briefly review three of the ways in which experience with the design of software-based systems is codified and transferred. The following sections then go on to elaborate further upon how these roles are performed.

Codifying and transferring knowledge about the form of detailed design *solutions* for 'representative' problems has sometimes been provided through the use of case studies, but only recently has a more general framework been devised that can be used to record and codify ideas about the higher-level form of design solutions. The concept of a **software architecture** (Perry and Wolf, 1992; Shaw and Garlan, 1996) is one which seeks to classify the more abstract features of a design solution. So this concept provides a basic vocabulary that can assist with describing solution *forms* to others.

Transferring knowledge about design *processes* is a more established approach. The early forms of **software design method** came into accepted usage in the 1970s, and provided a procedural form of guidance on how to develop solutions for specific classes of problem. The form of knowledge employed is largely about the sequences of decisions that can lead to a particular form of solution (methods tend to implicitly assume a particular form of architectural style).

More recently (and within the context of a particular architectural form), the idea of the **design pattern** has provided an alternative form for use both in codifying and transferring knowledge about how a design might be structured (Gamma *et al.*, 1995). Superficially, patterns would appear to codify knowledge about design products, since they describe particular solutions to commonly occurring problems. However, this is to misunderstand the role of a pattern, in that it is not a solution template within which the user has only to 'plug' some code, but rather a solution *strategy* which the designer can then adopt for a particular problem. So patterns are really much more about the 'how' of design development. In that sense, therefore, their role is closer to that of the design method, being more concerned with transferring knowledge than codifying it.

The following sections examine each of these concepts in rather more detail, while still focusing on their roles as mechanisms for knowledge codification and transfer. However, since the concepts of *architecture* and of *architectural style* provide a framework for much of the rest of the book, and since we will be discussing the roles of methods and patterns in later chapters, most of the emphasis has been placed upon architectural issues.

6.2 The architecture concept

Since this concept provides some important ideas that we will be using throughout the rest of this book, we provide quite a detailed description in this section. (The other two topics are addressed more extensively at a later point and so get a briefer treatment here.) We begin by identifying what we mean by a software architecture; look at how different architectural styles can be described; examine three simple examples; and then briefly consider how the concept provides aid for our theme of transferring knowledge about design.

6.2.1 What is architecture?

The term *architecture* has been used for many years within the software development world in a very informal manner. Unfortunately, as with so many descriptive terms, it has also been used by different people to mean rather different things. So before going on to look at the way in which this has been drawn together by the work of a number of people, and especially by Dewayne Perry, Mary Shaw and David Garlan, it is useful to consider what we mean by the term in a more general sense.

The role of the *architect* has long been one that is associated with a quite specific domain of design, namely buildings. This is also a role with a very clear design responsibility, in that no-one expects the architect involved with developing a new building to actually take part in managing its construction. The architect *may* choose to do so, but in general, it is not expected of him or her. The term is used in other domains too, although usually by analogy. For example, we may speak of 'naval architects' as being people who design ships (usually warships, but not necessarily so); and also of 'landscape architects' whose domain of design is that of gardens, estates, etc. Again, in both of these cases, we associate the term very much with those people whose role is to undertake the more abstract design tasks, rather than managing the details of the actual implementation.

Closer to our own domain, we also have the concept of the 'computer architect' who designs the top-level structures of a computer, usually referred to as its 'architecture'. Indeed, this has been one of the more important concepts in the development of computing. Beginning with the IBM 360/370 range, the idea of a 'family' of computers with a generally consistent form (typically described using such terms as RISC, pipeline, etc.) became the norm. By providing a (largely) consistent platform for executing software elements, this opened up great opportunities, both in terms of the marketplace, and also by making it possible for software to evolve and migrate, rather than needing to be rewritten for each new generation of computers. Indeed, it is this very success that has provided part of the motivation for seeking to adapt this concept to software. However, Perry and Wolf (1992) have rightly cautioned against drawing the analogy too far. As they have observed, a hardware architecture makes use of a relatively small number of design elements, with scale being achieved by replication of these. With a few exceptions (such as neural networks), this is rarely true for software, where any increase of scale generally involves adding further distinct design elements.

Perhaps a little inconsistently though, an architect does not design an *architecture*, but rather a solution to address a particular need.* The role of architectural style is to provide a framework for that design task, by identifying a general set of characteristics (the style) that relate to the problem and which have been employed successfully on similar problems. As such, the 'physical' concept of architecture is more a reflection of common patterns than something that is itself designed (Buschmann *et al.*, 1996).

---

* A personal bête noire here is those who speak of *architecting*, when what they really mean is *designing*! While it might be possible to 'verb any noun', this one is particularly inappropriate.

So that begs the question of whether we can usefully speak of a system as having an *architecture*? In practice, most authors seem to consider this to be an abstract top-level description of a design, expressed in terms of its major elements and their general form. The way we express this is also apt to provide a description of its *style* and, for our purposes, the term **architectural style** is often the most useful one to employ, and one that we will use extensively in this book. For example, when speaking about buildings we might say that a given building is in an 'Elizabethan' or a '1960s' style. (When describing buildings we often seem to use temporal classification of styles, perhaps because, as new building materials have come along, so architects have developed particular ways of employing them. In contrast, in the domain of ships, role is more likely to be the basis for classifying architectural style. If we describe a ship as an 'aircraft carrier', then we know that it is likely to have such characteristics as a flat 'through deck' to allow aircraft to land and take off, and a small 'island' for its superstructure, etc.)

So the notion of an *architectural style* can perhaps best be viewed as something that provides a very abstract description of a particular set of general characteristics of a solution. When provided with such a description, we will then know something of the general form of a particular solution, but within that there may still be great variation in detail. More specifically, and this is a point that we will return to later, such a description may also enable us to make a fairly broad assessment of the likely consequences of mixing items of software that have different architectural styles. (Returning briefly to the analogy with buildings, we can easily see that adding a 1960s-style flat roofed extension to a cottage that was built in the Tudor period is unlikely to be visually harmonious, nor are they likely to 'bond' well physically! Both may well be quite functional in their own way, and be constructed in a style that is appropriate for the materials employed in their fabrication, but as these are so very different, some degree of 'mismatch' is almost guaranteed.)

So what roles can the idea of architectural style provide when applied to software systems? Firstly, the role of providing a very abstract description of the overall form is still an appropriate one, although this is more likely to be expressed in terms of constructional forms than epochs. (Of course, we may also refer to buildings in this way, as in 'wattle and daub' or 'glass and concrete', where such a description provides some idea of what the likely form of the building will be.) Descriptive terms such as 'client–server' and 'pipeline' are widely employed, although not necessarily well-defined. One view of this role is that it 'defines constraints on the form and structure of a family of architectural instances' (Garlan and Perry, 1995). Secondly, as mentioned above, the concept may assist with identifying where there is potential for some degree of 'mismatch' to occur between the forms of the elements used to construct a software-based system (Garlan *et al.*, 1995). Thirdly, it tells us something about the type of constructional notations that are likely to be useful for describing a particular solution.

In addition, although the concept is primarily concerned with categorizing the *form* of a particular design solution, it may also tell us something about the design processes involved. Indeed, a rarely recognized characteristic of software design methods is that the use of any method implicitly imposes a particular architectural style upon the designs that are produced. This is a point that we will return to in the next section.

One of the clearest discussions about the roles of software architecture and architectural style is provided in a short paper by Garlan and Perry (1995). Writing as an introduction to a collection of papers on software architecture, they capture many of the key issues very elegantly and in a concise manner. The authors also argue that the concept of architecture can have an impact upon at least the following five aspects of software development.

- **Understanding**. This stems from the way that architectural concepts provide an abstract vocabulary that aids understanding of a system's high-level design.

- **Reuse**. This partly relates to the idea of the *component*, which we will be examining in Chapter 17.

- **Evolution**. Garlan and Perry argue that 'software architecture can expose the dimensions along which a system is expected to evolve'. As such, therefore, it provides a guide to the ideas and aims of the originators, for use by those entrusted with its later maintenance and change.

- **Analysis**. Here an architectural style offers a framework that can provide the basis for checking various features of a design (including its conformance to the style!).

- **Management**. The arguments here are largely concerned with the role of architecture as an aid to planning and, in particular, of planning for change.

Some of these are issues that we have already encountered in the discussions of earlier chapters, and all of them are issues that we will return to in later ones.

Various authors have suggested some ways in which we might classify architectural styles so that these can be used to describe software systems. We now go on to review some of these, in order to illustrate some of the points made in this sub-section.

6.2.2 Classifying architectural styles

For the concept of an architectural style to be of use to us, we need to be able to provide a specification of its characteristics in some way. Not unreasonably, since a style describes 'a family of instances', we might also expect that the notation we use to describe the architectural form of individual systems should also be suitable for describing the more general concept of an architectural style too.

In Perry and Wolf (1992), the authors proposed an initial classification scheme in the form of:

Software Architecture = {Elements, Form, Rationale}

through which an architecture (and hence a style) could be considered as being defined by a set of (design) elements that have a particular form. The particular *elements* that they identified were:

- processing elements
- data elements
- connecting elements

where the connecting elements could also be processing or data elements. (Examples of connecting elements include such mechanisms as procedure calls, messages, shared data repositories, etc.). *Form* was then described as a set of 'weighted properties and relationships', which constrains the choice of elements and how they can be used.

Finally, the *rationale* was intended to capture the motivation for particular choices (although, as we have observed previously, this information is too rarely recorded).

Subsequent authors have often tended to adopt simpler schemes of classification. For example, Shaw and Garlan (1996) employ a basic framework based only upon *components* and *connectors*. In contrast though, the scheme adopted in Shaw and Clements (1997) is somewhat more elaborate (and in some ways, also returns to some of the ideas used by Perry and Wolf, although organized in a different way). Here the authors categorize architectural styles in terms of the following major features:

■ the kinds of components and connectors that are used in the style;

■ the ways in which control (of execution) is shared, allocated and transferred among the components;

■ how data is communicated through the system;

■ how data and control interact;

■ the type of (design) reasoning that is compatible with the style.

For our purposes, this scheme has the benefit of making explicit many of the issues that we should be considering in the context of this and later chapters. So, in the next sub-section, we employ it to briefly examine and categorize some examples of different architectural styles. Table 6.1 summarizes the styles identified by Shaw and Clements.

Various efforts have also been made to codify such descriptions of architectural style using a more formal basis, largely to aid with analysis, although also to provide a more formal basis for these concepts. In Shaw and Garlan (1996) examples are provided of specifications that are represented using the Z formal description language, and there is also a discussion of their own *UniCon* architectural description language. Whether this is a realistic goal is open to debate, since there is the inevitable conflict between the needs of abstract description and those of the detail needed for specification (a conflict that we examine more fully in the next chapter). However, for the purposes of this book we will only be concerned with the concepts and with their categorization in general terms, as above.

Table 6.1 Major categories of software architectural style

Category	Characteristics	Examples of Styles
Data-flow	Motion of data, with no 'upstream content control' by the recipient	Batch sequential Pipe-and-filter
Call-and-return	Order of computation with a single thread of control	Main program/subprograms 'Classical' Objects
Interacting processes	Communication among independent, concurrent processes	Communicating processes Distributed Objects
Data-centred repository	Complex central data store	Transactional databases Client–Server Blackboard
Data-sharing	Direct sharing of data among components	Hypertext Lightweight threads

6.2.3 Examples of some software architectural styles

One qualification that does need to be made right at the outset (and which is firmly made in Shaw and Clements (1997) is that real systems are not necessarily 'pure' in terms of their architectural style, and so may possess the characteristics of more than one style. (This is not inconsistent with what we see in other domains. Buildings may well be altered and extended with the passage of time, and the changes may not necessarily be consistent with the original style – which should not be taken to imply that there is necessarily a mismatch.) As with buildings, the presence of 'hybrids' does not render the basic idea of classification any less useful.

The descriptions provided in the rest of this section are of necessity brief ones, and for fuller discussion of these issues the reader should consult a specialized source such as Shaw and Garlan (1996) or Shaw and Clements (1997). To illustrate the concepts involved, we will look at three examples of widely encountered architectural styles.

1. Pipe and filter

This style (which from the 1970s onwards has been embodied within the architecture of the Unix operating system) is essentially one based upon the transformations that are centred around the **dataflow** that occurs within some form of network. Indeed, although the Unix variant is essentially linear, many non-linear topological forms exist, such as the MASCOT approach described in Simpson and Jackson (1979). Examples of these are shown in Figures 6.1 and 6.2.

In a pipe and filter architectural style, the components are typically processes that transform an input data stream into an output stream (the 'filters'), connected together by some form of dataflow mechanism, which may occur in a synchronous or asynchronous manner. A widely-cited example is the 'classical' approach to compiler design, in which a series of operations are performed to gradually transform the source code into some form of binary code. Each element, such as a lexer or parser, acts as a filter, transforming a stream of input tokens into the form required by the next stage. For example, the lexer inputs a stream of characters and splits this into the 'lexemes' or groups of characters that have meaning in the context of the program. So the input expression

count = count + 1;

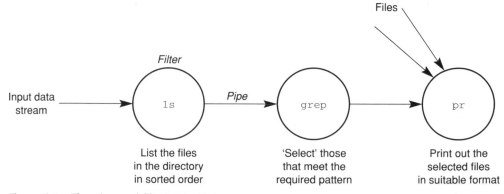

Figure 6.1   The pipe-and-filter style: Unix processes.

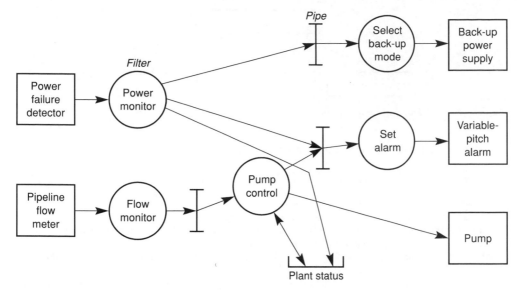

Figure 6.2   The pipe-and-filter style: MASCOT diagram.

Table 6.2   The pipe-and-filter architectural style

Feature	Instantiation in pipe and filter
Components	Data transformation processes.
Connectors	Data transfer mechanisms (e.g. Unix pipes, files, etc.).
Control of execution	Typically asynchronous, control is transferred by the arrival of data at the input to a process. Upstream processes have no control of this.
Data communication	Data is generally passed with control.
Control/data interaction	Control and data generally share the same topology and control is achieved through the transfer of data.
Design reasoning	Tends to employ a 'bottom-up' approach using *function* due to the emphasis placed upon the filters (components). A design method such as JSP (Chapter 14) may generate this style of solution.

will be output as the stream of lexemes: 'count', '=', 'count', '+', '1', ';' regardless of the presence or absence of intervening space or tab characters.

More complex forms of this style (such as that used in the MASCOT system cited earlier) may incorporate more complex dataflow control, including allowing for the retention of data, its synchronization and, where appropriate, having mechanisms to allow data to be over-written where it is time-expired and not yet processed.

Table 6.2 provides a brief summary of this style using the general classification scheme adopted in Shaw and Clements (1997) described in the preceding sub-section.

2. Call and return

The concept of an ordered and hierarchical transfer of control from one processing element to another underpins this style. Unlike the more data-driven 'pipe-and-filter' style, which is essentially non-hierarchical (filters have no control over the actions of other

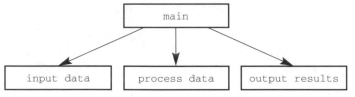

Figure 6.3 The call-and-return style: subprogram invocation.

Table 6.3 The call-and-return architectural style

Feature	Instantiation in call and return
Components	Subprogram units.
Connectors	Subprogram invocation (calling).
Control of execution	Sequencing is controlled through the calling hierarchy and (in detail) the algorithms in the components.
Data communication	Data is passed via parameters and can also be accessed directly (global access).
Control/data interaction	This is relatively limited, beyond the linking of parameters and return inform within the 'calling stack'.
Design reasoning	Encourages use of a 'top-down' strategy, based upon *function*. A design method such as the 'traditional' Structured Analysis/Structured Design will produce solutions that employ this style (Chapter 13).

filters), the call-and-return style places much greater emphasis upon control aspects rather than upon data transfer issues. A call-and-return style is therefore closely linked to the traditional program structuring form of 'main program' and 'subprograms' as illustrated in Figure 6.3. The main program (which itself is really a top-level subprogram when viewed from the operating system) may well perform no role other than that of controlling and sequencing the subprograms that perform the actual processing tasks. Table 6.3 summarizes the main features of this style.

3. Data-centred repository

This style describes systems in which the key element is some central mechanism used for the persistent storage of information which can then be manipulated independently by some arbitrary number of processing units. Examples that embody such a style are database systems and blackboard expert systems. Shaw and Clements (1997) also argue that client–server forms come into this general category, on the basis that the server acts as a repository and, indeed, often incorporates a database. Figure 6.4 provides an illustration of the general form of a client–server system.

In the case of a database system, the central mechanism is generally concerned with providing some form of indexed access to a (potentially) large volume of data. Blackboard systems can be regarded as rather more 'freestyle' variants on this, with the data now being representative of some form of 'knowledge' and with the control and sequencing of any updates being much less tightly controlled. Table 6.4 provides a summary of this architectural style.

There are obviously many other styles, of which good examples include *object-oriented* and *event-driven* architectural forms, and some of these will be discussed in

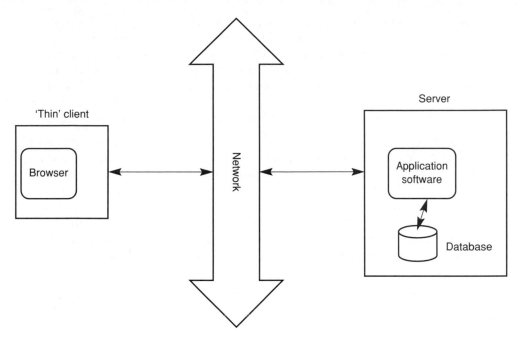

Figure 6.4   The data-centred repository style: simple client–server system.

Table 6.4   The data-centred repository architectural style

Feature	Instantiation in data-centred repositories
Components	Storage mechanisms and processing units.
Connectors	Transactions, queries, direct access (blackboard).
Control of execution	Operations are usually asynchronous and may also occur in parallel.
Data communication	Data is usually passed via some form of parameter mechanism.
Control/data interaction	Varies quite widely. For a database or a client–server system, these may be highly synchronized, whereas in the case of a blackboard there may be little or no interaction.
Design reasoning	A *data modelling* viewpoint is obviously relevant for database and client–server systems. The wider variation of detail that occurs in this style tends to preclude the widespread use of more procedural design approaches.

later chapters on design practices. However, the above three offer good examples that illustrate the basic concepts.

6.2.4 The role of the architectural concept in knowledge transfer

At this stage, the obvious question is: 'what role do these ideas perform in terms of the task of designing software?' A number of answers to this question were suggested by Garlan and Perry (1995) and were reviewed in Section 6.2.1. Taking a slightly narrower focus, in terms of the issues that are more directly the concern of this book, we can identify the following key roles.

■ **Providing a framework and vocabulary for top-level design ideas.** An important element in designing is to determine what the overall form (architecture) of a system is to be. Is the best choice to use a set of processes connected as a pipeline; a network of distributed processing elements; or a centralized database? Sometimes this choice is more or less pre-determined by context, but this is not always the case. These ideas therefore provide both a framework for deciding on the overall form of a solution, and a vocabulary for describing it to others and hence for discussion.

■ **Determining the choice of design strategy.** One of the consequences of choosing an architectural form for a solution is that we then need to find some way of achieving that solution, whether it is by using the forms described in the rest of this chapter, or by less 'formal' means. Choice of a style affects both the strategy and the choice of notations used to support it and describe the eventual solution. For example, choosing a call-and-return style would suggest that we might begin by considering the functionality of the overall system, or choosing to use a transaction-centred form may suggest that we should begin by thinking about the data forms involved.

■ **Assisting with later changes.** An important element in successfully updating an existing system is to understand the ideas and intentions of the original designer(s) (what Perry and Garlan refer to as 'evolution'). Changes that preserve the overall architectural integrity are likely both to be more successful and to leave scope for further changes in the future. Since many design tasks occur within a larger operational context, these concepts provide a valuable aid to identifying such constraints and hence to preserving the structure of a system.

This section has introduced some important ideas that will be employed in the later chapters. Like so many of the elements that make up the software design context, the major value of the concept of architectural style lies in this ability to describe the broad picture, and placing too much emphasis on detailed classification may risk being counter-productive. Most of our use of this concept will therefore be for describing high-level characteristics of different design forms, although occasionally we may need to be specific about some of the more detailed characteristics that were described in the previous subsections.

6.3 Design methods

The preceding section has described a means of codifying knowledge about the *form* of a design solution. In this section we discuss the role of design methods in terms of codifying knowledge about *how* to generate design solutions. We will not be describing design methods in any real detail, since we have much fuller descriptions in the rest of this book. Our only real concern here is with their role in transferring knowledge, or rather with the detailed forms used to do this.

A design method can be regarded as providing a *procedural description* of how to set about the task of producing a design solution for a given problem. That is, a method describes the tasks that the designer is to perform and the order in which they should be performed. However, since design is a creative process, a method cannot provide actual guidance about exactly how each task should be performed for any specific problem.

While the idea of design *methods* is not one that is confined to software, as demonstrated in Jones (1970), software design methods are generally much more detailed and prescriptive than those which arise in other domains. (Another example of this is provided by the 'classical' engineering design text by Pahl and Beitz (1996), which takes a quite different and much less prescriptive approach to teaching about the design process than is commonly adopted with software.) Why this should be so must remain partly a matter for conjecture, but we can suggest a number of reasons.

- The rapid development of the computing industry since the 1960s has led to a drastically escalating need for design and development skills over the past 30 years. Traditional master/pupil mechanisms for transferring knowledge could not have coped with this, and the design method has provided one of the ways in which design knowledge could be conveyed to large numbers of people with design responsibilities.

- Rapid developments in software technology have also meant that some means of providing peer-to-peer knowledge transfer has also been needed if practitioners are to be kept informed, and again this role has been partly filled by the use of design methods.

- The *invisibility* of software (Brooks, 1987) has made it necessary to create artificial frameworks for its description (including design notations) and the design method has become an integral part of that framework, providing both an explanation of how these abstract forms can be developed and deployed and also a vocabulary for doing so.

Through its procedures and notations, a design method implicitly produces a design solution that embodies a particular architectural style. This leads to one other observation about the rather unique role that design methods play in the software domain. In no other domain is there quite the same expectation that following a given design *process* will ensure the production of a sound design *product*. (In fairness, software design method developers do not necessarily make this claim, but of course it is implicitly assumed. No-one would be expected to adopt a method that was thought to result in poor design solutions!)

Studies of experienced designers have tended to suggest that they are only likely to follow design method practices where they do not feel confident about their 'domain knowledge' (Adelson and Soloway, 1985; Guindon, 1990; Visser 1987). In other words, an expert in designing compilers might feel less confident when asked to design (say) a transaction processing system for a bank and hence might employ a design method for this, when they would certainly not do so in developing a new compiler. Similarly, studies of method use also suggest that few designers follow a given method completely, and that they tend to use experience to adapt the procedures in varying degrees (Hardy *et al.*, 1995). This suggests that once some degree of knowledge about how to design has been acquired, the framework offered by a method becomes less valuable, supporting the view that methods are more a means of *transferring* knowledge than of generating specific solutions.

One other question is why the development of new design methods enjoyed greater popularity and importance during the 1970s and 1980s, whereas, since the early 1990s, they have played a less prominent role, at least in the software engineering literature. Again, this is partly a matter for conjecture, but one possible reason (apart from a growing maturity of design expertise in the community) is the increasing complexity of software structures. We have argued elsewhere that this also leads to increasing complexity of design methods (Budgen, 1995; Budgen, 1999), in which each of the procedural steps is likely to require greater maturity of design thinking. In other words, the only people able to use such methods effectively are those who probably already have sufficient expertise not to need the detailed procedures, or whose need is mainly to adapt their expertise to a new architectural style.

While the above arguments should not be seen as a claim that 'design methods are dead!', they do suggest that there are limits to their degree of usefulness in transferring design knowledge and, indeed, in reading the later chapters of this book, we need to keep this in mind. In terms of the roles that we identified at the beginning of this chapter, it is probable that, while design methods continue to play a useful role in transferring knowledge to the novice designer, their value in terms of peer-to-peer exchange has been reduced.

Having looked at how knowledge about design is transferred through the concepts of architectural styles and the practices of design methods, we now look at one of the other developments of the 1990s, the *design pattern*. While design patterns are not procedural, they share some of the role of methods in that they are concerned with the *processes* of producing a design solution, but also retain a strong element of product modelling.

6.4 Design patterns

The detailed form and application of design patterns is a topic that we will be addressing much more fully in Chapter 10. So, as with design methods in the preceding section, our main concern here will be to consider design patterns in the context of their role as a mechanism for knowledge transfer.

The concept of the design pattern is very much associated with the object-oriented architectural style, although in principle there are no reasons why patterns could not be employed with other styles. To some extent, this reinforces the arguments of the preceding section: the object-oriented architectural style is one that has necessitated the use of much more complex (and hence less accessible) design methods, leading to a search to find alternative ways of developing such designs.

The concept of the design pattern is rooted in the work of the architect Christopher Alexander (Alexander *et al.*, 1977), who describes it in the following words:

'Each pattern describes a problem which occurs over and over again in our environment, and then describes the core of the solution to that problem, in such a way that you can use this solution a million times over, without ever doing it the same way twice.'

This concept has been taken up for software (or, more specifically, for object-oriented software) by the 'pattern community', with the core work on the topic being the book by Gamma *et al.* (1995).

Essentially, a pattern is a generic solution to a problem, which itself is likely (almost certain) to be a part of a bigger problem. In terms of knowledge transfer, therefore, it conveys information about a particular problem that a designer might encounter, together with a strategy for addressing that problem (as well as some notes about the possible consequences that might need to be considered when performing design trade-off decisions).

In some ways, the idea of the pattern comes much closer to embodying the traditional master/apprentice model for transferring knowledge and expertise than design methods can possibly achieve. Methods also concentrate on 'teaching' about solutions, while patterns educate about problems too, and the recognition of these is an equally important part of learning about design, if generally much more difficult to achieve! Patterns can also have a role in terms of providing peer-to-peer exchange of design knowledge in much smaller 'chunks' than can be achieved through the use of methods. The pattern idea also matches some of the observed practices of designers. One of the characteristics of expert design behaviour that was observed in Adelson and Soloway (1985) was the employment of 'labels for plans', where a designer would recognize and 'label' a sub-problem that they knew how to solve, leaving them free to concentrate on the less familiar aspects of a problem.

Patterns are of course no more of a panacea than any other approach that we might choose to adopt for organizing the transfer of design knowledge. Indeed, the very mechanism itself effectively imposes limitations: to be successful, patterns need to be readily accessible and recognizable, which in turn suggests that too large a set of patterns is likely to be unmanageable, presenting problems for indexing and remembering the relevant bits of knowledge. (We might note that in Gamma *et al.*, (1995), the authors concentrate on a catalogue of 23 design patterns. In other words, they keep their vocabulary to a manageable limit, which is perhaps one good reason for its wide acceptance.) That said, of course, very few design problems present features that are entirely new and original and so, as such, the pattern concept does recognize and embody a useful level of reuse of design knowledge.

As with design methods, one question that we need to ask is whether the use of patterns will lead to 'good' solutions. While the process of pattern use does not seem to have been studied, there are some experimental findings regarding how maintainable the end product is likely to be (Prechelt *et al.*, 2001). While not conclusive (few empirical studies ever are!), these findings certainly indicate that design patterns can be used to produce solutions that have a consistent style, especially in terms of enabling future change.

The design pattern concept is not restricted to use in 'detailed design' activities. At the programming level it is generally referred to as an **idiom** (Coplien, 1997) and, at the architectural level, the concept of an **architectural design pattern** has been explored in Buschmann *et al.* (1996). The latter authors look upon many of the architectural styles such as *pipe and filter* as architectural patterns and, as such, they also extend the pattern concept beyond a purely object-oriented context.

6.5 A unified interpretation?

This chapter has introduced some very important material in terms of providing a framework for our understanding of the ways in which software design practices are organized. However, as always, it can become difficult to 'see the wood for the trees' when faced with so many concepts. This short section is intended to provide a rather personal interpretation of how these ideas complement each other. While the interpretation provided draws upon the observations from a number of academic studies, it has not itself been subjected to either analysis or empirical study, hence the emphasis on it being a *personal* interpretation, based largely upon experience.

Our starting point is some of the earliest studies of how people actually design software. One particular observation of Adelson and Soloway (1985) was that experienced designers would 'execute' their designs in order to explore their ideas about how well a design would meet its purposes. If to this we add the observation in Curtis *et al.* (1988) that expert designers are not necessarily good programmers, we are left to conclude that one of the characteristics of the experienced designer is the ability to form and use some intermediate level of 'mental model'. In other words, the experienced designer uses a set of abstractions of their design elements without needing to think about how these will be implemented. In contrast (as many teachers will know), the inexperienced designer lacks this intermediate level of thinking, and can easily become entangled in consideration of an undue degree of detail about implementation. Figure 6.5 shows this schematically.

This model is not inconsistent with some of the other observations made by Adelson and Soloway and by other researchers. Concepts such as 'labels for plans' can be considered as being part of this 'underpinning knowledge' that a designer brings to a task. So one of the roles of design methods (and, to some degree, of design patterns

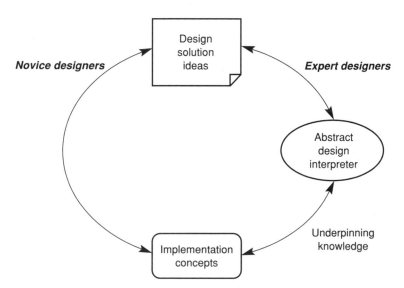

Figure 6.5   A simple model contrasting expert and novice design contexts.

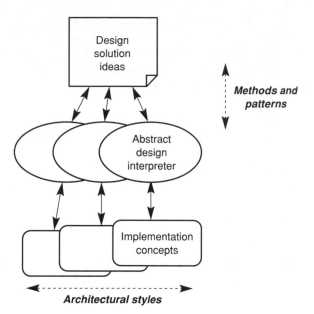

Figure 6.6 An extended model describing an expert's design context.

too) is to help the inexperienced designer develop such intermediate models of their ideas.

If we pursue this further, we can note that where designers tackle unfamiliar tasks, they may well have problems in building such a model (and hence may revert to using a method). So this suggests that there are likely to be potentially many forms of intermediate model, where each form loosely corresponds to a particular architectural style. A designer who is an expert in using the object-oriented paradigm might feel less confident about developing a solution for a transaction-based architectural style because of this lack of an intermediate model. Figure 6.6 extends the original concept as described in Figure 6.5 to include this possibility.

The detailed form of any particular intermediate model is almost certainly a very personal one, and this is not itself the object of our attention in the rest of this book. Rather, our concern is with the ways in which a designer develops the ability to form and employ such intermediate models and, where appropriate, to express their ideas using particular notations.

One question that this leaves is just how the 'underpinning knowledge' is developed. In other words, how much does a designer need to know about implementation? Such questions are, of course, almost impossible to answer. Certainly most of us would accept that the task of designing software does require an understanding of its general properties, of what is possible, and of what are the 'good' ways of deploying it. The observations of Curtis and his co-workers also suggest that, while such knowledge is necessary, a high degree of programming expertise may actually be a distraction. This underpinning knowledge will also be linked to particular architectural styles, at least to some degree.

A specific feature of this book is that, for just such reasons, no code-based examples have been used to illustrate points. The assumption throughout has been, and will be, that the reader has a basic understanding of the basics of programming, and that the role of this book is to help further with developing an understanding of how to form and employ these 'intermediate models'.

Summary

This chapter has examined some of the principal ways in which software design knowledge and expertise can be codified and transferred. Particular issues addressed here have included:

■ the reasons for transferring design knowledge, and (where known) for codifying the rationale behind such knowledge;

■ the role of the concept of architectural style in providing a framework and a vocabulary for top-level design ideas, and for assisting with the choice of design strategy;

■ the use of design methods to codify design practices and strategies;

■ the rationale for using design patterns and their ability to describe the core features of reusable design solutions.

Further reading

Monroe R.T., Kompanek A., Melton R. and Garlan D. (1997). Architectural styles, design patterns, and objects. *IEEE Software*, **14**(1), 43–52

A very readable paper that draws together many of the concepts discussed in this chapter and explores their capabilities and roles, as well as their strengths and limitations, with some simple examples for illustration.

Shaw M. and Garlan D. (1996). *Software Architecture: Perspectives on an Emerging Discipline*. Prentice-Hall

This is the definitive reference text for the subject of software architecture. Although in terms of developing the theme its structure is rather fragmented, it contains a wide set of examples and illustrates all of the key ideas.

Exercises

6.1 The concept of *architectural style* can be recognised in many domains. Identify some examples of architectural styles and their principal characteristics, for the following domains:

(a) ships;
(b) motor vehicles;
(c) publications;

(d) websites containing static pages of information about a topic such as a sport (tennis, hockey, cricket, etc.).

6.2 While many systems can be implemented using a range of architectural styles (there is a good illustration of this in Shaw and Garlan (1996)), there are usually features of a problem that encourage the choice of a particular style in the absence of any other constraints. For the following types of system, identify what you consider to be their major features and identify the architectural styles that are likely to be most appropriate:

(a) a bank auto-teller machine;
(b) a spell-checker used to analyse static files of text;
(c) a program that reformats 'raw text' into the page description language employed by a particular printer.

6.3 Identify any other mechanisms that might be used to codify design knowledge for software, based upon analogies with the practices of any other disciplines that also involve significant elements of design activity.

chapter 7

Some Design Representations

The abstract nature of software means that it lacks any readily visualisable images. This chapter reviews and describes a selection of the forms that are adopted for describing the properties of software. We begin by reviewing the choice of examples and then go on to discuss each one: identifying its form, and the role(s) that it generally plays in the design process. For convenience, these example forms have been loosely grouped into two sets: the 'black box' forms that are used to describe *what* a system does, and the 'white box' forms that are concerned with describing *how* it is to do it. Finally, we briefly examine some of the ways of checking and developing diagrams.

7.1 A problem of selection

This chapter examines a selection from the many design representation forms that are used in software design methods. There are very many such representation forms, as well as variants on some of the more popular forms, and rather than producing a 'laundry list' of these, this chapter focuses upon a fairly small sample, chosen to give as wide a spectrum as possible.

Chapter 5 provided a framework for describing the roles and forms of representations, and gave some general classifications for these. For this chapter, which looks at specific examples, the selection from these forms has been made so as to range across the spectrum of:

■ *form*, including textual and diagrammatical forms of notation;

■ *viewpoint*, in terms of the ideas described in Chapter 5, where we considered constructional, behavioural, functional and data-modelling viewpoints;

■ *use*, in terms of the form's role during the phases of design, the type of problem domain in which it might be appropriate, and the extent to which it is used.

(Remember too that some notations used for software design may well have originated with quite different purposes – in some cases, even before the invention of computers!) The selection is not exhaustive, nor is it likely to meet with universal agreement. As emphasized throughout this book, the activity of design is a creative process, and hence the forms that go with it are also subject to personal preference when it comes to a question of use.

Descriptive forms, such as those reviewed in this chapter, are not particularly amenable to being neatly classified and categorized, not least because some forms play multiple roles in the design process. However, the idea of 'black box' and 'white box' descriptions (roughly corresponding to 'what' and 'how' respectively), has been adopted here as providing a useful indication of the roles that a given notation can perform. In addition, all of the forms described are ones that can be easily produced with the aid of pencil and paper alone. In Chapter 5, we identified this as an important criterion that any diagrammatical form should meet, and hence it has been used as one of the selection criteria for this chapter.

These are not the only forms of representation that will be met in this book, since further examples will be encountered when specific methods are reviewed. (In particular, the examples of mathematical forms have been deferred until they can be shown in a fuller context.) However, the ones discussed in this chapter are considered to be of enough significance to be introduced in advance of the description of the techniques for their use. Tables 7.1 and 7.2 provide a summary of the viewpoints on the design model that each of these forms can provide, and list the characteristics of the design that can be captured through its use.

We should also note that some of these notations may well be known under more than one name. (Michael Jackson's Structure Diagram is a particularly good example of this, with different names for each role and method.) Where possible, the most generic or widely adopted name has been employed here.

Table 7.1 The selection of black box design representations

Representation form	Viewpoints	Design characteristics
Data-Flow Diagram	Functional	Information flow, dependency of operations on other operations, relation with data stores
Entity–Relationship Diagram	Data modelling	Static relationships between design entities
State Transition Diagram	Behavioural	State-machine model of an entity
Statechart	Behavioural	System-wide state model, including parallelism (orthogonality), hierarchy and abstraction
Structure Diagram (Jackson)	Functional, data modelling, behavioural	Form of sequencing adopted (operations, data, actions)
UML: Class Diagram	Constructional	Interactions between classes and objects
UML: Use Case Diagram	Behavioural and functional	Interactions between a system and other 'actors'
UML: Activity Diagram	Behavioural and functional	Synchronization and coordination of system activities

Table 7.2 The selection of white box design representations

Representation form	Viewpoints	Design characteristics
Structure Chart	Functional and constructional	Invocation hierarchy between subprograms, decomposition into subprogram units
Class and Object Diagrams	Constructional	*Uses* relationships between elements, interfaces and dependencies
Sequence Diagrams	Behavioural	Message-passing sequences, interaction protocols
Pseudocode	Functional	Algorithm form

A final point that follows on the one that was made in the previous paragraph: the level of detail provided in the descriptions of the following sections is not intended to be consistent. In particular, those notations that will be used in the later chapters on design methods are not normally described in such complete detail as others, since further examples of their use will be provided in the relevant chapters.

7.2 Black box notations

To remind ourselves of the discussion in Chapter 2: a **black box** notation is one that is concerned with the *external* properties of the elements of a design model. That is, it is used to describe *what* an element will do, rather than *how* it is to do it. We can also consider such forms as performing the role of 'external memory devices', used to help increase the limited capacity of human working memory (Vessey and Conger, 1994).

Our choice of forms is a mixed one, in terms both of historical and technological factors. We begin with the Data-Flow Diagram (DFD), a form which is generally considered to have been employed for system modelling well before the computer era began and which is, of course, strongly related to an important architectural style. The Entity–Relationship Diagram (ERD) is again related to an important architectural style, albeit a very different one (transaction-based forms). We then consider two behavioural forms, the State Transition Diagram (STD) and the Statechart, each with its particular strengths and limitations. The Jackson Structure Diagram offers a quite different example of such a notation: being more concerned with 'structure' and hence less explicitly related to any one viewpoint. Finally, we examine the recent development of the Unified Modeling Language (UML), and examine some representative black box forms from this (Rumbaugh *et al.*, 1999).

7.2.1 The Data-Flow Diagram

The DFD is mainly used for describing a very problem-oriented view of the workings of a system. It provides a description based on modelling the flow of information around a network of operational elements, with each element making use of or modifying the information flowing into that element.

The use of some form of DFD for describing the operation of complex systems almost certainly predates the computer era, and Page-Jones (1988) has suggested that it is likely to have originated in a number of places and times, all quite independently. The earliest reference that he can find (although admittedly this one is largely folklore) dates from the 1920s.

The general nature of the DFD concept has been shown very effectively through an example used by Tom De Marco (1978). In the introduction to his book *Structured Analysis and System Specification*, he gives an example of an informal flow diagram being used to clarify the assembly instructions for a kayak. While obviously the 'data flow' in this case is physical (consisting of subassemblies), the principle is the same as for software, and the example provides an excellent demonstration of the effectiveness of such a form when it is used to describe a *process*. In the same spirit, the simple flow diagram in Figure 7.1 shows how this form can be used to describe the assembly of a garden shed.

Even this simple example is sufficient to show one of the strengths of the DFD when used to describe a sequence of operations, namely that one can readily see the prerequisites for any operation at a glance. For example, if we take operation 5, 'fit door to walls', we can see that it is dependent upon having the completed results of operations 3 and 4 available, and we can see why. Sequential lists of actions may be able to convey the same information, but the dependency aspect, which is so easily visualized through the use of a DFD, is generally less clear in such forms. The benefits of this ready visualization become even more important for operations that involve much greater complexity than this simple example.

The DFD has been widely used for software design purposes over many years, and a number of variations in the exact forms of the symbols used for drawing DFDs are to be found in the literature. This chapter will concentrate on describing the form that has been popularized through the work of De Marco (1978) and others, since Chapter 13 will be making use of this. Another example form, which uses a more 'formal' notation and performs a somewhat different role in the design process, is that used by the Structured Systems Analysis and Design Method (SSADM) (Longworth, 1992).

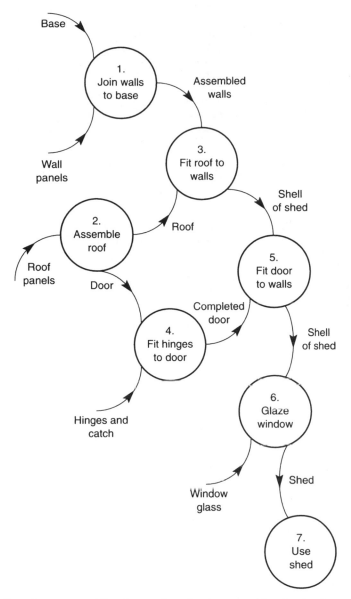

Figure 7.1 A flow diagram providing instructions for the assembly of a simple garden shed.

The form of the DFD

The DFD is a graphical representation, and it makes use of only four basic symbols. Because of its highly abstract nature, in terms of the level of description provided, it is chiefly used during the early design stages that are often termed 'analysis' – at a time when the designer is likely to be making major architectural design decisions.

Figure 7.2 shows an example of the use of a DFD to describe the operation of a bank autoteller (cashpoint) system. The four basic elements that are used in the diagram are:

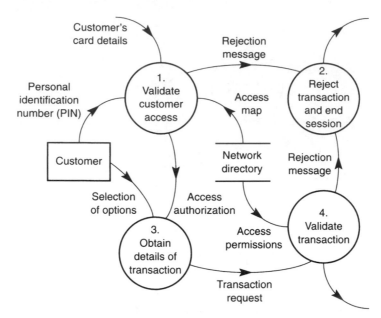

Figure 7.2 A top-level DFD describing the operations performed by a bank autoteller machine.

- the circle (or, as it is popularly termed, the bubble), which is used to denote an operation, and is labelled with a brief description of the operation;

- the box, used to denote an external source or sink of information;

- the parallel bars, used to denote a data store or file;

- the arc, used to denote the flow of information between the other three components.

(The form used to describe a data store seems to vary in practice; other conventions include denoting it by the use of a single bar or by an open-ended box.)

To take an example from the operations described in Figure 7.2; the validation operation requires inputs from the customer's card, from the customer (in the form of the personal identification number or PIN) and from an internal directory. The first two of these are used to authenticate the customer's identity, while the third ensures that the card (which may be issued by a different financial institution) is acceptable to the machine. The outputs from this process are then concerned with either acceptance (proceeding to the selection of the required transaction by the customer) or rejection (which may involve returning or retaining the card). Even if permission is given to proceed further with the transaction, there will be a further validation process involved to ensure that the option selected is permitted for this customer.

So essentially this DFD provides a top-level 'model' of how the designer intends the autoteller to operate. It is expressed in terms that are part of the *problem* domain (customer, PIN, transaction), rather than of the *solution*, and as such it identifies the main architectural tasks for the autoteller system.

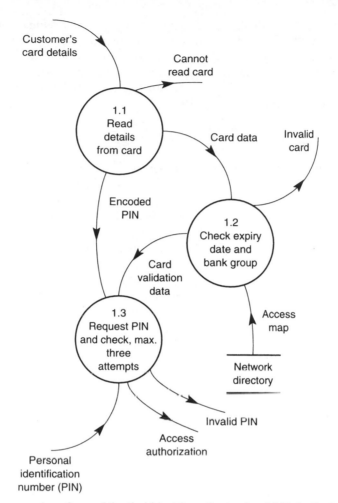

Figure 7.3 An expansion of one of the 'bubbles' from the top-level DFD for the bank autoteller machine.

An important characteristic of the DFD is that it can be expanded in a hierarchical fashion, with the operation of any bubble being described by means of a further DFD. As an example of this, Figure 7.3 shows an expansion of bubble 1 of Figure 7.2, using the same symbols. This also emphasizes the significance of the numbering scheme used for identifying the bubbles, since the identity number indicates the 'level' of a bubble, its position within an expanded description of the system.

In this example, the designer has elaborated on his or her ideas for the operation 'Validate customer access'. Note particularly that in the operation represented by bubble 1.3, there is no attempt to show the structure of the *control* flow that is associated with the possible iteration required to permit the customer three attempts at entering the PIN. The DFD is not concerned with the control logic involved in performing this operation, and its details will need to be elaborated later, using other forms for its description.

While expansion is valuable in allowing for the gradual refinement of a design, it can also lead to problems of inconsistency: changes may be made to a lower-level diagram that alter the number and/or form of the information flow arcs in the parent diagram. Consistency checking of such changes (as well as automatic numbering of bubbles) is generally provided by the specialist drawing tools that are quite widely available to assist with the production of DFDs.

The DFD viewpoint

Data-Flow Diagrams are primarily concerned with describing the architecture of a system in terms of its *functions*, in that they identify the operations that need to be performed by the system, using an abstract level for the description. The data-flow element is used to identify the information that is needed for the appropriate operations to be performed, as well as that which is generated by them.

The point about abstraction is an important one when it comes to the conventions that should be used when drawing such diagrams. Figure 7.3 has already raised this point: bubble 1.3 describes the number of tries that the user is permitted when entering the PIN, but the diagram does not show the iteration directly in any way. On this same point about sequencing information, the form of the diagram makes no statement about whether the operations are to be performed sequentially or in parallel. The convention is usually to assume sequential operations (see Chapter 13), but the DFD can equally be used to describe parallel operations. Indeed, some design methods make use of it in this way.

Using the DFD

Because of its abstract nature and ability to describe function, the DFD is widely used for the initial modelling of systems (often termed 'analysis'). It is a major component of the widely used SSA/SD (Structured Systems Analysis and Structured Design) approach, which is described in Chapter 13, and it is also used in the various derivatives of this method.

In this role, one of its benefits is that it can fairly easily be understood by the user, since it is used to model the *problem* rather than a computer-oriented solution. De Marco makes a distinction here between 'logical' and 'physical' DFDs, which it is useful to consider.

The **physical** DFD is used to model a system in terms of the physical entities concerned, rather than their functions. For example, Figure 7.4 shows a physical DFD that is used to model the workings of the booking system in a travel office. The labels on the bubbles in this diagram indicate who does a job, rather than describing the job in any detail. (For example, Roger clearly handles all arrangements concerning rail travel, although we can only conclude this by examining the data-flow arcs.)

Figure 7.5 shows the equivalent logical DFD, in which the bubbles are now labelled to show what is being done to the data, rather than who is doing it. This is a more abstract and more structured view of the system described in Figure 7.4, but is clearly derived from it. Both of these forms are important: the physical DFD helps with initial modelling tasks and with communication with the customer, while the logical DFD is necessary when the designer begins to build up the architectural model

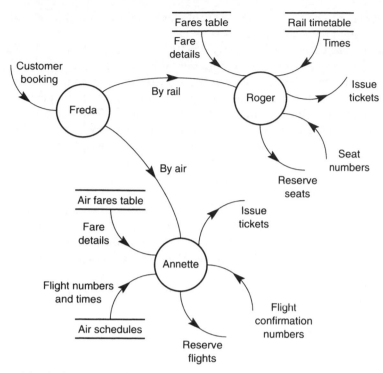

Figure 7.4   A 'physical' DFD describing a travel agency booking system.

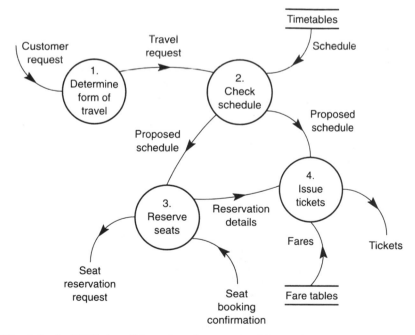

Figure 7.5   A 'logical' DFD describing a travel agency booking system.

required in order to build the system. (In this case, the system will presumably be some sort of automated reservation system.)

As mentioned earlier, other forms of DFD are used to help with more detailed modelling of a design, a point that emphasizes the general usefulness of this tool. This in turn reflects the fact that it is often relatively easy to think in terms of actions (as is demonstrated by the emphasis that older programming languages place on providing forms that describe actions rather than data structures). There is therefore a strong intuitive appeal to the DFD: it can be understood relatively easily, and can often be developed more easily than could many other forms of description.

7.2.2 The Entity–Relationship Diagram

This form of diagram is principally used to capture the relationships that exist between static data objects in a problem model or a design model. In particular, the *Entity–Relationship Model* has provided an essential foundation for the development of the relational models that are used in many database systems (Batini *et al.*, 1992; Stevens, 1991).

However, ERDs can play other roles apart from their use in database design. For example, they are sometimes used to model the detailed form of the data stored in a system (Page-Jones, 1988; Stevens, 1991), while on a larger scale they can be used to model the relationships that occur between more complex and abstract design 'objects' (Booch, 1991).

The Entity–Relationship notation

In their detailed form, many ERD notations exhibit 'local' variations, but most of the widely used forms seem to have been derived from the notation devised by Peter Chen (1976). This section will seek to concentrate on the more 'generic' elements of the notation, and will not explore the more detailed nuances of the form.

Figure 7.6 shows the three principal symbols that are used in these diagrams, together with their meanings. (The symbols for entities and relationships are fairly standard, but beyond that the representations of attributes and other qualities are apt to differ in detail.) These basic elements are defined as follows:

- *entities* are real-world objects with common properties;
- a *relationship* is a class of elementary facts relating two or more entities;

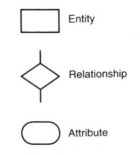

Figure 7.6 The basic Entity–Relationship notation.

- *attributes* are classes of values that represent atomic properties of either entities or relationships (attributes of entities are often the more recognizable, as can be seen from the examples).

The nature of an entity will, of course, vary with the level of abstraction involved, and so, therefore, will the form of its attributes and the nature of the relationships between them. Entities may be connected by more than one type of relationship, and attributes may be composite, with higher-level attributes being decomposed into lower-level attributes. (For example, the attributes student and teacher might be connected by the relationships attends-class-of and examines, while the attribute position might later be decomposed into range, bearing, and height.)

Relationships are also classified by their 'n-ary' properties. Binary relationships link two entities, such as the relationship 'married to' occurring between the entities 'husband' and 'wife'. Relationships may also be 'one to many' (1 to n) and 'many to many' (m to n). Examples of these are:

- books (entity of order n) held in library (of order 1)

- authors (n) having written books (m)

(In the latter case, an author may have written many books, and a book may have multiple authors.) The effect of the n-ary property is to set bounds upon the cardinality of the values that are permitted by the relationship.

The development of an ERD typically involves performing an analysis of specification or design documents, classifying the terms in these as entities, relationships or attributes. The resulting list provides the basis for developing an ERD. Figure 7.7 shows an example of the ERD form being used for describing information about some fairly recognizable entities, and so describes the data structures that might be used in some form of indexing system.

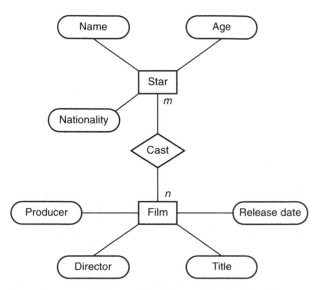

Figure 7.7 An ERD showing a simple relationship between two classes of entity.

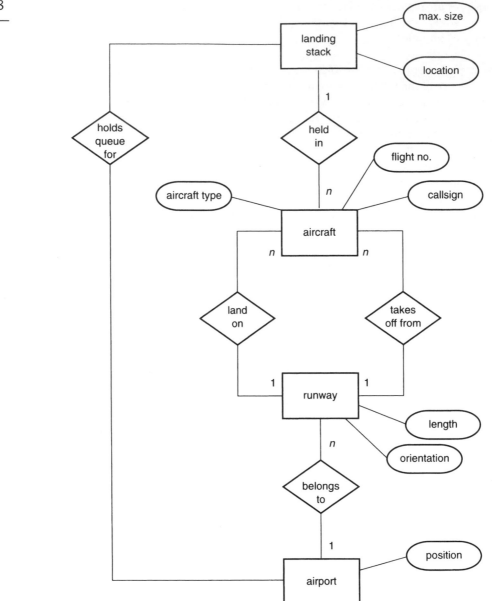

Figure 7.8 An ERD relating some of the major entities in an air traffic control system.

In contrast to this, Figure 7.8 offers an example of a more system- and design-related use of the ERD form to model the entities that might be involved in a basic air traffic control system. This figure also provides a simple illustration of a point that was made earlier, concerning the possible existence of multiple relationships between two entities.

ERDs are purely and simply concerned with providing a data-modelling viewpoint of a system. As with many notations, they can be used both during the analysis of the problem and during the development of the solution (design).

Use of the ERD

ERDs are widely used for developing the schema used in relational database modelling (Batini *et al.*, 1992). This is a rather specialized area of system design, and as such has not been addressed in this book. (The design of databases probably fits somewhere between the 'template' form of design that is widely used for producing compilers, and the more general-purpose systematic forms described later in this book.)

The data-modelling viewpoint is also used as a subsidiary viewpoint in a number of design methods. One example in which it occupies such a role is the SSA/SD (Structured Systems Analysis and Structured Design) method described in Chapter 13: other examples are the 'object' forms of Chapter 15 and SSADM, which uses a variant of the notation described in this section. However, it plays a relatively minor role in the procedures of all these methods, when compared with its central role in database design and development.

7.2.3 The State Transition Diagram

Some classes of problem (and solution) can usefully be described by considering them as 'finite-state automata'. Such a system can be considered as existing in a finite set of possible 'states', with external events being the triggers that can lead to transitions between the states.

A process executing in a computer fits this model quite well. Its 'state' at any point in time can be described fully in terms of the contents of its variables and the values of any associated registers in the CPU, most notably the program counter register, whose contents determine which instruction will be executed next. While we might not wish to model the complete behaviour of a process in terms of all its possible states, there might be some useful supersets that can be considered.

As an example, the popular Unix screen editor **vi** (pronounced 'vee eye') has two basic states of operation, which are termed its current 'modes'. These are:

- **command mode,** in which keystrokes are interpreted as commands to the editor to perform such operations as opening a file, moving the position of the screen cursor, or beginning to insert text at some point;

- **insert mode,** in which any keystrokes are interpreted as data to be stored in the editor's buffer.

Transitions occur between these modes according to certain forms of 'escape' command. There are many commands that can be used to make the transition between command mode and insert mode, but only one that can be used for the reverse transition (namely, pressing the Escape key). Figure 7.9 shows a simple diagrammatical description of this model of the **vi** editor, in which the bubbles represent the states

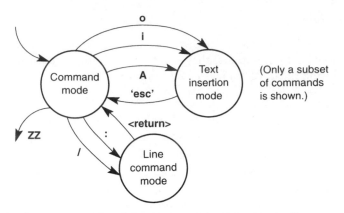

Figure 7.9 A simple state-transitional description of the Unix **vi** text editor.

(modes), and the arcs correspond to the transitions, labelled by the events (commands) that cause these to occur. (Not all the commands that cause the editor to enter insert mode are shown, in order to maintain clarity, as **vi** has a rich set of commands for this purpose.) *Line command mode* can be considered as a substate of command mode.

Figure 7.9 is a simple example of a form of STD (several conventions for these are in use), and it provides a convenient means for modelling many other systems too. Indeed, the general class of real-time (or 'reactive') systems can often be usefully modelled in this way, since their event-driven nature leads readily to the use of such a form.

The form of the STD

In Chapter 13, when we come to consider the extensions to SSA/SD, the Structured Systems Analysis and Structured Design Method, we will encounter a number of extended methods that are aimed at real-time systems. In the extension devised by Ward and Mellor (1985), they introduced a form of STD that will now be considered in a little more detail.

The form of this is a little more structured than that which was used in our first example. There are four principal components to this representation of an STD.

■ The **state** represents an externally observable mode of behaviour, and is represented by a box, with a text label that describes its behaviour.

■ The **transition** is described by an arrow, and identifies a 'legal' change of state that can occur within the system.

■ The **transition condition** identifies the condition that will cause the transition to occur – usually in terms of the event that causes the transition – but is not concerned with the actual mechanism. It is written next to the transition arrow, *above* a horizontal line.

■ The **transition action** describes the actions that arise as a result of the transition (there may be several, and they might occur simultaneously, or in a specific

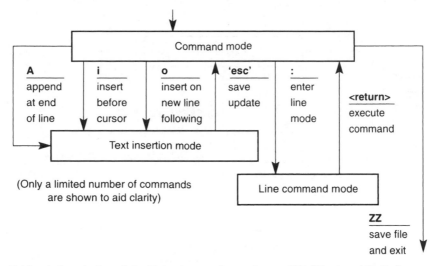

Figure 7.10   A description of the Unix **vi** text editor using an STD (Ward and Mellor).

sequence). These are written *below* the horizontal line and the details of the transition conditions.

To complete the diagram, we also need to identify a default **initial state** (which has an arrow pointing in to it, with no source state attached), and may (possibly) need to identify a **final state** (which will have transitions into it, but none out from it).

Figure 7.10 shows how the earlier example of the **vi** text editor can be modelled using this form of STD. Note that multiple transitions are still permitted between a given pair of states. (Once again, not all possible transitions are shown, in order to avoid too complex a diagram.) An action has been identified to determine when the editor terminates, and command mode has been identified as the initial state when the editor begins operation.

Figure 7.11 shows a rather more complicated system modelled in this way (complicated in the sense of having many more states). In this case, the system described is the behaviour of an aeroplane modelled as a component of an air traffic control system. The event that causes the initial state to be entered is the primary radar detecting the aircraft as it enters the airspace. The complexity of the transitions involved in this example arises because of the sheer number of actions that the aircraft might take, from simply flying through the airspace, to being stacked before landing, and of combinations of such events.

The STD viewpoint

The STD is our first example of a representation that is used to capture a behavioural viewpoint of a system, and so it is concerned with modelling dynamic attributes of the system in terms of entities such as states, events and conditions. It only identifies the possibility that particular transitions will occur, with no indication as to how these will be sequenced.

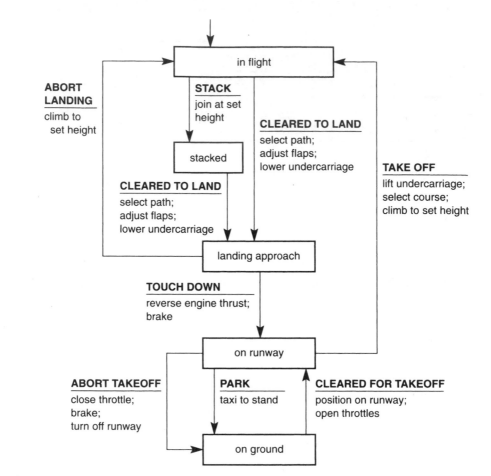

Figure 7.11 An STD describing the behaviour of an aircraft in an air traffic control zone.

Use of the STD

A major role for the STD is in modelling problem entities: although it can have a role in building models of solutions, this is less significant. It is also particularly useful in modelling some of the real-time needs of a system, hence its popularity in real-time variants of design methods.

The STD is a useful modelling tool, but as with all diagrammatical forms, it has limitations. As the example of the **vi** editor has shown, if there are a lot of transitions between a small number of states, the diagram can become very tangled. Similarly, large and complex systems result in large and complex diagrams, as the form does not lead directly to any form of hierarchical layering of diagrams. In the next section we describe another state-oriented form of description that overcomes the problem of layering by adding a hierarchy to the states themselves.

Like the STD that was described in the preceding section, the Statechart is concerned with describing the behaviour of a system as a form of finite-state automaton, or finite-state machine. Like the STD, it is a form that is particularly well suited for use in describing reactive systems, in which the main functions arise in response to particular events.

The Statechart was devised by David Harel (1987; 1988) and he has observed that it is based on the more general concept of the 'higraph', which in turn has a range of applications. (We should perhaps discount his claim that 'this rather mundane name was chosen, for lack of a better one, simply as the one unused combination of "flow" or "state" with "diagram" or "chart".') It provides a rather more abstract form of description than the STD, and in particular it adds to the state-oriented viewpoint the ability to create a hierarchy of abstraction in the description, as well as permitting the designer to describe transitions that are 'orthogonal' in that they are completely independent of each other – so making it possible for the transitions to occur in parallel.

The Statechart shares a generality of role with the STD too. Both of these forms can be used for describing the structure of a problem, as well as the functioning of a solution. (However, the better examples generally come from the former.)

By far the best tutorial on Statecharts and their powers of description is provided in Harel (1987), where the author uses the functions of the Citizen Quartz Multi-Alarm III watch as the basis for his examples. The examples below are rather less inspired, but should at least provide some basic ideas about the scope of this particular form of description.

The form of the Statechart

In this notation, a state is denoted by a box with rounded corners, labelled in the upper left corner. Hierarchy is represented by encapsulation, and directed arcs are used to denote a transformation between states. The arcs are also labelled with a description of the event and, optionally, with a parenthesized condition. (Conditions are quite common in real systems. For example, it might not be possible to engage a cruise control mechanism in a car while either accelerating or braking.)

Figure 7.12 shows an example of the use of this notation, to describe the operation of a Teletext television set. Figure 7.12(a) shows that the set has two states, 'standby' and 'display'. The transition between 'display' and 'standby' occurs in response to the operation of the 'standby' button on the remote control. The reverse transition will occur when any button on the control is pressed. In Figure 7.12(b) the description of the state 'display' is expanded further, and it is now elaborated into the three encapsulated states, which are labelled as 'picture', 'text' and 'mixed'. The small arrow above 'picture' shows that this will be the default state, which will be entered when the set is switched to 'display' (an extension of this particular convention can be used to indicate when selection is made by means of some 'history' mechanism that remembers the previous use of these states). Note also that the state 'mixed' can only be entered from 'text'.

The elaboration of the description of a state is similar to the form used in the Jackson Structure Diagram, described in the next section, in that the state 'display' is an abstraction of the three states 'picture', 'text' and 'mixed', so that selecting 'display'

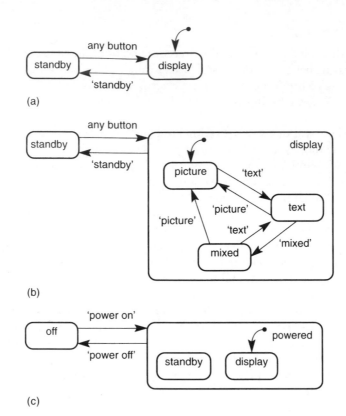

(a)

(b)

(c)

Figure 7.12 A Statechart describing a Teletext television set. (a) The two main states of the television set. (b) An expanded description of the states shown in (a). (c) A more abstract description of (a).

must result in selecting one of these three states. In the Jackson Structure Diagram abstraction is denoted by the levels of a tree, while in the Statechart it is denoted by encapsulation. One benefit of this latter form is that it makes it relatively simple to denote any transitions that apply equally to all the encapsulated states, by showing them as applied to the outer box as in, for example, 'standby' in Figure 7.12(b).

Figure 7.12(c) shows the first diagram expanded in a bottom-up rather than top-down fashion. The two initial states are now shown to be within a superstate 'powered'. (There are no specific limits about how many levels of a hierarchy can be shown in a diagram, but obviously there are practical issues of notational complexity that limit this. About two or three levels seem to be as many as can fit easily on a single diagram and be readily comprehended. Of course, the diagrams themselves can also be layered in a hierarchical fashion.)

The Statechart viewpoint

Like the STD, the Statechart is concerned with providing a behavioural description of a system. However, there are some significant differences between them in terms of the attributes that they each capture.

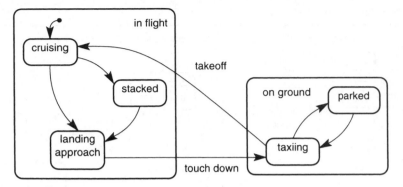

Figure 7.13   Statechart describing the actions of an aircraft in an air traffic control system.

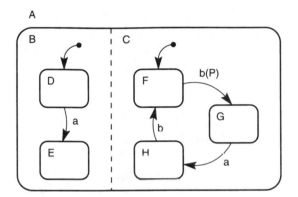

Figure 7.14   Describing orthogonality in the Statechart notation.

Watches and television sets have the advantage that the events that cause state changes are directly identifiable in terms of button presses, and hence are readily described. Figure 7.13 reworks the example of Figure 7.11 into this form, and shows a description of an aircraft in an air traffic control system, this time using the Statechart.

When comparing this with the STD form used in Figure 7.11, we can see that while the descriptions of state, event and transition are common to both, the STD provides a more detailed description in terms of the actions that occur, while the Statechart has more refined mechanisms for describing abstraction, defaults, history, and, of course, scale. The STD's lack of hierarchy also limits it largely to describing the behaviour of individual design elements, whereas the Statechart can describe whole systems through a hierarchy of diagrams and states. In that sense they are largely complementary, with the STD perhaps being more suited to modelling problems, and the Statechart being better suited for modelling detailed solutions.

The remaining major feature of the Statechart that ought to be described here is **orthogonality**. Figure 7.14 shows an example of a state A that can be described as a superstate of two orthogonal states B and C. B and C can in turn be described in terms of further states, but these are essentially independent groupings. Events may be common, as can be seen from the description of the transformations due to event a. Also,

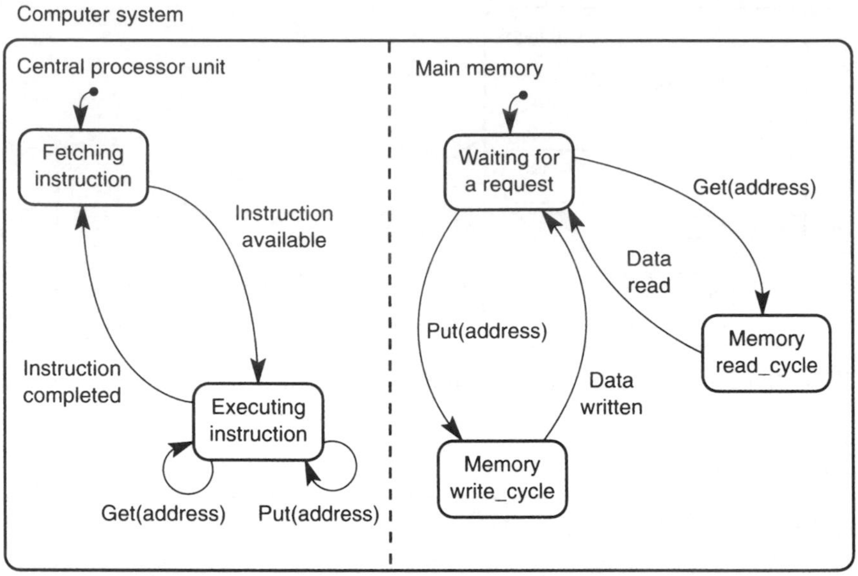

Computer system

Figure 7.15 A Statechart describing the architecture of a computer.

in describing A, note that we need to identify the default entry to states B and C, shown here as being the inner states D and F.

Orthogonality is important in reactive systems, where we expect to observe a suitable separation of concerns between groups of parallel functions, although all might be working towards the same objective. (Switching on the lights of a car should not cause its cruise-control system to change its setting, for example, and lowering the undercarriage of an aircraft should not affect the settings of the wing surfaces. In the latter case, the wing surfaces may well be changed by the pilot when lowering the undercarriage, as a part of the general routine for landing, but the two should not be linked automatically in any way.)

Figure 7.15 shows this concept in terms of the basic architecture of a computer. The state of the computer is shown as a compound of the state of the CPU and the state of the main memory (this is obviously something of a simplification). The two have various substates, and there are some events that are common to both. When the computer is first powered up, they each assume a default state that is expressed in terms of their internal operations. While there is communication via some memory bus, and hence some synchronization, the memory might also be accessed by device controllers or the like, and so its operations are suitably separated from those of the CPU.

Use of the Statechart

The Statechart is clearly a powerful and useful tool, and like the STD it has an important role in modelling reactive systems. Both forms are generally used to support other design viewpoints such as data flow. (To reinforce this point: Harel's 'STATEMATE' system uses two other viewpoints of a system, in addition to this form (Harel *et al.*, 1990).)

Although similar in appearance to the Structure Chart notation that is described in Section 7.3.1, the Structure Diagram describes a very different set of attributes, and performs a very different set of roles (Cameron, 1988a). It is basically concerned with describing sequential structure, in terms of the three 'classical' structuring forms:

- sequence

- selection

- iteration

In many ways this is an especially abstract notation, since it purely describes sequential structuring, with no particular interpretation being assumed about the type of entity whose form is being described. Indeed, it can be used to describe the form of a data structure (data modelling viewpoint); the sequencing of program actions (functional viewpoint); or the sequencing of 'states' that might occur for some form of 'object' (behavioural viewpoint). This feature is almost certainly unique to this notation; all of the other notations that we describe in this book are effectively linked to a particular viewpoint, and generally are also linked to a particular form of design entity. (Arguably, the one exception to the above statement is the ERD. Although this might be true for the original notation, many 'class and object' notations are loosely based upon its form.)

Since this notation will be used extensively in the later chapters of this book (albeit under a variety of names), this section will concentrate on the basic 'rules of form' involved, leaving the main examples of its use until later.

The form of the Structure Diagram

The Structure Diagram takes the form of a 'tree', constructed from a set of boxes and arcs. Each set of 'child' boxes provides an elaboration of the description contained in the parent box, and hence the full description of a complete sequence is described by the lowest boxes on each branch. (In that sense, the parent boxes are themselves abstractions of the lower boxes.)

The basic notation is very simple, and is based upon three forms of box:

1. A simple box denotes a component of a sequence – so in Figure 7.16(a) the action of making tea is described as a series of actions.

2. A box with a circle in the upper right corner denotes selection from an option, and so in Figure 7.16(b) the previous description of tea-making is extended to include the possibility of using either China tea or Indian tea.

3. A box with an asterisk in the upper right corner denotes an iteration, and so in Figure 7.16(c) the description is further extended by including the possibility that we might put more than one spoonful of tea into the pot.

There are a number of rules used in constructing these diagrams, but the most important is: 'forms cannot be mixed within a sequence'. Applying this rule shows that

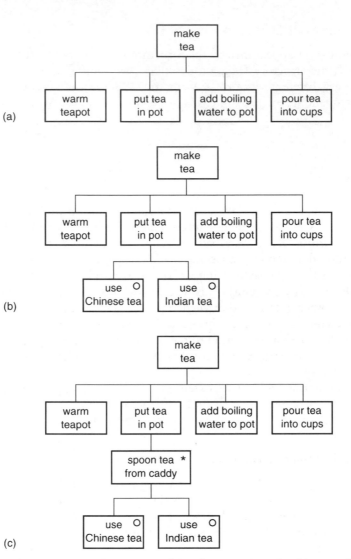

Figure 7.16 A Jackson Structure Diagram describing the operation of making tea. (a) A simple sequence of actions. (b) Adding a choice. (c) Adding iteration and choice.

Figure 7.17(a) is incorrect. To correct it, it may be necessary to add an additional abstraction of 'carriages' above the iteration box, as shown in Figure 7.17(b), in order to keep the first level of abstraction as a pure sequence.

The viewpoints provided by Structure Diagrams

As already indicated, Structure Diagrams can be used to provide a *data modelling* viewpoint, when used to describe the sequential structuring of data objects. They can also be used for describing a viewpoint that has elements of both *functional* and

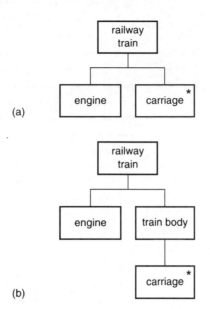

(a)

(b)

Figure 7.17 An example of an incorrect Structure Diagram. (a) The sequence and iteration forms are wrongly mixed on a single level. (b) How this can be resolved by adding a further level of abstraction in the description.

behavioural viewpoints, when they are used to describe the actions of a program or an entity. In particular, they provide a much more abstract form of sequencing description than can normally be provided through pseudocode (see Section 7.3.4).

Figure 7.18 shows an example of a data structure described in this manner. In this case, the data structure happens to be a physical one, as the diagram is used to describe the structure of a textbook such as this one. A more conventional programming data structure is shown in Figure 7.19, where a simple file of text is described using this form.

In Figure 7.20 an example of this form is used to describe the dynamic form of a program. In this example, the task of the program is to print out a page of a monthly bank statement. Clearly this is closely related to the appearance of the statement on the page.

Uses for the Structure Diagram

As already indicated, this form is ubiquitous. In examining the JSP design method (described in Chapter 14), it will be used to describe the structures of the input and output data streams. In both the JSD (Chapter 15) and SSADM (Longworth, 1992) design methods it is used to describe the 'evolution' of entities over time. The title of the form might vary, but the basic notation does not.

Since this form will occur so often later in the book, these roles will not be outlined any further at this point, and fuller descriptions will be left to the appropriate chapters.

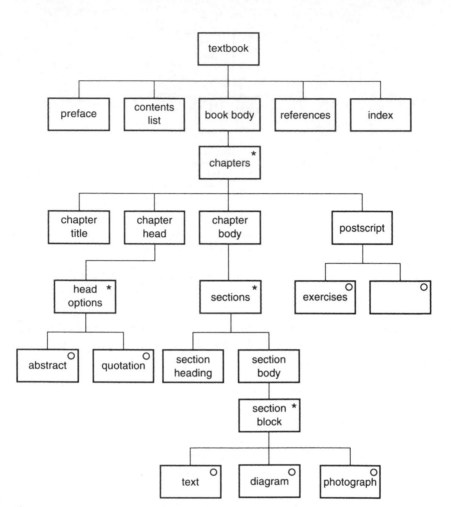

Figure 7.18 A Jackson Structure Diagram describing a static object (the structure of a textbook).

7.2.6 UML Modelling Forms

The UML emerged from the efforts made to bring together the ideas of three of the 'gurus' of the 'object community': Grady Booch, Ivar Jacobson and James Rumbaugh. As such, the term *unified* can be misleading as it refers to the unification of their methodological ideas, rather than of the notations making up the modelling language. Indeed, one criticism that can be made of the UML is that this process has resulted in an excessive number of notations, especially when compared with other design practices. Since 1996, the responsibility for the development of the UML has been vested in the Object Management Group (OMG), and it was adopted as an OMG standard in 1997, although work continues to develop and extend it further as the relevant technologies themselves progress.

This section differs from the others in this chapter in that it describes several notations. What is perhaps most striking to the reader is that these are much less distinctive than any of the other notations that we have discussed. (One exception to this obser-

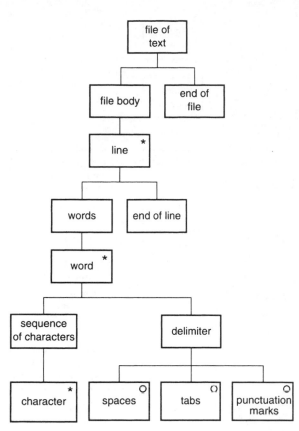

Figure 7.19 A Jackson Structure Diagram describing a simple file containing text.

vation is the **sequence diagram,** which is described separately in Section 7.3.3.) To some extent this probably reflects the 'unification' processes involved. It also (partially) reflects the nature of the object paradigm itself. When we come to examine this later we will see that an early emphasis upon constructional detail is characteristic of the development processes for the object-oriented architectural style, and hence this influences the nature and form of the notations adopted. As a further consequence, in a book such as this, which addresses wider conceptual issues relating to software design, the more 'fussy' aspects of the UML are also of less interest.

The UML has already generated quite an extensive literature of its own. The definitive reference text is Rumbaugh *et al.* (1999) although, as often occurs with 'reference' works, this does not provide a reader with the most accessible introduction to the UML. The text by Stevens and Pooley (2000) provides a rather more user-focused introduction, although the examples provided in this could be regarded as rather lacking in depth for anyone wanting to make serious use of the UML. In addition, most textbooks that describe the associated *Unified Process* do also contain some discussion of the UML and examples of its use. At the time of writing there is no single text that is widely recognized as offering a particularly clear and authoritative exposition of the UML and its application.

Since the rest of this section draws upon 'object model' concepts, the reader who is unfamiliar with these might want to read the opening section of Chapter 16 first.

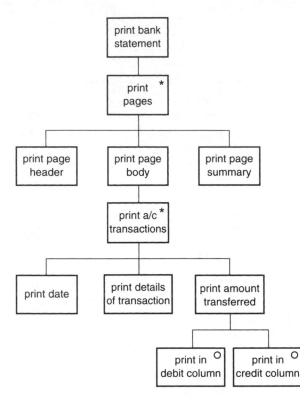

Figure 7.20 A Jackson Structure Diagram describing the actions of a program (printing a bank statement).

UML Forms

The UML forms are classified in Rumbaugh *et al.* (1999) into:

- *structural forms* (relating elements of a system);
- *dynamic forms* (concerned with describing system behaviour);
- *model management* (concerned with the organization of the model itself).

The first two can be recognized as corresponding to the *constructional*, *functional* and *behavioural* viewpoints that were introduced in Chapter 5. We will examine three of the nine UML notations in this section: the **class diagram** (structural); the **use case diagram** (structural); and the **activity diagram** (dynamic). A further dynamic form, the **sequence diagram** is covered separately in Section 7.3.3 and UML also makes use of a form of **statechart** that is essentially equivalent to that described in Section 7.2.4, although some of the notational details differ slightly.

In terms of conventions, it is useful to note that the UML makes extensive use of 'box and line' forms and, in particular, often employs variations of line and arrowheads to distinguish between different forms of relationship. By convention, where the form of relationship needs to be made explicit, this is placed between double arrows, as in <<extend>>.

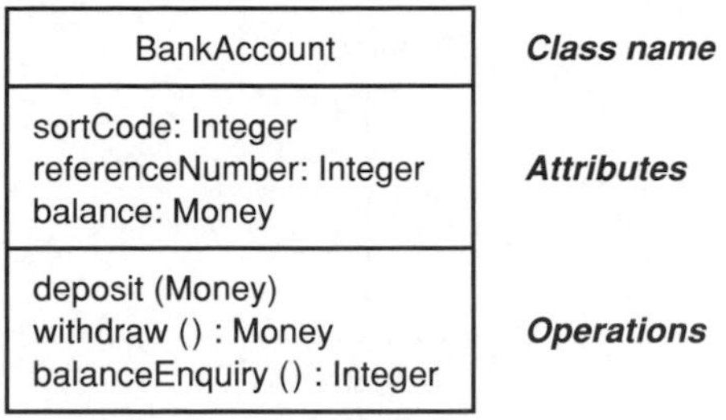

BankAccount	*Class name*
sortCode: Integer referenceNumber: Integer balance: Money	*Attributes*
deposit (Money) withdraw () : Money balanceEnquiry () : Integer	*Operations*

Figure 7.21   The UML class notation.

The Class Diagram   A core concept of the object model is centred upon the relationships that involve **classes** (where a class roughly performs the role of a 'template' that describes a general concept) and any **objects** that are created from these (where these are specific instances of a given class, possessing an individual state and identity). Identification of candidates for classes is one of the primary activities in object-oriented design practices. We will return to look more generally at the ways of describing classes and objects in Section 7.3.2.

The UML class diagram therefore provides a means of describing both the classes themselves, and also the interactions between these (particularly those based upon the *uses* relationship (Parnas, 1979) and the concept of *inheritance*). Figure 7.21 illustrates an example of a simple class as it is described in the UML, and this form can be used at different stages in the development of a design. For early design stages, the details of attributes and operations might well be omitted or curtailed to the bare minimum required to represent the appropriate logical concept embodied in a particular class. At later stages, as design decisions are made, so the description can be elaborated. In terms of the viewpoints model used in this book, it is therefore largely an element used for *constructional* viewpoints, being concerned with relationships that exist between (potential) implementation elements, albeit at a very high level of abstraction.

Classes can be related in a number of ways. The UML recognizes six forms of relationship (association, dependency, flow, generalization, realization and usage) with appropriate distinctions in the notation (which draws quite extensively on that employed in the ERD described earlier). Figures 7.22 and 7.23 show simple examples of two of these. Figure 7.22 shows a very simple association relationship indicating that any customer of a bank may be associated with any number of accounts (for simplicity, we have limited joint accounts to being held between only two customers). Note too that in this figure, the classes are only represented by name, as further details are not considered necessary when describing this particular relationship. Figure 7.23 shows an example of generalization through inheritance. The general class Bank-Account forms the basis for creating subclasses DepositAccount and CurrentAccount which, although having different modes of operation, will still possess the basic attributes and operations of the parent class BankAccount.

The Use Case Diagram   While the concept of the *scenario* of system use is one that has been employed informally over many years when determining how a system is to be used, the work of Ivar Jacobson has formalized both the concept and also its role in the design process (Jacobson *et al.*, 1992; 1999). From this has emerged the more general concept of the **use case**. Indeed, we can draw an analogy between the use

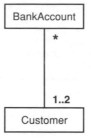

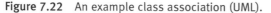

Figure 7.22 An example class association (UML).

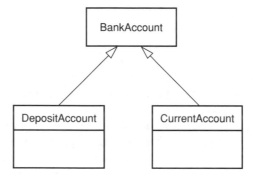

Figure 7.23 An example of class generalization via inheritance (UML).

case/scenario relationship and that of program and execution thread. In the way that a program describes a general set of possible actions, and an execution thread is a particular instantiation of these, so a use case describes a set of possible interactions between a system and other *actors* (which can be hardware, people or other systems), and a **scenario** describes a particular sequence of these interactions.

The UML **use case diagram** expresses this idea at a fairly high level of abstraction. Figure 7.24 shows the basic elements of a use case diagram. The use case itself is shown as an oval, and represents 'a logical description of a slice of system functionality' (Rumbaugh *et al.*, 1999). Actors are (rather confusingly and not very elegantly) represented by stick figures, and there are four kinds of relationship shown, although two of these share a single representational form and hence need to be labelled using the form indicated previously (this 'overloading' occurs elsewhere in UML).

Classifying the **use case diagram** in terms of our viewpoints model does offer rather more of a challenge! Use cases are concerned with the interactions that occur between a system and its environment, and hence have a *behavioural* aspect. However, they are also concerned with the tasks that a system performs, and so we can also ascribe a *functional* categorization to them too. There is nothing inconsistent about doing so. While the viewpoints framework is a useful classification mechanism, the boundaries are not firm, and many notations have elements of more than one viewpoint, although usually in a major/minor balance. What perhaps does distinguish the use case diagram is that the balance of these viewpoints is rather more even than is usual.

Figure 7.25 shows an example use case diagram, together with a textual example of one of the component use cases. We should perhaps note that the notations

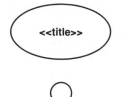

<<title>> — Use case (title indicates the activity covered by this use case)

Actor (not necessarily a human) describing a role in a use case

Indicates **<<communication>>** between actor and use case (only form of link that is employed between these two elements)

<<generalization>> that links the varieties of a use case with the more general form of these

<<include>> or **<<extend>>** relationships between use cases where one use case makes use of other use cases, labelled to indicate the form that a particular relationship has

Figure 7.24   Elements of a use case diagram (UML).

(a) The use case diagram

(b) A simple use case specification

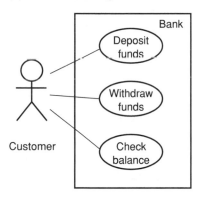

USE CASE: Withdraw funds

ACTORS: Customer

PRE-CONDITIONS:
  User is a customer of the bank

BODY:

1. User enters card in machine and establishes their identity using their PIN.
2. User enters a request for funds and specifies the amount required.
3. The system checks to ensure that this will not exceed the customer's credit limit.
4. If request is valid, and cash is available in the machine, system directs the machine to deliver the cash and debits customer's account, else request is refused.
5. System directs machine to return card.

POST-CONDITIONS:
  User's account is debited by the amount withdrawn

Figure 7.25   Simple example of use case modelling (UML).

provided in the UML are not particularly concerned with representing the details of the use case itself, so much as its context. A fuller review of some ways in which use cases themselves might be modelled is provided in Ratcliffe and Budgen (2001), and we will return to this concept when we later come to examine the wider issues of designing object-oriented systems, since the use case plays a pivotal role in the procedures of the *Unified Process*.

Use case modelling is perhaps one of the most disappointing elements of the UML. Use cases represent a powerful and distinctive element, but one that is not really supported by the UML notations anything like as fully as might have been hoped.

The Activity Diagram   The **activity diagram** can be thought of as a variant upon the state machine. Rather than modelling the states of the system and the events that cause transitions between these (as in our earlier example of Statecharts), the activity diagram is rather vaguely described as 'modelling computations and workflows' (Rumbaugh, 1999). Stevens and Pooley (2000) offer a rather clearer description, which can be summarized as one of modelling the essential dependencies and orderings that arise when operations have multiple goals.

The activity diagram is therefore useful for modelling the type of 'coordinating' situation where a given computation cannot proceed until certain conditions are met (for example, new data is available *and* a previous computation has completed). So the states in such a diagram now represent executions of statements, or performance of actions, and the focus of interest is upon the 'firing' of transitions between the states of such a system, and hence upon the synchronization and coordination of the various computations and actions. The activity diagram therefore resembles, at least in part, the Petri Net Graph (Stevens, 1991). We can classify this primarily as a *behavioural* description in terms of our viewpoint model, although with some *functional* elements too.

Key elements in the notation are as follows.

- The *activity*, shown as a named box with rounded sides.

- The *transition* (between activities), shown as an unlabelled arrow. The lack of a label is because, unlike the case of the Statechart, the transitions arise from the actions of the activities themselves, not because of external events.

- The *synchronization bar* is a thick horizontal line that represents the coordination of the activities. When all of the transitions into a bar are complete (the coordinating bit) then the outward transitions are 'fired'.

- A *decision diamond* that effectively 'routes' outgoing transitions (this is in preference to using a notation that shows multiple possible outgoing transitions). When this is used, then it becomes necessary to label the transitions to indicate which condition is employed for a particular route.

Figure 7.26 shows a simple example of an **activity diagram** that describes the operation (in part) of a bank autoteller machine. Only two synchronization bars are used here, one showing division of transitions (where multiple actions occur after a coordinating action, termed a **fork**), and the second the opposite case where the operation proceeds only after two transitions have completed (a **join**).

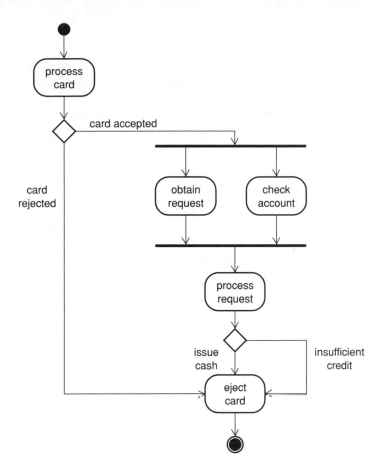

Figure 7.26 Example UML activity diagram: the bank autoteller.

UML *viewpoints*

One consequence of the plethora of UML notations is to produce some muddying of the 'viewpoints picture'. Indeed, one of the more disappointing aspects of the UML is the lack of any clear framework for integrating the different viewpoints within a model. In some ways, the UML is rather inward-looking, in that the only notation relating to 'model management' is one that is really intended to help with managing the complexity of the UML itself rather than the end problem which is the subject of the modelling process.

Uses of the UML *notations*

The strong links between these notations and the object-oriented architectural style means that we will be revisiting their roles more fully in a later chapter, and so we will not expand further on this aspect in this section.

7.3 White box notations

A **white box** notation can be viewed as one that is largely concerned with describing some aspect of the detailed realization of a design element. So, not surprisingly, such notations tend to be associated with the *constructional* and *functional* viewpoints. We should, however, be cautious of regarding these as being the equivalent of the draughtsman's 'blueprint'. There is still a design process to be performed in translating a white box description into the final system (essentially, the various detailed design activities of programming).

In this section we review a smaller choice of forms than in the previous section, and most of these are also quite closely related to particular architectural styles (perhaps we should not be too surprised at that!). We begin with the Structure Chart, which provides a classical form of description for the call-and-return architectural style. After that, we review two of the object-oriented notations that seek to describe the implementation details that relate to the concepts of **class** and **object**. Sequence Diagrams are also widely employed in object-oriented design, although strictly there is no reason to restrict their use to that particular architectural style. Finally, we examine the role of pseudocode, a venerable form of description that is not strictly a diagrammatical one, but which is often used to supplement diagrammatical forms in a very effective way.

7.3.1 The Structure Chart

The Structure Chart provides a visual 'index' to the hierarchy of procedures within a program, using a treelike format. It is therefore very much a solution-oriented form of description and, when allied with an algorithmic form such as pseudocode, can be used to provide a fairly comprehensive implementation plan for the programmer.

Its origins lie in the research performed at IBM to understand the problems encountered with the design of the OS/360 operating system, which in many ways was the first real example of an attempt at programming in the large. A major problem that the researchers identified was that of complexity, and the Structure Chart was one of the means suggested for helping to resolve and understand the structuring of a program (Stevens *et al.*, 1974).

The Structure Chart provides a means of recording the details of a program's structure in a form that is of great value to anyone who is trying to understand its operation. It is particularly useful to the maintainer, who needs to understand the general architecture of someone else's design, in order to make changes that are consistent with its form.

The form of the Structure Chart

The Structure Chart uses a treelike notation to describe the hierarchy of procedures (subprograms) in terms of the invocation relationship between them (sometimes termed a **call graph**). It therefore highlights the dependence of a procedure on the lower-level procedures that it invokes. Figure 7.27 shows an example of a Structure Chart, in which the three main components are:

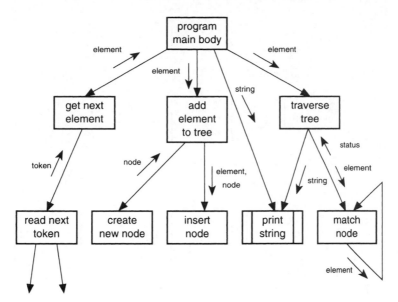

Figure 7.27   A Structure Chart describing a small program (first form).

■ the *box*, which denotes a procedure (subprogram);

■ the *arc*, which denotes invocation;

■ the *side-arrows*, which provide information about information flow in terms of parameter-passing (sometimes termed *couples*).

There are a number of conventions that can be identified from this example. Three in particular are as follows:

■ Procedures are drawn below the level of the lowest calling unit – in Figure 7.27, the procedure PrintString is drawn at the lowest level, because it is called by procedures in both the top (first) and second levels.

■ Double side-lines (again using PrintString as the example) are used to indicate where the designer expects to be able to use a standard 'library' unit. There will therefore be no further design details for such a unit.

■ The use of recursion can be indicated in a fairly simple manner. For example, in the procedure MatchNode, the recursive calling is indicated by the closed invocation arc.

The form of the Structure Chart is also hierarchical, in the sense that any box on the diagram can itself be expanded using the same form, although normally this would only apply to a box drawn at the lowest level. In the example of Figure 7.27, the procedure ReadNextToken is an obvious candidate for such treatment, since it is likely to call a number of other procedures in performing its task.

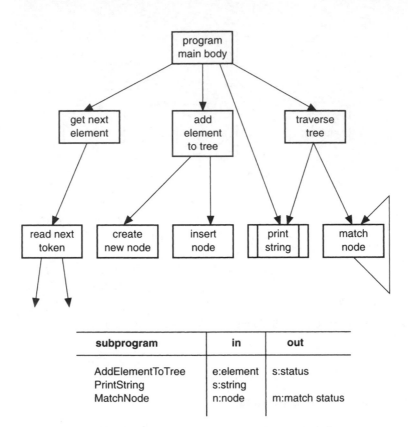

subprogram	in	out
AddElementToTree	e:element	s:status
PrintString	s:string	
MatchNode	n:node	m:match status

Figure 7.28   A Structure Chart describing a small program (second form).

An alternative notation that is sometimes used for drawing Structure Charts is shown in Figure 7.28, and this is more akin to that which was originally proposed in Stevens *et al.* (1974). Instead of annotating the diagram with text describing the parameter flow, which can rapidly become cumbersome, this form uses a separate table to indicate the parameters for each procedure.

One of the benefits of this latter form is that it can easily be extended for use with programming languages that support local permanent data structures, such as Java, C++, Ada and Modula-2. In using a Structure Chart to record the design of a program written in such a language, a third column can be added to the table, in which to record the details of any local or 'instance' variables that are used by the procedure. In designing for such programming languages, the use of direct references to such structures can be an important practice, and one that supports the use of information-hiding. It is important to record the details of such a direct access form in order to clarify the use of such practices.

The Structure Chart viewpoint

The principal role of the Structure Chart is to describe the way in which a program is assembled from a set of procedures. Its primary features are the description of procedure function and of connectivity with other procedures through invocation, although only the presence of the latter is recorded, with no attempt to indicate anything about frequency or sequencing of calls. While the transfer of data via parameters is recorded, it is not a primary feature of the diagram.

The Structure Chart contains some information about the organization of a program, and can therefore be regarded as also providing a certain amount of constructional information.

The use of the Structure Chart

The Structure Chart provides a relatively low degree of abstraction from the final implementation of a solution and, as was observed earlier, it can form a useful index to the structure of a program. (Some tools exist for 'reverse engineering' program code in order to construct the details of the Structure Chart.) For this reason, it not only provides a plan for the programmer to use, but also gives information that will be useful to the maintainer of a program (or to the marker of student programs!).

Chapter 13 provides an example of a widely used design method in which the output from the design transformations consists mainly of Structure Charts. When combined with pseudocode to describe the algorithmic portion of the design, they form a quite detailed set of outputs from the design process.

7.3.2 Class and object diagrams

A description of the UML **class diagram** was provided in Section 7.2.6, where the roles considered were essentially those that were relevant to black box modelling activities. However, one of the characteristics of the object-oriented paradigm is that such notations are used both for analysis purposes and also for quite detailed design, and so this section is chiefly concerned with the needs of the latter role.

Once again, the proliferation of object-oriented practices and programming languages has resulted in the creation of a range of notations and, for the same reasons as previously, we will mainly concentrate our attention upon the provisions made for such modelling needs within the UML. (Also, since this section is largely a continuation of Section 7.2.5, it has a less 'formal' structure and we will omit the usual sub-headings.)

The UML component diagram

The class notation introduced in Figure 7.21 already incorporates the main features that are needed for white box modelling, namely the descriptions of 'state' variables and of the methods provided by a given class/object. Where such diagrams differ from such forms as the Structure Chart is that they are not concerned with invocation hierarchy, instead seeking to model such dependencies as the *uses* and *inheritance* relationships. For constructional purposes, both of these are quite important.

The UML development of the class diagram that is used to describe 'physical' implementation issues is the **component diagram**. In the UML, the term 'component' is used to describe 'a physical unit of implementation with well-defined interfaces that is intended to be used as a replaceable part of a system' (Rumbaugh *et al.*, 1999). Also, 'each component embodies the implementation of certain classes from the system design' (*ibid.*).

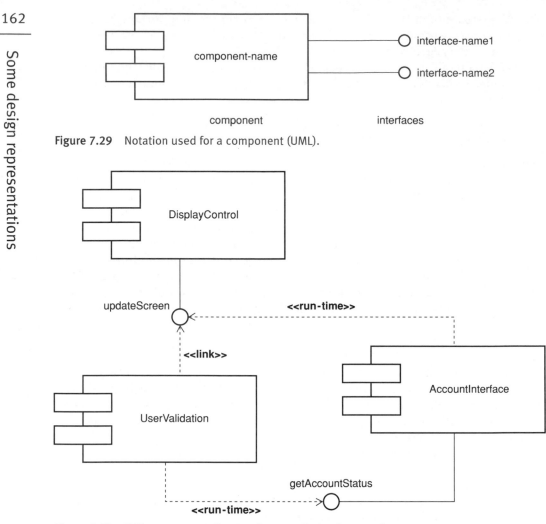

Figure 7.29 Notation used for a component (UML).

Figure 7.30 UML component diagram for part of a bank autoteller.

While this is a more specific view of the term *component* than is used in the wider software engineering context (and will be used later in this book), we will confine ourselves to using this definition within this section. Figure 7.29 shows the basic UML notation for a component. Such a component has interfaces that are *provided* for use by other components, and interfaces that are *required* to be supplied from other components; both of these are represented by a small circle attached by a line, with an identifier that represents the given interface.

Because components supply information to each other, the details of the interfaces may need to be available when a given component is compiled, or when a set of components are linked together. Such dependencies can also be shown on the diagram by dashed arrows, which may be labelled to show the details of the dependency concerned (usually in terms of binding time, as in <<compile>> or <<link>>). Figure 7.30 shows an example of a component diagram that describes some of the elements forming an implementation of a bank autoteller.

In its most simple form, such a component may be an object that is created from its parent class. Equally, since realizations such as the Java programming language permit the use of the class mechanism in a 'library' role, a component may be a class. In both cases, a component is therefore modelled directly from the description of the parent (or 'dominant') class.

Strictly, the UML component is more than the direct instantiation of a class or object, since it may represent a grouping of classes or objects too. However, viewed as a building block, we can effectively regard it as being the white box realization of these concepts, with the white box aspect being achieved through the additional information provided about both interfaces and dependencies.

The Fusion notation

The rather aptly-named *Fusion* method was one of the first of what we can term second-generation object-oriented design methods (Coleman *et al.*, 1994), and we will look at its practices in Chapter 16. Like other object-oriented methods, Fusion makes limited use of box-and-line notations for detailed design, and the main form it employs is that of the **object interaction graph.** What is interesting is that such a diagram is constructed for each system operation (although, again, this is not inconsistent with the object-oriented architectural style, which tends to place less emphasis upon overall constructional issues). The basic notation employs boxes to represent *design objects*, linked by labelled arrows that represent *message passing*. One box (and only one) has an external arrow as input, representing the system operation that the interaction graph is intended to implement. Collections of objects are represented by a box drawn with a dotted outline. Figure 7.31 shows a simple example of an interaction graph.

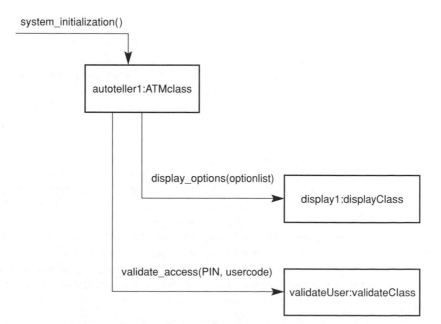

Figure 7.31 A simple example of an object interaction graph (Fusion).

Fusion does use other box-and-line notations (such as its **visibility graph**), and we will consider the roles of these further in Chapter 16. However, it lacks any notation that describes any form of overall picture of the constructional aspects of a particular design.

Viewed as a whole, this general category of class and object notations is rather a disappointing one. Those available are mostly based upon fairly basic box-and-line combinations, depend heavily upon textual decoration, and provide limited scope for hierarchical structuring. This should perhaps not be too surprising. The 'object concept' is a complex one that has many ramifications, and so this is hardly likely to encourage the evolution of so clean a form as Jackson's Structure Diagram, to take one example. However, it does also seem an area where there is scope for new developments, as anyone who has ever tried to produce a graphical illustration of the workings of a Java program will be only too well aware!

7.3.3 Sequence Diagrams

The UML **sequence diagram** represents an interesting form of notation that has gained particular popularity for object-oriented design, although there is no real reason why its use should be confined to that particular architectural style. Essentially, the purpose of this notation is to detail the interactive message-passing sequences that occur between a set of elements (which can be objects, actors, remote processes, client and server, etc.), when they collaborate to perform a given task.

So another example of a use for a sequence diagram is to describe the interactions that may be involved in a use case (or, more correctly, in a specific scenario). It might also be used to describe the exchanges involved in a network communications protocol, as well as more general aspects of the interactions that occur between any group of cooperating system elements, whatever their architectural form.

The Sequence Diagram notation

The organization of a sequence diagram is dominated by the need for a *timeline*, which conventionally runs from the top of the page downwards. (Obviously, where there is a need to indicate specific time intervals this might be drawn to scale, but generally only the sequential aspects are described.) Each processing element, usually an object, but also possibly some other system 'actor', is allocated a column, and messages are shown by arrows between the columns.

The sequence diagram has some additional and optional notational elements. Since objects can be created and destroyed during a sequence, and since their methods can themselves be activated or otherwise, the vertical line below each element can be modified to show the changes in element state. While the element exists, its timeline can be shown as a dashed line and, when it is active, this can be shown as a pair of solid lines.

Figure 7.32 shows a simple example of a sequence of basic operations using this notation, based upon the interactions between a web browser and an applet. In the example, the user invokes the applet when a particular web page is selected and then interacts with the applet, causing it to redraw its image on the page (which requires it to request the browser to organize this, since the applet can only draw with the facilities provided by the browser). Finally, the user selects another page and the applet is terminated.

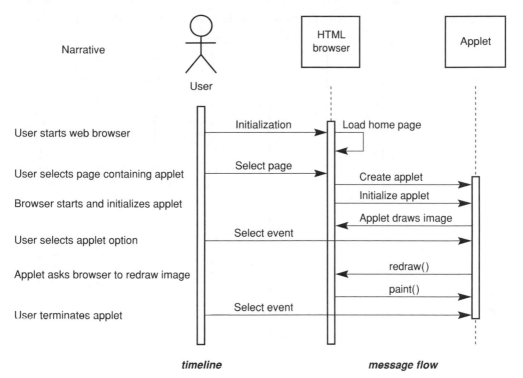

Figure 7.32 A simple example of a sequence diagram (UML).

The Sequence Diagram viewpoint

We can regard this notation as being mainly concerned with providing a *behavioural* description of a system. It is a white box notation because its primary concern is to describe how a particular behavioural response is to be produced. Like many behavioural forms it is intrinsically non-hierarchical and, indeed, one problem this can easily create is the difficulty of comprehending relatively large and complex diagrams of this form.

The sequencing aspect does mean that there can also be a degree of *functional* information provided in such a diagram, although this is very much a secondary role.

Uses for Sequence Diagrams

As indicated above, sequence diagrams are essentially concerned with modelling the detailed sequence of actions taken by a set of collaborating elements (which can be regarded simply as processing 'threads' for this purpose), and with the messages that they use to coordinate these actions. This is obviously an important role when expanding object-oriented design models, and one which we will be examining in Chapter 16. So for the rest of this section, we consider briefly some other roles that this notation can perform.

One of these is to describe exactly how a proposed set of objects will be able to meet the needs of particular *use cases*, and indeed, the use case is a rather practical way

Some design representations

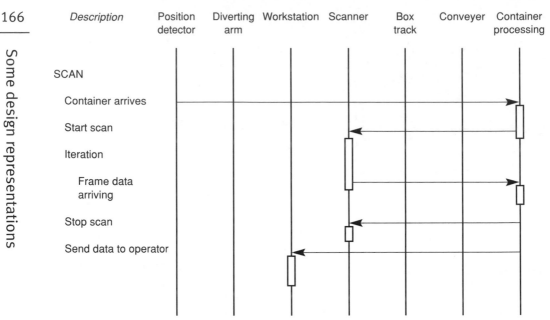

| Description | Position detector | Diverting arm | Workstation | Scanner | Box track | Conveyer | Container processing |

Figure 7.33 Example of a use case described using a sequence diagram.

of identifying the external stimuli involved. Conversely, a sequence diagram can also be used to describe a use case (or, more correctly, a *scenario*). Some examples of sequence diagrams used for this role are provided in Ratcliffe and Budgen (2001), and Figure 7.33 shows a short sequence taken from one of these (the unused elements are activated in a later part of the sequence). One attraction of using this form is that it can help end users to gain an understanding of the use cases, and hence make it easier for them to assist with identifying any inconsistencies or errors in these.

One other area where the sequence diagram can offer a useful form of visualization is in describing *protocols*. In many ways, the interactions of objects can themselves be regarded as a form of protocol, but we more usually employ the term when describing more general sequences used in communications networks.

Overall, the sequence diagram offers a rather useful notation that is not confined to one architectural style (this is generally true of behavioural descriptions of course), and forms a useful addition to the designer's 'visualization portfolio'. The main limitation is the lack of any hierarchical organization, although there may sometimes be scope to structure through subgroups of sequences. (As a rough guide, descriptions of sequences that span more than a single page can become difficult to comprehend and manage.)

7.3.4 Pseudocode

Pseudocode is, of course, used very widely indeed. It sometimes appears under other (more imposing) titles such as PDL (program description language), but it is easily recognized, even when concealed behind such grander titles.

If anything, pseudocode is used rather too much, as the low level of abstraction that it provides tends to conceal the wood within the trees as far as design abstraction is concerned. Perhaps some of its attraction lies in the ease with which it can be maintained using an ordinary computer terminal and keyboard.

That said, the level of abstraction that it provides is an important one, in that it permits a designer to think about the detailed sequencing of a solution while still remaining distant from the detailed forms of the solution. However, in order to do this effectively, it is necessary to ensure that pseudocode does not become too much like the programming language!

Pseudocode form

Like the Structure Diagram that was described in Section 7.3.1, pseudocode is concerned with describing a solution in terms of sequence, although it is restricted to describing the sequencing of operations alone. Figure 7.34 shows a typical example of this role, and expands upon the tea-making example of the previous section. Figure 7.35 shows a more typical example of the use of pseudocode for program design.

To be effective, there are some useful rules of thumb for writing pseudocode. The principal ones (as illustrated in the example of Figure 7.35) are:

- Use indentation to emphasize structure (it aids the eye in following the form of a sequence and finding other nodes in a branch).

```
boil water;
pour some water into teapot;
empty teapot;
REPEAT
    place spoonful of tea in pot
UNTIL enough tea for no. of drinkers;
REPEAT
    pour water into pot
UNTIL enough water for no. of drinkers;
```

Figure 7.34 The use of pseudocode to describe an algorithm.

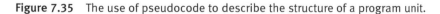

```
INITIALIZE line buffer;
READ first character from keyboard;
WHILE not the end of line DO
    IF character is terminator of a word
    THEN
        mark end of word in buffer;
        SKIP any trailing word separators
    ELSE
        copy character to buffer
    END IF;
    READ next character;
END WHILE;
```

Figure 7.35 The use of pseudocode to describe the structure of a program unit.

■ Pull out 'language keywords' in some manner, perhaps by typing them in upper case or underlined.

■ Try to 'bracket' executable blocks such as the body of a loop, or a branch clause in a conditional structure, by using such paired keywords as LOOP and ENDLOOP or IF and ENDIF.

■ Avoid referring to the identifiers of program variables or the values of constants. For example, the line check for the end-of-line character is more abstract and much more easily comprehended than check for #15, which requires a knowledge of the significance of #15.

While these practices cannot guarantee better levels of abstraction, they can certainly help to avoid writing pseudocode that is little better than poorly documented code!

The pseudocode viewpoint

As already mentioned, this is basically a functional one, based upon the sequencing of operations, expressed at quite a detailed level. There is also a small constructional element, but this is relatively minor in terms of importance.

Uses for pseudocode

Pseudocode is widely used to complement and augment other forms of description used in the later stages of design. It is hard to develop a design using pseudocode alone (one hesitates to say 'impossible'), but it is certainly undesirable, not least because of the restricted viewpoint it provides when making design choices.

Pseudocode can be used to complement the Structure Chart by providing the details and sequencing information that elaborates on the boxes in the diagram. It can of course be generated directly from a Structure Diagram. Indeed, almost all forms of diagram can usefully be augmented with a textual description of this form, since its disciplined format can help to maintain the relevant levels of abstraction.

Pseudocode will rarely appear in the examples of this book, since we will not be taking any segments of our larger examples down to quite this level of detail. However, its use for detailed design should be taken as assumed, even if it is not mentioned explicitly in the context of a particular design method.

7.4 Developing a diagram

Having considered a range of (largely diagrammatical) forms of design notation, two obvious and related questions that might arise are 'how are these diagrams developed?' and 'how can they be checked for consistency?'. Obviously, there is no one answer to either of these questions and, for design methods at least, both the tasks of producing and verifying diagrams may be partly driven by the procedures of the method. In this last section, however, we briefly review one means of checking and producing diagrammatical forms, namely the use of tabular structures.

Many notations can be conveniently reduced to a tabular form to assist in checking them for completeness and consistency. Conversely, starting from a tabular form can assist with generating a diagram. Tabular forms are generally better at handling large-scale descriptions, while diagrams make it much easier to visualize and recognize relationships between elements. The two are therefore largely complementary in nature, and there are good arguments in favour of recording the details of a design using both formats.

To illustrate these points we will briefly examine two examples. In the first we will transform a diagram into its corresponding tabular form, while in the second we will begin with a table and then develop the diagram. As examples, the choices of the particular forms used in these are purely illustrative, and both techniques are capable of being adapted for use with a wide range of diagrammatical forms.

7.4.1 A tabular representation of a diagram

For this, we will return to the STD that was described in Section 7.2.3. As we noted there, this is a non-hierarchical form of diagram, and hence becomes complex to manage when used to describe systems with large numbers of states and transitions.

The tabular form of the STD is generally referred to as a **State Transition Table** or **STT**. A common convention used is to plot the set of states down the left hand column and the events as column headers to the remaining columns. Entries in the table then denote the final state that results when a given event occurs at a time when the system is in the state denoted at the left hand edge of the row.

Figure 7.36 is an example of an STT that corresponds to the 'simple' STD describing the Unix vi text editor that was originally depicted in Figure 7.10. For convenience and as an aid to comparison, both are shown, with the STD being slightly abbreviated to show only the events and not the actions and, again, with only a small subset of the vi command set being described.

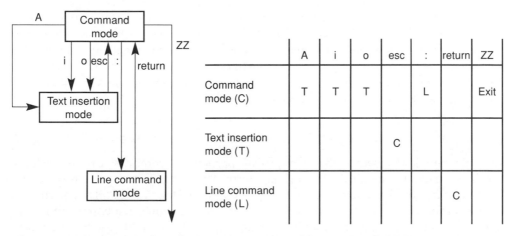

Figure 7.36 An STT describing the Unix **vi** text editor, with corresponding STD.

	stack	cleared to land	abort landing	touch down	take off	abort take off	park	cleared for take off
in flight	stacked	landing approach						
stacked		landing approach						
landing approach			in flight	on runway				
on runway					in flight	on ground	on ground	
on ground								on runway

Figure 7.37   An STT describing an aircraft in an air traffic control zone.

Simple though this example is, it does demonstrate the way in which a tabular form can aid with checking a model and identifying any questions about its completeness or correctness. For example, the table in Figure 7.36 might rightly lead the designer to question whether there should be any way of moving between (say) *line command mode* and *text insertion mode* (probably not), and also whether there are actions that might usefully need to be defined, such as the effect of pressing the 'esc' key when in *text insertion mode*. Finally, we can also note that, in this particular example, the STT's tabular form can more readily accommodate the structure of **vi** than the STD can, since it is more easily extended to include the many other command options.

A slightly fuller (or, at least, more balanced) STT describing the behaviour of an aircraft in an air traffic control zone, is shown in Figure 7.37. The corresponding STD was shown earlier in Figure 7.11. Again, this provides a form that might be used for checking the analysis model with users, since each combination of state and event can be considered in turn (and decisions about each recorded).

While the STT is by no means the only form that can be readily transformed into a table, it does provide a particularly clear illustration of the concept, as well as of the trade-offs between the two formats. On the one hand we have ready visualization of the model itself, while on the other we have easier visualization of any omissions or inconsistencies. We can also see that a tabular form is likely to be convenient only where a particular notation combines two major elements in some way. So while an ERD might be easily transformed into a table (if not so usefully as an STD), it is slightly less convenient, although not impossible, to transform a DFD, where auxiliary elements such as datastores need to be included.

7.4.2 Developing a diagram from a tabular representation

One software design method that does provide particularly comprehensive procedures for diagram development is SSADM (Longworth, 1992). To illustrate this process, we briefly consider the development of an Entity Life-History Diagram (ELHD) (a particular interpretation of the Jackson Structure Diagram). All we should really note about the SSADM model at this point is that it is strongly data driven, makes use of a variation upon the DFD, and hence is based upon the use of processes rather than objects.

ENTITIES	EVENTS					
	Post bulletin	List b-b contents	Read bulletin	Delete expired bulletin	Mail bulletin author	Save bulletin in file
Bulletin	*		*		*	*
Bulletin board	*	*				
User	*	*	*		*	*
Daemon				*		

Figure 7.38   Example of an Entity Life-History Matrix (SSADM).

The strategy that is recommended for developing these diagrams involves using a matrix or grid (the 'ELH matrix') to help with identifying the basic links between system events and the individual data entities. So the basic steps are:

1. *Listing the entities.* This task is largely performed as part of a previous task in SSADM and so, at this stage, one of the main roles of the ELHDs is to provide a further degree of validation for the choice of entities made previously.

2. *Identifying and listing the events.* This is a task that normally involves an analysis of the DFDs produced for a system in order to extract the details of those events that are:

   ■ *external* (arise from things occurring outside the system);
   ■ *temporal* (occur at a particular point in time);
   ■ *internal* (arise when some condition is satisfied within the system itself).

3. *Creating the ELH matrix.* Figure 7.38 shows a simple example of such a matrix. The first substep in developing this is to identify links between events and entities; a further analysis substep is then performed to determine whether a particular link leads to entry creation, modification or deletion, and hence provides further guidance on the development of the ELHD itself.

4. *Drawing the ELH Diagram.* This is likely to involve several evolutionary stages for each such diagram. While diagrams can be powerful descriptive forms, creating a clear diagrammatical description is not always an easy task, especially where layout issues are concerned,* and so there may need to be several iterations in order to develop such a diagram. Indeed, since a poor diagram can be confusing and misleading, it is important to recognize the possible need for iteration here. The diagram resulting from the above matrix is shown in Figure 7.39.

---

* Indeed, the task of drawing a diagram can be considered as a microcosm of the 'wicked' nature of the wider design process: there is no prescriptive way of doing it; there are many possible ways of organizing the layout; and there is no way of knowing when a 'final' form has been achieved!

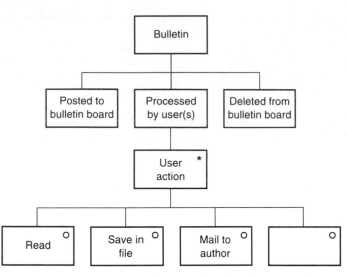

Figure 7.39   Example of an Entity Life-History Diagram (SSADM).

Again, the effectiveness of this procedure is strongly assisted by the 'dual-element' nature of the representation, although this should not detract from its wider useful-ness. Indeed, a useful starting point in drawing *any* diagram is to list the elements, then to try to identify the dependencies between these using one or more tables as necessary.

Summary

This chapter has examined a wide range of notations that can be used to support and document the development of a design model. The examples chosen illustrate the forms used for both white box and black box modelling across the set of viewpoints (functional, behavioural, data mod-elling and constructional). The choice of any particular notation will of course depend upon many factors, including the problem domain, ideas about the architectural form of the eventual system, and also any particular design practices being used. We have also briefly reviewed the use of tabular forms to help with checking and developing diagrammatical descriptions.

Further reading

There is surprisingly little literature that considers representational forms used in software design, other than from method-based aspects. Even Détienne (2002) contains no real discussion of the cognitive aspects of design notations and their influence upon the design process. The two items listed below provide further illustrations of some of the issues described in this chapter.

Wieringa R. (1998). A survey of structured and object-oriented software specification methods and techniques. *ACM Computing Surveys*, **30**(4), 459–527

The discussion of 'techniques' in this paper does include a review of notations which provides some good examples, as well as a discussion of their role in the conclusions.

Stevens P. with Pooley R. (2000). *Using UML: Software Engineering with Objects and Components*. Addison-Wesley

This concise book gives a good summary of the main notational forms used in the UML, together with examples, although not in very great detail.

Exercises

7.1 Identify the principal viewpoints and forms that you would consider suitable for describing the modelling involved in each of the following design tasks:

(a) the top-level design for a Java compiler;

(b) the detailed design for a program that will be used in a microprocessor-controlled washing machine;

(c) the design of a payroll-processing program.

7.2 Why are the diagrams in Figure 7.40 wrong? Redraw them using the correct forms.

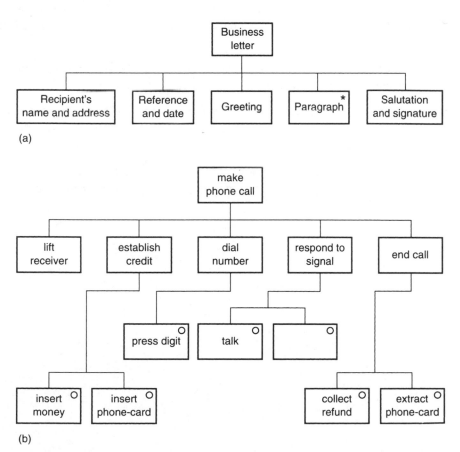

Figure 7.40 Diagrams for Exercise 7.2.

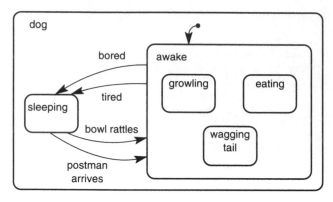

Figure 7.41   Diagram for Exercise 7.3.

7.3 Complete the Statechart in Figure 7.41 by adding the internal transitions and any further external ones.

7.4 Draw a Statechart that describes the operation of a simple electric cooking ring. (Remember, even if the ring is switched on, it will not need current whenever its temperature is higher than the selected level.)

7.5 Choose a set of representations that you consider suitable for the most recent program that you have written, and use them to describe (or document) its structure.

7.6 Draw a DFD that represents the processes involved in cooking and serving a three-course dinner, including all such associated tasks as laying out the table. Seek to ensure that your solution does not impose any unnecessary assumptions about the sequencing of actions.

7.7 Transform the Statechart in Figure 7.41 into an STD (consider only the lowest level states) and then into an STT. Using the latter, identify any inconsistencies and redraw the STD.

chapter 8

The Rationale for Method

This chapter introduces the initial steps in the study of design methods. It considers the nature of a design method, its component parts, and some of the reasons why design methods are used. As well as identifying the benefits that can be obtained from the use of a design method, it also reviews the limitations on what they can provide for the user, and examines the extent to which particular classes of problem may be suited to the use of specific design methods.

8.1 What is a software design method?

The concept of the *software design method* is one that has played an important role in software development since the late 1960s. A major motivation for employing such methods, that of assisting with *knowledge transfer*, was discussed in Chapter 6. There we suggested that some of the reasons why thinking about software design has been so directed towards the use of methods (when compared with the practices adopted in other domains) included the following.

- The need for a rapidly expanding industry to educate a continuous supply of new designers and developers, in circumstances where the traditional master/pupil approach would simply have been inadequate to cope with demand.

- The way that the continual rate of technological change and development has also required readily usable peer-to-peer updating about how to employ new concepts and new architectural styles most effectively.

- The need to create artificial frameworks that can be used to assist with structuring ideas about a medium that is intrinsically *invisible* in nature.

The last of these more or less directly leads into the material of this chapter (and of many of the following chapters). Here we take a rather wider view of the roles that methods perform, look more closely at the actual mechanisms that they employ, and consider some of the consequences (including the limitations) that may arise from their use.

In Chapters 1 and 2 we examined the nature of the design process in general, as well as its role in the development of software. There, we particularly emphasized the non-analytical nature of the design process: it is highly unlikely that different designers will come up with exactly the same solution to a problem; there are no clear criteria that allow us to select one of these as being *the* solution and our understanding of a problem is bound up with our ideas about its possible solution.

Based upon these observations, one view that can be taken of the design process is that it corresponds to a process of 'navigation through a solution space'. Each step in design may provide the designer with many options, and it is a part of the design task to identify these and to choose among them. One of the major roles of a design method is therefore to assist the designer by providing some guidance as to how the choices should be made, and how to assess the likely consequences of a particular decision in terms of the constraints it may impose on subsequent structures and choices.

However, before we can begin to examine the structure of a design method, we need to have a better understanding of what a method is, and hence how it can fulfil the roles identified above. A typical dictionary definition of the word 'method' is couched in such terms as the following: 'a way of doing things, especially a regular, orderly procedure'. It is this view that will form the main theme for the remainder of this book. (As we have previously observed, it is unfortunate that, in software development at least, a habit has arisen of using the rather grander-sounding term 'methodology' as if it were a synonym for 'method'. The correct meaning of 'methodology' is 'the science of method or orderly arrangement'. Indeed, this book is intended to provide a methodological analysis of design methods, by trying to analyse their forms and to classify them in some way.)

The idea of a method as a structured and 'procedural' way of doing things is one that should be familiar enough. 'Methods' are used to structure the way that we perform many routine tasks, such as making a cup of tea:

> Boil the kettle; warm the pot; add the tea; pour on water; wait a number of minutes; pour the tea into the cup.

Like most methods, this puts a strong emphasis on the ordering of actions (if you don't think so, try changing the order of any of the operations in the above example, and see what results!). However, it provides little or no guidance on those issues that are more a matter of taste, such as:

- how much tea to add

- how long to wait for the tea to brew

since these are personal preferences of the tea-maker. Since they are also essential to the success of the tea-making process, we can reasonably conclude that 'procedural' guidance alone is insufficient for this purpose, and that some 'domain knowledge' is also required.

We can devise methods for organizing many other activities, from driving a car to constructing kitchen units, model aircraft and so on. However, such methods are rarely *creative* in quite the same sense that we consider the act of design to be creative. Rather, these methods are *recipes* for doing something that we have learned to do through 'experiment' or 'theory' (or some combination of both). We might be able to adapt a method like that in the example above for other tasks (for making coffee instead of tea, perhaps), but we cannot easily change its basic domain (that of making hot drinks).

A design method is generally much less prescriptive than the kind of method that we might use for making tea, or for assembling a new garden shed. Indeed, in some ways a software design method can almost be considered as a 'meta-method', in that it is used to develop new processes, which in turn are ways of doing things – where the 'doing' that is involved will be the task of the computer. Returning to the tea-making example the analogy in this case would be using a design method to design the form of the tea-making process itself.

So we can reasonably expect that a design method should identify a general strategy to be used by the designer, and provide some rather general guidelines on its use, based upon experience. However, a method cannot be expected to be very prescriptive about how the ultimate solution to a problem is to be attained, since the specific design decisions required will be determined by the nature of the problem, rather than by the method. (Think of all the different processes that are used for making coffee!)

Vessey and Conger (1994) have suggested that the knowledge involved in successfully employing a design method can be categorized into two forms:

1. *declarative knowledge*, describing what tasks need to be performed at each step in the design process; and

2. *procedural knowledge*, consisting of knowledge about how to employ a given method in a particular situation.

In terms of our example of making tea, the declarative knowledge would include the tasks to be performed, and the order in which they should be performed (boiling water, adding tea to pot, adding water to pot), while the procedural knowledge would address such issues as how much tea to add and how much water to use when making tea for four people.

Declarative knowledge is therefore fairly readily conveyed through the use of a 'do this, then do that' form of description, whereas procedural knowledge is more likely to be acquired through experience. This experience may itself be acquired directly (as is likely when the knowledge is about how to make tea) or through exposure to case studies (which is probably more practical when the knowledge is about how to design software). Since we often express the declarative knowledge in what we term a procedural form, by specifying a sequence of actions that should be performed, this terminology can be a little confusing, although both uses of 'procedural' are quite reasonable ones! (It is also worth noting that Détienne (2002) uses the terms declarative and procedural in yet another, slightly different, way.)

Returning to the need to find ways of designing software: in Chapter 2, the following three main components of a software design method were identified, and their relationships are shown in Figure 8.1:

■ The *representation* part consists of one or more forms of notation that can be used to describe (or model) both the structure of the initial problem and that of the intended solution, using one or more viewpoints and differing levels of abstraction.

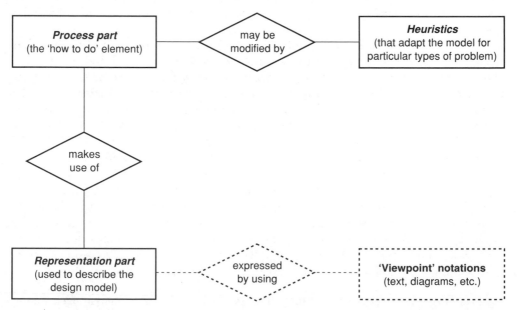

Figure 8.1   The three components of a design method.

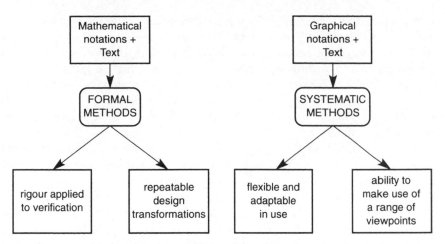

Figure 8.2   Some properties of formal and systematic software design methods.

- The *process* part describes the procedures to follow in developing the solution and the strategies to adopt in making choices. This generally involves the designer in making a series of transformations on the different forms that comprise the representation part.

- A set of *heuristics* or *clichés* provide guidelines on the ways in which the activities defined in the process part can be organized for specific classes of problem. These are generally based on experience of past use of the method with a particular problem domain, or for a particular form of structure.

In terms of the classification of knowledge discussed above, the process part can be considered as embodying the declarative knowledge, while heuristics are more concerned with procedural knowledge. This description will be elaborated further in the next chapter; for the moment these terms will provide a very general descriptive framework.

Software design methods fall into two very broad and general categories. These are essentially distinguished by the forms of representation that are used, although in turn the representation forms have some influence upon the forms of process that can be used within them. This division is illustrated in Figure 8.2.

Formal methods largely depend on the use of mathematical notations for the representation parts. These notations permit a degree of consistency checking between the descriptions used in the different stages of design, as well as more rigorous design transformations. However, while the representation parts for such methods have been the subject of considerable research and development, the process parts are less well refined and are apt to be developments of the 'top-down' strategy which is discussed more fully in Section 9.3.

This imbalance leads us to ask whether the term 'Formal Method' is really the most appropriate description. Because of this, the term *Formal Description Technique* (FDT) is sometimes preferred, as one that emphasizes the powerful notational aspects while playing down the much weaker procedural element.

Systematic methods are generally less mathematically rigorous in form, both in terms of the representation part – which normally consists of one or more forms of diagram – and also of the process part. This is true even for those methods that are generally considered to be more prescriptive in their form, such as JSP and SSADM. As a consequence, there is far more scope to use 'mix and match' techniques with systematic methods, in which ideas or representation forms from one method can be used to help resolve a particular issue, even though the design is being developed using the strategy of another method.

The third component of a design method, the *heuristics* (or *clichés*) usually consist of a set of techniques that are recommended for use in handling particular situations that may be encountered across a wide variety of problems. These heuristics are generally built up over a period of time, as experience is gained with using the method in a wider problem domain, and so they are essentially experiential in origin, although they may be highly systematic in form. We will encounter a number of examples of these in later chapters, and they play an important role in allowing a designer to reuse the experience of others. Examples of heuristics can be found in both systematic and formal methods.

The design methods discussed in this book are all systematic in their form, although we will also examine an example of an FDT in Chapter 18. This bias partly reflects the relative preponderance of systematic methods in current industrial practices, and partly the wider variety of design models that they tend to provide. The rest of this chapter will examine in greater detail the rationale for using any method to design software, and will consider some of the limitations that generally apply to the use of a design method.

8.2 The support that design methods provide

Since this is a book about design and design methods, it is not unreasonable at this point to raise the question: why should anyone use a method at all? Indeed, probably considerably more software has so far been produced without the use of an explicit design method than through the use of such methods – so what benefits might be expected from making use of a software design method (whatever form this might take)?

Some answers to this were identified in Chapter 6 and were summarized at the beginning of this chapter. The last of these, that of providing an artificial framework to assist with thinking about an intrinsically invisible set of elements, is an important one, and one that is largely addressed by the representation parts of design methods.

A second reason, and one that draws upon both the representation and process parts, is simply that of scale. Software-based systems increasingly underpin almost all aspects of a modern society. Some, such as those used to handle financial transactions within banks and similar institutions, were designed with the expectation that they would be large systems, while others may have become large through an undirected process of aggregation. (An example of the latter is the growth of many websites, where different elements are owned and maintained by separate individuals or organizations, but the site may still form a virtual whole.) For the former in particular, the cognitive tasks involved in planning and understanding such degrees of complexity are ones that may be usefully supported by using a systematic and structured approach to development and maintenance. For the latter, the need to ensure consistent behaviour and the need to facilitate integration between diverse elements also imply the need for some degree of standardization, at least to the level of being able to describe the structures involved. While such systems are less obviously candidates for the use of design methods, there is certainly scope to employ the representation elements and possibly some of the more strategic ideas.

One of the implicit features of design methods is that the use of any method will lead to designs that employ the architectural style associated with that method. With the long service life of much software, one way of preserving the integrity and structure of a system is to develop and maintain it by using a single design method.

There are therefore two aspects of the software development process (and of the subsequent maintenance task that normally goes with software systems) that can be expected to benefit from using a method to provide a structured and systematic approach to the development process. These are:

- *technical* issues

- *management* issues

and so both of these are considered in this section.

'Technical issues' consist of the problem-related aspects of design. There are a number of these to consider, with the relative importance of each one being somewhat dependent upon a range of external factors such as the structure of the development organization (Curtis *et al.*, 1988), as well as the nature of the design problem itself. So the following points should not be considered as ranked in any particular order.

- The 'knowledge transfer' mechanism discussed earlier in Section 6.3. Studies suggest that experienced designers may often work in an opportunistic manner, but that this practice may be less well-formed and reliable when the designer is less familiar with a problem or its domain (Adelson and Soloway, 1985; Guindon and Curtis, 1988; Visser and Hoc, 1990). So for the inexperienced designer, or the designer who is working in an unfamiliar domain, the use of a design method may assist with the formulation and exploration of the mental models used to capture the essential features of the design. In this way, therefore, *method knowledge* may provide a substitute for *domain knowledge*, where the latter is inadequate or lacking.

- The use of a design method should help the designer to produce a system that is structured in a consistent way, which may be particularly important if the design is being produced by a team of designers who will need to ensure that their contributions fit together correctly. In such a case, the use of a design method both helps with defining the chosen architectural form and also establishes a set of common standards, criteria and goals for use by the team.

- The use of a method should lead to the production of records and representations in standard form that can be used by a maintenance team to capture and understand the intentions of the original designer(s) (Littman *et al.*, 1987). This allows the system maintainers to make changes consistent with the overall structuring of the system, as originally planned, and so to help preserve its integrity. (However, as Parnas and Clements (1986) have observed, for this to occur it is important that the documentation should reflect the idealized design process rather than the actual one used!)

- The use of a method should aid with managing the 'cognitive load' involved in designing a system. This should reduce the likelihood of errors in the logical structuring of the system, and should ensure that all of the factors involved in a problem are properly weighed and considered by the designer(s).

While each of these points is particularly significant for large systems, they are valid for smaller ones too. The lifetime of an item of software, and the extent to which it is subsequently modified in maintenance, are not directly related to its size. (The only advantage of working with a smaller system is that if it proves impossible to understand its structure, the maintenance team can choose to recreate all or part of it from scratch – an option that is quite impossible to consider for medium or large systems.)

Each design method provides a particular form of 'Design Virtual Machine' (DVM), which in turn supplies the framework needed by the designer to develop his or her model of a solution. (One reason why experienced designers may be able to work in an opportunistic manner is that they have developed their own DVMs for particular classes of problem.) While the concept of an architectural style forms one of the key components of a DVM, determining the form of the set of design elements as well as defining the run-time environment that will be used for the eventual implementation, a DVM is rather more than just an architectural style.

The concept of a virtual machine is not a new one, although it is not usually applied to design methods. In computing terms, a virtual machine provides a layer of abstraction above that of the physical machine. An operating system provides a number of virtual machines, to allow programmers to access the resources of a computer at different levels of abstraction. (For example, a file may be treated as a sequence of characters, a sequence of records, or a sequence of blocks on a disk.) Programming languages also provide virtual machines: the programmer works with what is effectively a Java computer, or a C++ computer, without needing to understand the underlying architecture of registers, buses and processors. Figure 8.3 illustrates the basic ideas behind this.

The user of such a virtual machine structures his or her ideas around the behavioural model that it provides. It is then the job of some 'interpreter' to translate this into the form of a machine of lower level, and ultimately to that of the bare computer architecture itself. For example, when using Java, programmers are concerned only with making decisions such as determining that they need the features of (say) a `while` loop, and not with how that is to be achieved in terms of skip instructions and registers. They are therefore using a Java machine.

Each programming language therefore provides a virtual machine, whose architecture and form are determined by the features and semantics of the programming language. In the same way, a design method provides the user with a virtual machine that can be used to express ideas about program forms at a very high level indeed; although unfortunately, owing to the imprecise semantics of current representations, the resulting design model has to be translated into a lower level of abstraction by the designer and the programmer together.

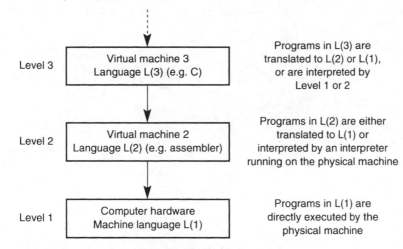

Level 3	Virtual machine 3 Language L(3) (e.g. C)	Programs in L(3) are translated to L(2) or L(1), or are interpreted by Level 1 or 2
Level 2	Virtual machine 2 Language L(2) (e.g. assembler)	Programs in L(2) are either translated to L(1) or interpreted by an interpreter running on the physical machine
Level 1	Computer hardware Machine language L(1)	Programs in L(1) are directly executed by the physical machine

Figure 8.3 The use of virtual machines in the design process.

This is performed by following the process part of the method: as Figure 8.4 shows, the task really involves two levels of DVM. One is used for architectural design (often termed 'logical' design or 'analysis'). The model produced is then translated into the 'design plan' (physical design), which is effectively another level of DVM with more precise characteristics than the initial DVM, and with structures that are much closer to the eventual implementation form. A further process is required to translate this into a programming language, which can then be translated by machine and eventually leads to the execution of the system on the physical machine.

The DVM that is embodied in a particular design method is characterized by such factors as:

- the architectural style implied by the forms of design element used;
- the viewpoints used in the various phases of the modelling process;
- the relationships between these that are established by the form of the design process;
- the basic strategy of the method itself, since this determines how the design models will be elaborated.

Together these create a set of assumptions about the general form of the solution (sequential, parallel, data-centred, object-centred . . .) that in turn form an essential part of the framework used by the designer.

In the ideal, the DVM should be matched to the virtual machine provided by the eventual implementation form that is to be used. While a DVM that is based upon defining sequences of actions to be performed on data structures may map well onto many imperative languages, it is unlikely to help with determining how best to use the packaging features of a language, or a feature such as inheritance, as provided in many object-oriented programming languages. For example, it could well be argued that one of the problems created by the introduction of the Ada language was that it

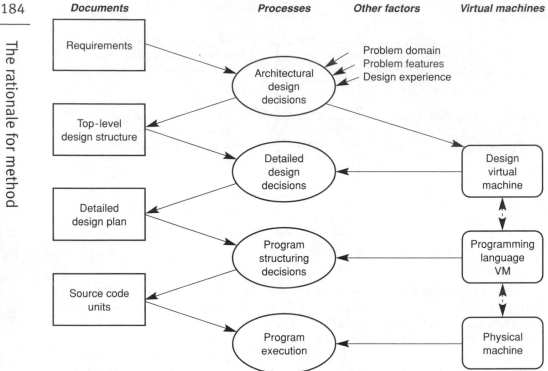

Figure 8.4 The link between the DVM and the virtual machine levels used on a computer. (Each method has a design virtual machine embodied within it, helping to determine such aspects as the set of viewpoints used, the strategy, architectural assumptions, etc.)

incorporated a virtual machine that was not well matched to that of any existing design method. Features such as the *package* and the *task* model that is provided for parallel operations required a DVM that addressed such issues as packaging and parallelism, a problem that has yet to be resolved in a completely satisfactory manner.

The design methods that provide the topics of Chapter 13 and the following chapters have been selected precisely because they provide a set of very different DVMs. Perhaps the main feature that they possess in common is that they all assume that the final system will be implemented using imperative programming forms.

The management benefits of using design methods are (not surprisingly) linked to many of the same issues as the technical benefits. In particular, the documentation of a system is important both for the development of the system and for its maintenance.

So from a management viewpoint, using a recognized design method will provide:

- a framework for recording decisions and reasons in a systematic manner;

- a set of procedures that should ensure consistency in the structure of a design, and in the structure of the interfaces between design components, so making it easier to use a team of designers on a large project;

- a framework that helps with identifying important progress milestones.

In particular, the use of a design method helps with structuring the design *process* as well as the design *product*.

All of the above issues become even more important when we consider the extent to which designers spend their time modifying existing systems, rather than developing new ones. For much of the time, a designer is likely to be performing tasks that can be regarded as 'perfective maintenance' rather than undertaking original design work. Even for a totally new system, the designer is unlikely to be completely unconstrained in terms of the available choices, and so much of the work is likely to involve adaptation of existing structures. In this context, one of the strongest benefits that a design method can offer is that it encourages the designer to plan for change, and to think ahead in terms of subsequent developments and extensions. Some methods do this explicitly, others less so, but, whatever the method, its use should lead the designer to explore the solution in a structured manner that is likely to encourage consideration of later modifications.

The need to design for change was strikingly demonstrated when the British government changed the rate of Value-Added Tax (VAT) in 1991. The billing software used by one major utility to issue its bills could not cope with a split rate of VAT – one rate applying until a given date, and a new rate after that. So all bills covering that period were issued with VAT charges set at the new rate, with refunds to follow! Whereas software designed to cope with income tax rates will normally allow for such changes, because they tend to occur annually, VAT rates change only very infrequently – with embarrassing consequences for some hapless design team.

8.3 Why methods don't work miracles

The preceding sections have explored some of the major reasons for using design methods to help with solving software design problems. However, it is important to appreciate that a design method does not offer a panacea that will automatically remove all problems. In the first two chapters, we examined the nature of the design process, and the reasons why it is so difficult to impose any structure on its form, and the points that were made there need to be kept in mind in assessing the usefulness or otherwise of specific software design methods.

A design method provides the designer with a framework within which to organize the development of a design. It provides a set of recommended representation forms that can be used to give insight into the issues that are significant for that DVM. It provides guidance on the steps that the design process should follow, and advice on the criteria that should be considered when making design choices. However, none of this guidance can be problem-specific, and hence the emphasis must very much be on the notion of providing guidance. For an actual design task, the designer's choices and decisions will need to be resolved solely on the basis of the needs of the particular problem that requires to be solved.

One analogy that it may be helpful to repeat here concerns the use of a recipe for cooking. A recipe is a process that determines how a particular dish will be produced – much as a computer program is a process that determines how a graph will be drawn, or how tax rebates will be calculated. Designing software is therefore rather like designing a recipe – it requires the designer to possess insight into the problem domain, to be aware of the potential that is present in the basic materials, and to know the bounds upon the capabilities of the system that will execute the process (whether this be a cook or a computer!).

A design method intended for producing recipes might be able to provide some guidance as to how a recipe should be organized, presented and described, and would be able to provide advice on:

- how to lay out the instructions to the cook (for example, terms to use and/or appropriate forms of measure);

- the best use of photographs, tables and so on;

- making suggestions about possible variants.

But it cannot be more specific than this. Decisions about detailed issues – such as the choice of ingredients and the amounts of each to be used, the length of time in the oven, the oven temperature to be used – must all depend upon the nature of the dish and the materials, not upon the format used for developing the recipe.

Because a software design method provides a form of 'process' that is used to design another process, it is all too easy for the inexperienced to fall into the trap of believing that a design process is itself a recipe – but that is not so at all, as the above example demonstrates. Instead, a recipe is something that is output from the design process, rather than being the model for the design process itself.

One way in which it is possible to increase the amount of guidance from a method slightly is to focus it upon a particular domain of problems. By concentrating upon (say) data-processing problems, or information-retrieval systems, it is possible to give somewhat tighter guidance for some of the decisions that the designer needs to make. However, even this will be limited in the extent to which it can be usefully carried out. (In the ultimate, of course, we could narrow down the problem domain until the method would be only suited to one problem!) In practice, most methods are aimed at reasonably wide domains so as to try to optimize their use: hence the benefits of familiarity with the method.

To make their forms as prescriptive as possible, design methods are based on defining a set of carefully itemized sequences of actions that should be performed by a designer. Indeed, it is usually the only practical way of describing the process part of a method – as an analogy compare the complexity of writing and comprehending programs that contain parallel threads of execution with that of writing and comprehending sequential programs. However, observed design practices suggest that experienced software designers may work on several different threads of action in parallel, and that these may also be at different levels of abstraction (Guindon and Curtis, 1988; Visser and Hoc, 1990). So a design method that is described purely in terms of sequential actions can provide only a very inadequate approximation to expert behaviour, although this might be partly offset by the iterations that are necessary in design activity. (A further factor that may offset this disadvantage is that, as designers gain expertise, they may be better able to adapt a method to their needs, and so employ parallel activities where their use would be appropriate.)

The purpose of this section is not to encourage the idea that design methods should not be used, but rather to point out that they have limitations and that these need to be recognized. Unfortunately the purveyors of courses and textbooks on

187
methods are sometimes guilty of encouraging exaggerated expectations about their
wares, and it is important to be able to keep these in perspective.

8.4 Problem domains and their influence

The concept of a problem domain figured in the preceding section, and this section
elaborates a little the implications of the concept as applied to the design process.

Almost all software design methods expect the designer to begin the design process by building some form of model of the real-world problem that is to be solved.
The form of this model is essentially based on the underlying DVM, and hence is highly
method-specific. Ultimately, therefore, the chosen method will strongly influence the
form of the solution that is derived from it, including its architectural style.

The basis for model-building can vary quite considerably, but usually involves
mapping the characteristics of the original problem into one or more of the following
viewpoints:

- function

- information flow

- data structure

- actions

- data objects

- time ordering of actions

(Of course, some of these descriptions may utilize a range of possible forms.) The form
of this initial model is a major factor in determining how well the method will map
onto particular problem domains. For example, real-time problems will normally
require that the initial model incorporate timing issues in some way; while data-
processing problems will be likely to incorporate models of data structures or information flow.

Sometimes a method may be very specialized. An example is the design of compilers. For imperative programming languages there are some very well-established
techniques (with supporting software tools) that can be used for constructing compilers. However, this is a relatively unusual situation, and most problem domains are
much more general in form. In addition, domains are not necessarily mutually exclusive, so that a design method that is targeted largely at one class of problems might
still prove useful with other problems that can be considered as belonging to quite a
different class. An example of such a design method, and one that we will be meeting
later, is JSP. This method is essentially intended for use with designing algorithms for
data-processing problems, but it can sometimes be used to help solve other types of
problem too.

One question that arises here is whether the problem characteristics should determine the design approach and the eventual architectural style of the system, or whether

the choice of preferred architectural style should determine the design approach? While the former may well be the 'ideal' or certainly the more 'pure' approach, pragmatic factors may favour the latter more strongly! Software is rarely constructed in isolation from other software, so that the needs of compatibility with existing software may need to be considered. Equally, designers and programmers gain expertise with certain styles, which may be particularly important if time to delivery is a major factor. Unfortunately, fashion too cannot be ignored; particular styles often have periods of being 'in vogue' and hence may be preferred within an organization.

Of these, the only legitimate argument is really the first and, indeed, if we consider the need for compatibility as being one of the 'domain' issues, this is not really inconsistent. Indeed, architectural mismatch can easily become a major hurdle and is certainly one to anticipate and avoid (Garlan *et al.*, 1995).

An important point arises from this concept of the problem domain that is relevant to the remaining chapters of this book. Because the domains of application for software design methods are essentially ill-defined, it is generally impractical to seek any form of 'comparative methods' evaluation of design methods, along similar lines to those performed for programming languages, which have a well-defined syntax and semantics.

Any attempt to classify problem domains in other than a very general way will usually lead to difficulties, because real problems are rarely easily categorized in a simple manner. However, some rather general domains can be identified, and there are three in particular that are useful.

- In **batch systems** the main feature is that all the operating characteristics of the system are essentially determined when it begins processing one or more data streams. Any changes in these characteristics arise because of the contents of the streams, when considered as sequential flows of data. Such a system should therefore perform operations that are *deterministic* and *repeatable*. An example of a batch system is a compiler, all the actions of which are determined by the nature of the input source program. It goes without saying that compilation should be deterministic!

- The principal characteristic of **reactive systems** is that they are event-driven. For such systems, the events are almost always asynchronous and non-deterministic. An obvious example of such a system is a screen editor, for which the operations of the process depend upon the events that are generated externally, by the user. A commonly encountered subsidiary characteristic of such systems is that the specifications of the required responses to events will often include explicit requirements about timing.

- **Concurrent systems** are characterized by the use of multiple threads of execution within the problem, so that a solution might utilize one or more processors. For such systems, the process of design may need to consider such issues as the overheads of process scheduling, as well as the need for mutual exclusion and synchronization between processes.

These classifications should not be considered as mutually exclusive: while a system is unlikely to have both batch and reactive aspects, either of these forms could well have concurrent features.

A somewhat different approach to classifying problem domains is to consider how these influence the designer's goals. To illustrate this, consider the distinction between the following two classes of design problem.

■ Problems where the *form* and content of the data guide the designer's actions. Examples occur in such applications as transaction-processing systems, in which the key criterion is to process the data correctly (where the data may be financial information, hotel bookings, and so on), and there is no time constraint beyond that of processing the necessary volume of transactions within a particular time interval.

■ Problems where the *existence* and content of data will guide the designer's actions. This is more typical of the domain of real-time systems, where the occurrence of the event will be highly significant (this may be the detection of a gas leak, or an approaching missile, or an aircraft that is too close), together with the need to process the data within a time interval determined by the nature of the data itself and before it is replaced by new data.

In the former case, the important thing is for the system to generate a correct response (it will not be disastrous if some small delay in processing is involved on occasion, but debiting the wrong bank account by several million pounds may well be considered catastrophic!). In the second case the important thing is to generate a response within a critical time interval. The response needs to be a correct one, but an approximation may suffice: disaster *will* occur if an approaching missile is ignored for too long, while an 'inexact' response that fires two counter missiles, because there is not time to ensure that one will be accurate enough, will be acceptable.

In the first case a design method is required that allows the designer to check thoroughly for correct behaviour, and to verify this in some way. The second case also has these needs, but adds the requirement that correct performance of the eventual system must be guaranteed. Each of these domains will require design practices that help to focus attention on the aspects that are most critical, as illustrated in Figure 8.5. The next chapter begins to examine what forms these might take.

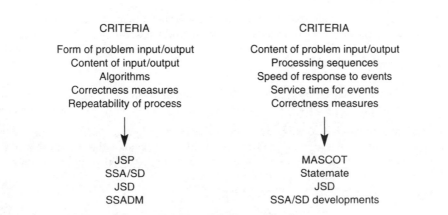

CRITERIA

Form of problem input/output
Content of input/output
Algorithms
Correctness measures
Repeatability of process

↓

JSP
SSA/SD
JSD
SSADM

CRITERIA

Content of problem input/output
Processing sequences
Speed of response to events
Service time for events
Correctness measures

↓

MASCOT
Statemate
JSD
SSA/SD developments

Figure 8.5 Some design criteria and related design methods.

The rationale for method

Summary

This chapter has considered the nature of the software design process in terms of its components and of the potential for providing these with a structure.

In the design process itself, the following three principal components have been identified:

- a *representation* part
- a *process* part
- a set of *heuristics*, or *clichés*

and their roles have been discussed. The rationale for using a design method has also been considered, and how 'method knowledge' may provide a substitute for 'domain knowledge' when necessary. By looking at the nature of the design process in this way, it has tried to determine what the limitations on the form and applicability of *any* software design method are likely to be.

As a final step before a fuller consideration of the structure of design methods, the nature of problem domains was considered. In particular, the characteristics of the

- batch
- reactive
- concurrent

problem domains were identified.

Further reading

Parnas D.L. and Clements P.C. (1986). A rational design process: How and why to fake it. *IEEE Trans. Software Engineering*, **SE-12**(2), 251–7

This paper starts from a recognition that software design is not a precise and systematic process, and argues that we should, however, seek to document a design as though it had been produced by such an ideal process. The paper provides a valuable discussion of the issues of the documentation of design features.

Visser W. and Hoc J.-M. (1990). Expert software design strategies. In *Psychology of Programming* (Hoc J.-M., Green T.R.G., Samurçay R. and Gilmore D.J., eds). Academic Press

This is a review of research involving observations of expert designers of software and the strategies that they use when designing systems. While it does not examine the relationship of these actions to specific design methods, it does identify the design practices that should be approximated through the use of a design method.

Exercises

8.1 How would you classify each of the following systems in terms of one or more of the domains batch, reactive or concurrent?

(a) A bank autoteller machine.

(b) A system utility program used to list the contents of a user's directory (such as the Unix **ls**).

(c) An interpreter for a programming language.

(d) A multi-user operating system.

(e) An airline seat reservation system with terminals in travel agents' offices.

8.2 Making tea (or coffee) is a process executed in a manner influenced by the conditions that apply at the time of execution (the preferences of the drinker, the amount of tea or coffee available, and so on). Find examples of similar everyday processes that are not based on the kitchen and identify the relevant operations.

8.3 Faced with the need to understand and modify a simple interactive 'client program' used for e-shopping purposes that was originally written by another person, list five forms of information about its design that you would like to have available to you, and rank these in descending order of importance.

chapter 9

Design Processes and Design Strategies

Each design method embodies a design strategy within its process part, which gives a sense of direction to the procedures of the method and forms one of the elements that make up its basic philosophy about designing. Following a discussion about the roles of strategy in design, this chapter introduces some simple process modelling forms which can be used to help with describing the design processes themselves. It then goes on to examine some of the more widely adopted strategies, together with the principles that underpin these. Strategies are not necessarily wholly based upon technical factors, and so we also examine how they can be influenced by the needs of organisational users of software.

9.1 The role of strategy in methods

Chapter 8 examined the nature of design methods in a rather general way, and identified the major components that a design method might be expected to possess. In this chapter, our ideas about the roles of these components are developed a bit further, and we begin to examine the principal strategies encapsulated in the process parts of some major software design methods. This completes the groundwork needed to undertake the more detailed study of specific software design methods in the remaining chapters of this book.

We begin with a reminder of the form used for describing the structure of a design method, first introduced in Chapter 2 and further developed in Chapter 8. There it was suggested that a software design method could be described in terms of the following principal components:

- *representation* part

- *process* part

- set of *heuristics*, or *clichés*

The properties of some widely used forms of representation have already been described in Chapters 5 and 7. In Chapter 8 it was further observed that the set of these used in a method are important in defining the Design Virtual Machine (DVM) that is embodied in a method, since they determine the type and form of design model(s) that a designer is encouraged to produce when using the method.

The process part of a method is closely entwined with the representation part, since it provides 'procedural' guidelines on how the models should be developed. We

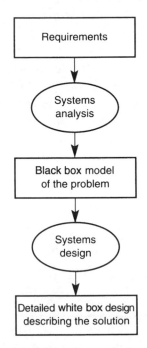

Figure 9.1 General procedural model of the software design process.

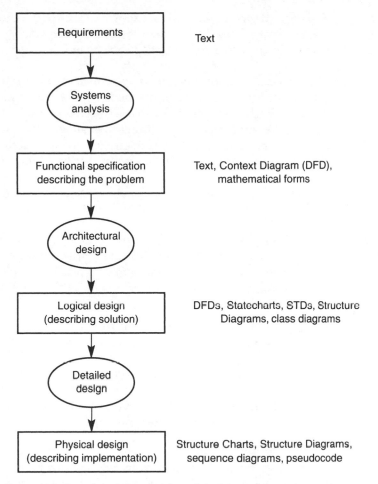

Figure 9.2 Expanded view of the procedural model of the software design process.

now look more closely at the nature and form of the process part, while in later chapters the three components are brought together when we look at examples of design methods and examine the specific forms of heuristic that are associated with them.

Figure 9.1 shows this procedural model of the software design process in a symbolic fashion, and we will be making use of this form throughout the rest of this book. The basic symbols it uses to describe a design method are:

■ an oblong to denote a representation form;

■ an oval to denote a procedural step;

■ an arc to denote the sequence of steps.

These can be seen more fully in Figure 9.2, which shows a slightly expanded form of Figure 9.1. (Note that our notation possesses the important property of being hierarchical, as discussed in Chapter 5, in that the description of any transformation step can be expanded further using the same three components.) The iterations that occur between phases of the design process are not shown explicitly: the model is concerned with describing overall strategy rather than the detailed sequencing of actions, since these will be driven by the needs of a specific problem and the experience of the designer.

Back in Chapter 2, in a brief and introductory discussion about the form of the typical process part of design methods, we made the distinction between a 'transformation' step and one concerned with 'elaboration'. Now that we need to consider design processes and strategies in rather more detail, it is useful to examine this categorization more closely. This is because each of the procedural steps of any design method, regardless of the strategy employed, can usually be classified as being one of those two forms.

These two forms have quite distinctive roles and characteristics, which can be described as below.

- A **transformation step** is one where the designer modifies the structuring for their model of the 'system' in some way. Typically this consists of reinterpreting it using a different viewpoint (ultimately, of course, the aim is to produce a constructional model). Such a step will require the designer to make some fairly major design decisions and is clearly a strongly creative one.

- An **elaboration step** is one which does not usually involve any change of viewpoint, but is more concerned with restructuring or reorganizing the design model within the current viewpoint. (Examples might include expanding the bubbles in a DFD, or grouping states within a Statechart.) The purpose of an elaboration step is usually either to add further information to the model, or to obtain greater insight into the current state of the design plan through restructuring, and as such it may be an essential preliminary to a successful transformation step.

When we come to examine some examples of design methods, we will see that many of these have only one transformation step, usually preceded and followed by elaboration steps. Important factors from a methodological aspect are whether the transformation step appears early or late in the sequence of steps, and the number (and types) of viewpoint that may be involved.

It is important to recognize that both types of step involve creative actions, although the forms that the creativity takes are somewhat different. The transformation process typically requires the designer to be able to bridge their ideas across two or more different sets of properties, while the elaboration process is more concerned with recognizing patterns and structures (or the potential for forming these), while also possibly anticipating the needs of subsequent transformation. Figure 9.3 illustrates these distinctions in an abstract manner. We might also note that the issues of *strategy* that we discuss later in this section are more likely to be embodied in the procedures employed in the elaboration steps of a method.

This general model, in which a sequence of procedural steps make up the process part, is one that we will use extensively in analysing design methods, and the notations shown in Figures 9.1 and 9.2 will be used for this. In the next section we will introduce a slightly more 'formal' notation that complements this, and which places more emphasis upon the use of the viewpoints model, so making a more explicit distinction between transformation and elaboration steps.

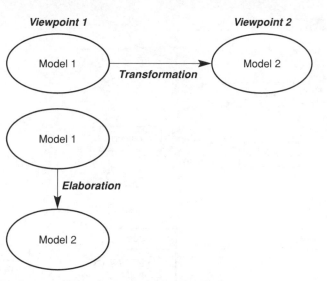

Figure 9.3   Contrasting transformation and elaboration design steps.

These models were largely chosen because they are convenient forms for aiding the analysis of the procedural aspects of design methods. Although we do not have scope in this book to utilise more detailed models of the actual procedural steps, the ability to describe these can be useful when we need to review particular processes. As an example of such a more detailed process model, that developed by Potts and Bruns (Potts and Bruns, 1988; Potts, 1989; Lee, 1991) does provide the means of performing a more detailed analysis of the factors involved in making individual design decisions, and an example of this is shown in Figure 9.4.

Their model is based on the use of five entity types (the boxes) and eight binary relationships (the arcs). The relationships operate as follows (Potts, 1989).

- Steps *modify* artifacts. In 'derivation', a new artifact is created. In 'revision', a new version of an existing artifact is created.

- Steps *raise* issues. This may occur automatically, but the issue may not have to be addressed immediately.

- Issues *review* artifacts. An issue may be raised to review the property of an artifact.

- Positions *respond to* issues.

- Arguments *support* positions.

- Arguments *object to* positions. Arguments are often paired, with one supporting a position and the other opposed to it.

- Arguments *cite* artifacts. The artifact provides evidence for the argument.

- Positions *contribute* to steps. A step is performed because a set of commitments has been made.

In Potts (1989) this model has been used to analyse the initial stages of the JSD method, and to model the processes involved. This form therefore provides a useful

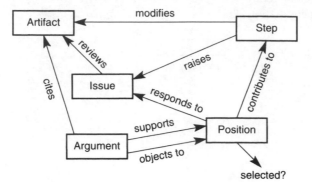

(a) The generic form

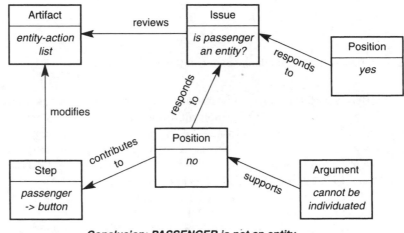

Conclusion: PASSENGER is not an entity.

(b) An example from the JSD method (applied to a passenger lift)

Figure 9.4 A Potts and Bruns model of the processes involved in design steps.

(After Potts (1989) © 1989 IEEE)

supplement to our basic process model, since it can be used to elaborate on the form of specific components from the process model.

The design transformation and elaboration steps in a method can be considered as embodying local tactical decisions, which are in turn guided by the strategy that is adopted by a particular method. Strategic issues, for their part, are generally concerned with large-scale factors such as the domain of a particular problem, specific constructional and behavioural characteristics and likely forms of implementation.

Where strategy does play a particularly important part is in determining the form of the initial model that a designer will create in order to describe the problem. While almost all design methods claim to begin by modelling the 'real world', the form of the Design Virtual Machine (DVM) that is used for this description can vary very widely, and can make use of a wide variety of viewpoints.

There is also a historical perspective to this issue of how the design process is performed. David J. Koepke (1990) has recorded his research into the evolution of software design ideas and has described how thinking about software design has developed and evolved. A particularly important element of this work is that it included making contact with some of the pioneers of the field, in order to obtain their impressions and recollections.

A major factor in the development of thinking about software design has been the way that the concept of a module has been interpreted and defined. In the earliest stages, the goal of physical modularity was achieved through the development of the subprogram mechanism, which then provided the basic design element that could be modelled in the design process. Only later did such concepts as that of information-hiding provide a basis from which to develop a quite different view of how modularity might be used in a logical manner.

The form of module employed in a design model is clearly related to the ideas about architectural style introduced in Chapter 6, and the evolution of the two has largely gone in parallel. Changes in the form of module employed have reflected the evolution of ideas about how systems should be structured, and how those structures might be achieved. Early thinking about design was concerned with making effective use of the subprogram's strengths, and so was focused on partitioning system functionality into sub-tasks, well summarized in Niklaus Wirth's (1971) classic paper. Structuring a design solution around the principle of information-hiding has proved to be a rather more difficult goal to achieve through procedural forms but, since the late 1980s, applying these to the object-oriented architectural style has attracted considerable attention and effort. In such a style, the basic module concept (the *object*) is correspondingly more complex in its nature and properties than the subprogram.

Software design methods are not influenced by technical issues alone, of course. There are environmental, cultural, organizational and national influences, as well as the continually increasing scale of user expectations and need as systems have become ever larger and more complex (Curtis *et al.*, 1988).

Clearly, many factors have influenced the development of design methods, and for that reason they are difficult to classify in any very systematic manner. For the purposes of the rest of this chapter, though, we will use the following broad groupings in order to discuss how strategy is incorporated into a design method:

■ *decompositional* methods, which generally take a 'top-down' view of the design process, developing the design model through a process of sub-division;

■ *compositional* methods, whereby the basic design model is built up from the identification of 'entities' of some form;

■ *organizational* methods, for which the structure of the design process is strongly influenced by the requirement that it should conform to non-technical requirements that are based on the form of the organization;

■ *template*-based methods, where a specific problem domain provides a class of problems that can be tackled using a fairly standard strategy.

The rest of this chapter examines the characteristics of each of these strategies (with the exception of the last, which is addressed in the next chapter), and makes an initial classification of methods in terms of them.

Before proceeding, however, one other point should be mentioned here: the relationship between strategy and such ancillary aspects as the design of the user interface and the design of error-handling strategies.

Design strategies (and associated methods) tend to encourage the designer to focus on structuring core activities of the eventual system in building up a model of a problem. As a result, such issues as the organization of human–computer interactions (HCI), and the handling of error (exception) conditions, are generally deferred until a later stage in the design process, when the design model is being refined and elaborated.

This is generally a reasonable practice to adopt, particularly for such issues as exception-handling, since any attempt to include these in the initial model may lead to it becoming excessively complex. The designer is then faced with the following alternatives when determining how to incorporate these issues:

- to incorporate them into the later stages of design refinement, by which time architectural decisions may have been made that are inconsistent with their needs;

- to repeat the design process from a much earlier stage, using the experience gained from producing a design for the basic problem to help with the greater complexity of the fuller problem.

As always with design, there is no hard and fast rule about which of these strategies may be the most appropriate. Constraints such as project deadlines may push the designer towards the former choice but, where significant HCI elements are involved, or where error-handling is an important element, this may lead to considerable distortion of the design structure.

On the whole, existing design practices do not help greatly with either of these issues. HCI design is now a rather specialized field in its own right, and designing for exceptions is a relatively unexplored field in design theory.

Before reviewing the major design strategies, we now examine a 'viewpoints-centred' notation that will aid with modelling the procedural steps of a method.

9.2 Describing the design process – the D-Matrix

The forms used for modelling a software design process discussed in the previous section are largely concerned with identifying the sequence of steps that make up a particular design process. In this section, we introduce a formalism that seeks to unite the concepts of *transformation* and *elaboration* with the viewpoints model that was introduced in Chapter 5. To do so, we use what we have termed the **D-Matrix** (short for 'Design Matrix') notation, which is intended to provide an abstract description of the state of the 'design model' at any point in its evolution (Budgen, 1995). The D-Matrix is totally independent of any specific methods; indeed it can be used to describe not only method processes, as we will do in later chapters, but also to record quite opportunistic sequences of design activities.

Despite its rather formal and mathematical appearance, we should emphasize that this notation is solely concerned with providing a *description* of design states. Its chief attraction for our purposes is that it offers a very compact notation that can be used to describe particular design steps.

The basic assumption for this notation is that any design (or requirements) specification can be composed from the specifications for a set of 'design elements' (or 'requirements elements'), where each element can itself be described in terms of a set of attributes that describe the properties associated with the four major viewpoints (function, behaviour, data model and construction). The actual form of the elements, the set of attributes, and their description, will of course be dependent upon the design approach adopted and the architectural style that this employs.

At any given point in the design process, the current state of the 'design model' is therefore represented by a matrix. This has a column for each of the elements (which might be subprograms, objects, processes, etc.), and four rows that represent the attributes of each element within one of the viewpoints. Rather than ordering the rows, the superscripts **b**, **f**, **d** and **c** denote the viewpoints (the last of these was denoted by **s** in Budgen (1995)). Similarly, numerical subscripts are used to identify individual design elements.

So, an example of such a matrix, describing n design elements, with full descriptions available for each element, will have a form such as:

$$\begin{pmatrix} D_1^b & D_2^b \ldots D_n^b \\ D_1^f & D_2^f \ldots D_n^f \\ D_1^d & D_2^d \ldots D_n^d \\ D_1^c & D_2^c \ldots D_n^c \end{pmatrix}$$

where the column

$$D_i^b$$
$$D_i^f$$
$$D_i^d$$
$$D_i^c$$

represents the attributes that describe the properties of the ith design element.

Specific design *representations* (for example, a set of STDs) can then be regarded as being projections from the set of attributes that are described along a single row, as in the set:

$$\{D_1^s, D_2^s, \ldots, D_n^s\}$$

Of course, since any one diagram may omit the states of certain elements, not all of these will necessarily be present in such a projection. However, in practice, we will be more interested in columns and matrices than in rows when modelling design processes.

At the beginning of the design process itself, the requirements specification will usually describe the black box properties of the system as though it were a single element. So this can be described as a matrix with one column (and hence no subscripts), as in:

$$\begin{pmatrix} R^b \\ R^f \\ \varnothing^d \\ \varnothing^c \end{pmatrix}$$

Here the empty set symbols $\varnothing^d$ and $\varnothing^c$ are used to indicate that there are no data modelling or constructional attributes present in the specification (which of course may not necessarily be true!).

To conclude this introduction to the basics of the notation, we need to consider how it can be adapted to cope with the abstractions that are created when we employ a hierarchical representation such as the DFD or Statechart form. With one constraint, this can be achieved by only a slight extension, which involves replacing the column in the matrix that is currently representing the ith design element

$$\begin{matrix} D_i^b \\ D_i^f \\ D_i^d \\ D_i^c \end{matrix}$$

by a set of columns that represent the properties of the sub-elements. These are in turn distinguished by using a second index value in the subscript, so that if the ith element were to be replaced by three sub-elements (say), we would now have the columns

$$\begin{matrix} D_{i1}^b & D_{i2}^b & D_{i3}^b \\ D_{i1}^f & D_{i2}^f & D_{i3}^f \\ D_{i1}^d & D_{i2}^d & D_{i3}^d \\ D_{i1}^c & D_{i2}^c & D_{i3}^c \end{matrix}$$

(and of course, there is scope for the reverse when we group a set of elements into a 'super-element').

The only constraint that this imposes (for pragmatic reasons) is that a given abstraction needs to be described in terms of the same set of sub-elements in each of the different viewpoints. In practice this does not create any real problems when describing the practices of design methods, although it does limit our ability to describe some opportunistic design sequences.

9.2.2 Describing design transformations

Since we will be providing examples of these in later sections and chapters, we will only provide a fairly brief description of these here, in order to show how this notation can be deployed.

If we begin with a very global view of the design process as a whole, then we can consider it as consisting of a transformation which takes a requirements specification and produces a complete design description. Using the elements we have already met in the previous section, this can then be expressed as

$$\begin{pmatrix} R^b \\ R^f \\ \varnothing^d \\ \varnothing^c \end{pmatrix} \quad D \rightarrow \quad \begin{pmatrix} D_1^b & D_2^b \dots D_n^b \\ D_1^f & D_2^f \dots D_n^f \\ D_1^d & D_2^d \dots D_n^d \\ D_1^c & D_2^c \dots D_n^c \end{pmatrix}$$

Again though, we should not assume that this use of mathematical formalism implies that the 'design transformation' involved is in some way a mathematical procedure related to matrix algebra. We are simply using it as a convenient shorthand that can help to make explicit the manner in which particular software design methods encourage the designer to develop a design solution.

As discussed earlier, the process parts of procedural design methods generally consist of a sequence of *elaboration* and *transformation* steps, and these will be denoted by the transformation symbols E^i and T^i, where the superscript indicates that this is the ith step of the process. (Use of the general design symbol D will be kept for non-specific steps, such as those arising in opportunistic processes.) To conclude our introduction to the D-Matrix concepts, we therefore examine two very simple examples of elaboration and transformation steps.

In our first example, the designer expands the DFD shown in Figure 9.5(a) into that shown in Figure 9.5(b), by restructuring one of the bubbles into three bubbles. Since we are using our notation to show how such a step is represented in this particular case, we will not be too concerned about the reuse of the index value 3 for a different element, although obviously this would be significant in practice! Assuming that this is the designer's third design 'step', then the step of elaborating Figure 9.5(a) into Figure 9.5(b) will be described in our notation as:

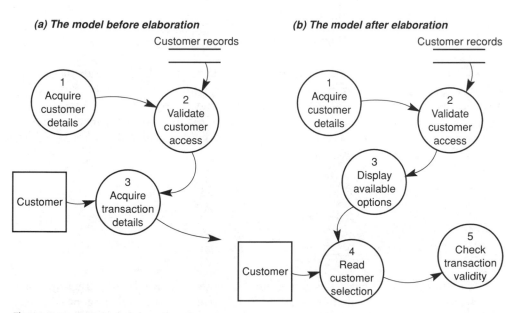

(a) The model before elaboration

(b) The model after elaboration

Figure 9.5 A typical elaboration step.

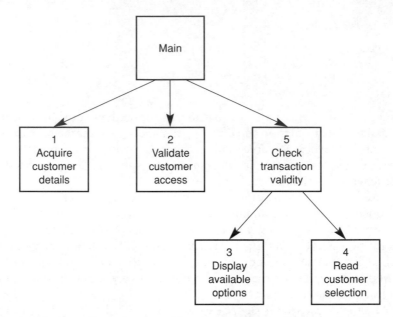

Figure 9.6 A typical transformation step. (Transforming the functional model of Figure 9.5(b) into a constructional viewpoint.)

$$
\begin{pmatrix}
\varnothing_1^b & \varnothing_2^b & \varnothing_3^b \\
D_1^f & D_2^f & D_3^f \\
\varnothing_1^d & \varnothing_2^d & \varnothing_3^d \\
\varnothing_1^c & \varnothing_2^c & \varnothing_3^c
\end{pmatrix}
\; E^3 \rightarrow \;
\begin{pmatrix}
\varnothing_1^b & \varnothing_2^b & 0_3^b & \varnothing_4^b & \varnothing_5^b \\
D_1^f & D_2^f & D_3^f & D_4^f & D_5^f \\
\varnothing_1^d & \varnothing_2^d & \varnothing_3^d & \varnothing_4^d & \varnothing_5^d \\
\varnothing_1^c & \varnothing_2^c & \varnothing_3^c & \varnothing_4^c & \varnothing_5^c
\end{pmatrix}
$$

For our second example, the designer takes the DFD created above and, as their fourth design step, restructures this into a Structure Chart, with each DFD 'bubble' becoming a sub-program unit. This is shown in Figure 9.6, and the transformation step (which involves making decisions about invocation hierarchy and data flow mechanisms) is demonstrated below. Note that the new design model is considered to consist of both the DFD and the Structure Chart.

$$
\begin{pmatrix}
\varnothing_1^b & \varnothing_2^b & \varnothing_3^b & \varnothing_4^b & \varnothing_5^b \\
D_1^f & D_2^f & D_3^f & D_4^f & D_5^f \\
\varnothing_1^d & \varnothing_2^d & \varnothing_3^d & \varnothing_4^d & \varnothing_5^d \\
\varnothing_1^c & \varnothing_2^c & \varnothing_3^c & \varnothing_4^c & \varnothing_5^c
\end{pmatrix}
\; T^4 \rightarrow \;
\begin{pmatrix}
\varnothing_1^b & \varnothing_2^b & \varnothing_3^b & \varnothing_4^b & \varnothing_5^b \\
D_1^f & D_2^f & D_3^f & D_4^f & D_5^f \\
\varnothing_1^d & \varnothing_2^d & \varnothing_3^d & \varnothing_4^d & \varnothing_5^d \\
D_1^c & D_2^c & D_3^c & D_4^c & D_5^c
\end{pmatrix}
$$

While obviously the D-Matrix is rather cumbersome when used with larger and very specific examples, we will mainly be using it to illustrate fairly simple or general design steps such as the two above.

The top-down (decompositional) approach to the design of software has a long pedigree. Most of the earliest programming languages to become widely available, such as assembler and FORTRAN, provided quite powerful mechanisms for describing action-oriented structuring of a program through the use of subprograms, but rarely provided the means of creating and using complex data structures. Given such an emphasis among the implementation forms, a natural design strategy was one in which the main task of a program was subdivided into smaller tasks, with this subdivision being continued until the resultant subtasks were considered sufficiently elemental to be implemented as subprograms. This strategy has been elegantly summarized in a paper by Niklaus Wirth (1971), which suggested practical ways to implement this approach. Wirth used the term 'stepwise refinement' for this strategy; the phrase 'divide and conquer' has also sometimes been used.

In its most basic form, the success of this approach of finding a good solution will be highly dependent on the way in which the original problem is described, since this forms the model that is the basis for the designer's initial choice of subtasks. Indeed, it can be argued that this approach is therefore inherently unstable, in that small differences in the decomposition of a task can lead to solutions that are functionally equivalent, but structurally very different. Figure 9.7 provides just such an example of how we can easily find two ways to decompose a given problem. It may be that these two

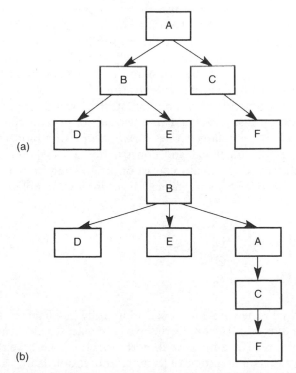

Figure 9.7 Decompositional solutions to a simple problem. (a) Solution 1. (b) Solution 2.

structures will converge following further decomposition, but this cannot be guaranteed by the use of the strategy alone. (We might usefully note here that a D-Matrix description would not distinguish between the two solutions, since its emphasis lies on describing the presence or absence of state information about the design elements, and not the relationships between them. While information about the relationships is part of the detail making up the states of the individual elements, the D-Matrix model does not show this in any explicit way – a limitation of any use of abstraction of course.)

This instability arises because, when following a top-down strategy, the important decisions about basic structures have to be made at the beginning of the design process, so that the effects of any poor decisions will be propagated through the following steps. This in turn may lead to significant problems at a later stage of design, and even to the need to totally redesign a system. When using a top-down strategy, it is particularly important to explore the design options as fully as possible at each stage of decomposition.

The top-down strategy also illustrates one of the characteristic features of the design process itself. When discussing Rittel's definition of a 'wicked problem', we identified one of the characteristics of such a problem as being the lack of a 'stopping rule' that the designer can use to determine that the design process is complete. This feature of the design process is particularly evident in functional decomposition, since there are no generally applicable criteria that can be used to determine how small a task should be to be considered as suitably elemental.

One other consequence of using this strategy that should also be mentioned is the problem of duplication. Because the strategy consists of a sequence of (essentially divergent and disconnected) refinements, there is potential for full or partial duplication of functionality when the low-level operations are defined. The scope for this is, of course, even greater if the design is the responsibility of more than one person. So the use of a refinement process implies the need to explicitly check for, and resolve, any such duplications. Figure 9.8 shows a simple example of how such duplication can easily arise during such a process of decomposition.

We will return to a discussion of how this strategy can be applied in Chapter 11. In terms of the concepts discussed in the first two sections of this chapter, we can view the process involved as being largely one of *elaboration* of a model that is expressed mainly in terms of the functional and constructional viewpoints. So a D-Matrix description of each step will normally consist of progressing from a model with a few elements (columns) to one with many elements, as in, for example

$$\begin{pmatrix} \varnothing_1^b & \varnothing_2^b & \varnothing_3^b \\ D_1^f & D_2^f & D_3^f \\ \varnothing_1^d & \varnothing_2^d & \varnothing_3^d \\ D_1^c & D_2^c & D_3^c \end{pmatrix} E^n \rightarrow \begin{pmatrix} \varnothing_1^b & \varnothing_2^b \ldots \varnothing_n^b \\ D_1^f & D_2^f \ldots D_n^f \\ \varnothing_1^d & \varnothing_2^d \ldots \varnothing_n^d \\ D_1^c & D_2^c \ldots D_n^c \end{pmatrix}$$

and again, we will be reviewing this process more fully in Chapter 11.

Because of its long history and the relative ease with which it can be applied, the top-down strategy has played quite an important role in the development of design methods, and ways of avoiding some of its more undesirable features have been developed and used in the methods that are based upon it. Indeed, even where other design

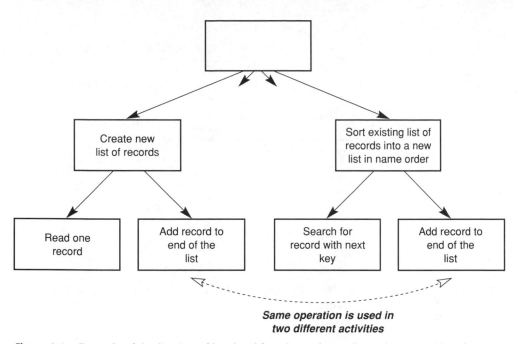

Figure 9.8 Example of duplication of low-level functions when using a decompositional structure.

strategies are to be used for developing a system, it is not uncommon for the initial design steps to consist of a functional decomposition, using a top-down strategy to identify the major functional modules of the system, with the design of these then being elaborated using a quite different strategy.

The SSA/SD (Structured Systems Analysis and Structured Design) method, evolved by Yourdon and coworkers (Page-Jones, 1988; Gane and Sarsen, 1979) is an example of a widely used method based on an enlarged version of this strategy. Chapter 13 will show how the recommended process steps incorporate ways of handling these major criticisms of top-down design. Even in more recently developed methods, such as SSADM (Longworth, 1992), there is still a significant top-down aspect to the process model itself.

9.4 Design by composition

In a top-down strategy for design, the emphasis is heavily focused on identifying the operations that need to be performed by the system. So the model of the problem that results is based almost entirely on consideration of the functional viewpoint, although the refinement of the model may make use of other viewpoints.

The reverse of this approach is to use a compositional strategy for building the designer's model. In this, a model of the problem is constructed by developing descriptions of a set of particular entities or objects that can be recognized in the problem itself, together with a description of the relationships that link these entities. The

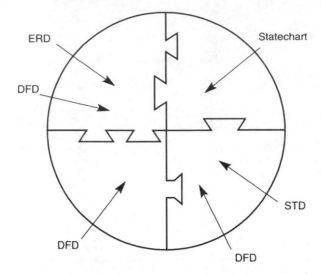

Figure 9.9 The compositional design strategy. An important feature is the design of the interfaces between the elements of the model.

nature of the entities used in the model will vary with the method, as will the viewpoints chosen for describing them. Figure 9.9 shows a schematic view of this strategy.

In a method that uses a compositional strategy, such as JSD (Chapter 15), and the 'object-oriented' approaches (Chapter 16), the relevant entities are normally identified by analysing an initial description of the problem. A complete and detailed model of the solution is then developed by elaborating the descriptions of the entities and the interactions occurring between them. While the type and form of entity and interaction may differ considerably (as indeed they do in the two examples cited above), the overall strategy of composing the design model by grouping elements together is the same.

We can again model these processes using the D-Matrix, but now the process is more likely to be one of grouping columns of the matrix to create new abstractions, as well as elaborating more complex combinations of viewpoints. Indeed, as we will see when we come to examine methods that employ such models, the philosophy behind this strategy tends to result in design processes that are largely sequences of elaboration steps, with any transformations being essentially 'spread out' across a number of steps, rather than forming explicit steps in the process.

JSP (Chapter 14) is another design method that can be regarded as using a compositional strategy. In the case of JSP, however, the model of the problem is created using a data-modelling viewpoint, by assembling a set of descriptions of the structures of the input and output data streams. While these are rather less concrete forms of entity than those used in the two methods referred to above, the basic strategy involved in the design process is still a compositional one.

It is reasonable to consider the process of using a compositional strategy as rather less directly intuitive than the top-down strategy (Vessey and Conger, 1994). However, it can also be argued that this 'intuition' is partly a matter of familiarity, since programmers are generally more experienced with function-oriented (imperative) programming languages, and therefore have acquired greater experience with a function-oriented view of systems. We can therefore expect that this bias can be offset by training in a compositional method, and this view seems to be borne out by experience (Fichman and Kemerer, 1997).

If compositional methods are more complex and less directly intuitive than those methods that are based on a top-down approach, and so perhaps require more discipline in their use, it can be argued that they are also:

- more *stable*, in that their use will tend to lead to similar solutions for a problem, regardless of the user, since the design strategy relates the structure of the solution to the structure of the problem (Détienne, 2002);

- more *even* in terms of the transformation steps involved, with a more gradual progression of design development than is common for top-down methods;

- better able to provide a good *verification* process between the design and the original specification, since there is usually an explicit 'audit trail' between solution objects and problem objects.

A particular benefit of the compositional strategy is that it gives more opportunity for using multiple viewpoints to exploit the use of such important design concepts as modularity and information-hiding (Parnas, 1972) in the structuring of a designer's solution. This arises from the emphasis on 'grouping' that occurs in the elaboration of a design model, with scope to group elements by considering different relations between them, including shared data structures, shared data objects, function, and so on. This is a process that is difficult to achieve (if not impossible) through the use of a top-down strategy.

These points will be examined as part of the descriptions of specific methods given in the following chapters, in order to show how well this view of the compositional strategy is justified.

9.5 Organizational influences upon design

For our purposes, an organizational design method can be considered as one in which the form of the process part of the method is strongly influenced by a set of non-technical factors, arising from the nature and structure of the organization using the method. While these factors do not usually affect the representational part so directly, their influence may still have the effect of extending or formalizing it in some way. To understand the nature of such a method, the rationale that lies behind their adoption and use must be considered.

International agencies, as well as central and local government bodies, are major customers for software-based systems. These range from specialized defence real-time systems to applications for stock control or taxation. Many of these systems are very large; they are difficult to specify; the requirements may change with technology, legislation or internal reorganization; and they may be produced by in-house teams or by outside contracting agencies.

A significant feature of such organizations is that they are highly likely to provide their staff with career structures that are geared to overall organizational needs, and hence are not directly related to project needs. As a result, staff at all levels may be transferred in and out of a project team (and the project management) at times that are determined by factors largely or wholly independent of the state of the project.

The British Civil Service is an example of just such an organization, and it is mirrored by similar bodies in Britain as well as in other countries. During a civil servant's career, he or she may expect to progress through a series of grades, and may well be required to occupy a number of positions for fixed intervals of (say) two or three years. Each transition between grades or posts will therefore occur at an externally determined time, regardless of the state of any software-based project that they might be involved in. While this view is perhaps a little simplified, it does embody the main principles and practices that are used by such organizations.

To help with control of the increasing number of large software-based projects needed in such organizations, there was in the 1980s, continued into the 1990s, a corresponding growth in emphasis upon the use of 'standard' methods for analysis and design. The use of a standard method or strategy within an organization (and preferably beyond it) has a number of benefits:

- there is minimum disruption of a project when staff changes occur;

- a change of project manager should not lead to a change of technical direction;

- standardization of documentation allows for better management of maintenance;

- there is scope for better planning, costing and control of projects, based on the use of past experience, which can be related directly to current practices.

There are, of course, some negative features of such methods to offset these positive ones. Perhaps the major negative aspect is that they tend to be overly bureaucratic, with the attendant risk that creative options may not be adequately explored, and also that the overall technical direction can be lost.

There are a number of methods that can be classified as having an organizational element. These include:

- SSADM (Structured Systems Analysis and Design Method), which has been produced for use with data-processing projects by central and local government agencies in the UK (Longworth, 1992);

- MERISE, which is a French equivalent to SSADM;

- HOOD (Hierarchical Object-Oriented Design), which has been developed on behalf of the European Space Agency for use in designing Ada-based systems;

- MASCOT (Modular Approach to Software Construction, Operation and Test) is intended for use in real-time systems, and originated in the UK defence sector. (Strictly, MASCOT is not a method as we have defined the term, having only a representation part and no well-defined process part.)

These are all examples from Europe, as the development and use of such methods does not seem to have been common practice in the USA, nor elsewhere, as far as can be ascertained.

At a technical level, in terms of the strategies involved in their use, these methods differ quite considerably, according to their domain of application. In that sense, therefore, we can regard the 'organizational' category as being essentially independent of strategy, so that a method can be both top-down and organizational, or compositional and organizational.

Summary

This chapter has provided the basic material needed for the study of a number of design methods in greater detail. In particular, it has outlined the forms of the principal technical strategies that are currently used in software design methods, and has examined some additional ways in which the attributes of a design method can be classified and its processes can be modelled.

From this, it can be seen that the major division in terms of design strategy lies between the

- top-down, or *decompositional* strategy; and the
- *compositional* strategy

and that design methods can further be classified according to whether they consider the effects of

- *organizational* structures and rationale.

Having examined the conditions for classifying software design methods in this manner, the following chapters are concerned with describing and assessing a number of widely used design methods, relating them to these issues in each case.

Further reading

Wirth N. (1971). Program development by stepwise refinement. *Comm. ACM*, **14**(4), 221–7

This can be considered one of the classic papers in the area of software design. It is primarily concerned with the use of the top-down strategy for detailed program design, and is based around a worked example.

Parnas D.L. (1972). On the criteria to be used in decomposing systems into modules. *Comm. ACM*, **15**(12),1053–8

This too is considered a classic paper in terms of its influence on software design (and the design of programming languages). It introduces the concept of information-hiding through the use of a worked example, before proceeding to discuss the consequences of such a strategy for design practices.

Exercises

9.1 Consider the task of designing the organization and layout of the garden for a new house. (For the purpose of this exercise, assume that the space for the garden is a rectangle 20 metres by 25 metres.) How would you set about this task using a top-down strategy, and what would be the criteria to use? (As a suggestion, the first-level decomposition might be into *lawn*, *vegetable plot* and *flower-beds*.) Would a compositional approach be better? If so, why, and how would you expect this to proceed?

9.2 The D-matrix notation can be used to describe the development of a program (since this is detailed design). Here we might consider decisions about the tasks performed by subprograms (procedures, methods) as *functional* design decisions; the choice of the subprograms and any larger packaging units (such as classes) as *constructional* design decisions; and the choice of data structures as *data-modelling* design decisions. (Behaviour doesn't fit quite so well.) When you next write a program, keep a note of the development process and then try to describe this using the D-matrix form. (You may need to group related actions to make this manageable.)

9.3 When anyone moves house, do the removal men organize their work on a top-down basis or a compositional one? What criteria do they use in selecting objects to pack into boxes, and in organizing the packing of the van in a particular order?

9.4 List in order the factors that you think might influence the software design practices that are likely to be used in each of the following organizations:

(a) a large petrochemical company;
(b) a Local Government Authority;
(c) a small (three-person) software developer producing business packages for personal computers.

Why would the order of the common factors be likely to change between these?

Design Patterns

Codifying design experience for reuse by others is not solely embodied in procedural forms such as design methods, and the concept of a design pattern offers an important alternative (and complementary) approach to recording design experience. In this chapter we begin by examining the wider issues of reuse in software design and establish some criteria for a 'template-based' approach to be practicable. We then examine the nature and form of *design patterns* as used for Object-Oriented design, identify some of the implications of their use in terms of design practice, and finally consider how easily the concept can be expanded to use with other architectural styles, and what factors might aid or limit this.

10.1 Design by template and design reuse

In Chapter 6 we examined the principal ways in which a software designer could reuse the experiences of other designers. While design methods have been a widely-adopted and rather dominant mechanism for this, their general-purpose nature makes them unsuitable for giving detailed guidance about the particular form of solution that might be adopted by a designer when faced with a problem having specific characteristics. While the component of a method that we have termed a *heuristic* (sometimes also referred to as a 'cliché') does provide some scope to address the question of how to approach certain well-defined classes of problem, the heuristics for most methods are neither well codified nor even recorded and, even when they do exist, they are still apt to be rather general.

An alternative way to reuse experience of what has worked for others when faced with similar problems is through the concept of some form of 'design template'. Such a template then provides an abstraction of the knowledge that others have acquired about how to structure solutions for a particular type of recurring problem. (A rather more visual example of this from another domain is the development of the arched bridge. Once the basic idea had been established, this model could be adapted and extended to create a whole variety of bridges, large, small, single or multiple arches, etc. Regardless of detailed form, all of these could still be readily recognized as fitting into the 'pattern' of the form of an arched bridge.) However, prior to the development of the **design pattern** concept (Gamma *et al.*, 1995), such templates, when used for software design, were largely informal in nature. They were also relatively few in number, since the basic requirements for developing and using a template are that the problem domain should:

- be very well-identified, well-defined, and tightly constrained; and

- contain a significant number of problems that each need a design solution;

and further that there should be some accepted form of constructional description that could be used for describing the design template. (We can easily see that these conditions are met in the case of the example of the arched bridge: crossing streams is a well-defined need; there are lots of streams needing to be crossed; and it is possible to describe the template by a drawing.) Indeed, one might argue that this last factor has been a, if not *the*, major problem in terms of adapting this concept for use with software. The descriptive forms used with software that we reviewed in Chapter 7 are organized more for describing the details of specific solutions than for portraying their general forms, not least because any diagram still depends quite heavily upon the use of supplementary text.

At the level of detailed program design, the idea of 'solution patterns', often referred to as **idioms**, is fairly well-established (even if still not particularly well codified). At a very basic level of 'coding-as-design', the problem characteristics that determine which form of looping construct a programmer should employ are familiar enough 'templates' to most programmers. (For example, when reading data streams of unknown length, some form of `while` construct is generally advocated. Similarly, when manipulating data structures of known size, allowing for counting, some form of `for` loop is regarded as being the most suitable to employ.) Equally, at a rather more advanced and slightly more abstract level, the basic structure that needs to be employed for interrupt-handling is a recognizable pattern which must then be adapted if it is to be mapped on to both the specific features of a particular processor architecture and the particular device characteristics.

At more abstract levels of design, the one good example of wide reuse of design experience is that of compiler-writing. No-one would now begin to develop a new compiler from scratch by using a general-purpose design method, since the basic rules for the organization of compilers are particularly well understood. (The adoption of such a compiler-writing 'pattern' is further encouraged by the availability of tools to perform such tasks as lexical analysis and parsing, which in turn exist *because* the form of compilers is standard enough to merit putting effort into developing such reusable components.)

In a somewhat different way, window-based user interfaces provide another example of template use, at least in terms of user interface design. Widget sets such as that provided in the `Tk` toolset enable the development of systems that have a visual style that is consistent with other systems, and hence with the user's expectations. In this case, the design template does not consist of the widgets themselves, but rather comprises the conventions that the designer adopts for assigning functionality to particular forms of widget. The user may, for example, expect to have the option of selecting an input file through the use of a *ListBox* widget, which displays a list of candidate files, and here the 'template' is the convention of using such a widget for the task of file selection. (Once again, file selection is a recurring need, it is well defined, and the widget set provides a standard set of constructs that enable the solution to be described.)

All of these examples do tend to place the relevant 'template' in a fairly recognizable context (building bridges, developing user interfaces). However, the somewhat broader concept of a 'pattern' is one that does cut across domains and, in the case of software especially, the fact that it does so provides it with an important element of 'added value'. This point is illustrated in the quotation below, taken from Mellor and Johnson (1997).

> *'People who work with design patterns observe that certain patterns manifest repeatedly across applications, but in different guises. Contention for a resource, for example, appears in hotel reservation systems, and in printer managers.'*

In that sense, the evolution from template to pattern removes the domain-specific constraint, and so the (broad) terminology of architectural style is probably the best way to describe patterns.

In addition, for the idea of the design template/pattern to be effective as a means of sharing experience (rather than facilitating reuse by a single designer), it needs to be supported by some form of 'pattern book' mechanism that can be used to record and describe the template. Here, the invisibility and ill-defined form of software does present something of a problem. So it is perhaps not surprising that the pattern or template concept was not successfully realized in the context of software design until the emergence of an architectural style that was both widely adopted and also sufficiently standardized (at least at the conceptual level) to meet the criteria that we identified at the beginning of this section. In the following sections we will look at the use of design patterns for object-oriented design, consider the consequences of their successes, and finally consider what scope there is for this approach to be adopted for use with other forms of architectural style.

10.2 The design pattern

The concept of the **design pattern** was briefly introduced in Section 6.4, and we begin this section by reminding ourselves of the basic characteristics of the pattern. We then go on to examine the ways in which design patterns can be codified and catalogued within an object-oriented architectural style, and then to look at some examples of their use.

10.2.1 The pattern concept

It is useful to begin by recapping the basic elements that make up a pattern, as described in the original ideas about patterns developed by Christopher Alexander (Alexander *et al.*, 1977):

- the pattern describes a recurring problem;
- it also describes the core of a solution to that problem;
- the solution is one that can be reused many times without actually using it in exactly the same way twice over.

So any form of *pattern description* will need to identify both the characteristics of the problem and the general solution to it. Adaptation of the general solution to meet the specific local need remains a creative task for the designer, much as the programmer who knows which looping construct is best employed for a problem must still decide how best to organize it to fit the specific context of their particular program and its data structures. For our more physical example of the arched bridge, the designer of such a bridge must make local decisions about how they will employ the form for crossing a particular river at a given point. Determining the number of arches to use and their individual spans remains a creative decision, albeit one that is made within the context of a particular pattern. We should also note that in this case particularly, the design 'experience' provided by the pattern is not just through the idea of the arched bridge, but is also contained in the various exemplars of its use that can be found and the knowledge of any difficulties that occurred with constructing these.

The non-physical and invisible qualities of software present some obstacles when we seek to employ the pattern concept. If we employ it at the more detailed level of program design, then recurring problems can be recognized fairly readily (for example, handling interrupts or reading files of data), partly because their context provides a framework that helps with recognition. (Again, for the example of interrupt-handling, this context could be the structures of a particular operating system.) When we seek to employ it on a larger scale then such frameworks are less readily found, as we observed in the preceding section, so it is perhaps not surprising that the 'patterns movement' only developed with the evolution of a widely-adopted architectural style (object orientation), within which such higher-level patterns could be recognised (Gamma *et al.*, 1995).

217

The design pattern

As we noted in Chapter 6, the pattern concept is also one that fits well with some of the observed characteristics of designer behaviour. In Adelson and Soloway (1985), one of the forms of behaviour they recognized in the actions of their subjects was the use of 'labels for plans'. This occurred when a designer recognized that they were encountering a subproblem that they already knew how to address and so 'labelled' it in order to indicate the plan that they would later employ. Such plans could be thought of as rather informal patterns owned by particular designers. Détienne (2002) uses the term **schema** to describe this form of design knowledge, and considers programming expertise to be partly based upon the possession of a set of constructional schemas, which may be further reinforced by a set of domain-specific schemas that map the programming schemas on to certain types of problem.

10.2.2 Describing object-oriented design patterns

In architectural terms, the evolution of the 'object concept' has been one of the major developments of the 1980s and 1990s. While our main discussion of this will be provided in Chapter 16, we have inevitably needed to consider some of its characteristics in earlier chapters, and in this chapter we again adopt the view that only those characteristics of specific relevance to the use of design patterns will be considered here.

In brief, an 'object' can be viewed as being an evolutionary development of the concept of the *abstract data type*, that provides an abstraction of a part-solution that:

- possesses a *state* which is encapsulated within the object;
- exhibits *behaviour* in that it responds to external events;
- possesses an *identity* (there may be more than one object of a given type);

where the inspection/modification of its state can only be achieved through the use of those external *methods* that are provided by the object as its interface to the outside world. Figure 10.1 shows a simple illustration of this idea.

For the purposes of this chapter, the key features of an object are that it provides an *abstraction* of the part-solution, that it incorporates the notion of *encapsulation* of state information, and that it provides externally accessible *methods*. We should note here too that, while the object concept is essentially a constructional solution-centred one, some have argued that many 'real-world' problems can themselves be modelled in terms of 'real-world' objects. Hence one approach to object-oriented design is to identify these real-world objects and develop a solution by providing corresponding implementation objects that model their behaviour. For most purposes, however, the design patterns community has concentrated on describing implementational objects that provide reusable elements of solutions rather than on describing problem objects.

A key text for any student of design patterns is the 1995 book by the 'Gang of Four' (often abbreviated to *GoF* in the patterns literature): Erich Gamma, Richard Helm, Ralph Johnson and John Vlissides. This is not to imply that the development of pattern thinking ended there – for example, while their book provides a catalogue of some 23 design patterns, at the time of writing over 200 patterns have been

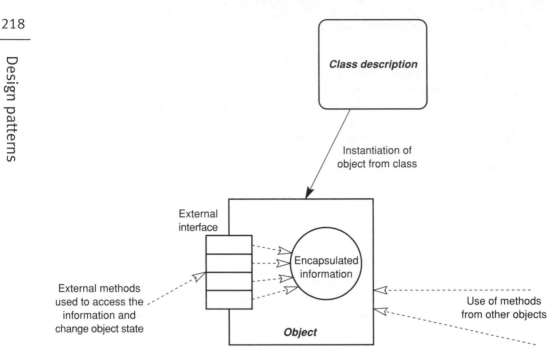

Figure 10.1 A simple illustration of the 'object concept'.

catalogued. However, their book does lay down many of the foundational elements of this approach to design. A rather different, slightly more academically-oriented interpretation of the role of patterns is presented in Buschmann *et al.* (1996). Their view is one which spans a rather wider context from architectural styles to programming idioms, and so provides an interesting and complementary view to that of the *GoF*.

Within a catalogue, design patterns can be classified in various ways. The one adopted by the *GoF* was along two 'axes', which were as follows.

1. Their **purpose**. The purpose describes what a pattern is used for, and is usually described as being one of the following three types:

   ■ *creational* patterns are concerned with object creation;
   ■ *structural* patterns address the way in which classes or objects are composed;
   ■ *behavioural* patterns describe the way that classes or objects interact, and how responsibility is allocated between them.

2. Their **scope**. This describes whether the pattern is primarily one that addresses the use of classes or the use of objects (where we can regard classes as being the 'templates' from which objects are instantiated). Most patterns deal with objects, and we will not attempt to discuss the use of class patterns in this book.

This catalogue structure is shown schematically in Figure 10.2.

In contrast, Buschmann *et al.* (1996) use a framework that is much more concerned with design hierarchy. Whereas the *GoF* focus upon design patterns Buschmann *et al.* takes a wider view of pattern applicability, including for:

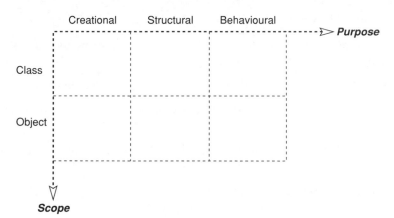

Figure 10.2 Pattern classification scheme used by the 'Gang of Four'.

- *architectural style* (architectural patterns relating to the form of the overall system);
- *design* (design patterns that relate to the detailed form of subsystems);
- *programming* (idioms that describe the broad structure of code).

For the case of design patterns, they adopt a scheme of grouping patterns under the following set of role-based headings.

- *Structural decomposition* where patterns 'support a suitable decomposition of subsystems and complex components into cooperating parts', with the term 'structural' being used in a similar sense as by the *GoF*.
- *Organization of work* which is concerned with component collaboration (a bit like the *GoF*'s concept of 'behaviour').
- *Access control* describes patterns that 'guard and control access to services or components', which we can again recognize as a form of structural grouping.
- *Management* where patterns address the organization of collections of objects (roughly structural again).
- *Communication* which is concerned with (obviously) communication between system components.

We will return to this issue in Section 10.3. For the moment, the main observation from the above is that there is no particular consensus about how to categorize design patterns!

If we now turn to the issue of how the patterns themselves are codified, normal practice is for design patterns to be described using a **pattern description template**. Again, there is no real standard for this, and a comparison of the forms used in Gamma *et al.* (1995) and Buschmann *et al.* (1996) suggests that the following core set of headings provides a fairly good description of a pattern (both of these texts use slightly fuller sets of headings).

- **Name** used to identify and (ideally) describe the essence of the pattern.

- **Also known as** identifies other names (if any) that might be used for the pattern elsewhere (a rather pragmatic touch).

- **Problem** is the design problem that the pattern is intended to address.

- **Solution** is the way that the pattern addresses the problem, and any design principles behind this.

- **Example** (or **Motivation**) provides a real-world illustration of a particular design problem and shows how the pattern addresses this.

- **Applicability** (or **Context**) is a description of the situation in which a pattern might be employed, and includes any hints for recognizing such situations.

- **Structure** provides a detailed description of the solution using graphical notations (usually employed to describe it in terms of both the *behavioural* and the *constructional* viewpoints).

- **Implementation** provides a set of guidelines for implementing the pattern, and notes about any possible pitfalls that might arise.

- **Known uses** is a set of examples to be found in existing systems, ideally taken from more than one domain.

- **Related Patterns** (or **See Also**) identifies any patterns that address similar problems or which complement this one in some way.

- **Consequences** identifies any design trade-offs that might be involved in using the pattern as well as any constraints that its use might impose in terms of system structure or behaviour.

For our purposes, this common subset should be quite adequate especially as, when looking at the following examples of specific patterns, we will be mainly concerned with those headings that relate to the more abstract design issues.

10.2.3 Examples of design patterns

In this subsection we examine two example patterns:

- *Proxy (GoF(207), Bu(263))*

- *Chain of Responsibility (GoF(223))*

(Note that the convention in books such as Gamma *et al.* and Buschmann *et al.* is to identify the page where the description of a given pattern begins. Here we have extended this slightly by using the prefix *GoF* or Bu to indicate which of these two texts is involved.) These two are relatively uncomplicated patterns, and so provide a good basis for illustration of the basic concept, without a need to get ourselves too involved in the subtleties of design pattern use.

The *GoF* classify this pattern as *Object Structural*, whereas under the scheme used in Buschmann *et al.* it is classified as *Access Control*. The core set of headings from Section 10.2.2 can then be used to describe this as follows.

Name	Proxy
Also known as	Surrogate
Problem	Proxy addresses the problem where direct provision of access to an actual object will represent a significant overhead in some form (loading time, space, communication, etc.). As such, the use of proxy may be particularly relevant when developing distributed systems.
Solution	This is to provide a *representative* of the object, and to let the user object communicate with the proxy rather than the real thing. The proxy provides the same interface as the actual object and ensures correct access to this object, while possibly performing additional tasks such as enforcing access protection rules. Where necessary, it may organize the creation and deletion of instances of the 'real' object.
Example	The *GoF* offer the example of a complex image in a word processing document. Rather than incurring the overhead of loading the (potentially) large and complex drawing object to produce an image on the screen, it may be possible to employ a much simpler proxy object that ensures that key properties (such as position and boundaries) are correctly represented in the screen image. So this example of a proxy may just display an outline box to represent the image so that the user may adjust text flow, positioning, etc. However, if further information is needed, or if it is necessary to manipulate the image itself, these can be invoked in the original via the proxy. Buschmann *et al.* offers a rather different example which is based upon optimizing repeated accesses to remote databases to obtain images which may be large and complex. Here, the proxy plays a role which is closer to the concept of a *cache* and, like a cache, it is clearly most effective in situations where the predominant access forms are for reading rather than for updating.
Applicability	Proxy is concerned with access to relatively complex objects which may be in a different space, such as a remote database (**remote proxy**), involve significant overheads in object creation, as with the example of the graphical image (**virtual proxy**), or where different access rights may be involved (**protection proxy**).
Structure	Figure 10.3 illustrates the idea of proxy using a class diagram. Normally, the client requests will be serviced by the proxy, which relays these to the original where necessary. Figure 10.4 demonstrates this role in terms of a sequence diagram that describes one possible way of working.

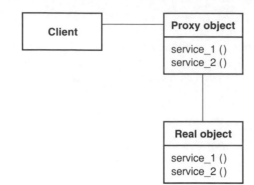

Figure 10.3 The proxy design pattern (class diagram).

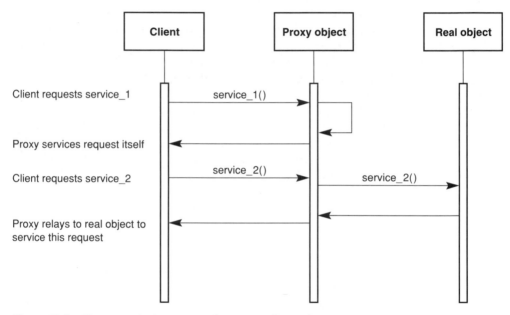

Figure 10.4 The proxy design pattern (sequence diagram).

Implementation	Since this aspect is not directly relevant to the theme of this book, we omit such a detailed level of discussion.
Known Uses	Both the *GoF* and Buschmann *et al.* provide examples here, with the latter being the more extensive and varied and, in particular, relating more strongly to web-based forms of implementation where this pattern is quite widely employed.
Related Patterns	The *Adapter* (*GoF*(139)) and *Decorator* (*GoF*(175)) patterns are both concerned with interfacing issues.
Consequences	There is some discussion of these in both reference texts. Perhaps the most obvious is the correspondence to the use of a cache in a situation where an object is extensively updated. In this context,

the proxy may offer few benefits and even impose a slight over-head. Proxy also adds a level of indirection to object access, which is a design benefit (largely), but may add some implementational overheads.

The *proxy* pattern provides a good example of where the ideas from 'conventional' software merge with those of the 'web' in its various forms. Although there can be different roles for *proxy* (as described under **Applicability**), and some of these may be more relevant to one form than the other, the basic design principle is common to both.

Chain of Responsibility

This pattern is classified by the *GoF* as *Object Behavioural* (it is not discussed in our other reference), and hence offers a somewhat different style of example to that of proxy.

Name	Chain of Responsibility
Also known as	(none)
Problem	Here the problem to be addressed is one of needing to avoid the coupling of a request (event) to a particular receiver, so allowing more than one object the chance to respond to it. (There is some analogy to the idea of 'broadcast' used with networks here.)
Solution	The request is passed along a chain of objects until one of them accepts and handles it.
Example	Windowing systems often contain such a chain. An event corresponding to the pressing of a mouse button may be passed to the window manager, on to the window object, and on to an element in the window (such as a button) until one of them accepts and handles the event.
Applicability	In essence, this pattern is an appropriate one to employ wherever the issuer of a request does not, or need not, know which object is to handle it. (Implementations of object-oriented systems often require that the sender and receiver of a message are bound together early, which is inappropriate for this need.) It may also be the case that the set of possible receivers is only determined dynamically at run-time.
Structure	Figure 10.5 provides an object diagram that describes the structure of Chain of Responsibility. Figure 10.6 provides a sequence diagram describing this (rather inevitably, this is not particularly complex, even though in this case we have made the last handler in the chain respond to the request!).
Implementation	Again, we omit any details of this. However, we should note that implementation does require each object in the chain to share a common interface for handling requests and also for obtaining access to the next element in the chain.

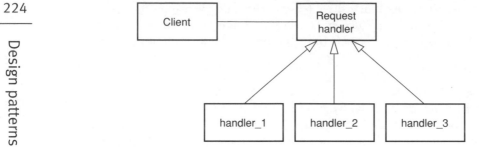

Figure 10.5   The chain of responsibility pattern (class diagram).

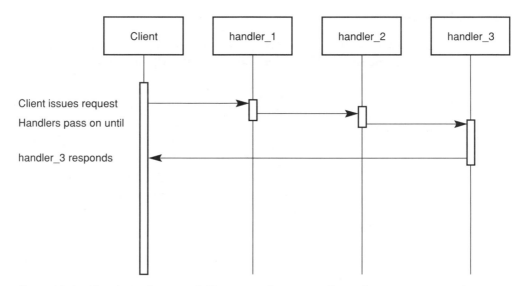

Figure 10.6   The chain of responsibility pattern (sequence diagram).

Known Uses	The *GoF* provide a set of examples of this, mainly from graphical contexts.
Related Patterns	The *Composite* (*GoF*(163)) pattern has been identified as being one that can be used in conjunction with Chain of Responsibility.
Consequences	Chain of Responsibility does reduce the coupling in a system and provides scope for dynamic modification of the chain during system execution. In terms of design consequences, one possible issue to consider is what is to happen if *no* object accepts a request.

Chain of Responsibility offers an interesting contrast to *proxy*, since it is much more concerned with patterns of behaviour than with the way that objects are configured (hence its classification as *behavioural* of course). As such, it illustrates the way that patterns may take quite different forms, and so leads on into the topic of how we can use patterns when designing software. Before that though, we briefly digress to examine the complementary concept of the design anti-pattern.

Thinking about software reuse (as exemplified by the concept of the design pattern) understandably tends to focus upon how we can find ways to reuse *good* experiences. But of course, it is sometimes important that we should also promulgate experiences of unsuccessful attempts at design solutions too, if only to ensure that others avoid the same pitfalls. So, not surprisingly, although much less well codified than the concept of the design pattern, this has led to the concept of the **design anti-pattern**.

As described in Long (2001), design anti-patterns are 'obvious, but wrong, solutions to recurring problems'. In a very readable, if rather tongue-in-cheek, paper John Long provides a number of examples of this concept, largely focusing on the processes involved. Indeed, the anti-patterns literature does tend to put more emphasis upon the *reasons* why wrong solutions are adopted, rather than on the forms of the wrong solutions themselves (Brown *et al.*, 1998).

This emphasis is quite understandable, since technical solutions are rarely completely wrong in themselves, although a given solution may be the wrong one to adopt in a particular context. So, while the literature on design patterns emphasizes solution structures, although recognizing the influence of context and motivation, the anti-patterns literature chiefly emphasizes motivation.

For our purposes, the main message here is that *reuse* (a concept which underpins the whole rationale for patterns) is not automatically a 'good thing'. While reuse of experience, especially where it concerns workable solutions, represents desirable practice, it does always occur within a larger context which may itself act to increase or reduce the benefits. We will return to some of these issues when we later come to examine component-based design practices.

10.3 Designing with patterns

Having established just what a design pattern is, and examined examples of how they are structured and organized, the next obvious question is 'how do we use design patterns to solve design problems?'. In this section we examine such guidance as is available, and consider one of the consequences of pattern use, which is how these are most effectively indexed.

10.3.1 How to use patterns

Books that describe design patterns, such as Gamma *et al.* (1995) and Buschmann *et al.* (1996) very much function as **catalogues** of design patterns. In the early chapters which looked at the wider context of software design, we observed that catalogues are more common in other domains and uncommon for software design, where most of the literature addresses design processes. Unfortunately, much as a garden catalogue full of glorious colour photographs of healthy, thriving plants provides little real aid to the task of planning a new garden, beyond telling us which plants like shade and how tall the various varieties (may) grow, so it is with design patterns. Possession of the catalogue provides a source of ideas, it provides information that helps with planning and with anticipating any possible consequences, but the design task of working out how to produce a particular plan of action is still a creative activity. (Actually, the analogy with gardening is not a bad one, since gardens do evolve and exhibit *behaviour*, even if over longer periods than we commonly employ when thinking about software. Trees grow and shade new sections of the garden, some plants take time to become established, but then take over adjacent sections, etc. Like the software designer, the gardener's planning requires them to envisage some future state, while having inadequate control of both the conditions and the quality of the materials that will determine the exact form that it takes.)

How then do we use catalogues of design patterns? Well, the *GoF* advice is very much along the lines that patterns need to be *learned*, and that by studying patterns, the designer will acquire both insight into why the pattern works, and also a familiarity with it that will enable he or she to recognize those situations where it can be used to effect. They also advise the designer to follow the two principles of:

- *programming to an interface, not an implementation* so that a client object need not be aware of the actual object that is used to service a particular request, as long as its form and behaviour adhere to the interface specification;

- *favouring object composition over class inheritance*, which is not to deny the usefulness of inheritance as a reuse mechanism, but rather to observe that it should not be over-used.

From this, we can recognize that the minimum conditions for the successful use of patterns will require that the designer should:

- acquire a 'vocabulary' of design patterns;
- be able to recognize where a pattern would provide a suitable solution;
- have an understanding of how to employ the pattern within the particular solution.

While indexing and cataloguing of patterns forms a useful and important step towards the first of these goals, finding ways to support the other two is rather more problematical, although provision of case studies of pattern use may be helpful.

The authors in Buschmann *et al.* (1996) advocate a rather different strategy, although the basic conditions for pattern use are the same as those specified above. They argue in favour of classifying a given problem in the same way that the patterns themselves are classified, as a step towards identifying the set of potentially useful patterns. (One thing in favour of their suggested scheme of classification is that it appears more suited to supporting such a process than that adopted by the *GoF*.) Their basic process can then be summarized as follows.

1. Specify the problem (and, if possible, any subproblems involved).

2. Select the category of pattern that is appropriate to the design activity involved (*architectural* or *design* patterns).

3. Select the problem category appropriate to the problem.

4. Compare the problem description with the available set of patterns taken from the selected category.

5. Compare benefits and liabilities (assess the design trade-offs).

6. Select the pattern variant that most fits the problem.

(There is a seventh step too, which is essentially an iterative recycling of the previous steps should no match be found to any existing patterns.)

Since their categorization structure includes architectural styles as well as design patterns and idioms, the above process is potentially one that could be employed from top-level down to detailed program design. This is illustrated in Figure 10.7. We might also note that it implies use of a top-down strategy, which is perhaps unexpected, given that patterns are essentially a compositional concept.

Of course, we should not assume that there is always going to be a suitable pattern when using such a process. Indeed, trying to force all problems into a 'pattern framework' is likely to produce exactly the opposite of what is intended. So step 5 in the above process is an important one, where the designer may well need to recognize that there is no 'ready-made' pattern for a given problem.

Finally, of course, the more 'implementational' guidelines advocated by the *GoF* are still applicable when using this strategy.

10.3.2 Indexing and classifying patterns

The concept of patterns carries within it a self-limiting aspect that is clearly difficult to overcome. This is the problem that, as more patterns are identified and added to the corpus of pattern knowledge, so the ability of the individual designer to *learn* all of these becomes strained. The only way to address this is to index patterns in some way, so that a design process similar to the one outlined above can be adopted.

Unfortunately, as already demonstrated, there is (at the time of writing) no widely agreed scheme for indexing patterns. There are also no empirical studies into the use of design patterns that might assist with establishing the most effective ways of indexing patterns for ease of use (rather than ease of cataloguing). In the absence of such knowledge, we can only say that of the two schemes examined in this chapter, the one of Buschmann *et al.* would seem to provide better support for the design process itself.

10.4 Patterns in the wider design context

The enthusiasm of the pattern community, and the attractive nature of the concept (which appeals to experience in related areas of design), has led to considerable interest in seeking new design patterns. Indeed, it can be argued that the enthusiasm for *writing* new patterns has acted to expose two weaknesses in the 'pattern concept', namely:

■ the difficulty of *indexing* patterns in any consistent way; and

■ the lack of any well-established practices for *using* patterns during the design process.

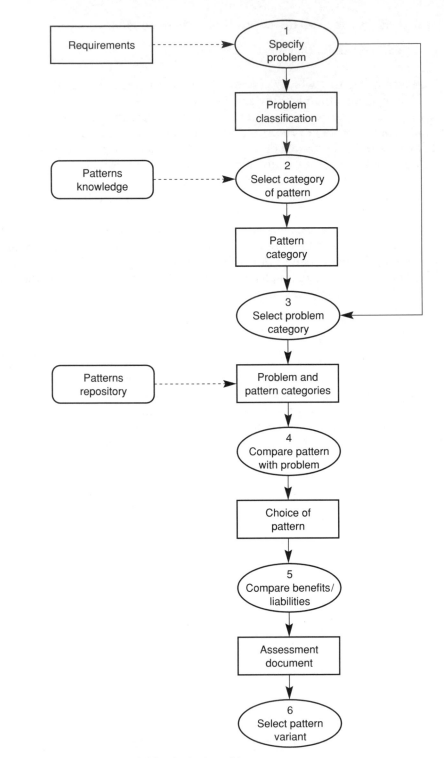

Figure 10.7 A process model for designing with patterns.

Neither of these weaknesses invalidates the concept, but they do raise the question of how useful it is to have an ever-increasing stock of patterns.

Although there are many books about patterns (including books that cover quite specialized areas), there has been little to date in the way of systematic empirical evaluation of the effectiveness of the pattern concept.* The one such study that has been conducted (Prechelt *et al.*, 2001) is overall one that is supportive of the idea that the use of patterns can often result in designs that are more easily maintained and modified. Given the frequency with which the need for modification arises in software development, the added *flexibility* which comes from using a pattern seems to more than offset the greater complexity that tends to result from using a pattern rather than an optimized structure. Indeed, this trade-off between flexibility and the complexity that arises from generality is one that clearly needs to be explored more fully.

So, patterns are clearly a useful addition to the designer's vocabulary and skill-set. Indeed, it can be argued that even if patterns are not widely employed in practice (possibly because of the trade-offs referred to in the previous paragraph), simply studying them will itself encourage the development of clearer thinking about design, and will convey some of the benefits of experience.

In that sense too, design patterns are no more a 'silver bullet' than are design methods, or any other systematic design practice. It would be as naive to expect that we can design entirely by using patterns as it would be to expect that the use of design methods will *always* lead to good designs. The act of designing software requires a wide vocabulary of ideas and techniques, and the pattern concept is clearly one of these.

One last question that we need to consider is how widely the pattern concept can be applied across different architectural styles. Much of the basic development has been centred upon the object-oriented style (which, equally, is one that has proved particularly intractable for the use of procedural forms for design methods (Budgen, 1999)). However, there is no particular argument that suggests that this is in some way the 'only' architectural style; simply this is the one where the need has been greatest. Indeed, while looking at the pattern repositories available on the web tends to reveal a preponderance of patterns for object-oriented design, there is a growing set of design patterns that are used within other styles or, at least, with forms of implementation that are not particularly centred around objects. From this, we can perhaps conclude that the pattern concept is applicable across different architectural styles, but that it is only likely that pattern repositories will develop where there is a community that is sufficiently motivated to share ideas by writing patterns.

Summary

Our discussion of the use of the *design pattern* as a means of transferring knowledge about design experiences has examined both the concept and also its application, along with two examples as (rather outline) illustration. We have also briefly considered the wider applicability of the pattern idea, beyond its use simply within the object-oriented architectural style.

---

* In fairness, this is by no means a problem that is specific to design patterns and their use. Few widely-used software engineering practices can be said to have been subjected to any effective empirical evaluation.

The patterns community is an enthusiastic, if often rather evangelical, one. That said, while writing *new* patterns is perhaps understandably a more interesting task than developing better ways of *using* patterns, it is sometimes hard to avoid the feeling that a 'write-only' mentality prevails rather too much! To really become useful, there still seems to be a need to explore and evaluate the most effective ways to index and classify patterns. So, while the pattern concept is undoubtedly a valuable addition to the software designer's repertoire, the process for *using* patterns to solve problems may benefit from further refinement and development.

Further reading

The information available about patterns is quite extensive, but also rather mixed in terms of quality and quantity. There are various websites that are devoted to patterns, with the *Patterns Home Page* at http://hillside.net/patterns being probably the best starting point. This site lists a wide range of information, including pattern repositories, books, papers and tutorials.

The patterns literature is very book-centred (maybe this should not be entirely surprising, since the books are often themselves catalogues of patterns), and to date there are very few tutorial papers or papers that report experiences of pattern use. The January 1997 issue of *IEEE Software* contains a number of papers on patterns, including a rather reflective one by James Coplien (Coplien, 1997).

Exercises

10.1 In what other spheres of design activity can you readily recognise the use of patterns? Identify the benefits and limitations that result from their use.

10.2 How might *chain of responsibility* be used in a system where an input positional event may originate with a mouse, a keyboard or a touch-screen. How might the handlers for these be prioritised?

10.3 Suggest how the *proxy* pattern might be used in a web-based client-server system that provides a web mail service, and identify the elements that might benefit most from its use. Would these be sufficient to make it worthwhile?

Design Practices

Stepwise Refinement

Historically, this can be regarded as the first form of 'design method' to be used for software design on any scale. Although much of its importance lies in its influence upon the form and strategy employed in many later methods, its universality has also meant that it has been used widely for software development, and so it does merit a short chapter in its own right. We review both its role and form, and consider some of the consequences that arise from its use.

11.1 The historical role of stepwise refinement

Since the early days of computing, the designer of software has been faced with the need to address complex problems using a medium that is enormously powerful and flexible, and yet is also ill-defined in terms of the way in which its detailed form is organized. As already observed, the subprogram (whether termed a subroutine, procedure, function or method . . .) has probably formed the most important mechanism for providing structural organization in many programming languages. Indeed, it has long been the norm for computer hardware to support this by providing special instructions for the transfer and restoration of control.

So it is not surprising that some of the first ideas about how the characteristics of software could be abstracted, in order to aid thinking about its structure, were largely concerned with finding ways of mapping the overall program functionality on to a set of subprograms. In a pioneering paper, as already mentioned in Chapter 9, Niklaus Wirth (1971) addressed the question of *how* such a mapping could be created through a process of gradual decomposition of the problem into smaller problems (usually termed **stepwise refinement**).

In this approach, a top-down 'process of successive refinement of specifications' led to 'the decomposition of tasks into sub-tasks and of data into data structures'. The latter phrase is significant, since Wirth sought to consider how both function and data could be structured within the same process, although subsequent thinking would appear to have placed much more emphasis upon the question of function. This may be partly because in his example solution to the classical *eight-queens problem,*[*] the refinement of ideas about data representations was performed at a relatively late stage in the process. Indeed, Wirth argued that, because it could be difficult to foresee the operations on the data that might eventually be needed, it was 'advisable to delay decisions about data representation as long as possible'. (That said, his discussion about the data structures occupies quite a large segment of the paper.)

In the conclusion of Wirth (1971), five lessons about this process were identified, and these can be paraphrased as follows.

1. Program construction consists of a sequence of *refinement steps*, in each of which a task is divided into a number of subtasks, accompanied where appropriate by a further refinement of any data structures involved. In other words, and using the notation introduced in Chapter 9, the process of stepwise refinement consists of a set of *elaboration* steps, of the form shown below (where $n > m$ and where the later stages will also contain some details of the elements D_i^c that describe how the functional elements are to be mapped on to constructional ones).

$$
\begin{pmatrix}
\varnothing_1^b & \varnothing_2^b \ldots \varnothing_m^b \\
D_1^f & D_2^f \ldots D_m^f \\
D_1^d & D_2^d \ldots D_m^d \\
\varnothing_1^c & \varnothing_2^c \ldots \varnothing_m^c
\end{pmatrix}
E^i \rightarrow
\begin{pmatrix}
\varnothing_1^b & \varnothing_2^b \ldots \varnothing_n^b \\
D_1^f & D_2^f \ldots D_n^f \\
D_1^d & D_2^d \ldots D_n^d \\
\varnothing_1^c & \varnothing_2^c \ldots \varnothing_n^c
\end{pmatrix}
$$

---

[*] This problem is attributed to C.F. Gauss, and can be stated as follows: Given are an 8×8 chessboard and 8 queens which are hostile to each other. Find a position for each queen (a configuration) such that no queen may be taken by any other queen (i.e. such that every row, column, and diagonal contains at most one queen).

2. The degree of *modularity* resulting from this process will determine the ease with which a program can be adapted to meet changes in the requirement or context. Although this idea is demonstrated in the paper, the changes illustrated are very much extensions of the functionality involved in the original problem and, indeed, the ideas about *information hiding* that were subsequently presented in Parnas (1972) provide a much more coherent strategy for determining the choice of modular structure.

3. The need for a *notation* that relates to the problem in hand. In Wirth's paper this was an Algol-like extension, since his example was relatively close to the programming level. The later development of such ideas as the *Structure Chart* (Section 7.3.1), and indeed of many other diagrammatical notations, reflect this particular lesson.

4. Each refinement embodies a set of *design decisions* that are based upon specific criteria. This lesson reflects the recognition that designing is not an analytical process, and that there is a need to assess (and re-assess) the influences of a range of factors at each design step.

5. The last lesson is an interesting one in terms of books such as this one, and observes the difficulty of describing even such a relatively small problem without needing to create a 'long story' for the purpose.

While this paper is undoubtedly a seminal one, it can be argued that, although centred upon the concept of modularity, it provided no criteria that a designer could employ for comparing possible choices of modules at any stage (Shapiro, 1997).

The ideas about such criteria put forward by David Parnas in the following year (1972) were somewhat in conflict with the ideas of stepwise refinement, since the key axiom was that information about how a module performed a task should be kept concealed! However, the idea of module **coupling** introduced in Myers (1973), and later used as one of the foundations in the more developed design thinking involved in the 'structured design' school (Stevens *et al.*, 1974), did provide criteria that could be used with the process of stepwise refinement.

Myers argued that the 'primary goal in designing a modular program should be to decompose the program in such a way that the modules are highly independent from one another'. He advocated the use of 'strong modules', which performed a single, well-defined function (essentially describing what later became known as *functional cohesion*), and examined some of the ways in which coupling between modules could arise. Since these issues were reviewed in Chapter 4, we will not repeat them here.

The role of stepwise refinement as a foundational element of the highly influential 'structured design' school (in which issues of *scale* were addressed more effectively) means that interest in developing it in its own right largely faded out in the mid-1970s. Since then though, it has still continued to be used in various roles, and often as a primary technique used to decompose a top-level task into more manageable units. Some of the consequences of this role are examined in Section 11.3.

11.2 Architectural consequences

The strategy and processes of any design method implicitly assume one or more forms of 'target' architectural style – which is not to say that human ingenuity cannot adapt

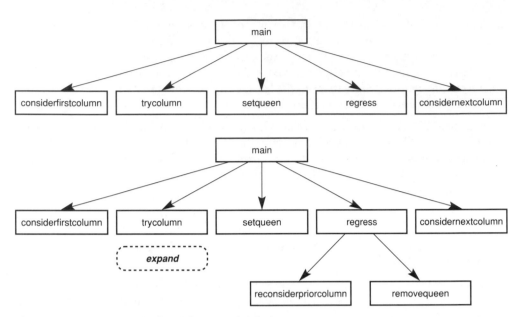

Figure 11.1 Two steps in the eight-queens solution.

this as and when necessary! In the case of stepwise refinement, a **call-and-return** architectural style is implicitly assumed through the emphasis placed upon function as the primary basis for making design decisions. Figure 11.1 illustrates this using Wirth's own solution to the eight-queens problem, and shows (as an informal 'call graph' style of Structure Chart) the effects of one of his design transformations.

The first step has established an algorithm that uses five operations: considerfirstcolumn, trycolumn, setqueen, regress, and considernextcolumn. Then in the following step he has done two things:

- expanded the detail for trycolumn, although no new operations are invoked by this; and

- expanded the detail for regress, which now makes use of two further operations, reconsiderpriorcolumn and removequeen.

(The detailed reasoning behind choosing to expand these particular operations at this stage is explained in the paper.)

While a hierarchical process such as stepwise refinement is readily associated with a hierarchical constructional form such as the subprogram, the link is by no means an essential one. Indeed, if we consider the rather different interpretation of hierarchy used by Michael Jackson in his Structure Diagram notation (Section 7.2.5), then here, the only nodes of interest are those at the ends of the branches, with inner nodes being simply abstractions of these.

Indeed, where the higher level units in a call-and-return style of solution have roles that involve little more than co-ordinating and sequencing the lower units, it may well be worth considering the use of a **pipe-and-filter** architectural style. We can see this if

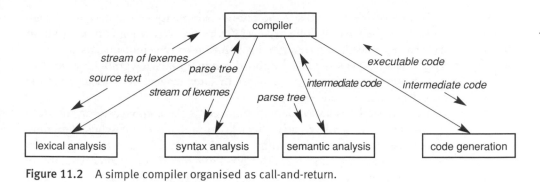

Figure 11.2 A simple compiler organised as call-and-return.

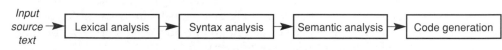

Figure 11.3 A simple compiler organised as pipe-and-filter.

we consider the traditional model of a compiler. Figure 11.2 shows a (rather simple) model of a compiler, expressed in a call-and-return style. In this, the functionality is strongly partitioned into the lower units, with the main body doing little more than sequencing these, so that the more traditional pipe-and-filter format shown in Figure 11.3 is clearly quite a practical alternative to employ.

The choice between such forms of solution may depend upon many factors. One of these is the data design and data access issues. (Indeed, Shaw and Garlan (1996) argue that, due to the incorporation of such features as shared symbol tables and attributed parse trees, modern compilers employ an architectural style that is intermediate between the pipe-and-filter and data-centred repository styles.) One of the benefits of a pipe-and-filter solution is that it may be better able to incorporate such ideas as information hiding. This highlights one of the problems of call-and-return, which is that, when using this style, knowledge about data is not easily confined within particular elements.

However, since the elements of a pipe-and-filter solution may well themselves be constructed using a call-and-return style, we can regard this as further reinforcing the above argument that both of these styles are compatible with the use of stepwise refinement! In such a case, all that differs is the implementational mappings that are used for different levels of the process. High-level refinement steps lead to identification of the filter processes, and then lower-level refinement steps, applied to each of these processes in turn, structure them using subprograms.

11.3 Strengths and weaknesses of the stepwise strategy

Perhaps it is inevitable that, in a book of this form, we are likely to be more interested in identifying the weaknesses of particular design practices than the strengths, not least because the advocates of methods provide plentiful arguments for the latter. However, before examining the limitations of stepwise refinement, we should at least briefly review its strengths.

Undoubtedly one of the strengths is the relative simplicity of the design process, although even that can be partially illusory, as Wirth observed when commenting on the 'long story' that was needed to describe his solution to the eight-queens problem. Indeed, although the emphasis is placed upon the functional viewpoint, the need to consider the data modelling viewpoint, at least in later stages, does mean that the simplicity of the process is indeed relative.

A second strength, perhaps less widely recognized, is the emphasis upon the *stepwise* nature of the process. While creative 'leaps' can and do occur when designing software, the stepwise process which favours a gradual development has its benefits too. In particular, it encourages an orderly development of ideas and (if suitably documented) a means of managing backtracking in a controlled manner. An important element of this is to accept (as Wirth did) that backtracking is a normal feature of any design process. (This aspect of design is rarely given much emphasis in design textbooks, not least because case studies of design are already 'long stories' and adding episodes of backtracking makes them even longer!)

Turning now to the issue of weaknesses, we begin by reminding ourselves of the limiting characteristics of a top-down strategy that were identified in Chapter 9. These included:

- the *instability* that can arise from making key decisions at early stages (which to some extent is countered in stepwise refinement by its emphasis upon the ability to backtrack, providing that the process is managed adequately);
- the *lack of a stopping rule* which, although inconvenient, does not render the process invalid in any way; and
- the problem of *duplication* of lower-level units.

The last of these relates to the issue of *scalability*, which Wirth did not try to address in his 1971 paper. (His chosen problem was also relatively small and particularly well-specified.)

Duplication of functionality is only one aspect of scalability. A related issue is the way that the data is employed in large systems. Zahniser (1988) argues that where 'resident data' is involved (as opposed to 'transient data' or 'control data'), then the complexity of data access and manipulation can lead to further duplication and complexity, requiring a more data-centred approach to design.

Perhaps the main conclusion from this section is that stepwise refinement, while it is an eminently practical strategy, is most effectively employed on a limited scale (often as an initial design phase), and on problems that are not data-centric in nature. In the next chapter we see how some of the benefits of stepwise progression can be realized using larger and more self-contained process steps.

Summary

Stepwise refinement has been examined as a design strategy in its own right. From this we can see that, while applicable within a limited range of problem size (and with well-specified problems that are strongly functional in their emphasis), it becomes less satisfactory for larger problems and for those that involve more than a minor element of data modelling.

Further reading

Wirth N. (1971). Program development by stepwise refinement. *Comm. ACM*, **14**(4), 221–227

An eminently clear and lucid paper that, among other things, is particularly useful for its narrative form. Each design step, together with the reasoning behind it, is clearly explained.

Exercises

11.1 How well is stepwise refinement suited for use in designing systems that are to be realised through media other than 'traditional' forms of software? In particular, how would it be suited to the design of:

a) motor cars
b) hi-fi systems
c) web-based e-commerce systems

Explain why you think it would or would not work for each of these.

11.2 Use of a *call-and-return* architectural style can lead to the use of 'global data structures'. For any programming language of your choice, consider what mechanisms are provided in the language to avoid the need for this.

chapter 12

Incremental Design

| 12.1 Black box to white box in stages | 12.2 Prototyping |
| | 12.3 An example – DSDM |

In a book such as this, where software design activities form the principal object of study, it is easy to develop a rather compartmentalized view of design activities and of the context within which they are performed. This chapter considers how design activities are organized within a more dynamic context, where they need to be interleaved with other developmental tasks, and where they may be constrained by having only limited time available for completion. In such a context, the control of design activities becomes of paramount importance. Indeed, when we examine an example of a design method that supports this style of development, we find that its main elements are those concerned with the organization of the processes involved.

12.1 Black box to white box in stages

In some ways, this chapter can be considered as representing something of an 'aside' when it is viewed from the context of the design practices that form the dominant theme of the preceding and following chapters. Yet it deals with an important issue and, indeed, highlights some of the underlying assumptions adopted in many of our approaches to the task of designing software.

The title of this section (which, as we will demonstrate, is probably not very accurate) emphasizes the key tenet of incremental development through the term 'in stages'. Implicit in almost all procedural approaches to software design is the idea that we begin with some form of 'requirements specification' that is agreed with the customer and which then forms the basis for developing a black box model, and eventually from this a white box model that conforms to that specification.

In practice, it is widely recognized that this is a rather unrealistic situation, although it is one that is often necessitated by contractual or other factors. There are situations where a very comprehensive and inclusive requirements specification can be provided at the start of development, but these are relatively uncommon. In addition, over the period needed for the development of any sizeable software system, the requirements may evolve or even change dramatically, for both technical and organizational reasons. So, the development of any design solution is very likely to involve some degree of interaction with the customer throughout the design process. The difference this then highlights is between conventional procedural design approaches, which try to minimize the perturbations that this creates for the design solution, and incremental approaches, which seek to incorporate this interaction as a fully-fledged element of the design process and so control and manage its effects.

Incremental development is often termed **Rapid Application Development**, or **RAD**, and the approaches used for RAD are sometimes termed **Agile Methods**, with the development practices of *Extreme Programming*, or XP, representing the 'outer limits' of such approaches (Boehm, 2002). In terms of the philosophy that underpins Agile Methods, Boehm suggests that they favour:

- individuals and interactions over processes and tools;

- working software over comprehensive documentation;

- customer collaboration over contract negotiation;

- responding to change over following a plan.

Of course, taken to the extreme, both Agile Methods and procedural development practices can be abused and misused. The agile approach can degenerate into unstructured 'hacking' of code, while the procedural approach can become bureaucratic and document-bound. However, an awareness of the strengths and limitations of both forms should be a part of any software developer's knowledge-set, along with an appreciation of how they are best (and least-suitably) deployed.

In Chapter 3 we identified some reasons why an incremental development process might be adopted, which included situations where:

- there may be a need to demonstrate that an idea is feasible;

- it may be necessary or even essential, for business purposes, to establish a market position as rapidly as possible;

- the 'customer' may wish to establish whether a market exists for a product before committing to large-scale investment.

Underlying all of these is the concept of *risk*, whether it be a risk that a given solution is not feasible; one of missing out on a market opportunity; or that no real market may actually exist. Risk is also an important element in Boehm's *spiral model* (Boehm, 1988) that was shown in Figure 3.2, and in which risk evaluation forms a key activity which needs to be performed at each step of development. Incremental development processes effectively assume a lifecycle model of this form, rather than the more linear 'waterfall' forms that tend to be implicitly embodied in procedural design methods.

The adoption of an incremental development process is therefore likely to be favoured in those situations where an organization needs to maintain its position in volatile and rapidly-changing markets, and where minimizing time-to-market is a particularly important constraint. (This applies whether the software is itself being marketed or whether, as is more likely, it is being used to market an organization's services or products.) Such organizations are sometimes characterized as being **emergent** in nature. An emergent organization can be defined as one that is 'in a state of continual process change, never arriving, always in transition' (Truex *et al.*, 1999), and hence is one where continual change is regarded as being a 'normal' state of the business context. While the internet-centred 'dot com' organizations are often seen as being of this form and, indeed, many may be so, a more extensive domain of this form is probably that of those organizations dealing in financial markets of any type, where new services may need to be introduced rapidly in order to meet legislative or other changes. If the organization is continually re-shaping itself to meet new business opportunities, then any software used to support the business will need to evolve in parallel with the business itself.

From the designer's point of view, we can identify two major technical reasons why an incremental design approach might be adopted.

1. To develop the 'black box' model for the system, in a situation where the purpose of the eventual system may need to be explored with the customer. (This is less likely to be a situation where the customer doesn't know what they want, than one where they don't know what is really feasible, especially if there are severe time constraints on implementation.) Such a role corresponds roughly to the idea of *exploratory prototyping* that was discussed in Section 3.3, where this was described as 'enhancing the information that is provided from the requirements analysis and functional specification activities', with the distinction that here we are to some extent undertaking the second of these tasks.

2. To develop a working solution (white box) within a set of resource constraints. Time is probably the most likely form of resource constraint although, where new developments are concerned, an organization may be unwilling to invest heavily in terms of staff effort until convinced of the likely benefits. Here, the key need may

well be to deliver a solution on time, even with some elements of functionality missing or curtailed.

For the rest of this chapter we are largely concerned with the second of these roles for incremental development, since this is more in keeping with our emphasis upon studying design activities. It is also more in keeping with the notion of the emergent organization, where there is no real likelihood or expectation of ever creating a 'final' system, since such organizations are characterized by a 'continuous redevelopment perspective' (Truex *et al.*, 1999).

Moving on to the design process itself, our first observation is that the use of an incremental design approach is not closely tied to any particular design strategy or architectural style. This is not to say that architectural style is not important. Achieving the goal of 'continuous change' requires an overall framework which enables extensive use of 'plug-and-play' extensions to a system, a theme that we will return to in Chapter 17. Indeed, an important technical factor is to recognize that a system is being designed for change, and to facilitate this as far as possible. Maintaining the 'separation of concerns' needed for plug-and-play is more a matter of attention to detailed design, rather than one that is affected by the choice of a specific architectural style. Where the use of an incremental approach to design does affect the act of designing is in the way that the design process needs to be organized in order to provide the degree of control necessary to meet the constraints. Section 3.3 looks at this issue more closely where we study a particular approach to incremental design.

Last, but certainly not least, alongside the evaluation of risk, and planning for change, we can regard the issue of *control* as being a key distinguishing feature of an incremental approach. By its nature, incremental development provides more 'degrees of freedom' than is usual, and so the need to organize the design process so as to maintain control of it within this more unconstrained context becomes an important task.

Since the role of the individual tends to be emphasized in this type of development, one question that it raises is whether agile approaches require the employment of 'premium people' (in the sense of people whose skills are in short supply) to lead a development team (Boehm, 2002). As Boehm observes on this issue: 'agile methods derive much of their agility by relying on the tacit knowledge embodied in the team, rather than writing the knowledge down in plans.' Certainly the availability of individuals with appropriate skills does need to be one of the risk factors to be considered when deciding whether to adopt such an approach.

Incremental design is an approach that is less commonly encountered in conventional forms of engineering design. As a technique it is unlikely to find much favour with civil engineers ('after we have built the central span of the bridge, we'll work out how to construct the approaches'), any more than with their chemical or electrical counterparts. This is not to argue that it is not a valid engineering approach, given adequate planning and control, but rather that it is an approach which only makes sense when used with a medium such as software, and within the type of dynamically changing context often met in software-based business use and in the emergent organizations that such software makes possible.

One issue that can easily become blurred where incremental development is employed is the distinction between design and implementation. Indeed, this was touched upon in Chapter 3 when we discussed the use of prototypes. Certainly, an

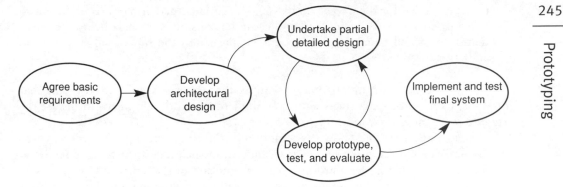

Figure 12.1 Profile of an incremental design process.

incremental approach is likely to involve some interleaving of design stages with implementation. However, the design stages are likely to be 'detailed design' activities, occurring with a context established by a set of overall architectural design decisions that are made before the incremental phases begin. Figure 12.1 illustrates this point and, indeed, when we examine the form of DSDM in Section 12.3, we will see that its organization broadly conforms to this type of structure. This then leads us on to the topic of the next section, where we examine the issue of prototyping more fully.

12.2 Prototyping

In Chapter 3 we examined Floyd's classification of the reasons why prototyping might be employed in software development (Floyd, 1984). To recap these briefly, the three roles she identified were as follows.

■ *Evolutionary*. This is the form closest to our idea of 'incremental development' of a system. The software for a system is adapted gradually, by changing the requirements step by step as these become clearer with use, and changing the system to fit them. In this form, prototyping is used to develop a product and the prototype gradually evolves into the end product.

■ *Experimental*. This role is distinguished by the use of the prototype for evaluating a possible *solution* to a problem, by developing it in advance of large-scale implementation. The reasons for doing this may be manifold, including the assessment of performance and resource needs, evaluation of the effectiveness of a particular form of user interface, assessment of an algorithm and so on. This form of prototype is essentially intended to be a 'throw-away' item, and might well be implemented in a quite different form to that which will be used for the final system itself.

■ *Exploratory*. In this role a prototype is used to help with clarification of user requirements and possibly with identifying how introducing the system might lead to the need to modify the wider work practices of an organization. One purpose might be to help with developing an analysis of users' needs by providing a set of possible models for them to use and assess. Essentially this form of prototype is also likely to be a 'throw-away' item, and it can be considered as enhancing the information provided from the requirements analysis and the functional specification activities.

For the purposes of this chapter, we can see that the two roles of prototyping that are most likely to be extensively employed in incremental development forms are the *evolutionary* and the *exploratory*.

The evolutionary role fits with the notion of the emergent organization that was briefly described in the preceding section. Indeed, in such a context there is really no notion of there being an 'end product', only the notion of the 'current state' of a system. Each new state of the system is then achieved by modifying a previous state (not necessarily the 'current state'), or even by creating a completely new implementation. So in a context where the incremental design process is continuous and on-going, the development of software may closely approximate to a continuous process of evolutionary prototyping.

One of the characteristics of incremental design is that it usually involves some degree of interaction with the 'customer' (or with 'end-users', who may or may not be the customer.) Here we can see a role for the exploratory prototype, which may address anything from very specific aspects of some element of a system through to the functionality or behaviour of the complete system.

Of course a prototype need not actually be an item of software, especially where such aspects as possible scenarios for the use of a system are being considered. Indeed, prototypes are commonly used quite extensively in the design of human-interactive systems, and the forms employed may include such forms as mock-ups of the layout or format of user interfaces, intended simply to gauge responses from eventual users (Preece *et al.*, 2002).

At a very abstract level, one of the prototyping forms sometimes used in system design is the notion of the **story-board**. Design reviews, both with other team members and with end-users, form an important element of incremental design, and the story-board is a useful means of conveying ideas about system behaviour without needing to get into technical detail. An example of this idea is shown in Figure 12.2. We can regard the story-board as a form of 'design execution' mechanism, and hence as a high-level prototype. It also has the benefit of avoiding one of the hazards of prototyping identified earlier, in that it cannot be delivered as the eventual product!

An intermediate level of prototype is one provided by using a more formal notation than that of the story-board. Executable diagrammatical forms such as Petri Net Graphs (Birrell and Ould, 1985; Stevens, 1991) and Statecharts (Harel and Gery, 1997) can provide powerful mechanisms for modelling system states and transitions between these. The use of such semantically well-defined forms is not only able to provide a valuable prototyping mechanism in itself, but also, with suitable tools support, can result in the automatic generation of outline code in implementation languages such as Java and C++.

At a lower level, prototypes can be built with a variety of tools, depending upon their purpose. Scripting languages such as Visual Basic, tcl/tk and perl or perl/tk are some popular mechanisms for building exploratory prototypes, especially where the user interface is an important element of a system. As always with software, one

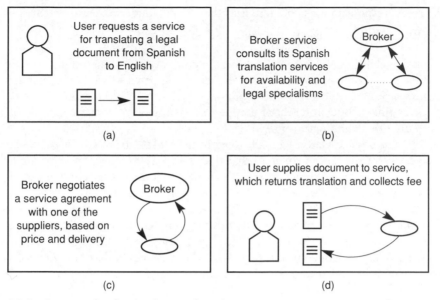

Figure 12.2 An example of a simple story-board.

person's implementation language is another person's prototyping tool, and so the list is really an endless one.

So having examined some of the reasons why an incremental design approach may be the appropriate one to adopt, and then briefly considered some of the mechanisms for organizing the feedback needed for incremental design, we now need to consider how the process might be structured. In the next section we examine an example of one approach to RAD, in the shape of the DSDM method.

12.3 An example – DSDM

In this section we examine an example of how a 'design method' that is based around an RAD strategy is structured. The method that we will examine is the **Dynamic Systems Development Method**, generally known as DSDM. This originated in 1994, and is managed by the 'not-for-profit' UK-based DSDM Consortium (the associated trademark has a reversed second 'D' character), which is mainly made up of representatives from the business community. At the time of writing, following a typical process of evolution, the 'current' version of the DSDM method is 4.1.

DSDM is quite unlike any of the other design methods that we examine in this book. It is almost entirely concerned with managing and controlling the RAD process, and makes no assumptions about design strategy, notations or any of the other classical 'method features'. This is not to say that these issues are ignored in the DSDM design process, simply that DSDM makes no assumptions about their particular form. Indeed, throughout the DSDM lifecycle, there are two distinctive elements that emerge very strongly:

■ the roles, responsibilities and activities that *people* undertake and perform;

■ the effect of *business* needs upon design decisions.

As much as such things can be placed in neat compartments, these factors mean that DSDM as a method can be considered as belonging in what we sometimes term the *Information Systems* category. This is not to say that it would never be used by (say) software engineers but, in terms of emphasis, it is far more concerned with business issues than with technological ones.

In the rest of this section we seek to examine DSDM from two aspects. The first of these concerns the set of *principles* that underpin DSDM, since these principles provide the rationale for its particular structure and practices. The second aspect that we examine is the DSDM development cycle, which is where these principles are interpreted to create its particular approach to systems development. We should also note that the DSDM practices are concerned with the complete development life-cycle, from establishing requirements through to planning maintenance although, as usual in this book, we will chiefly concern ourselves with those elements that are concerned with the roles generally described under the headings of 'analysis and design'.

12.3.1 The DSDM principles

DSDM is based around nine principles, which are invoked as necessary in order to decide on the way that the development process should be structured. In brief, these are as follows.

1. *Active user involvement is imperative.* As mentioned above, DSDM has a very strong 'people' element and users are seen as being active participants in the development process. Two examples of very specific user roles encouraged in DSDM are the *ambassador*, who 'guides the developers in their activities to ensure that the solution being developed will accurately meet the needs of the business'; and the *advisor*, who is tasked with representing a particular user view (which might stem from marketing issues, the IT operational support, etc.).

2. *DSDM teams must be empowered to make decisions.* This can be seen as being partially a corollary of the previous principle. For active user involvement to work effectively, it is essential to avoid the need for frequent consultation with higher-level management.

3. *The focus is on frequent delivery of products.* The DSDM process is based upon favouring a product-focused view over an activity-focused one. There is also an emphasis upon allocating short periods of time for performing various activities. (We should also note that the resulting products can be interim design documents, as well as prototypes or executable code.)

4. *Fitness for business purpose is the essential criterion for acceptance of deliverables.* DSDM places the main emphasis upon 'delivering the necessary functionality at the required time'. In that sense, it again takes a very different approach to those employed in the methods discussed in the following chapters, where issues of structure are also considered as important criteria. The DSDM view is that, once the functionality has been established, the solution can be re-engineered as necessary.

5. *Iterative and incremental development is necessary to converge on an accurate business solution.* While iteration is a normal element in any development process, it is not always easy to incorporate this into an organization's procurement procedures. DSDM, however, explicitly makes this an expectation, with the aim of achieving continuous improvement in the system through its use.

6. *All changes during development are reversible.* Basically this means that configuration control is an essential and all-pervasive element of the DSDM development context. As and when necessary, it should always be possible to backtrack to reuse an earlier version as the basis for the next incremental step in development.

7. *Requirements are baselined at a high level.* In contrast to 'traditional' approaches, where the documentation of system requirements may occupy several volumes of very detailed specification, the DSDM approach is to freeze the requirements at a high level, but allow more detailed aspects to evolve as necessary.

8. *Testing is integrated throughout the lifecycle.* Rather than being a separate 'end of project' activity (as implied in the waterfall model) user acceptance testing of only partially-complete software proceeds throughout the development process.

9. *A collaborative and co-operative approach between all stakeholders is essential.* The main concern here is to involve stakeholders, implying that change control procedures should be kept as 'light' as possible, so that short-term redirection of a project can be achieved through a shared understanding, rather than as the outcome of an adversarial conflict between developers and users.

Enumerating these principles does reinforce the earlier point that the focus of attention in DSDM is really upon business aims and people. Before going on to see how the principles are embodied in the process, we need to examine two other aspects of the 'DSDM philosophy', both of which form important concepts for the method.

The first of these is the importance of *time* in the process. In a more conventional approach to software development, the functionality that the system is intended to provide is fixed, and the time and resources that are needed to achieve this are varied as necessary. In the DSDM approach this emphasis is inverted, the time and resources are fixed, and the deliverable functionality is allowed to change. Figure 12.3 illustrates this difference.

This distinction is an important one. While, in principle, all of these attributes (which ought really to include *quality* too) can be regarded as being variable parameters of the development process needed for a system, the need to *manage* this process generally requires that one or more of them be fixed. Since a key element of most design methods is that they develop models of system functionality at an early stage, understandably they seek to fix this parameter, while regarding delivery time as a variable. In contrast, the DSDM processes are geared around working to a set of fixed time intervals, and the deliverable functionality is regarded as being a variable element.

Obviously this philosophy is one that very much constrains the set of domains for which a RAD approach such as this can most effectively be employed. No-one would advocate DSDM as the most suitable strategy for producing avionics software ('we didn't have time to complete the module which allows the aircraft's landing gear to be lowered, but go ahead with the test flight anyway'). On the other hand, within a

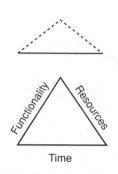
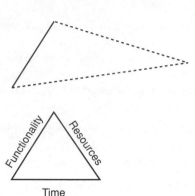
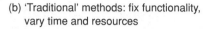

(a) DSDM: Fix time and resources,
vary the functionality delivered

(b) 'Traditional' methods: fix functionality,
vary time and resources

Figure 12.3   Varying the design constraints (time, functionality and resources)

context where (say) gaining a marketplace advantage by getting a new financial service out first is the all-important consideration, then some limitations in the initial facility might be acceptable. (The latter is a bit simplistic of course, the degree of functionality available for an early release still has to be acceptable to supplier and end-user, but DSDM does consider such factors quite explicitly when deciding when a release can be made, as we explain below.)

An important concept in DSDM is that of **timeboxing**. This is a process 'by which defined objectives are reached at a pre-determined and immovable date through continuous prioritisation and flexing of requirements using the *MoSCoW* rules' (DSDM Consortium, 1999). (Note that timeboxing is a process, rather than an object of some form although, of course, DSDM does then refer to individual 'timeboxes'!) In essence, the role of timeboxing is to maintain project control and to ensure that a project team has a clear focus and deadline at any point in time. It is also the mechanism used to control the fixed-time aspect of RAD development by providing the means of determining the acceptable degree of functionality for an increment. This last aspect is the role of the MoSCoW rules, which provide the second key element of DSDM philosophy that we examine here.

The **MoSCoW** rules provide a mechanism for prioritization within DSDM activities. If a deliverable (in whatever form) is to be produced by the due date (within the timebox), then the requirements need to be prioritized to ensure that the essential work is completed, and that only less critical elements are omitted. The rules therefore describe the following four categories of priority.

- *Must have* is the category that includes those requirements that are fundamental to the system, such that it will be unusable if they are not met. This category effectively identifies the minimum usable subset of system functionality.

- *Should have* describes important requirements which would be mandatory if more time were available, but for which some degree of workaround can be achieved in the short term.

- *Could have* is the category of requirement which can be safely left out of the current deliverable. In other words, features which are nice to have, but are not essential for the functioning of the system.

- *Want to have but won't have this time* is the category that forms the 'waiting list' of requirements that can be addressed in the future.

Of course, the assignment of requirements to categories can be quite a difficult process and, again, this is where the emphasis that DSDM places upon a collaborative approach to development is important. Users who insist that all *their* requirements are (by definition) in the 'must have' category are unlikely to prove useful members of a development team!

Returning briefly to the use of these rules within timeboxing, we can also see that this is something that can be employed at various levels of the development process, which will include:

- at the 'top' level, to establish the date for final system delivery and the set of overall requirements that will be met at that point;

- within project cycles, to set an end date for a particular increment and to define the related deliverables;

- within individual project activities such as workshops, or prototype development, to set deadlines for these and to specify their objectives.

From this, we can also see that timeboxing will operate in a hierarchical fashion, with smaller timeboxes within larger ones. However, it can be argued that the really key use of timeboxing is to provide control of the prototyping activities that occur within the different phases of the development process, and we now move on to examine these.

12.3.2 The DSDM process

Having discussed the ideas that underpin the organization of DSDM's particular approach to RAD, we now go on to examine how the process is itself structured. (We do not have space to discuss any details of its management, and for those aspects the reader is advised to consult the DSDM literature described at the end of this chapter.)

The DSDM process is generally described as being a *framework*, and in that sense it is less prescriptive than the processes that we will examine in the next few chapters. (For that reason, coupled with the absence of a specific design strategy, we have not attempted to model this process using the D-matrix notation.)

The basic framework incorporates five development phases, that can be summarized as follows.

1. The *Feasibility Study* assesses whether DSDM is a suitable approach to use on a given project.

2. The *Business Study* looks at how the business processes of the organization are (or will be) affected by the project and prioritizes the requirements accordingly.

3. The *Functional Model Iteration* can be considered as developing the 'black box' model of the system.

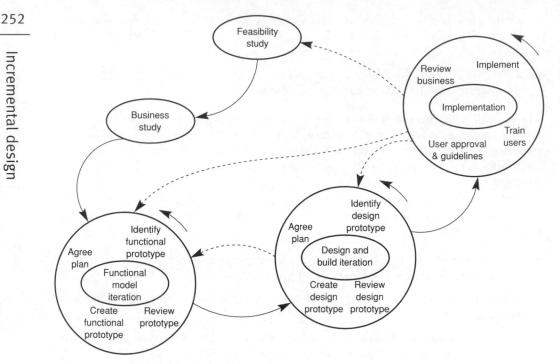

Figure 12.4   The DSDM development process.

4. The *Design and Build Iteration* provides a mix of 'white box' solutions and proto-typed elements.

5. Finally, the *Implementation* phase provides the final deliverables, which will include user training and evaluation.

Figure 12.4 illustrates the way in which these are organized and interact. From this, we can see that the first two phases effectively form a sequence, while each of the following phases is seen as being individually iterative in form. While in principle these three make a sequence, the form of DSDM makes it possible for them also to form a larger cycle of iteration.

In the rest of this section we expand briefly on the activities that each phase incorporates, and identify where some of the key design decisions are made.

Feasibility Study

This is concerned with examining both the nature of the problem and the practicality of using the DSDM approach to meet its needs. The DSDM literature places considerable emphasis upon keeping this phase short, on the quite reasonable basis that RAD approaches such as DSDM are intended for use in developing systems that are needed urgently.

The Feasibility Study is expected to deliver a (short) **Feasibility Report**, together with an **Outline Plan** for development, giving more detail to the arguments of the report. Optionally, it may also be appropriate to develop a **Feasibility Prototype**, which can be regarded as exploratory in nature, and which provides a demonstration that a solution is possible. Indeed, this prototype need not be software; it could be a story-board (as described in the previous section) or take other forms.

Business Study

Again, this is expected to be of short duration, for the same reasons as were given for the Feasibility Study. This element is strongly collaborative, since it needs considerable input from staff who possess knowledge about the organization and how its working will be affected by the project. A vehicle for identifying and agreeing business needs that is particularly favoured by the DSDM process is the **Facilitated Workshop**, bringing together developers and users.

The outcomes from this phase are important, and include the first elements of what we can consider to be design decisions. The four key outcomes in the form of deliverables from this phase are:

- The *Business Area Definition* document, which is rather similar to the Feasibility Report.

- A *Prioritized Requirements List*, developed by using the MoSCoW rules.

- A *Development Plan*.

- The *System Architecture Definition*. Since this document identifies both the architectural style to be employed and also the main elements, this phase can be regarded as incorporating the architectural design step of the method. The developers are also encouraged to look for scope to reuse existing components as a part of this activity.

So, at the end of this phase, the initial design framework should be established and, as a consequence, related decisions about the development platform and development tools should also have been made. While, like everything else, these are changeable, clearly alterations to them are likely to have fairly significant effects.

Functional Model Iteration

As described above, this essentially encompasses the 'black box' activities that aim to describe what the system is to do within the given business context. So the emphasis of this phase is on modelling the business needs, but without going into detail about non-functional aspects such as security and performance.

The main outputs from this phase are models (which may include models in the form of class diagrams, or data models using one of the data-modelling forms) and prototypes (termed **Functional Prototypes**), that will be more or less complete in terms of user interface, with basic levels of functionality too.

Design and Build Iteration

This is the completion phase of DSDM, with a strong emphasis upon testing incorporated within it. The main output produced is still classified as being a prototype, although it may well incorporate the key functionality of the system. For our purposes, this is where the detailed design decisions are likely to be made, and so the output can be considered as being a 'white box' model, although this is also likely to contain more elements of an implementation than is normal with other design approaches.

Implementation

As always with RAD, the distinctions between this step and the previous one can be rather difficult to identify, which is where a strong process management element is important in such a method. In many ways, this phase is more one of getting the increment into productive use, including any training and documentation needs. Again, it is considered important that these latter tasks, especially training, are collaborative in nature, so as to ensure that any training is appropriate to need.

12.3.3 DSDM in retrospect

As with all chapters that describe methods, we can only describe the essential features of DSDM in the space available in this book. However, based upon that, we can see a number of areas where the features of DSDM are particularly distinctive when compared to more 'traditional' approaches to design. These include the emphasis upon management and control (essential in a RAD context); the strong emphasis upon user involvement throughout the process; the fixing of delivery time and varying of functionality (timeboxing); the non-prescriptive view of architectural style; and the extensive use of prototyping (this last aspect is covered in much more detail in the DSDM literature than we have been able to do here).

In some ways, the characteristics of the target domains where DSDM is likely to be effective are also quite well defined. The close attention to business processes means that it is more likely to be used for projects within individual organizations than for producing 'shrink-wrap' solutions; the emphasis upon shortening 'time to market' that runs throughout its processes and techniques can offer much to organizations that face rapidly-changing market-places and hence which need to ensure the availability of new systems; and there is also a strong emphasis upon making a system accessible to end-users, in whatever form this might be appropriate.

All of these make DSDM a rather interesting subject of study, both as a method that provides a degree of formality for incremental development, and also as one in which prototyping plays so important a role.

Summary

Incremental systems development offers the opportunity to address software development needs that cannot be fully itemized or identified when development begins. Indeed, as we have seen, for *emergent* organizations, the continual need to reinvent the business means that its system requirements are likely to be in a continual state of change (arguably, a further characteristic of a 'wicked problem'). However, retaining control of what is effectively an opportunistic development process does then require a well-structured approach to the design task, in order that the development process does not degenerate into 'hacking', and so that it continues to provide a good fit to the business needs.

The example of the DSDM method that has been examined in this chapter illustrates the above issues well. The DSDM practices put considerable emphasis upon user involvement (see Barrow and Mayhew (2000) below) and, perhaps even more important, upon user commitment. The focus upon providing solutions within a fixed time interval is also very relevant to these issues. In contrast, DSDM is not prescriptive about technical issues such as architectural style or notations, leaving these to be adapted to the needs of a particular problem. Significantly too, the first phase of DSDM is a feasibility study, intended partly to determine whether or not a given project is a suitable candidate for using the DSDM approach!

As observed at the beginning of the chapter, the material in this chapter is rather different from that of the preceding and following chapters, not least in its focus upon management of processes rather than technical decision-making. Such management is an important part of designing, although what particularly differentiates the material of this chapter is its predominance in this type of design approach.

Further reading

Boehm B.W. (2002). Get ready for Agile Methods, with Care. *IEEE Computer*, 35(1), 64–69

This short and very readable article looks at and contrasts the approaches employed in agile methods and those used in procedural methods (which the author terms 'plan-based'). Highly readable, and provides a very useful context for anyone considering the use of agile methods.

http://www.dsdm.org

The website maintained by the DSDM consortium. Provides information about DSDM activities and literature, including educational support material which may be of interest for anyone wanting to learn more about DSDM.

Barrow P.D.M. and Mayhew P.J. (2000). Investigating principles of stakeholder evaluation in a modern IS development approach. *J. of Systems & Software*, 52(2/3), 95–103

This paper reports the results of a survey intended to examine the effectiveness of user participation in the DSDM process. While the results are supportive of the idea that the DSDM method encourages stakeholders to become involved, it also illustrates the diversity of practice that can occur in the use of DSDM.

Stapleton J. (1997). *DSDM: Dynamic Systems Development Method*. Addison-Wesley

The only textbook on DSDM available at time of writing. While covering an earlier version of the method than the one addressed here, much of the key material is largely unchanged, especially in terms of philosophy and overall structure.

Exercises

12.1 Write down a list of points *for* and *against* using an incremental development approach for developing the following systems.

(a) A web-based system that will provide on-line access to the facilities of a Bank. The Bank's customers will be able to transfer funds between their accounts, set up and cancel instructions for standing (annual, monthly or weekly) payments and purchase services from the Bank, such as foreign currency. The Bank is concerned that its existing system is too dated, and that failure to provide an upgrade is causing it to lose customers.

(b) A system for providing access to a digital library which contains a large set of digital images of specialist photographs. These will be used only within the organization, and across its internal network, so access does not need to be web-based. Important needs are for rapid delivery of digital or paper copies of images and for rapid searches of the index using a variety of search strategies.

(c) A system that will be embedded in mobile telephones to provide access to 'local' information, which will be linked to the geographical location of the user when this is requested. Key needs are to keep the size of the system small and to provide rapid access to the information. It is intended that the phone company's customers will be able to download the system to their phones from the company's website.

12.2 For each of the systems outlined in question 12.1 above, identify where *evolutionary*, *experimental* and *exploratory* prototyping might be usefully employed.

12.3 Taking each of the DSDM principles described in Section 12.3.1 in turn, consider how this might be interpreted for each of the systems described in question 12.1 above.

12.4 Student projects often use an incremental approach to development. Why is this so, and would employing a 'formal' structure such as DSDM be helpful?

Structured Systems Analysis and Structured Design

SSA/SD, the design method examined in this chapter, is one that has evolved over a relatively long period of time, and also during a period when thinking about software design was in a rapid state of evolution. Partly because of this, and also because it has been extended in a number of ways, this method draws upon a wide range of viewpoints, and has been applied across a wide range of application domains.

In its original form at least, the underlying design strategy can be considered as adapting the basic ideas used in stepwise refinement (Chapter 11) for use with larger-scale problems. However, many other influences have helped to shape its approach, and indeed, one of the hardest choices in a book such as this is to decide just which form can be considered as the core one!

So in this chapter, the aim is to identify the main design themes and philosophies, and to describe these within our general framework, rather than to attempt to identify or classify all of the variations.

13.1 Origins, development and philosophy

Although this method for software design was developed at much the same time as the JSP method described in the next chapter, there are extensive differences between them, both in origins and strategy. In particular, SSA/SD provides an example of a significantly broader approach than that of JSP to the activities involved in software design. This contrast is of especial interest given the very wide use that has been made of both methods.

A number of people have been closely identified with developing the various forms of SSA/SD over the years. Much of the foundation for this approach to thinking about the structuring of programs and design was developed by Larry Constantine and Ed Yourdon, in association with their coworkers at IBM (Stevens *et al.*, 1974; Yourdon and Constantine, 1979). A further name that has been closely associated with the development of the analysis component of SSA/SD is that of Tom De Marco.

As a byproduct of this evolutionary development, there is a spectrum of variations in the details of the method. It is widely termed 'structured analysis and design', but to avoid confusion with other methods (the word 'structured' has been used rather liberally by method designers – presumably because of its positive connotations), throughout this book the longer description preferred by some users will be employed. The variations in the detailed form of the method and notation, and its evolution over the years, have also resulted in a range of textbooks that describe its use (for example, Gane and Sarsen, 1979; Page-Jones, 1988; Connor, 1985), but for the descriptions in this chapter the forms that are described by Meilir Page-Jones (1988) will be used.

As a design method, this one is really a composite of two separate but related techniques. The first is Structured Systems Analysis, which is concerned with the modelling of problem-related features of a system (often termed 'analysis'), making use of a set of descriptive forms that can also be used for architectural design. The second is Structured Design, which in turn is oriented towards the solution-related aspects (detailed design). Some texts concentrate almost entirely on the analysis stages alone (for example, De Marco, 1978), while others combine descriptions of the two in their presentation (for example, Page-Jones, 1988).

The earlier forms of the SSA/SD design process essentially made use of a refinement of the top-down strategy for design, with the choices that are usually involved in the functional decomposition process being moderated and constrained by considerations of information flow and, to a lesser degree, of data structure. Subsequent variations adopted a more compositional approach to the analysis stages, based upon such techniques as event partitioning (Avison and Fitzgerald, 1995). Still later developments have sought to combine the techniques of the method with object-oriented ideas of design (Henderson-Sellers and Constantine, 1991). However, this latter development apart, the evolution of this method effectively came to an end in the late 1980s.

To some degree this decline of interest in further development reflected both the emergence of the object-oriented model as a major architectural style, and also the ever-increasing size of software systems. Whichever strategy is employed, the SSA/SD processes are essentially geared towards developing a design solution that uses a *call-and-return* architectural style based upon main program/subprograms; this is neither very compatible with object-oriented forms, nor is its 'monolithic' form as attractive when considering the structures of very large systems.

None of these points detracts significantly from its importance as a topic for study. As a method it remains highly usable and particularly well documented, and it is also one that has influenced many later developments. So within this chapter we will continue to regard this method as employing a largely top-down philosophy and will confine our examples to this 'core' form.

The basic problem domain assumed for this method (and hence that which is normally assumed by most textbooks) is that of data processing. However, the basic strategy seems to be capable of quite wide application, and it has been extended in a number of different ways, mostly intended to enhance its usefulness for the real-time problem domain (Hatley and Pirbhai, 1988; Ward and Mellor, 1985; Ward, 1986; Gomaa, 1986).

Because of this background in the domain of data processing, most of the textbooks describing the method concern themselves with problems that involve the use of only a single sequential process for their solution. However, this is not a restriction imposed by the method, apart from the design transformation stages of the Structured Design process, and certainly Structured Systems Analysis is well able to cope with problems that involve concurrent processing of information.

13.2 Representation forms for SSA/SD

All of the many variants of this method make extensive use of two of the forms of diagrammatical representation encountered in Chapter 7. The Structured Systems Analysis techniques are centred on the use of the Data-Flow Diagram, or DFD (described in Section 7.2.1), while the Structured Design process makes use of the Structure Chart that was described in Section 7.3.1.

13.2.1 Representations for Structured Systems Analysis

DFDs provide a problem-oriented and functional viewpoint that does not involve making any assumptions about 'hierarchy' (in the sense that all bubbles on the diagram are 'equal'). The techniques of Structured Systems Analysis guide the designer (or 'analyst') in building a model of the problem by using DFDs, elaborating this where necessary by using child DFDs in order to provide the necessary levels of detail. (This process of elaboration is rather confusingly termed 'levelling' of the DFD.) Figure 13.1 shows a simple example of a DFD, which we previously encountered as Figure 7.2.

The functional viewpoint provided through the use of DFDs can be augmented by means of more detailed descriptions in the form of 'process specifications', or 'P-Specs' (sometimes termed 'mini-specs'). A **P-Spec** is a textual description of the primitive process that is represented by a bubble in a DFD, and so can be regarded as a subsidiary functional viewpoint. A typical P-Spec will summarize the process in terms of its title, a description of the input/output data flow relating to the process, and the procedural tasks that it performs, couched in terms of the basic concepts of sequence, selection and iteration. An example of a simple P-Spec and its form is shown in Figure 13.2.

A **data dictionary** can also be used to record the information content of data flows. This typically includes descriptions of all of the data forms that are mentioned in the DFDs, P-Specs and any other forms of description that might be used. The initial

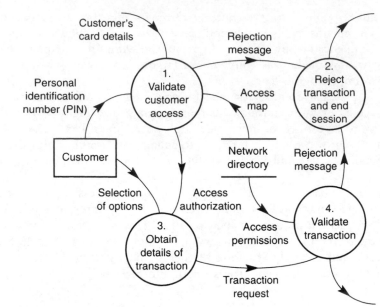

Figure 13.1 Example of a top-level DFD.

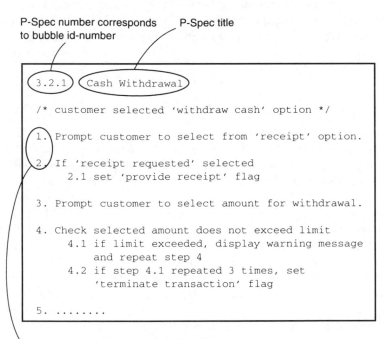

Figure 13.2 A simple example of a P-Spec (mini-spec).

Conventions

For clarity, the use of the following operators is helpful:

= means 'is' or 'is equivalent to'

+ means AND

[ ] means either/OR, so that one of the enclosed options will be selected

{ } means the components inside the braces are iterated

( ) means that the component is optional

A graphical equivalent is the Jackson Structure Diagram (Section 7.2.5).

Examples

customer-id = bank code + sort code + account number

transaction-req = customer-id + [withdraw I withdraw with receipt I
account-summary I new chequebook req]
+ (withdrawal-amount)

account-summary = account number + {transaction log entries}
+ current total

Figure 13.3   Conventions for use with, and examples of, data dictionary entries.

description provided by the data dictionary should be highly abstract, and should not focus upon physical format (Page-Jones, 1988). (While the term 'data dictionary' may sound rather grand, it simply takes the form of a list of the data components, with their structure being described in a suitably abstract manner, as demonstrated in the example of Figure 13.3.)

A later evolution in design practice has been to encourage the analyst to develop a set of Entity–Relationship Diagrams (ERDs) as a means of modelling the relationships between the data elements in a problem and determining their attributes in a suitably systematic manner. This data-modelling viewpoint can be regarded as complementary to that of the DFD, since it models static relationships rather than the dynamic flow of information.

13.2.2 Representations used for Structured Design

In comparison with the variety of forms that can be used for the task of analysing the structure of a problem, the Structured Design activities mostly make use of only one significant form of diagrammatical notation. As might be expected, the viewpoint adopted is a constructional one, and it is provided by the Structure Chart.

Appropriately for a notation that is concerned with recording the details of 'physical design', as is shown by the example in Figure 13.4, the Structure Chart is very much a program-oriented form of description in the call-and-return style. It is chiefly concerned with describing the functions of the subprograms that make up a program, together with the run-time invocation hierarchy that links them. It is therefore the task of the Structured Design part of the method to bridge the gap between the

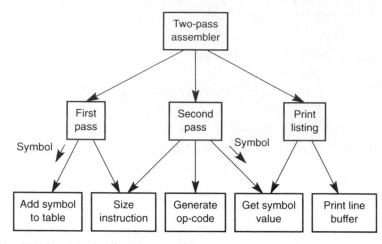

Figure 13.4   Simple example of a Structure Chart.

very different viewpoints and forms that are used for Structured Systems Analysis and for Structured Design, and the next section provides an outline of the way in which this is achieved.

13.2.3 Other descriptive forms

While the forms just described are the principal diagrammatical tools used in this method, they can also be supplemented with other forms. Probably the most common of these is plain pseudocode, which provides a means of describing the algorithmic elements of the design and a more detailed description of the initial structure of the procedural units identified in the Structure Chart. Depending on the nature of the problem, designers may find it convenient to make use of further representations in order to help with resolving particular issues, including such forms as decision trees, decision tables and ERDs (Page-Jones, 1988). While all of these can be useful, their prime role is to supplement the design transformations, which in turn are based on making use of the two main forms, and so the outline description here will not be concerned with the roles performed by these ancillary forms of design description.

Some of the ways in which the basic strategy of this method has been developed and enhanced were mentioned in the previous section. The real-time design methods based on the SSA/SD strategy have particularly developed the use of further diagrammatical forms, with these typically being used to capture the behavioural features of both the problem and the solution. These include such forms as the State Transition Diagram, as described in Section 7.2.3, and the Control Flow Diagram, a development of the DFD (Ward, 1986). These forms can assist the designer with modelling the time-dependent issues that predominate in a real-time system, as well as providing a means of describing the causal features that link external events to system reactions. Once again, though, these forms are not central to the present description of the basic strategy of SSA/SD, and so their use will not be explored in the description given in this chapter.

As already mentioned in Section 13.1, in its original form the over-arching strategy adopted in this method can be regarded as a refinement of the classic top-down strategy of 'divide and conquer' discussed in Chapter 11. The designer begins by constructing a model of the top-level problem in terms of the operations that are performed by the system, and then this description of the problem is transformed into a plan for a program; this plan is in turn described in terms of the set of subprograms that are used to perform the relevant operations, together with the details of the inter-actions between the subprograms.

The form of the design process is more subtle than that of the simple top-down design strategy, however: it extends the simple description of the system, expressed in terms of operations, by also considering the flow of information between the oper-ations. The wider foundation that this provides assists the designer in producing a more consistent structure for the eventual design than is likely to arise from the use of the simple top-down strategy, since the information-flow component of the model helps to reduce and constrain the 'solution space' available to the designer.

Returning to the framework that is provided by the transformational model of the design process introduced in Chapter 9: the design transformations involved in this method can be viewed as forming a set of sequential steps, with feedback occurring automatically between them. The five basic steps, shown in Figure 13.5, are:

1. Construct an initial DFD to provide a top-level description of the problem (the 'Context Diagram').
2. Elaborate this into a layered hierarchy of DFDs, supported by a data dictionary.
3. Use Transaction Analysis to divide the DFD into tractable units.
4. Perform a Transform Analysis on the DFD created for each transaction, in order to produce a Structure Chart for that transaction.
5. Merge the resulting Structure Charts to create the basic implementation plans, and refine them to include any necessary error-handling, initialization, and other exceptions.

Steps 1 and 2 are essentially those that make up the process that we are terming 'Structured Systems Analysis', while the other three can be considered as forming the process of Structured Design. This section concentrates on describing the nature of the first four steps, since the actions of step 5 do not involve major design decisions, although they play an important role in the form of the final design. (To do proper justice to the actions of step 5 also requires a more detailed description than can be provided in an overview such as this.)

13.3.1 Steps 1 and 2: Structured Systems Analysis

Most of the basic operations involved in these steps were outlined in Section 7.2.1, when discussing the use and the development of the DFD. However, as Structured Systems Analysis is quite a large topic, which merits textbooks in its own right, it is appropriate to add a few more comments at this stage.

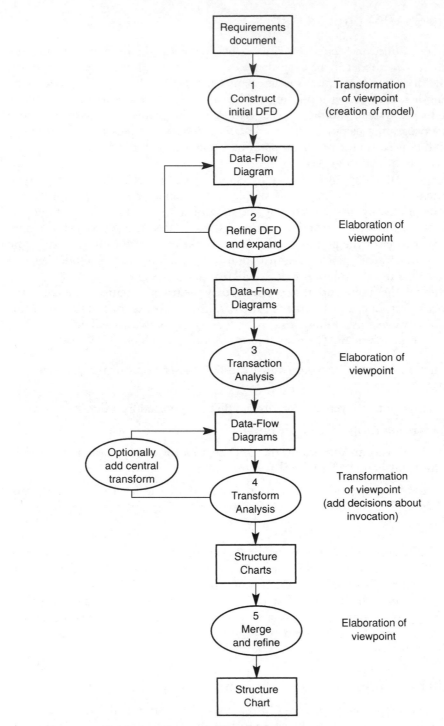

Figure 13.5 Transformation diagram for SSA/SD.

As might be gathered from their names, Structured Systems Analysis is essentially problem-driven in nature, while Structured Design is concerned with the form of the solution. For that reason, each process makes use of those diagrammatical forms that best support its particular purpose and provide for the necessary levels of abstraction.

The objective of the Structured Systems Analysis steps is to produce a functional specification that describes what the system is to do. Ideally this should constrain the form of the eventual implementation (solution) as little as possible. However, in practice it is often difficult to avoid making choices that will effectively constrain some architectural choices in the general form of the final solution, although the analyst is encouraged to avoid the former wherever possible. So, although analysis is not strictly a part of the design process, the reality of the situation is such that it should really be included in this chapter.

The most abstract description we can provide for a system is one in which the complete system is itself the process being described. This 'single-bubble' description is termed the 'context diagram', and it is basically the 'level zero' diagram that encapsulates the whole system with a single bubble; the only data flows described in it are those that are external to the system. Figure 13.6 shows an example of such a context diagram for a readily recognizable system. Of course, each system can have only one context diagram.

A context diagram having been produced (a valuable initial step), there are two commonly used strategies that can be adopted for producing the remaining levels of the DFD schema.

- *Top-down functional decomposition* is the 'traditional' approach, in which first the context diagram is divided into a set of 'functional' subtasks and then this process is repeated until the bubbles are considered to be sufficiently simple to be represented by P-Specs.

- *Event-partitioning* is a technique in which the thread of actions associated with each event is identified and used to form a simple bubble in the DFD. The process

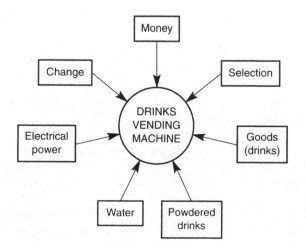

Figure 13.6 A context diagram for a vending machine.

from this point may then be either compositional, in the sense of grouping related functions to form a higher level of DFD, or decompositional, using top-down techniques to refine the description.

In producing the DFDs that form a major output from this step, the analyst (to employ the term usually adopted) is encouraged to use them for two purposes (De Marco, 1978; Page-Jones, 1988):

- drawing *physical* DFDs to describe the initial system model in terms of relatively concrete items (explicit names for users, form numbers, and so on);

- constructing *logical* DFDs, which use more abstract terms to describe the operations and data flow.

Examples of these roles were given in Section 7.2.1. The advantage of this subdivision is that the physical DFD is often easier to produce in the first place, and it can more easily be verified with the users (who can directly identify their problem in terms of its descriptive forms). However, the logical DFD is more valuable in terms of the next steps in the design process, and may also provide more insight into the design problem itself.

   Of course, there are many aspects of a problem that cannot be captured easily by using the DFD as the sole basis for the designer's model. Among other things, DFDs are concerned only with describing the flow of information, and not with its form or its persistence. For that reason, the DFD needs to be supplemented by other forms, with the choice of these depending on the problem itself. Besides the possible use of P-Specs, there will almost certainly be a need for some form of data dictionary. (In a large system, where the final DFDs identify very many processes, the data dictionary will be correspondingly large.) Other information about the problem may also need to be captured if the designer is to produce a complete model, such as

- frequency of information flow

- volume of data flow

- size of messages

- 'lifetime' of an item of information

In some cases, the flow of control may be a significant factor to be considered, in addition to any consideration of the data-flow element (Ward, 1986).

   As with all apparently simple notations, actually producing a DFD requires a degree of practice. Both De Marco and Page-Jones offer suggestions to assist the inexperienced with this task (as do most textbooks that describe the different variations of this method). Some of the useful practices that are recommended are:

- begin the task of identifying operations by considering the inputs and outputs of the system, since these are normally well defined in the user's requirements documents;

- work inwards from these, if appropriate, otherwise outwards from the centre;

- label carefully (following this advice is much harder than you might think);

- don't try to handle exceptions and error conditions at this stage, since they will obscure the rest of the model;

- don't flowchart (DFDs are used to model the *system*, whereas a flowchart models the operations of the *machine* that will eventually be used to implement the system).

Whatever the technique adopted (and however extensive the experience of the analyst), it is essential to be prepared to begin again, rather than to attempt to distort a model that is clearly wrong. (This provides one of the more convincing arguments for performing this task with paper and pencil rather than some unfamiliar CASE tool, since the cost in personal time and effort of starting again is then much lower!)

13.3.2 Step 3: Transaction Analysis

The description of this step will be relatively brief, partly because this is not a major design transformation and partly because for less complex systems it may even not be required. The main purpose of the actions of this step is to separate the components of a large design into a network of cooperating subsystems, and this is done by identifying the transactions that are involved in the problem as a whole. The DFD components that correspond to each transaction are then grouped together and used as input to a Transform Analysis step, after which the resulting Structure Charts are recombined to provide the design model for the complete system. Figure 13.7 shows this process, together with those of steps 4 and 5, in abstract form.

The Transaction Analysis step can therefore be regarded as being largely concerned with architectural design choices, with its process part being chiefly concerned with the identification of transactions. However, it is not quite so simple as that, as it is also necessary to consider some detailed issues about structure in anticipation of the final task of recombining the transformed transactions.

A transaction is usually considered to have five basic components:

- the *event* in the system's environment that causes the transaction to occur;

- the *stimulus* that is applied to the system to inform it about the event;

- the *activity* that is performed by the system as a result of the stimulus;

- the *response* that this generates in terms of output from the system;

- the *effect* that this has upon the environment.

Figure 13.8 shows a simple example of a transaction that might occur in a particular system (in this case, a banking system).

The later regrouping of the Structure Charts produced for each transaction may not necessarily be a complex one. For some problems, it may involve little more than organizing an initial CASE or `switch` statement in the program's main body to identify which transaction should be selected in response to a particular event.

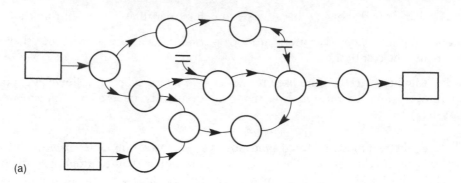

(a)

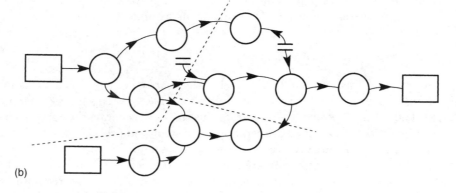

(b)

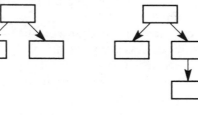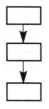

(c)

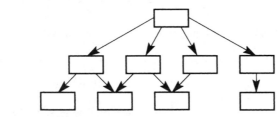

(d)

Figure 13.7 Transaction Analysis logic.
(a) A complete system DFD from steps 1 and 2.
(b) Step 3 Transaction Analysis divides into smaller DFDs.
(c) Transform Analysis creates Structure Charts in step 4.
(d) Structure Charts recombined in step 5.

- EVENT: Student 'signs up' for a bank account
- STIMULUS: Information about student; university/college;
  date of opening account; income source; etc.
- ACTIVITY: Add account details to bank's records
- RESPONSE: Free gifts to student; chequebook; monthly statements
- EFFECT: Student can spend money

Figure 13.8   A simple example of a transaction.

13.3.3 Step 4: Transform Analysis

Transform Analysis is the key transformation of this method, and is performed on the DFD that is created to describe a given transaction. It is in this step that the designer takes the non-hierarchical model constructed to describe the problem, modelled around the flow of data between operations, and transforms this to create a description of the structure of a computer program. This in turn is modelled in terms of the hierarchy formed from the order in which subprograms are called (invoked), together with the flow of information created through the use of parameters and shared data structures.

To see how this is done, we will first work through an outline description of the general form of this step, and will then seek to interpret the actions and operations in terms of our more general model of the design process.

The first action of the designer is to identify the operation or 'bubble' that acts as the **central transform** in the DFD. The central transform is the bubble that lies at the centre of input and output data flow – where these are considered to have their most abstract form (on the basis that they take their most concrete form when interacting with physical input/output devices). On occasion, however, it is not possible to identify a clear candidate to act as the central transform, and in such a case the recommended practice is to create one – adding a further bubble in the position where the designer feels a central transform should occur. (While this may seem to be a slightly odd practice, a rationale for it will be given when we seek to interpret the transform structures.)

The basic form of the operations that are involved in the Transform Analysis step is depicted in Figure 13.9. A useful analogy is that used by Meilir Page-Jones (1988), in which he suggests that we regard the DFD as being a 'set of balloons, linked by strings'. To create the hierarchy, pick up the central transform balloon, letting the others dangle from it, and then turn the central transform into the 'main body' of the program. To stretch the analogy (and the balloons) rather hard: square off the balloons, so that the 'operations' become first-cut subprograms, and turn the data-flow arcs into invocation arcs (together with data flow), in order to form the initial draft of the Structure Chart.

A feature of this process that sometimes gives conceptual difficulty is that the flow arrows on the arcs seem to change direction when this transformation is made. This is because the arc in a DFD depicts *data* flow, while that in a Structure Chart depicts *control* flow (via subprogram invocation). The latter are added in this design step, and the former are subsumed into the data flow that is conducted via the parameters of the subprograms.

Structured systems analysis and systems design

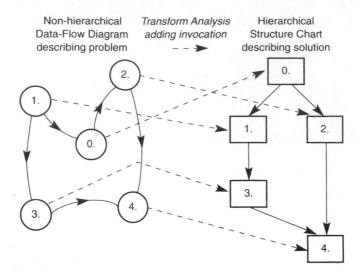

Non-hierarchical
Data-Flow Diagram
describing problem

*Transform Analysis
adding invocation*
- - ➤

Hierarchical
Structure Chart
describing solution

Figure 13.9 The operations of the Transform Analysis step.

While this is by no means all that is involved in the Transform Analysis step, since a lot of work remains to be done to produce a proper Structure Chart that describes the form of the eventual system, it is sufficient for our immediate purposes, since it explains the essential nature of the transformation it contains. We now need to consider the implications of this for the design process.

A major distinction between the DFD and the Structure Chart is that the former is non-sequential and describes the structure of the *problem*, while the latter describes a *solution* in terms of a hierarchy of program units. That apart, both describe a system in terms of operations (which, of course, can conveniently be packaged into subprograms), and in terms of the flow (or transfer) of information around the system. It is therefore reasonable to begin the transformation process by making a one-to-one mapping of bubbles to subprograms, even though this may later require refinement.

In order to do this, it is necessary to be able to identify exactly where in the eventual subprogram invocation hierarchy each operation will need to be positioned. Not surprisingly, the operations most closely concerned with physical input/output are mapped onto the procedures at the base of the Structure Chart, while the most abstract operations (as represented by the central transform and the bubbles immediately around it) are mapped onto the top level of the chart.

This explains why it is sometimes necessary to create a central transform in order to be able to perform the transformation process. A system in which this extra step proves to be necessary corresponds to a situation where the chief role of the main body of the final program is to organize the sequencing of the calls to the subprograms. Since such a program main body performs no specific problem-oriented operations, it is unlikely to be identified as a bubble in creating the DFD. This is why it needs to be added to the DFD in the form of an 'empty bubble', in order to 'complete' the DFD so that the Transform Analysis operations can be performed in a consistent manner.

Once the first-cut Structure Chart has been produced in this way, quite a lot of work remains to be done in revising its form into one that is appropriate for implementation with a hierarchy of subprograms. Almost certainly, there will be additional work needed to sort out the detailed forms of any input and output; the functions of the DFD operations may need to be split between subprograms, or combined in some cases; and the needs of initialization and exception-handling need to be met through the creation of additional modules. On top of all that, there is a need to consider the quality of the structures created, and to maintain these by considering such factors as coupling, cohesion and information-hiding.

Transform Analysis is therefore a complex step, and in this subsection only a very general outline of the principal actions that it involves has been given. However, this description should be sufficient to provide an understanding of the nature and form of this transformation, leaving the details of the various refinements to be described in a more specialized text.

13.3.4 Step 5: Completing the design process

Where the Transaction Analysis step has identified a number of separate transactions, step 5 will involve bringing together the Structure Charts produced for the different transactions and resolving any overlaps or mismatches between these. As already mentioned, for systems in which these are essentially distinct options (as, for example, in a bank autoteller system, where the user may opt to deposit money, receive money or receive information), the linking may involve little more than adding a new top-level module that selects among the transactions. Equally, there may be some need to rationalize the lower-level modules, since there is the risk of some duplication occurring in their operations.

13.3.5 Summary of the design process

The characteristic features of this method are particularly well illustrated by using the D-matrix notation which was introduced in Chapter 9. So in this subsection we employ this notation to provide a summary of the processes that were described in the preceding subsections.

Step 1: Constructing the initial DFD

Because the requirements document effectively forms its input, we can consider this initial step as being to produce an elaboration of this that concentrates on the functionality of the eventual system. This is particularly evident if we consider the creation of a 'black box' Context Diagram as being an intermediate step which has the following form:

$$
\begin{pmatrix} R^b \\ R^f \\ \varnothing^d \\ \varnothing^c \end{pmatrix} \quad E^0 \rightarrow \quad \begin{pmatrix} \varnothing_c^b \\ D_c^f \\ \varnothing_c^d \\ \varnothing_c^c \end{pmatrix}
$$

We have used the subscript c to indicate the Context Diagram. The elaboration of the Context Diagram then produces the top-level system description:

$$
\begin{pmatrix} \varnothing_c^b \\ D_c^f \\ \varnothing_c^d \\ \varnothing_c^c \end{pmatrix} \quad E^1 \rightarrow \quad \begin{pmatrix} \varnothing_1^b & \varnothing_2^b & \dots & \varnothing_n^b \\ D_1^f & D_2^f & \dots & D_n^f \\ \varnothing_1^d & \varnothing_2^d & \dots & \varnothing_n^d \\ \varnothing_1^c & \varnothing_2^c & \dots & \varnothing_n^c \end{pmatrix}
$$

Step 2: Refine the DFD and expand

If we stay with a 'vanilla' approach (ignoring the use of STDs or ERDs in this step) and assume that the functional description is the main element being developed, then this step is largely an expansion of the functional elements. However, we have included the elements D_i^d to represent the information that is added in the Data Dictionary:

$$
\begin{pmatrix} \varnothing_1^b & \varnothing_2^b & \dots & 0_n^b \\ D_1^f & D_2^f & \dots & D_n^f \\ \varnothing_1^d & \varnothing_2^d & \dots & \varnothing_n^d \\ \varnothing_1^c & \varnothing_2^c & \dots & \varnothing_n^c \end{pmatrix} \quad E^2 \rightarrow \quad \begin{pmatrix} \varnothing_1^b & \varnothing_2^b & \dots & \varnothing_m^b \\ D_1^f & D_2^f & \dots & D_m^f \\ D_1^d & D_2^d & \dots & D_m^d \\ \varnothing_1^c & \varnothing_2^c & \dots & \varnothing_m^c \end{pmatrix}
$$

When using a decompositional strategy we would normally expect that $n \leq m$, although, since there is also scope for rationalization of the elements, this is not necessarily always the case. Also, the numbering of the actual elements may be rather different as a result of this refinement. For this very simple demonstration we have ignored this, but when modelling actual design steps we should remember that the identity of element i may differ between the two matrices.

Step 3: Transaction Analysis

Since this partitions our DFD into a set of DFDs, we can represent this (in a slightly clumsy manner) by mixing elements of set notation with matrix notation! Again, this is an elaboration step:

$$
\begin{pmatrix} \varnothing_1^b & \varnothing_2^b & \dots & \varnothing_n^b \\ D_1^f & D_2^f & \dots & D_n^f \\ D_1^d & D_2^d & \dots & D_n^d \\ \varnothing_1^c & \varnothing_2^c & \dots & \varnothing_n^c \end{pmatrix} \quad E^3 \rightarrow \bigcup_j \quad \begin{pmatrix} \varnothing_1^b & \varnothing_2^b & \dots & \varnothing_{m(j)}^b \\ D_1^f & D_2^f & \dots & D_{m(j)}^f \\ D_1^d & D_2^d & \dots & D_{m(j)}^d \\ \varnothing_1^c & \varnothing_2^c & \dots & \varnothing_{m(j)}^c \end{pmatrix}_j
$$

where the number of transactions $j \geq 1$, and where $m(j)$ is the number of elements in the jth DFD.

Step 4: Transform Analysis

In this transformation step, we add the constructional information to each of our sub-matrices, which leads to a set of transformations of the following form:

$$
\begin{pmatrix}
\varnothing_1^b & \varnothing_2^b & \dots & \varnothing_{m(j)}^b \\
D_1^f & D_2^f & \dots & D_{m(j)}^f \\
D_1^d & D_2^d & \dots & D_{m(j)}^d \\
\varnothing_1^c & \varnothing_2^c & \dots & \varnothing_{m(j)}^c
\end{pmatrix}_j
\quad T^4 \rightarrow \quad
\begin{pmatrix}
\varnothing_1^b & \varnothing_2^b & \dots & \varnothing_{m(j)}^b \\
d_1^f & d_2^f & \dots & d_{m(j)}^f \\
D_1^d & D_2^d & \dots & D_{m(j)}^d \\
D_1^c & D_2^c & \dots & D_{m(j)}^c
\end{pmatrix}_j
$$

(One question that arises is whether the D_i^f elements should be preserved across this transformation. In Budgen (1995) the preference was to omit these. However, since they do form the basis of subprogram functionality, in this exposition we have retained them, while changing to the use of a lower case letter d to emphasize that this is an indirect description.)

Step 5: Completing the design process

For our purpose, this represents a 'bringing together' of the Structure Charts, which we can represent in a very simplified manner as shown below:

$$
\sum_j
\begin{pmatrix}
\varnothing_1^b & \varnothing_2^b & \dots & \varnothing_{m(j)}^b \\
d_1^f & d_2^f & \dots & d_{m(j)}^f \\
D_1^d & D_2^d & \dots & D_{m(j)}^d \\
D_1^c & D_2^c & \dots & D_{m(j)}^c
\end{pmatrix}_j
\quad E^5 \rightarrow \quad
\begin{pmatrix}
\varnothing_1^b & \varnothing_2^b & \dots & \varnothing_n^b \\
d_1^f & d_2^f & \dots & d_n^f \\
D_1^d & D_2^d & \dots & D_n^d \\
D_1^c & D_2^c & \dots & D_n^c
\end{pmatrix}
$$

13.4 The role of heuristics in SSA/SD

The relatively relaxed structuring of SSA/SD, and the number of variations in the form of the process, has the result that it is harder to classify and identify well-defined forms of problem that can lead to the development of heuristics. So the type of heuristic that has evolved is likely to be one that is related to the form of the solution rather than to the form of the process that led to it.

We have already encountered one significant example of a heuristic of this type, which is that of devising an 'empty' central transform when there is no obvious suitable candidate. This is a prime example of the use of a design heuristic to assist with the design transformations, as it provides guidance on the restructuring of a design model (which in itself may be quite correct) to allow a particular transformation to be applied to it.

Indeed, the very act of identifying the central transform during Transform Analysis is itself a form of heuristic. There are no prescriptive guidelines for performing this task, and the results of selecting different candidates will be quite different in their structure, as is demonstrated in the simple example in Figure 13.10, where the effects of selecting different candidates to be the central transform can be seen.

The technique of levelling, as used for developing a DFD, is probably a further candidate for classification as a heuristic, since the available guidelines are rules of thumb rather than systematic rules. However, since it is a normal operation during

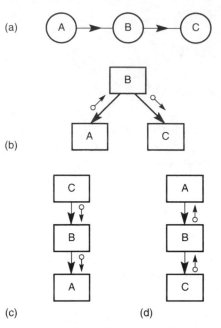

Figure 13.10 Selecting the central transform. (a) The DFD. (b) Choose bubble B. (c) Choose bubble C. (d) Choose bubble A.

Structured Systems Analysis, the heuristic element is really concerned with the rules used for performing the operation, rather than with the act of performing it.

A second heuristic of this type is known as 'factoring'. This is a technique used for separating out functions within a module, where the operations of one module are contained in the structure of another. There are a number of reasons why we might want to do this, some of which are:

- to reduce module size (and hence complexity);

- to help with clarification of functions (and hence to assist with future changes);

- to help identify and reduce duplication of operations;

- to help with reuse of code.

Associated with the idea of factoring are the concepts of coupling and cohesion, which were introduced in Chapter 4 (page 77). Clearly, any factoring that we perform will need to take these into account. So these too might be considered as design heuristics, in that they can be used to help resolve particular issues and to assist with design choices.

Evidently the heuristics in SSA/SD are very likely to appear during 'normal' use of the method, and so are largely concerned with assisting in the performance of the regular design transformations. This is in contrast to the use of JSP, described in the next chapter, where techniques such as program inversion are required only if the transformations generate a certain type of solution, and so where heuristics are used only during a later stage of the design process.

13.5 Extended forms of SSA/SD

This section should perhaps include the terms 'variations' and 'developments' in its title, since SSA/SD has spawned a wide variety of derivatives. These can be classified as:

- *Variations*: the overall form of the process does not differ significantly, but slightly different notations or process models are used. There are a number of these, with perhaps the best known being that popularized by Gane and Sarsen (1979).

- *Extensions*: new features have been added to the process model, and new viewpoints have been included in the representation part. Most of these have been directed at assisting with design in the real-time domain (remember that this method was essentially developed to meet data-processing needs), and so these have tended to enhance the use of the behavioural viewpoint in the design process. Particular examples are those due to Ward and Mellor (1985), Hatley and Pirbhai (1988) and Gomaa (1986; 1989).

- *Developments*: essentially refinements that have been added to the basic model over time without affecting the fundamental structure of the transformations. Much of the effort has been directed at improving the techniques used for data modelling (such as the addition of entity relationship models (Page-Jones, 1988)).

The development of the basic method can probably be considered as having reached its most refined state of development in the description provided in Yourdon (1989). The extensions are in many ways methods that have quite different design processes and models, in terms of both the analysis and the design parts. While, from a methodological point of view, these merit separate attention, time and space have not permitted a separate survey of their features in this book.

13.6 SSA/SD: an outline example

A fully worked out example of the use of an analysis and design method such as SSA/SD is outwith the scope of this book. However, as this is the first such method we have described, the fairly simple worked example that is provided here may help to give a strategic understanding of the mechanisms involved. It also provides an illustration of the 'exploratory' nature of the design process.

The problem

The problem chosen for this example is based on the development of a software utility that can be used to provide outline design documentation for an existing program, with the aim of using the documentation to help produce a 'call graph', using a form similar to that of the Structure Chart, that describes the invocation hierarchy of the input program. In effect this can be considered as a form of 'reverse engineering' process that can be used to aid the maintenance of a program, by ensuring that the working documentation faithfully reflects the actual structure of the program.

To make the task somewhat simpler, the program being analysed is to be written in a language such as 'standard' Pascal, so ensuring that all the subprograms (procedures) are contained in a single source file. However, even if we were to modify our goals to include programming languages that permitted separate or independent compilation, we should probably still adopt a strategy of 'separation of concerns' in the development of our solution, and begin the task of exploration by using the simplest case of the single source file.

Since the main requirement is to design a program that will be able to recognize any declarations of procedures and any calls to procedures in the input source file, the techniques involved are likely to be closely allied to those used in compiling. So, in an unconstrained situation, it would probably be most sensible to adopt a 'template' approach to the design of the system, involving the use of such software tools as the `lex` and `yacc` tools provided with the Unix operating system. However, to provide the desired example, we will use the SSA/SD strategies instead.

To perform its task, the program will need to read through the source code of a program and identify the extent and forms of the relationships among its procedures. So for each procedure that is declared in the input source program, this 'reversing' program will need to print out a list of the procedures that it calls, either directly, or by making use of other procedures. This information can then be used to construct the eventual Structure Chart. (We will not attempt to develop the graphical routines that would be needed for constructing this directly from our program.)

In its simplest form, the output from our 'reversing' program can simply show the calling hierarchy for the input source text, but of course there is also scope to include information about the formal parameters used for the procedures. Figure 13.11 shows a call graph that describes the form of a fairly simple program, while Figure 13.12 shows the type of output listing that our 'reversing' program might produce from its analysis of the code for the corresponding program, which can then be used to draw that call graph.

While this requirements specification is not a very rigorous or complete one, it is probably not atypical of those often encountered, since few end-users are likely to

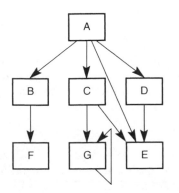

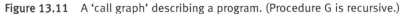

Figure 13.11 A 'call graph' describing a program. (Procedure G is recursive.)

					level	types
Level 1	A	>	B(list of formal parameters)		2	p
		>	C(	– ditto –)	2	f
		>	D(	– ditto –)	2	p
		>>	E(	– ditto –)	3	f
Level 2	B	>	F(	– ditto –)	3	p
	C	>	G(	– ditto –)	3	p
		>	E(	– ditto –)	3	f
	D	>	E(	– ditto –)	3	f
Level 3	G	>	G(	– ditto –)	3	p

>   procedure call at the next level
>>   call to a procedure at a lower level
p   procedure call
f   function call

Figure 13.12 Outline of the output form describing the program shown in Figure 13.11.

have the skills necessary to construct detailed requirements documents. (Indeed, where relatively new products are involved, attempting to identify the complete requirements in advance may not even be desirable.) One of the benefits of an initial pre-design stage such as that provided by Structured Systems Analysis is the opportunity to clarify and resolve any ambiguities and identify any significant omissions.

The Structured Systems Analysis step

We begin by producing the context diagram, which is shown in Figure 13.13. For this particular problem, which, like a compiler, has a fairly simple dataflow architectural

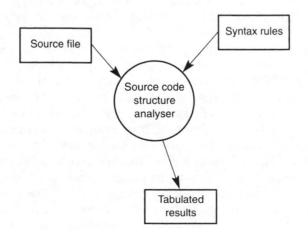

Figure 13.13 Context diagram for the 'reversing' program.

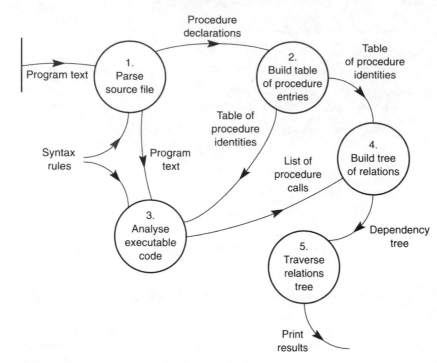

Figure 13.14 A first DFD for the 'reversing' program.

style, the context diagram is relatively simple, since there will be little or no interaction between the program and the user.

To develop the DFD, it is necessary to choose between top-down decomposition and event-partitioning. (Events are not necessarily associated with external actions: an 'event' in this context might well involve the recognition of a particular reserved word in the input.) In this case we will adopt the more basic top-down approach, in the absence of any features that indicate that either technique is likely to be the more appropriate.

Figure 13.14 shows a first attempt to produce a DFD describing this system. As often occurs in such a situation, this raises questions about the problem that lead us to refine or recreate the DFD. In this case, an obvious question that might arise is whether the solution will permit reading through the source file more than once. But we should avoid being diverted into considering eventual implementation in this way, and continue to concentrate on the more abstract task of analysis at this stage. (This point has been raised here to demonstrate how easily the task of analysis can overlap with that of design unless we take care to maintain an appropriate level of abstraction by a conscious effort. It also demonstrates how the design process might use note-making: a note of the above point should be made for consideration at a later stage.)

As it happens, further expansion of the DFD shown in Figure 13.14 leads rapidly to the conclusion that we have not chosen a particularly good set of basic operations. This is partly because operations such as 'parse' and 'build' are too vague, so

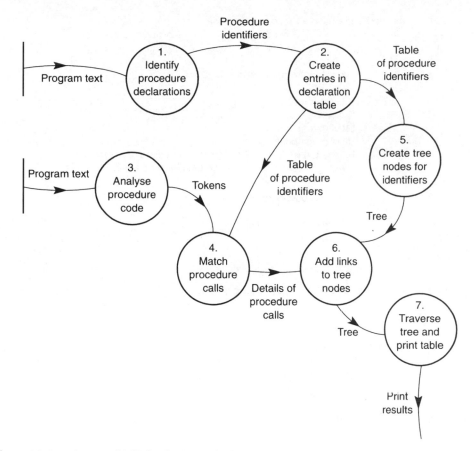

Figure 13.15 A second DFD for the 'reversing' program.

complicating the task of expanding the bubbles, and also because attempting to constrain the solution to one that reads through the program source file only once gives a convoluted form to the expansions of the operations in bubbles 1 and 3. Figure 13.15 shows a second attempt to construct a DFD, drawing on the experience of attempting to expand the first form. (Again, the point in showing this is to emphasize that we will not necessarily find a 'good' solution on the first attempt, and that a designer should be prepared to revise or even discard a model if it fails to meet all the requirements, and to develop anew with the experience so gained.)

The data elements involved in this problem are not particularly complex, and so the development of a more comprehensive description via such forms as the Entity–Structure Diagram is not really necessary. Figure 13.16 shows a simple first-level data dictionary, together with some notes that show where the designer has identified questions that will need to be resolved at some point in the future. The making of notes is, of course, a well-recognized practice already discussed in earlier chapters.

The process of levelling the DFD by expanding the bubbles can then be pursued until the designer determines that a suitable level of abstraction has been reached.

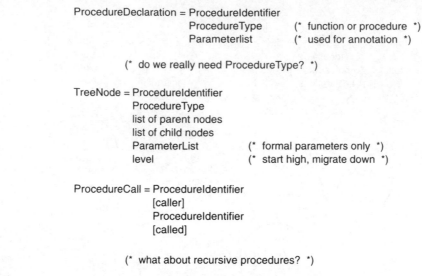

```
ProcedureDeclaration = ProcedureIdentifier
                       ProcedureType        (* function or procedure *)
                       Parameterlist        (* used for annotation *)

            (* do we really need ProcedureType? *)

TreeNode = ProcedureIdentifier
           ProcedureType
           list of parent nodes
           list of child nodes
           ParameterList        (* formal parameters only *)
           level                (* start high, migrate down *)

ProcedureCall = ProcedureIdentifier
                [caller]
                ProcedureIdentifier
                [called]

            (* what about recursive procedures? *)
```

Figure 13.16 A data dictionary for the 'reversing' program.

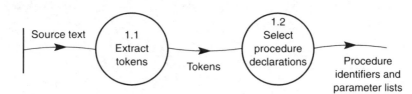

Figure 13.17 A first expansion of a DFD bubble.

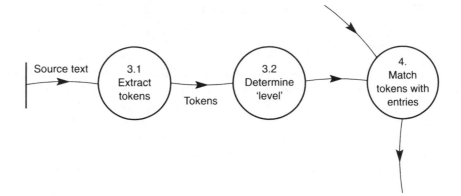

Figure 13.18 Further expansion of the top-level DFD for the 'reversing' program. It involves some global knowledge about 'level'.

Figures 13.17 and 13.18 show examples of such refinements for three of the bubbles in the top-level DFD (in the case of bubble 4, its description has been refined rather than levelled). For the moment there is no obvious expansion of bubble 2 and so this is left for future consideration.

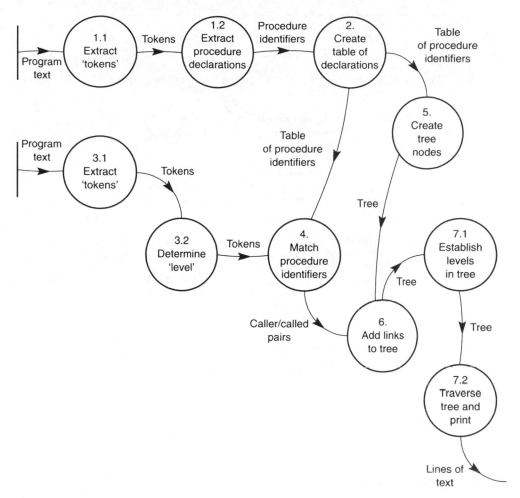

Figure 13.19 A more detailed DFD for the 'reversing' program.

The eventual DFD is shown in Figure 13.19, while Figure 13.20 shows a further refinement of the data dictionary; but there are still some issues needing to be resolved. For this problem, the eventual DFD is not particularly large, and so we can proceed to use it in full for the process of Structured Design. For a larger system, it might be necessary to use only the more abstract levels for the initial steps of the design process.

The analysis stage is also likely to form a significant source of designer's notes, where particular problems have been recognized but cannot be solved at this level of abstraction. One example of such note-making for this problem is likely to be prompted by the need to recognize the presence of recursive procedure calls, since too simple an approach to tracing procedure calls would be likely to throw the 'reversing' program into an infinite loop when it encountered a recursive procedure.

```
ProcedureDeclaration = ProcedureIdentifier
                       ProcedureType        (* function or procedure *)
                       ParameterList        (* formal parameters *)

ParameterList = NumberOfParameters          (* count of parameters *)
                {FormalParameter}

FormalParameter = ParameterIdentifier
                  ParameterForm             (* VAR or VAL *)
                  ParameterType

    (* do we really need procedure type ? *)
    (* procedure type is needed if we want to annotate with data-flow
        information, as a function procedure is another parameter for
        this purpose *)

TreeNode = ProcedureDeclaration
           linked list of parent nodes
           linked list of child nodes
           level in tree                    (* established by traversal *)

ProcedureCall = ProcedureIdentifier         (* caller *)
                ProcedureIdentifier         (* called *)

    (* what about recursive procedures? *)
    (* can be recognized by identical fields in ProcedureCall record *)
```

Figure 13.20 A revised data dictionary. While this has not been expanded fully, some of the questions raised have already been answered. Notes of both questions and answers should be kept on record in the data dictionary.

The Transaction Analysis step

For this particular problem, there is essentially only a single transaction, and so there is no need to separate out the DFD into separate transactions.

The Transform Analysis step

The key action that must be undertaken successfully to produce a well-balanced design is that of finding the central transform. In this problem neither the input data flows nor the output data flows are particularly significant features of the problem, which is mainly concerned with the creation and manipulation of the central information structures that describe the form of the program being analysed. Indeed, there are clearly two stages to the solution as adopted, namely:

- recognizing the procedure declarations; and

- recognizing the procedure invocations (calls) and linking these to create the data structure needed in order to produce the final output.

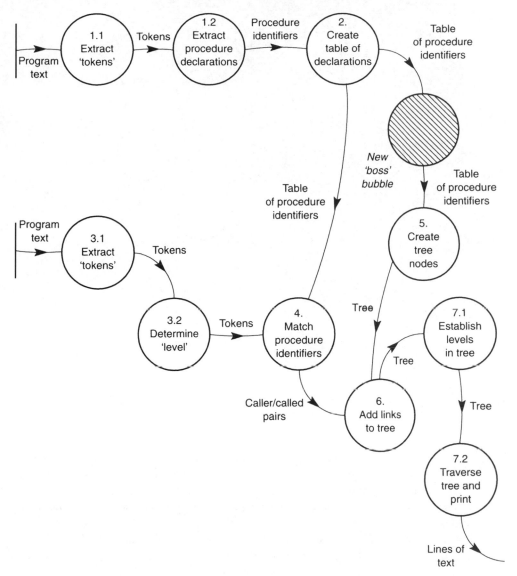

Figure 13.21 Adding the new 'boss' bubble to the DFD.

It turns out that, if we assess the qualities of any of the existing bubbles in the DFD (Figure 13.19) as candidates for the central transform, none of them are particularly suitable, since no bubble occupies a place between the two main tasks of the program as a whole. So this is where we create a further 'boss' bubble, positioned between bubbles 2 and 5. The new DFD that can then be produced from this is shown in Figure 13.21, and the new bubble will be used as the central transform.

Figure 13.22 shows the result of performing the first step in the transformation process, lifting the new bubble to the top of the diagram and letting the others

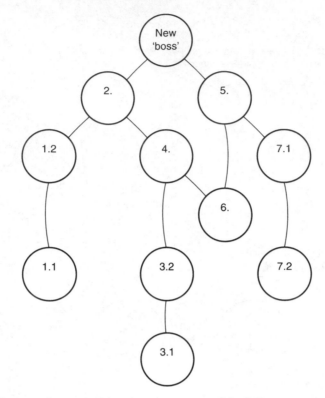

Figure 13.22 First step in reorganizing the components of the DFD.

trail below. The result of some squaring off and resolving of flows is then shown in Figure 13.23: the first rough Structure Chart describing the solution. This also reveals that the question of parsing the input has not yet been addressed and so will form a subproblem to be resolved separately (so perhaps we can make use of some degree of stylized design, anyway).

Finally, Figure 13.24 shows a rather more refined development of the Structure Chart, although obviously this is still by no means complete: lacking details of the 'parsing task', we still need to address such issues as:

- providing read and write modules;
- factoring out some of the functions that are really too large and complex to be contained in a single procedure;
- adding error-handling functions;
- adding the details for initialization and termination.

However, within those limitations the choice of the central transform has been fairly successful, in that the result appears to be a quite well-balanced tree of procedure calls.

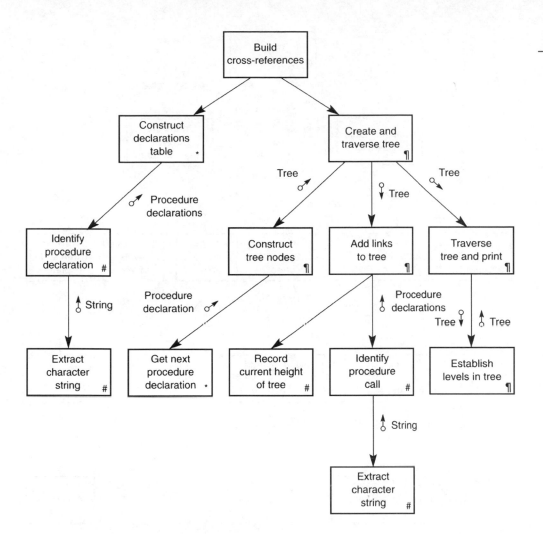

Identify procedure declaration

#	Indicates dependence on input program syntax
¶	Indicates 'knowledge' about the structure of the tree
*	Indicates 'knowledge' about the format of the data table

Figure 13.23 First rough Structure Chart.

As with all examples, this one is, of course, very much simplified. As a practical point, it should also be observed that producing even this first rough design required a number of attempts at performing the Transform Analysis step before the decision was made to adopt an empty central transform. The practical limitations of space prevent the inclusion of such iterations in this chapter, but their presence should not be forgotten.

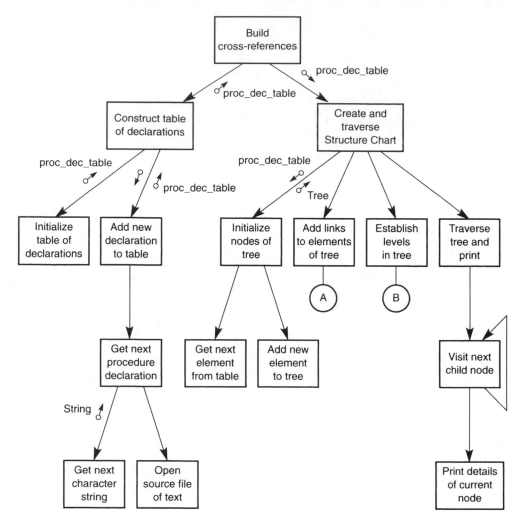

Figure 13.24 A more refined Structure Chart. (Items A and B require further expansion.)

Summary

The very widespread use of the various forms of this method, together with its historical role in the development of software design thinking, make this an important method to introduce at this point. Indeed, in much the same way that ALGOL 60 has influenced the form of many subsequent programming languages, so SSA/SD has influenced the thinking behind many subsequent developments in design methods. It also provides an important contrast with the JSP method described in the next chapter, both in its much wider scope and its (consequently) less prescriptive form.

The practices of Structured Systems Analysis have provided a very powerful set of techniques that can be used to assist with the initial stages of systems design. While analysis is not design, it is an essential precursor, and provides the initial problem modelling step that the designer is required to perform at some point. Indeed, there is a case for arguing that the distinction of title should not encourage a separation of role, in that it is the designer who should perform the analysis task as a part of gaining an understanding of the problem.

The Structured Design component would seem to be less widely adopted in its entirety, perhaps reflecting a general feature of design methods, that they are more prescriptive about the earlier activities of the design process than the later ones. Structured Design is certainly not a simple process if it is performed in a rigorous manner, although it can be very effective in practice.

Overall, the strong imperative content of Structured Systems Analysis and Structured Design practices has certainly assisted with their wide adoption by designers who have been brought up in the same imperative tradition. However, the limitations of placing undue emphasis on one viewpoint have also been recognized, as has been shown by the later developments and extensions that have been adopted into the method.

As a method, there have been no really significant developments since the late 1980s and the YSM form described in Yourdon (1989). However it continues to merit study both because of its influence on the development of later methods (Avison and Fitzgerald, 1995), and also because its widespread use means that any designer undertaking 'maintenance' activities may well encounter structures that were produced through its use.

Further reading

Connor D. (1985). *Information System Specification and Design Road Map*. Englewood Cliffs, Prentice-Hall International

Provides a quite comprehensive example of the use of this method and also shows how the same problem can be tackled using a number of other design strategies.

Page-Jones M. (1988). *The Practical Guide to Structured Systems Design*. 2nd edn. Prentice-Hall International

As the title implies, this is mainly concerned with the Structured Design process, although it also contains two useful chapters on Structured Analysis.

Yourdon E. (1989). *Modern Structured Analysis*. Yourdon Press

Provides the guru's own thoughts on developments in the method as a whole.

The real-time forms of the method are covered by rather fewer textbooks. Probably the most outstanding of these is:

Hatley D.J. and Pirbhai I. (1988). *Strategies for Real-Time System Specification*. Dorset House

Sets out one of the major forms of real-time extension in a clear and readable manner.

Exercises

13.1 Draw the context diagram for each of the following systems:

(a) a bank autoteller machine;

(b) a word-processing program;

(c) a payroll package that is required to produce a set of printed pay-cheques each month, and to provide pay statements showing amount paid and deductions (national insurance, pension, income tax, regular subscriptions or donations).

13.2 For the DFD shown in Figure 13.25:

(a) identify your choice of the bubble that should be used as the central transform;

(b) explain your reasons for rejecting the claims of each of the bubbles around it;

(c) produce a first-cut Structure Chart from it.

13.3 Consider the needs of any error-handling procedures in the example system used in Exercise 13.2. Describe what forms of error-handling need to be provided, and consider the effects of including these as:

(a) part of the Structured Systems Analysis model;

(b) extensions to the first-cut Structure Chart.

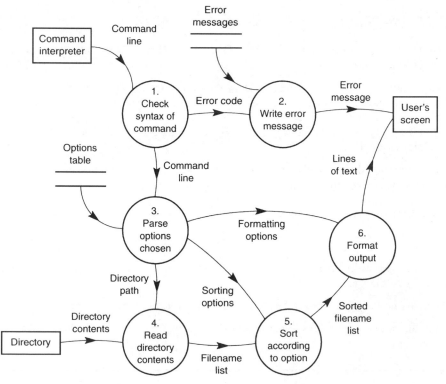

Figure 13.25 DFD for Exercise 13.2.

chapter 14

Jackson Structured Programming (JSP)

JSP is the first of two design methods developed by Michael Jackson that we will study. It can be considered as a 'design method in miniature', being directed at program design within a specific context and architectural style (data-processing using sequential processes, which is essentially a *pipe-and-filter* style). Its well-defined and well-constrained objectives make it a suitable candidate for quite detailed study, and it provides a set of examples for all the components of the framework that we have developed. Its use of a compositional strategy offers some interesting contrasts with the strategy employed in the SSA/SD method that was described in the previous chapter.

As a consequence, this chapter offers a rather more detailed 'method study' than we have generally provided in this book. Two worked examples are included that help not only to illustrate the method processes, but also to demonstrate some wider characteristics of the forms and limitations of design methods as a whole.

14.1 Some background to JSP

JSP is one of the two design methods described in this book that have emerged from ideas and experiences of Michael Jackson (the second is JSD, Chapter 15). It has been chosen as the second detailed example of a software design method for the following reasons.

- It has limited and well-defined applications, which make it possible to describe it more concisely yet fully than most other design methods. It is therefore a good choice for the second method in this book.

- Ever since its development in the early 1970s it has been widely used, and therefore has a historical claim to be discussed in depth.

- It is an excellent example of the use of a compositional design strategy.

- It is well documented and widely used.

However, some of the attributes that make JSP so valuable for developing ideas about design also have the potential to mislead. Because of its limited domain of application, JSP provides more *prescriptive* forms of design transformation than almost any other systematic design method, and this makes it possible to incorporate a greater degree of verification than is generally practicable with other methods.

JSP is essentially a *program* design method. It is concerned with the design of systems that

- are realizable as a single sequential process;

- have well-defined input and output data streams.

JSP is therefore particularly well-suited to developing systems that employ a *pipe-and-filter* architectural style. Despite this, while historically it has often been viewed as primarily of interest to the data-processing community, its use is by no means restricted to such problems, as will be illustrated here by examples and in the discussion in the final section. Indeed, because it is a program design method, there is scope to employ it in larger system design practices: one such example is SSADM (Longworth, 1992) where it can be used for detailed design tasks.

Because of the well-rounded nature of JSP, significant extensions to its structure have not been developed. So the method that will be described here is essentially the only form that is in widespread use.

In Chapter 8 it was suggested that all software design methods begin by building some form of 'model' of the problem that is to be solved. In the case of JSP, this model is constructed by modelling the sequencing of the elements in the input and output data streams; so the next section briefly reviews the forms of representation that are used for this purpose.

Since the forms of representation that are used in JSP have already been described in considerable detail in Chapter 7, the discussion of this section will be kept to a minimum.

JSP is unusual as a design method, in that it uses only a single diagrammatical form in its transformations. This is the Structure Diagram introduced in Section 7.2.5, where its use for describing the sequences involved in both static data structures and dynamic program behaviour was demonstrated. It is used in JSP for modelling both the structures of the data objects of interest, and the functional structuring of the program(s) that manipulate them. Figures 14.1 and 14.2 reproduce Figure 7.18 and 7.20, as examples of Structure Diagrams being used in both these roles; the rules for drawing them are shown in the box below.

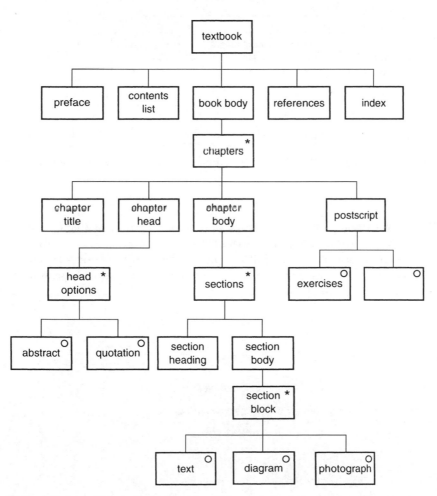

Figure 14.1   A Jackson Structure Diagram describing a static data structure (the structure of a textbook).

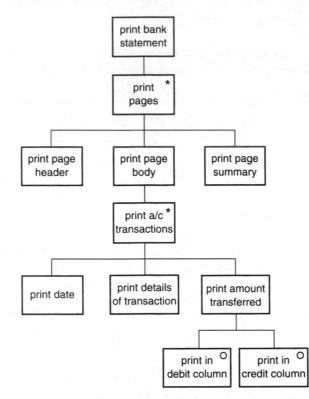

Figure 14.2 A Jackson Structure Diagram describing a program that prints out bank statements.

Because JSP is concerned with program design, it places a strong emphasis on the development of algorithms, and the detailed forms for these are usually better described through the use of text. So JSP also makes use of pseudocode forms for the later stages of design, with these being derived from the diagrammatical forms as a part of the design transformation process.

Some rules for drawing Structure Diagrams

- sequence is represented by unmarked boxes
- selection is represented by boxes marked with circles
- iteration is represented by an asterisked box
- sequencing is from left to right
- the three forms may not be mixed in a sequence
- the last selection part should always be conditionless (the ELSE clause)

The process part of JSP consists of five principal steps that are performed in sequence (although of course, as with all design problems, there will be iterations between these). The tasks performed in these steps can be summarized as follows.

1. Draw a Structure Diagram that describes each of the input and output data streams.

2. Merge these to form the program Structure Diagram.

3. List the operations that need to be performed by the program, and allocate each operation to an element in the program Structure Diagram.

4. Convert the program to text without specific conditions for any of the decision points.

5. Add the conditions used for each iteration and selection operation.

As this shows, the JSP design method is based on a strategy of producing a program structure that reflects the structure of the task itself. This structure is therefore based largely on consideration of algorithmic forms, and the JSP design process does not address issues of modularity, such as allocation to constructional units.

The first two steps are major ones, and may well require about half of the total design effort. While step 1 may seem relatively mechanical in nature, it is not necessarily so, and step 2 is far from simple. As a check on the results of step 2, experts generally consider that any problems encountered in performing the tasks of step 3 (allocation of operations) are likely to indicate that the structure produced by step 2 is not correct. JSP also incorporates a useful verification procedure that can be used to check that the structures generated by step 2 are consistent with those produced by step 1.

As already mentioned, JSP is unusual in that it uses only a single diagrammatical form of description. However, the transformation diagram in Figure 14.3 shows that this is perhaps misleading, since while the *form* of diagram used remains the same, the *interpretation* of it changes as a result of the transformation performed in step 2. Indeed, part of the complexity of step 2 is that it involves a transformation from a static model of sequential ordering of data elements to a dynamic model of time-ordered sequencing of program actions.

To illustrate the basic design process more fully, we will work through a short example of the use of JSP, concentrating on steps 1 to 3 of the design process, since it is these that form the major components of the method.

Since JSP is often (unfairly) associated only with 'classical' data-processing problems based on handling files, with the final structures expressed in COBOL, the example problem has been chosen to look as unlike this as possible. The basic system requirement is as follows:

A petrol filling station (shown schematically in Figure 14.4) has a number of self-service pumps, each of which can be used to dispense both diesel fuel and unleaded petrol. There is a small local computer in each pump that maintains the display of

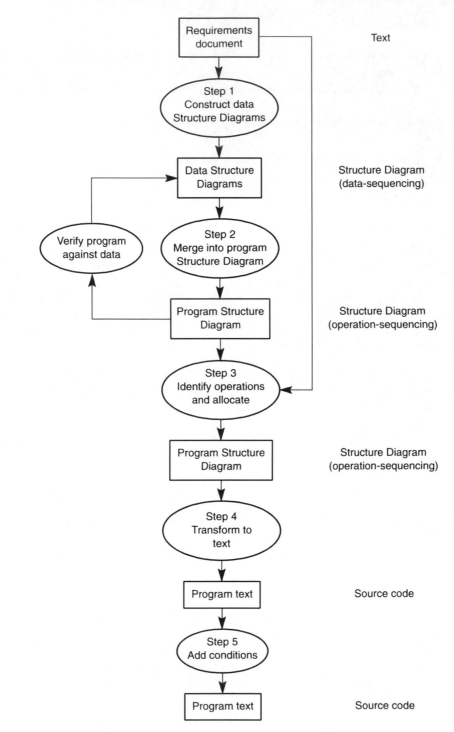

Figure 14.3 The JSP design process.

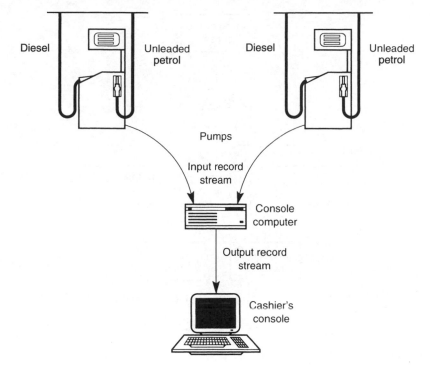

Figure 14.4 Schematic of a filling station.

price and volume on the pump; when the customer returns the pump nozzle to its socket, this computer sends a record to the cashier's console computer, containing the details of the current transaction as the sequence:

pump identity; type of fuel; volume of fuel

The problem is to design the software that receives these messages. For each message it receives, the program is required to generate a line on the printer positioned in front of the cashier, giving the details of the transaction in terms of

pump identity; volume of fuel; total cost

(Since there are many pumps, there is of course the possibility that contention could arise when more than one pump tries to send a message to the console. However, in the time-hallowed tradition of software design, we will leave this issue to be resolved by the designers of the communication hardware!)

As an initial design specification, the one given above is somewhat imperfect, in that although the computer in the pump calculates and displays the cost of the transaction, it does not send this information to the cashier's console. We therefore have a repeated calculation of the same 'object' value, which provides the potential for an inconsistency to occur. However, this is excused on the basis that the pump computer's software has already been designed and implemented (a not untypical situation); also, without this feature the problem would actually be a little too simple and so would fail to illustrate some of the desired points!

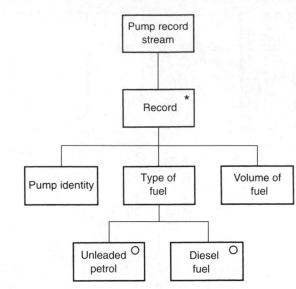

Figure 14.5 The filling-station Structure Diagram for the input data stream.

14.3.1 Step 1: Draw the input/output Structure Diagrams

On this occasion, this task is a fairly undemanding one, since the system has just one input data stream and one output data stream. The Structure Diagram for the input data stream is shown in Figure 14.5, and the levels of abstraction for this can be interpreted as follows:

- the *pump record stream* consists of many instances of a *record*;

- a *record* consists of the sequence:

  pump identity
  type of fuel
  volume of fuel

- the type of fuel field can specify the grade as either:

  unleaded petrol
  diesel fuel.

In this case, the structure of this record has been determined previously by the pump designers, and hence it is assumed that it cannot be modified as a part of the design process.

The form of the output data stream is shown in Figure 14.6, and again this can be interpreted as meaning that:

- the *sales record stream* consists of many instances of a *record*;

- a *record* consists of the sequence:

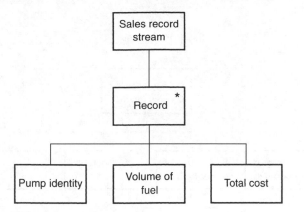

Figure 14.6 The filling-station Structure Diagram for the output data stream.

```
pump identity
volume of fuel
total cost
```

There is obviously some scope to improve on this. One such improvement would be to add some degree of page-handling, which would print headings on a page and begin a new page after printing the details of a set number of transactions. However, this is not fundamental to the problem and hence it would be better to add this feature after the basic structures have been established. Redesigning the system to include this feature is therefore left as an exercise for the reader!

Note that at this level of design the designer is solely concerned with handling abstractions such as pump identity and total cost. There is no attempt to consider how these are to be realized in terms of strings of text, number of digits and so on.

The apparent simplicity of this first step as demonstrated in our example risks being misleading. While many real problems can be described in this way, it should be noted that the task of producing correct descriptions in the form of Structure Diagrams can form a significant proportion of the overall design effort required.

14.3.2 Step 2: Create the program Structure Diagram

Without a doubt, this can be the hardest part of the JSP process, although for this example it happens to be relatively easy, as there are no contentions of structure to resolve. The resulting program structure is shown in Figure 14.7. The letters 'C' and 'P' have been added to the labels of the boxes in order to emphasize whether data is being 'consumed' or 'produced' in the given operation. (Much of the simplicity of this step as applied to the example comes from the relatively direct match between the input and output data forms. As a result, there is no need to introduce any new structures or extra levels of abstraction, which might occur with a less tractable problem.)

It is this step that leads to the conclusion that JSP should be classified as a method that uses a compositional design strategy, since the program structure is very much one that is 'composed' by bringing together the input/output data structures.

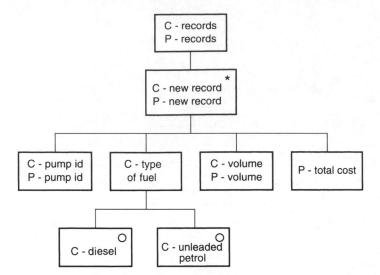

Figure 14.7 The filling-station program Structure Diagram.

Using the same process of step-by-step elaboration of the diagrammatical description as before, the operations of the program shown in Figure 14.7 can be described
thus:

▧ repeatedly consuming a new input record and generating a new output record;

▧ consuming and producing new records involves the following sequence of actions:

> consuming and producing the pump identity
> consuming the type of fuel
> consuming and producing the volume of fuel
> producing the total cost of the transaction

▧ consuming the type of fuel involves consuming information to indicate whether
it is

> unleaded petrol or
> diesel fuel

The basic verification procedure that forms a part of this design step can be easily performed in this instance. To check whether the program tree is consistent with the *input*
data stream, erase all lines beginning with a P, and delete all empty boxes. To check
whether the program tree is consistent with the *output* data stream, perform a similar
exercise, erasing all lines beginning with C and then removing any empty boxes. (Try
this as an exercise, and verify that each of these leaves the original input form.) Where
the process of merging trees is more complex, then the verification process will, of
course, be correspondingly more complicated.

Again, the nature of the chosen example is such that this is a relatively simple task to perform. Since most requirements place their emphasis on describing the outputs that are to be produced from a system, it may well be better to begin this task by considering the outputs first, and then using these to identify the necessary inputs and algorithmic operations. However, there seems to be no hard and fast rule about how this should be done, nor any direct way of checking for completeness.

For the filling-station system, the operations involved are the following:

Outputs   (1)   write pump identity
(2)   write volume of fuel
(3)   write cost to customer

Inputs   (4)   obtain pump identity
(5)   obtain volume of fuel
(6)   obtain type of fuel
(7)   multiply type price per unit by volume dispensed

Once again, the exercise of adding page headers and pagination to the output is left for the reader to consider.

These operations are then allocated to the elements in the program Structure Diagram, as shown in Figure 14.8 (the operations are shown as small numbered boxes). Note that it is only meaningful to attach an operation to a box at the base of any branch of the Structure Diagram, since higher levels within the diagram 'tree' are essentially abstractions of the base levels.

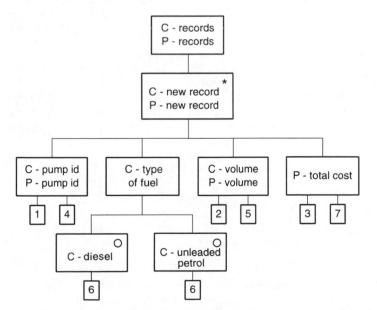

Figure 14.8   The filling-station program: allocation of operations to program elements.

(a) **Step 4:** Convert program to text without conditions

```
LOOP
    get pump identity
    get type of fuel
    get volume of fuel
    calculate price
    print pump identity
    print volume of fuel
    print price
ENDLOOP
```

(b) **Step 5:** Add conditions

```
LOOP
    get pump identity
    get type of fuel
    get volume of fuel
    CASE of type
        unleaded: price calculation 1
        diesel:   price calculation 2
    ENDCASE
    print pump identity
    print volume of fuel
    print price
ENDLOOP
```

Figure 14.9   The last two steps of JSP.

14.3.4 Steps 4 and 5: Convert program to text and add conditions

These steps are relatively straightforward for this simple problem. Figure 14.9 shows the basic program structure that is generated by combining the operations from step 3 with the program structure produced in step 2 (which provides the sequencing information). Step 5 then requires a simple extension of this to incorporate the conditional expression used to select price according to type of fuel. The remaining task is then to translate this into the chosen programming language in order to produce a usable program.

14.3.5 Summary of the design process

The relatively constrained nature of the JSP process means that using a D-matrix description offers only limited insight. However, not least because of its relative simplicity, this subsection uses the D-matrix to highlight the features of the first two key steps of the method.

Step 1: Draw the input/output Structure Diagrams

One point highlighted by this is that there is some initial expectation that these data structures will have been defined in some way. For that reason, we have modified the description of the 'requirements matrix' to explicitly recognize this. So our initial step consists of elaborating the requirements to create the first set of Structure Diagrams that are based upon the relationships in the data:

$$
\begin{pmatrix} R^b \\ R^f \\ R^d \\ \emptyset^c \end{pmatrix} \quad E^1 \rightarrow \bigcup_j \begin{pmatrix} \emptyset_1^b & \emptyset_2^b & \dots & \emptyset_{n(j)}^b \\ \emptyset_1^f & \emptyset_2^f & \dots & \emptyset_{n(j)}^f \\ D_1^d & D_2^d & \dots & D_{n(j)}^d \\ \emptyset_1^c & \emptyset_2^c & \dots & \emptyset_{n(j)}^c \end{pmatrix}_j
$$

Here we have used the same extended notation as was used in the previous chapter, where the subscript j denotes the jth Structure Diagram, and the elements $1 \dots n(j)$ represent the elements at the 'leaf' nodes of the jth Structure Diagram.

This step is clearly one of transformation, since it involves moving from a model based upon the structure of the data elements to one based upon function. (The representation form used for the inputs and outputs of this step happens to be the same one, a feature that is unique to JSP, but the *interpretation* is altered.) So now we go through a combination process to create a single Structure Diagram, and we can represent this as below:

$$
\sum_j
\begin{pmatrix}
\varnothing_1^b & \varnothing_2^b \dots \varnothing_{n(j)}^b \\
\varnothing_1^f & \varnothing_2^f \dots \varnothing_{n(j)}^f \\
D_1^d & D_2^d \dots D_{n(j)}^d \\
\varnothing_1^c & \varnothing_2^c \dots \varnothing_{n(j)}^c
\end{pmatrix}_j
\quad T^2 \rightarrow \quad
\begin{pmatrix}
\varnothing_1^b & \varnothing_2^b \dots \varnothing_n^b \\
D_1^f & D_2^f \dots D_n^f \\
d_1^d & d_2^d \dots d_n^d \\
\varnothing_1^c & \varnothing_2^c \dots \varnothing_n^c
\end{pmatrix}
$$

Again, we have left the data modelling element as being present in the model, but have represented it using *d* rather than *D* to show the change of emphasis to describing the structure of function.

The remaining steps of the JSP process are essentially concerned with elaboration, so that the final matrix description is really no different to the final one shown on the right hand side above (although obviously the details within each element are expanded). This highlights the point that this is a *program* design method, and that no decisions about constructional forms are developed through its processes.

14.4 Some JSP heuristics

With the extensive experience in the use of JSP that has accumulated since its development in the early 1970s, it is hardly surprising to find that some relatively systematic practices have been developed to provide guidelines for use in handling certain 'standard' types of problem that can arise.

These practices are needed in any design method, because assumptions that are made in its model-building process impose constraints on the form of solution produced. In the case of JSP, these constraints are chiefly placed on the forms of the input and output data streams (and they largely arise because no other viewpoints are used in composing the design model). Such constraints may not always map well onto some reasonably common situations and, as a remedy, the method developers evolve the ancillary strategies that we have termed 'heuristics' or 'clichés'.

This section will briefly describe three examples of such situations, together with outlines of the techniques for handling them. These examples respectively concern the use of the techniques of read-ahead, backtracking and program inversion. (For a more detailed account of how each of these is incorporated into JSP design practices, the reader is advised to consult one of the specialist texts identified at the end of this chapter.)

14.4.1 The use of read-ahead

JSP is essentially concerned with designing programs around algorithms that involve consuming and producing records (the 'filter' element of a *pipe-and-filter* style), as the example of the preceding section showed. The algorithms for these programs may involve resolving particular conditions in order to make decisions about how data should be processed, and on occasion it may be necessary to know something about the next item of data to determine how the current item should be processed.

Programmers who are familiar with structured programming languages derived from ALGOL will be familiar enough with the nature of this problem. In such a language the use of a WHILE loop, containing an input statement that determines the termination conditions for the loop, will usually require an initial input statement to be included before the start of the loop, as shown in Figure 14.10. This statement is needed to ensure that when the conditional expression used for the WHILE statement is first evaluated, it will not cause the loop to terminate incorrectly before it has begun. Even if the logic within the loop is correct, incorrect initialization will lead to problems if one (say) attempts to perform input from an empty file by using a loop that terminates on finding the end-of-line mark.

The initial abstract level of design that is involved in the JSP design process simply identifies that iterations occur: the detailed form of the iteration structure is not determined until the conversion to text in steps 4 and 5. However, as we have just seen, if the loop construct eventually adopted is similar to that of the WHILE loop, it may be necessary to adjust the logic of the program structure in order to allow for correct initialization. On such an occasion, a restructuring of the program structure to include a single read-ahead operation may well be required in order to solve the problem.

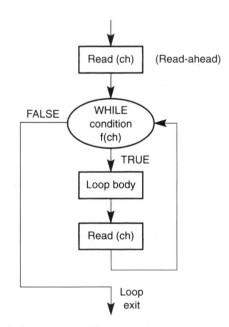

Figure 14.10 Read-ahead: the structure of a WHILE loop.

In many ways this is a specific instance of a much more general design problem. Software design methods normally encourage a design structure that is concerned with meeting the requirements of the 'steady state' of a system, and this is then adjusted to incorporate the needs of initialization and termination, and of any error-handling facilities required. In general, this approach of solving the general problem and then adapting to the exceptions is probably the most practical one, since attempting to incorporate all of these factors from the outset is likely to destroy any chance of establishing a clear design structure.

14.4.2 Backtracking

It is not always possible to resolve a condition by using a single simple read-ahead operation; when this occurs we have an example of a 'recognition difficulty'.

It is sometimes possible to use multiple read-ahead in such cases, where a predictable sequence can be determined that will be needed to establish the condition. However, where this cannot be used, the more general technique of backtracking will need to be adopted during step 4 of the basic JSP design process.

The basic steps of backtracking are as follows:

- posit a default condition for use in all cases, this being assumed to hold until proved false;

- at those points following at which it is possible to test the hypothesis, insert 'quit' operations (where a 'quit' is effectively a constrained GOTO operation);

- provide for any necessary 'undo' operations to reverse the effect of actions performed before the path was proved to be the wrong one.

Figure 14.11 shows the resulting structure. The last step of this sequence can make life rather complicated, and as a general rule the use of temporary storage for intermediate results is suggested, with the main data structures being updated only when the transaction has been completed.

The use of backtracking leads to much more complicated program structures, possibly including large numbers of conditions. Its use can be considered as important when it is necessary to handle various forms of error in the input data streams.

14.4.3 Program inversion and structure clashes

Like the other two problems described in this section, structure clashes occur because of the assumptions that are made in the initial JSP model about the mappings used for the data structures. To explain the issue a bit more clearly, we will use a further example of the JSP design process.

The problem involves the *Lotsalogs* company encountered in Chapter 1. The company has a tradition of giving its complete workforce a long break over the Christmas and New Year period. However, its generosity does not run to providing them with their pay in advance, and so, in order to pay its workers during the holiday period, it is necessary for the company to mail cheques to their home addresses.

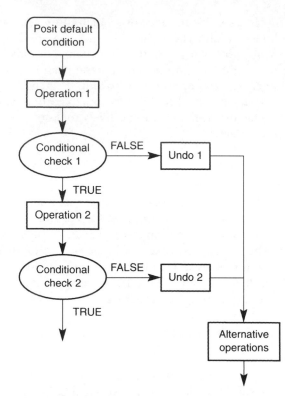

Figure 14.11 Backtracking: the basic strategy.

To complicate things a little further, the company employs people using two different types of contract. The permanent employees enjoy monthly salaries, while others are paid on a weekly basis. Also, all employees have a unique staff identity number allocated to them when they first join the company.

The company's finance department maintains a 'payments file' for the company, which is structured in the form shown in Figure 14.12. By now, this should be so familiar that there is little difficulty in identifying the structure of the file:

■ the salary file consists of many staff member records;

■ the record for each staff member begins with the staff identity number, followed by details of gross pay;

■ the details of gross pay are further structured according to whether the employee is paid on a monthly basis or a weekly one.

A full description of this file would obviously need to include further details about the structures used for monthly and weekly pay. However, for the purposes of this example, the description need not be elaborated further than this level of detail.

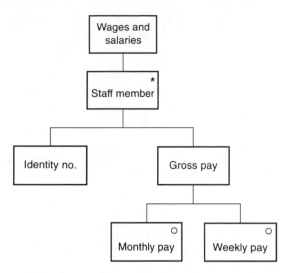

Figure 14.12 Structure of the finance file.

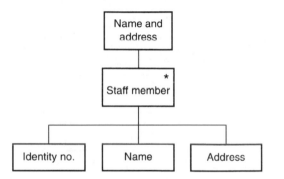

Figure 14.13 Structure of the personnel file.

In order to send out the Christmas pay cheques, this information from the finance department needs to be combined with further information about such details as the name and home address for each employee. Fortunately, these are held by the personnel section, and Figure 14.13 shows the format of the file that they maintain for this purpose.

Since each of these files has one record per employee, we can reasonably assume that each file will contain the same number of records (assuming no fraudulent behaviour) and that they can therefore be combined to create a file giving the information needed for addressing the envelopes to be used for sending out the Christmas payments. Figure 14.14 shows the structure of the file required for this purpose.

Step 2 of the JSP design process is slightly more complicated than it was for the previous example; we now need to combine three structures in order to create the

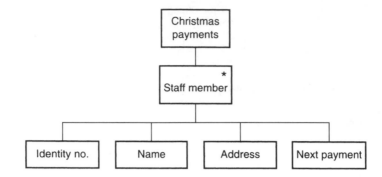

Figure 14.14 Structure of the output file.

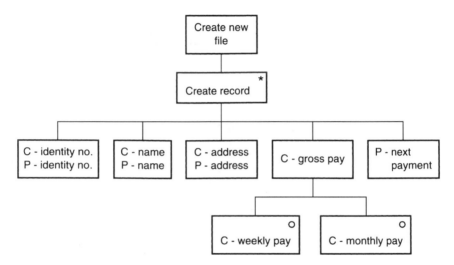

Figure 14.15 Structure of the Christmas payments program.

required program structure. However, as these data structures are not particularly complex ones, this can be done fairly easily, and the resulting program structure is shown in Figure 14.15. (This can again be verified against the data structures by the same process as before, although there are some slight extra complications involved in separating the inputs.)

So we now have a design for the required program, and the company should be able to proceed with generating the required output. Figures 14.16 and 14.17 show the first parts of the input files that are to be used for this purpose. Only at this point does it become evident that the design process has made a (flawed) assumption about the ordering of the records in the two files. The finance department likes to organize its files by using the staff identity numbers, while the personnel department prefers to use an alphabetical ordering based on the names of the employees. Unfortunately, unless the allocation of identity numbers is based on an alphabetical relationship – which is clearly not the case here – the records in the two files will be ordered quite differently. While Charlie Chips might be quite pleased to receive Sam Sawdust's salary payment,

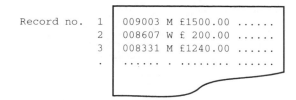

```
Record no.  1 │ 009003 M £1500.00 ......
            2 │ 008607 W £ 200.00 ......
            3 │ 008331 M £1240.00 ......
            . │ ...... . ......... ......
```

Figure 14.16 The finance department's file.

```
Record no.  1 │ 008607 Charlie Chips    9 Log Cabins Way
            2 │ 008721 Les Logjam       15 Sawpit Drive
            3 │ 009003 Sam Sawdust      14 Timber Mansions
            . │ ...... ...........      ............
```

Figure 14.17 The personnel department's file.

it isn't clear that Sam will be equally pleased with the size of his cheque, and so there obviously is a need to perform some form of remedial action.

This is an example of what Jackson terms a 'structure clash'. This particular form is an 'ordering clash', and occurs when one or more of the input streams are ordered using different keys. In the case of our example, the keys involved are the staff identity number and the name.

As it happens, this type of structure clash can often be resolved fairly easily, provided that the two files contain a common key. In this example, since both of the input files share a common key in the form of the identity number, the personnel data file can simply be reordered around this key by using an intermediate sorting program (an additional *filter* process), so that the file corresponds to the ordering used in the finance data file. Following this reasonably simple operation, the *Lotsalogs* employees can look forward to receiving their correct Christmas and New Year pay.

The other two types of structure clash that Jackson identifies are the boundary clash, in which data is broken up using different criteria, although ordered by the same keys; and the multithreading clash, in which data elements overlap in the input file. The idea of a boundary clash can be clarified by considering the two views that can be taken when describing the structure of a text file stored on a disk. At the programming level, it is considered to consist of a sequence of variable-length *records*, made up of strings of characters. However, to the low-level software of the operating system, the file is organized as a sequence of *disk blocks* of standard size. Figure 14.18 shows the Structure Diagrams that represent these two quite different views of the same file – one record-based, the other block-based. It is the task of the file-handling routines of the operating system to resolve these and to transform between them as necessary.

Structure clashes essentially arise because of some implicit assumptions that are made within the forms used in JSP. They are based on inconsistencies that arise in the ordering of components when these are viewed at a lower level of abstraction than is provided by the Structure Diagram. To handle these clashes without continual recourse to extra sorting and merging routines, JSP has developed an associated technique

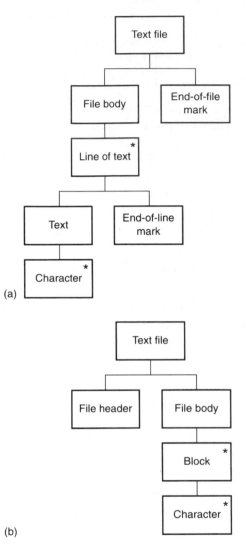

Figure 14.18 Example of a boundary clash: two views of a text file. (a) From the programmer's viewpoint. (b) From the operating system's viewpoint.

known as 'program inversion'. However, as has been observed by Cameron (1988a), it is unfair to regard program inversion as simply a means of resolving structure clashes. It can be used to assist with the structuring of solutions to other types of problem, including interactive programs and interrupt-handling programs (Sanden, 1985).

There is not enough space to give a detailed account of program inversion in this chapter, but the basic idea behind it can be summarized fairly briefly. In order to use inversion, we adopt the form of solution that was originally identified as appropriate for the example of the Christmas payments, which is to design *two* programs that share a common data structure. In that example, this requires that one of the original files be sorted into an intermediate file, and that the sorted file be the input to the

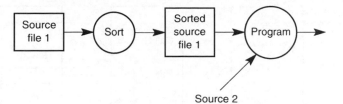

Figure 14.19   Program inversion: removing an ordering clash by a sorted intermediate file.

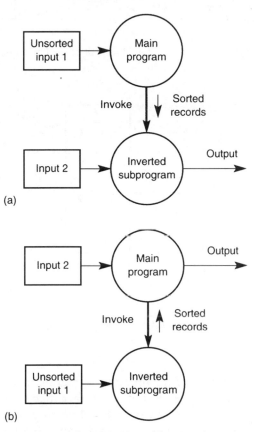

Figure 14.20   Program inversion: a schematic view. (a) Using the main program as the 'sort'. (b) Using the inverted subprogram as the 'sort'.

program. Figure 14.19 shows this idea schematically. The two programs are then used to create and consume this file. (We could, of course, just stop at this point, which might be adequate for a one-off situation such as the Christmas payments example.) The need for the intermediate file can be removed by 'inverting' one of the programs so that it becomes a subprogram of the other program (and similarly, we modify that program to call the inverted one). Figure 14.20 shows this form of solution schematically. In practice, as is shown in the diagram, either program can be inverted, for reasons now to be explained.

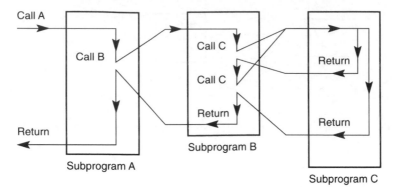

Figure 14.21 An example of the organization of flow of control for three subprograms.

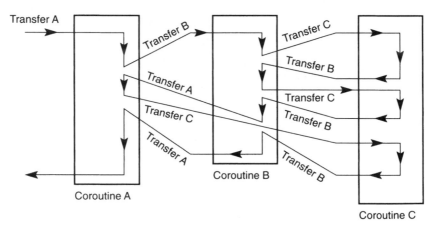

Figure 14.22 An example of the organization of flow of control for three coroutines.

A more correct description of the process of program inversion is that it leads to a solution based on the use of two coroutines, rather than of a main program and a subprogram. Figures 14.21 and 14.22 show the difference between the two types of construct. As they show, coroutines resume execution from the point at which they last transferred control, whereas, whenever a subprogram is invoked, it always begins execution at its first instruction. (Coroutines are effectively 'equals', and this is why either program can be inverted.)

Very few programming languages support the coroutine mechanism – Modula-2 is an exception to this rule, although even there, the implementation is in the nature of an 'add-on'. It is the need to create an approximation to this construct that usually leads to the use of subprogram. This in turn produces much of the messy control flow that usually characterizes the examples of program inversion to be found in many textbooks.

The nature of program inversion can perhaps be seen most easily for the example used above to describe a boundary clash. Figure 14.23 shows an example of part of a file of records, stored in a sequence of disk blocks (for artistic convenience, records are

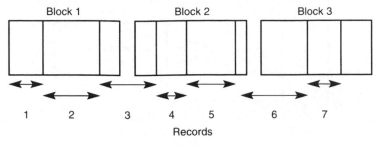

Figure 14.23 Mapping records onto blocks (boundary clash).

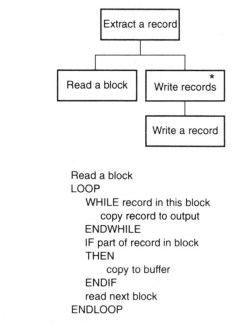

(a)

```
Read a block
LOOP
    WHILE record in this block
        copy record to output
    ENDWHILE
    IF part of record in block
    THEN
        copy to buffer
    ENDIF
    read next block
ENDLOOP
```

(b)

Figure 14.24 A simple program to extract records from blocks. (a) Structure Diagram.
(b) Pseudocode.

always shown as shorter than a block, but this is not a real restriction). Figure 14.24 shows the structure of the library routine that might be designed with JSP to extract records from the blocks and then pass them to a user program, one record at a time. Inversion of this program would then result in the construction of two coroutines: a section of their execution sequencing is shown in Figure 14.25.

So program inversion is a further example of a 'design heuristic', in the sense that it is a well-developed technique that can be used to overcome a problem that itself arises because of the needs and assumptions of the method. Because the method assumes the existence of certain ordering constraints upon the input streams, a technique is needed that can create these constraints whenever a particular problem does not fit the requirement.

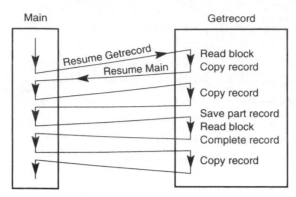

Figure 14.25   Execution sequence for inverted program.

Summary

Because JSP provides a rather good and concise example of the major characteristics of all design methods, it has been given fairly comprehensive cover in this chapter. In some ways this probably exaggerates its importance in terms of current design technology. Indeed, because JSP explicitly builds on knowledge of the detailed structure of data in the formulation of a design solution, it cannot readily be used to build structures that incorporate such ideas as information-hiding. Similarly, it lacks any means of modelling data stores or events. However, JSP does have an important historical place in the development of design thinking, not least through its introduction of the notion of composition as a design strategy. But today its main role is more likely to be confined to assisting with detailed tasks of algorithm design rather than larger-scale design.

This is not to suggest that the only good reason for studying JSP is as an exemplar of design methods. One of the benefits of using JSP is that it encourages the designer to think about a form of model different from that which emerges from the event-driven or top-down views, and so it has an important educational role in its own right. Indeed, the value of the Structure Diagram as a modelling tool is widely recognized in many other methods. Also, as with the Structured Systems Analysis and Structured Design method described in the preceding chapter, there is a large repository of designs that have been produced using JSP and related techniques, and their maintenance is likely to require that designers have some familiarity with JSP for many more years to come.

It is also important to reiterate the point that JSP is a *program* design method. Indeed, its main emphasis is on describing the time-ordered operations of the solution (sequencing), rather than on the derivation of any physical structure for the program, based on a hierarchy of subprograms. While it should be possible to develop this description relatively directly from the JSP solution, it is not explicitly included in any way.

As an aside, while JSP has spawned no real extensions or developments, there is an equivalent method in existence. This is Warnier's LCP method (Warnier, 1980), and while the notation is somewhat different, and LCP has some other restrictions when compared directly with JSP, it is much closer to it in philosophy than any other design method in use.

Jackson M. (1975). *Principles of Program Design*. Academic Press

The original work by Michael Jackson. While it is well written and gives a clear exposition of the basic ideas, it is probably rather too COBOL-oriented in its philosophy for many modern tastes.

Ingevaldsson L. (1986). *JSP: A Practical Method of Program Design*. Chartwell-Bratt

This short monograph provides a very concise introduction to JSP, and is not so heavily COBOL-oriented as Jackson's original work. It uses many illustrations and is permeated throughout with a very dry sense of humour.

King M.J. and Pardoe J.P. (1992). *Program Design Using JSP: A Practical Introduction*. 2nd edn. Macmillan

Very clearly written, and has examples that are described using COBOL, Pascal – and BASIC! A good exposition of the method.

Cameron J.R. (1988). *JSP and JSD: The Jackson Approach to Software Development*. 2nd edn. IEEE Computer Society Press

This IEEE Tutorial provides something of a sourcebook for JSP, full of details, examples and associated information. While perhaps not so suitable for a first introduction as the other three books, it surpasses them as a reference text.

Exercises

14.1 For the example of the filling station that was introduced in Section 14.3, extend the Structure Diagrams for the output data stream and the program to include:

   (a) a 'page throw' on the printer that occurs after every 50 lines of output, to be followed by the printing of a set of column headings at the top of the new page;
   (b) a total at the bottom of each page that shows the total value of the transactions on that page.

14.2 Taking your solutions to Exercise 14.1 above, identify the additional operations that will be involved, and allocate these to the program elements, as in step 3 of the JSP method.

14.3 Draw a Structure Diagram that describes the address of a person in the 'standard American' format of surname, forename, initials, number, street, city, state, zip code, elaborating on the details of each of these in turn. How would this model cope with Jim Smith, who lives in Blacksmith's Cottage with an address that has no street name?

14.4 The filling station example is a specific example of the general problem of producing a package for a point-of-sale system. Follow through the first three steps of the JSP method to design a program that will control a supermarket till: the program accepts input from a barcode reader and the keys of the till in order to read the details of each item and the number of items. The till should print out the details of each transaction, and should also print out the final total price when the 'total' key is pressed.

Jackson System Development (JSD)

The JSD method was developed in the 1980s as one that incorporated a large-scale 'compositional' design strategy, based on the use of 'long-running' virtual processes to model the required system. Its detailed form continued to evolve through the 1980s, although the changes were more in the nature of organizational refinements and incorporation of accumulated experience, rather than any significant revisions to the philosophy or concepts underpinning the method.

In this chapter we examine the concepts, forms and procedures that make up the JSD method, which shares much of the philosophy of JSP, although on a much larger scale of application. Also, as with JSP, the primary domain of application was intended as 'data-processing' tasks (in a fairly wide sense), although its use of parallelism and attention to time-ordering and event modelling has led to it also being employed for other types of problem.

15.1 The JSD model

Unlike the methods described in the preceding two chapters, which were devised in the early 1970s, JSD can be considered as a 'second-generation' software design method, since its development took place during the late 1970s and early 1980s. As a method, it encompasses both analysis and design activities, directed towards constructing a model of a system in terms of a set of 'long-running' interacting concurrent processes for its description, which is then transformed into a 'physical realization' of the model (namely, the detailed design).

Although originally intended for designing 'data-processing' systems, in a fairly general sense of the term, the JSD design model can potentially be applied to other problem domains, and especially those where time-ordering of actions may be a dominant characteristic. JSD is also concerned with modelling *processes* rather than objects, and hence its use usually results in a design that has an *interacting processes* architectural style (communicating processes). Arguably, JSD is also well suited to the design of client–server systems, with its emphasis upon long-term interactions and its explicit modelling of state information.

JSD is generally regarded as having its roots in the thinking that stems from Hoare's ideas on communicating sequential processes (Hoare, 1978). In contrast to the SSA/SD design method described in Chapter 13, JSD places emphasis on modelling the *actions* of the system in terms of their effects on the input and output data streams, rather than on using the direct functional tasks as the basis for the design model. As such, it is compositional rather than top-down in its form, and in some aspects it also comes close to the object-based paradigm that is described in the next chapter. Indeed, Henderson-Sellers and Edwards (1990) have argued that JSD occupies a midway point between these strategies.

JSD has undergone a certain amount of evolution since the original description in Jackson (1983). The form of the design process as described in Cameron (1986; 1988a) contains some revisions to the design steps, while the description in Sutcliffe (1988) shows a rather different view of the structure of the method. This chapter examines both the original form of the method and the revisions it has undergone, together with some of the reasons for these.

JSD shares a number of major structural features with JSP, although its much larger problem domain means that it is correspondingly less prescriptive in nature. One of these common threads is the importance ascribed to incorporating time-ordering in the modelling process. JSD also shares with JSP the philosophy of using a model of the real world as the basis for system structure, meaning that changes in the external world can be mirrored as changes in the structure of the model, and eventually emerge as changes in the structure of the program(s).

The best framework for describing the broad process of JSD design is that provided by Sutcliffe (1988) and also used in Cameron (1988a), where it is described in terms of the following three stages:

■ a *modelling stage*, in which the problem is analysed and modelled in terms of the constituent entities and the actions that they perform, and where these entities are represented by 'long-running' sequential processes in the model itself;

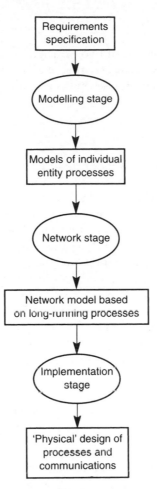

Figure 15.1 Top-level transformational model of JSD.

- a *network stage*, in which the overall structure of the system is developed from that of the model by adding the details of interactions between entities, and between the entities and the external world;

- an *implementation stage*, in which the abstract design is mapped onto a 'physical' design.

Figure 15.1 shows these stages using the general transformational model we have adopted. (Note too that the terminology of JSD is sometimes somewhat idiosyncratic, as in the use of the term 'implementation' for a process that more normally would be described as 'physical design'.)

The following sections describe and examine the major features of JSD, using the same general structure for presentation as was adopted in the previous chapters.

15.2 JSD representation forms

The JSD design process makes use of two principal forms of diagrammatical description. One of these has already been encountered earlier in this book, but it is used here to capture a different viewpoint; the second is essentially new (although not radically original in any sense).

15.2.1 The Entity–Structure Diagram

This is an adaptation (or, perhaps more correctly, an interpretation) of the Jackson Structure Diagram described in Section 7.2.5. In JSD it is used to describe the 'evolution' of an entity over a period of time. In this context, an entity is an 'active' element that is identified through the operations of the modelling process itself. (It can be loosely considered to be a form of 'processing agent' in the system.) The notation used for an Entity–Structure Diagram (ESD) is the standard form used for a Structure Diagram, and the main development involved is simply one of making a different interpretation of the diagram elements, in order to adopt a rather different viewpoint of the system model.

In the JSD model of a system as a network of long-running sequential processes, the ESD provides a means of describing the behaviour of the sequential processes. Figure 15.2 shows an example of such an Entity–Structure Diagram, as developed for one of the entities in an Air Traffic Control (ATC) system (namely, an aircraft). For

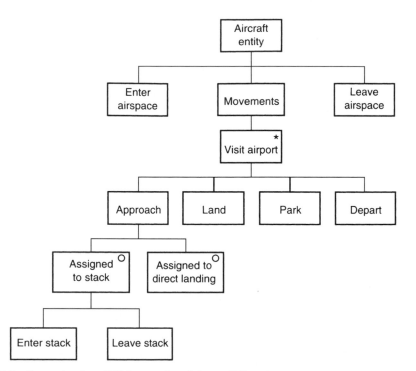

Figure 15.2 Example of an ESD for an aircraft in an ATC system.

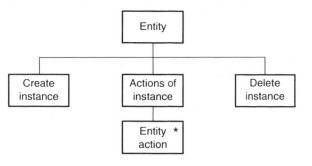

Figure 15.3 Generic form of ESD.

this problem, an aircraft has been identified as one of the entities whose behaviour should be modelled, and so this diagram is constructed as part of the modelling task. (The procedure for developing this diagram is described in the next section.)

Figure 15.3 shows the generic form of Structure Diagrams of this type; the overall basic sequence is concerned with:

- creation of the entity in the model;

- actions performed by the entity while in existence;

- deletion of the entity from the model.

An examination of Figure 15.2 shows that this conforms to this framework at the first level of abstraction. (Note that a JSD model is therefore essentially of a dynamic nature, being concerned with specifying time-ordered behaviour.)

In this example, an aircraft becomes an entity of interest to the ATC system only when it crosses a boundary to enter the controlled airspace and it ceases to be of interest when it leaves that airspace. Between those events it might perform a number of actions, which can include:

- doing nothing (the aircraft just flies through);

- landing and taking off;

- being 'stacked' before landing.

This model allows for multiple occurrences of an aircraft being stacked, landing and taking off – although most of us would probably prefer that these events should be exceptional! Once again, time-ordering is important: an aircraft must land before it can take off, and if it enters the landing stack, it must leave the stack before it can be assigned to the runway for landing.

For other systems, a suitable entity might be a person, as in Figure 15.4, describing a student who is on a course of some kind. Again, the person in question becomes of interest (in terms of the JSD model) only when undertaking those actions that make him or her into a student, and a specific type of student at that (one registered for this course); and ceases to be of interest to the model on ceasing to be a student, whether this occurs through passing or failing the course.

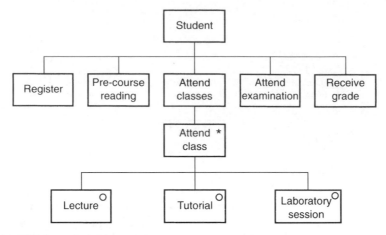

Figure 15.4 ESD for a student on a course.

Each of these examples of an entity might be of importance to a system designer using JSD. In the first case, we can assume that modelling aircraft behaviour would be required when constructing an ATC system intended to provide assistance to the human controllers. In the second, in order to create a system that will be used to maintain student records, the designer will need this model of student activity in order to help identify all the situations that the system will be required to handle. (We will examine the criteria used for the selection of suitable entities in Section 15.3, where we study the JSD procedures.)

15.2.2 The System Specification Diagram (SSD)

The SSD is basically a network diagram that identifies the interactions between the entities that make up the model of the system. These interactions take place by two basic mechanisms for interprocess communication, which are:

- A *data-flow stream*, in which messages are passed asynchronously between the entities concerned, using some form of pipeline mechanism, as shown in Figure 15.5. A data-flow stream acts as a FIFO queue, and is assumed to have infinite buffer capacity, so that the producer process is never blocked on a write operation to the buffer of the stream. In contrast, the consumer process *is* blocked if it tries to read from a buffer when no message is available, as it has no means of checking whether data is available before issuing a read request.

- A *state vector* that describes the 'local state' of a process at a given time. By inspecting this state vector, one entity can obtain required information from a second entity,

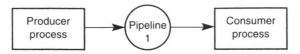

Figure 15.5 The SSD for a pipeline (data stream).

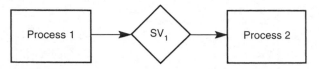

Figure 15.6 The SSD for a state vector inspection. Process 2 inspects the state vector of Process 1.

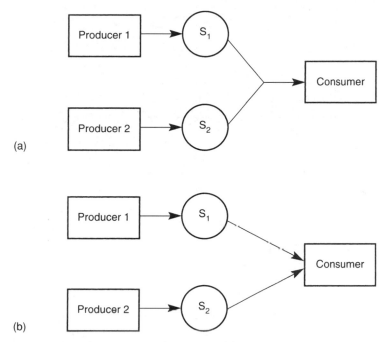

Figure 15.7 Processes with multiple input streams. (a) Using a rough-merged form. (b) Using separate 'read' operations.

where this is contained in its current state. The state vector will typically consist of the local variables of a process, including its program counter which is used to indicate the current state of execution. (This concept applies to the long-running 'virtual' processes used in the designer's model as well as to the 'physical' processes used in the eventual implementation.) Figure 15.6 shows an example of state vector inspection. Since the 'inspected' process may also be executing during the inspection process, there is a degree of indeterminacy present in this mechanism.

The notation used for SSDs has further elements to denote such features as multiplicity of data transfer operations and multiplicity of processes.

In particular, where a process reads from more than one stream, we can distinguish between the cases in which data is read from either stream as available using the 'rough-merged' scheme (Figure 15.7 (a)), and those in which the inputs remain distinct (Figure 15.7 (b)). In the first case, the consumer is required to organize the handling of

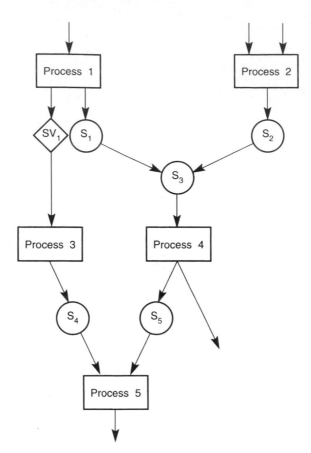

Figure 15.8 A simple example of a segment from an SSD.

multiple inputs through one read operation, while in the latter it must organize the sequencing of consumption from the two sources. However, beyond observing the presence of these structures, we will not explore the SSD notation in any further depth in this chapter.

Figure 15.8 shows an SSD describing a very simple network in a system. The circle is used to label a data-flow arc, and an entity is represented by using an oblong box. Those who are more accustomed to the conventional DFD notations might find this confusing. The diamond shape used to describe the state vector is associated with a particular entity by means of the labelling attached to it.

15.3 The JSD process

The procedures involved in the 'process part' of JSD have undergone a certain amount of revision and repackaging since the method was first introduced. Figure 15.9 uses an ESD to describe the JSD process as it was originally presented in Jackson (1983), while Figure 15.10 shows the form of the method as subsequently described in Cameron (1986). Two basic changes occurred in the method during this interval.

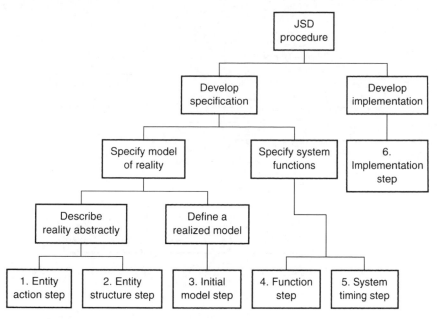

Figure 15.9 The JSD procedure as originally described in Jackson (1983).

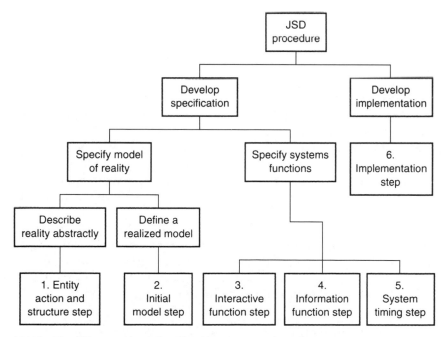

Figure 15.10 The JSD procedure as revised by Cameron (1986).

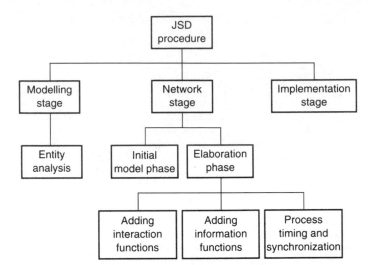

Figure 15.11   The three-stage model of JSD as used in Sutcliffe (1988) and Cameron (1988a).

■ The first two steps of the method as it is described in Figure 15.9 have been merged in Figure 15.10. The change involved can be considered as being largely cosmetic, as the two steps are so closely related.

■ The function step of Figure 15.9 has evolved into two separate steps in Figure 15.10 (the interactive function step and the information function step). We will examine the roles of these in a little more detail later. This modification is a more significant development than the previous one, since it gives additional structure to the design process for a task that is generally seen as posing difficult problems for the designer.

In Section 15.1 the JSD design process was also described in terms of the three-stage outline subsequently used by both Sutcliffe (1988) and Cameron (1988a). These stages differ slightly from the abstractions used in the other two forms, and the corresponding mapping of the design activities is shown in Figure 15.11. By comparing this with the descriptions of the earlier forms, it can be seen that the modelling stage can be identified as the first part of Jackson's 'specify model of reality', while the network stage comprises the latter part, together with Jackson's 'specify system functions'. (The implementation stage is common to all three.)

Sutcliffe's framework will be adopted for the outline description of the JSD process part in this section, since this is the most highly evolved structural description. However, the choice of framework does not greatly affect the description of the designer's activities, since these are based on the major steps of the method, which are, of course, essentially common to all the descriptions of the method.

15.3.1 The modelling stage

In many ways, the role of this step corresponds (rather loosely) to the 'analysis' phase of other methods such as SSA/SD, in that it is concerned with building up a 'black box' model of the problem, rather than considering the form of a solution.

Jackson and others have recommended that a designer should begin this task by analysing the requirements specification in order to identify the entities in the system, the actions that they perform, the attributes of the actions, and the time-ordering of the actions.

This task of entity analysis is based on making a study of the text of the requirements documents, augmented as necessary by questions and interviews with the client. A major objective for this task is to identify the entities of the problem. One strategy involves analysing the text of the requirements documents (and any other descriptions of the problem that can be obtained) in terms of the constituent verbs and nouns. The verbs can be used to identify actions, while the nouns are likely to describe entities, although the process of extracting the final lists of these requires quite a lot of work to refine and cross-reference the various candidates. In the process of doing so, the designer will also have to remove such extraneous items as synonyms, 'existence' or 'state' verbs, and entities that are not of direct relevance. In Cameron (1988b) the nature of this step and alternative strategies to use within it are explored more fully.

In practice, many problems turn out to have relatively few entities that actually need to be modelled, although the requirements documents may describe many other entities that are of only peripheral interest. These other entities are not included in the JSD model, and are described as 'outside the model boundary'. An entity that is outside the model boundary is one whose time-ordered behaviour does not affect the problem directly, but which may act to constrain the entities used in the design model.

As an excellent example of this distinction between entities and items outside the model boundary, Jackson (1983) develops an example of a simple banking system. A major entity that is identified for the model is the 'customer', which performs such actions as opening and closing accounts, and paying in and withdrawing funds. The bank manager, on the other hand, is dismissed as being 'outside the model boundary', because modelling the time-ordered behaviour of the bank manager does not help with developing a model of how the banking system operates, which is the purpose of this stage.

Once the entities and actions have been identified and correlated, the designer needs to add time-ordering to the list of actions for an entity. Figure 15.2 showed an example of the type of diagram that results from doing this, namely a Structure Diagram that describes an entity (in that case, an aircraft). As a further part of this task of analysis, the analyst will also seek to identify those attributes of the aircraft's actions that are of interest to the modelling. These may include information about:

- flight number
- call-sign
- position

and any other features that may be of assistance in distinguishing any one aircraft from the others in the airspace at a given time.

Figure 15.12 provides a symbolic illustration of the state of the JSD model at the end of the modelling stage. At this point in the design process the model consists of a set of (disjoint) process models for the major entities of the problem.

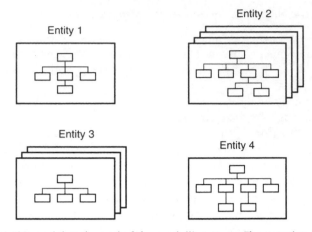

Figure 15.12 The JSD model at the end of the modelling stage. The notation is intended to indicate many instances of entities 2 and 3.

15.3.2 The network stage

The initial model phase

This phase involves the designer in linking the entities defined in the first step, and beginning the construction of the initial model of the system as a whole. Not surprisingly, as this initial model is concerned with modelling the interactions between the various entities, it produces a combination of SSDs and ESDs, with the added functionality arising from the fact that the operations of this step are contained in the SSDs.

The task of creating a model begins with the designer seeking to find the input that is required to 'trigger' each action of an entity that has been identified in the first step. Each such input will be either:

- an input corresponding to an event that arises externally to the system – for example, the radar detects a new aircraft in the control zone;

- an input generated internally by the system – for example, when interest is added to the bank account every six months.

This step is concerned with identifying instances of the first group of inputs, while the modelling task involving the second group forms the subject of the next phase (through the interactive function step).

The procedure for identifying the inputs is first to identify the external actions of the model, and then to determine how the corresponding event for each one of them will be detected in the real (external) world. For example, for the ATC system, we can see that a new aircraft entity will usually be instantiated when the radar detects a new signal in the area being controlled, and so this external event can be linked with a particular action of the entity (in this case, the 'action' of being created).

A part of this task of adding inputs (and outputs) to the model processes involves the designer in choosing the forms that these will take (data stream or state vector).

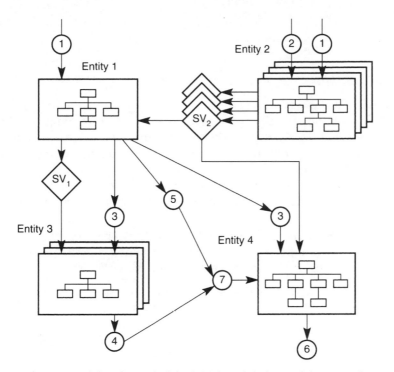

Figure 15.13 The JSD model at the end of the initial model phase of the network stage.

Initial decisions may also be needed where multiple data-stream inputs are required (for example, deciding whether or not to adopt a rough merge).

Tasks such as error-handling may also be included at this stage, although, as with all design methods, this needs to be kept at a suitable level of abstraction. However, such system needs as the detection of spurious events and their removal would certainly need to be identified in this phase.

On completion of this phase the designer should possess a fairly complete diagrammatical representation of the basic design model, together with textual descriptions of the properties that are to be associated with the actions performed by the entities.

It is during this second stage that the designer begins to transform the model of the problem into a model of the solution. However, it is important to appreciate that the model developed during this stage is still relatively abstract. It may well be expressed as being formed from a very large (often impractically large) number of sequential processes running concurrently. Figure 15.13 shows the state of the JSD design model at the end of this initial model phase, using the same symbolic form as before. Resolving this model into a practical detailed design is a task that is deferred until as late as possible, and so the elaboration phase continues to build on the same abstract model.

The first two steps of the elaboration phase (essentially corresponding to the rather complex function step of the original descriptions of the JSD process) provide a less well-defined set of actions for the designer than those of the initial model phase, since they are concerned with making a major design transformation, and one that is driven very strongly by the problem domain and the problem itself. While JSD is relatively prescriptive in the early analysis steps, this part of the network stage requires much more in the way of creative thinking.

The elaboration phase

The main role of this phase was identified in the description of the role of the previous phase. It is through the activities of this phase that the designer completes the creation of the basic model of the problem, and begins creating a model that is concerned with the solution, by adding extra processes to the network to perform the system-related tasks.

This major transformation was not particularly well defined in the earliest descriptions of JSD, but was later refined into two separate transformation tasks, which are:

- the *interactive function* step, concerned with identifying those events that affect the system and that cannot be derived from considering external actions, and then designing additional processes that will provide these events;
- the *information function* step, which adds the processes and data flows that are required for generating the eventual system outputs.

This phase is now also seen as incorporating most of the tasks of the former *system timing* step, which involves making decisions about the synchronization of the model processes.

Elaboration phase 1: the interactive function step

An example of such a function has already been mentioned, namely that of adding interest to a bank account at predetermined intervals. While 'normal' transactions can be identified through examination of a customer's actions (paying-in using a deposit slip, or withdrawing funds using an autoteller), this one arises as a function of the system, and so is not among the actions identified for a major entity of the design. So in this part of the modelling phase, the designer needs to identify such actions of the system, and to determine how they are to be incorporated into the design model.

The recommended procedure for this task is to examine the original requirements specification again, this time with the aim of identifying some of the issues that were not dealt with in the initial model. In particular, at this point the designer is required to consider in turn each action that needs to be internally generated, and *when* this action should be generated. The output from this analysis might be expressed in terms of other actions ('when the day of the week is a Friday') or of some form of external input. The designer may also need further information from the model to determine the details of the actions to be performed, together with the values of their associated attributes.

The refinements to the design model that result from the decisions made in this step will involve:

- adding ESDs that describe the behaviour of the new processes required for these functions;

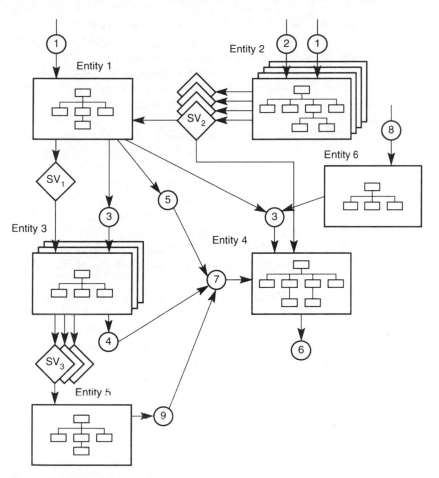

Figure 15.14 The JSD model at the end of the interactive function step (elaboration phase of the network stage).

- revising the SSD (or SSDs) which describes the system, to show the extra processes and the interactions that they will have with the rest of the model.

Figure 15.14 shows the state of the symbolic JSD model at the end of this step of the elaboration phase, including the new processes that have been added during this step. (In the example represented by Figure 15.14, it has been assumed for simplicity that the SSD is simply extended to incorporate the changes arising from this step. However, this is likely to be rather unrealistic for any real system, since adding new processes may well also require modifications to be made to the existing structure of the SSD.)

Elaboration phase 2: the information function step

Up to this point, the JSD modelling process has been concerned with handling system inputs, and it is only at this stage that the JSD designer begins to consider how the system outputs are to be generated. In particular, the design task involved in this step is centred on identifying how information will need to be extracted from the model processes, in order to generate the outputs required in the original specification.

Many of the rules for determining the outputs that are required from a system are likely to be provided in a relatively 'rule-based' manner in the original specification. They may well be expressed using such forms as 'when x, y and z occur, then the system should output p and q', as in the example requirement that:

'When it is Friday, and within six days of the end of the month, print a bank statement for the account, and calculate the monthly charges due at this point.'

The task of determining how such a requirement is to be met in terms of the model is somewhat less prescriptive than we might like it to be. One recommended procedure is first to identify how the information can best be obtained (through a data stream or from a state vector inspection); to assume that the task of extracting this can be performed by a single process; and then to use JSP to design that process. In practice, the complexity of the processing required may well need the use of several processes, in order to resolve JSP structure clashes.

Once again, the effect of this step is to further refine and extend the process network, and hence the SSD(s) describing it, and to create yet more ESDs to describe the actions of the additional processes. Figure 15.15 shows the effects of this step in terms of its effect upon the symbolic description of the JSD model. However, at this point the task of network development is relatively complete, and so the designer can begin to consider the behavioural aspects of the system in greater detail.

Elaboration phase 3: the system timing step

Up to this point, the JSD design model describing the designer's solution has effectively been based on the assumption that it consists of a network of essentially equally important processes. However, this will often be an unrealistic assumption, and one of the major tasks of the present step is to determine the relative priorities that will exist among processes. For example, in an ATC system, we may regard the processing of the signals from the primary and secondary radars to be of higher priority than (say) the updating of a display screen.

This in turn leads to consideration of the scheduling of processes (remember, though, that we are still talking about a model, not about actual physical processes). The consideration of how processes are scheduled, and by what criteria, helps with determining the basic hierarchy for these processes, and this hierarchy forms the principal output from this step.

It is perhaps this stage, in particular, that makes JSD appear very attractive as a design method for real-time systems, although on closer inspection the benefits are probably not as great as might be hoped. Certainly, though, although JSD was essentially developed with data-processing systems largely in mind, it is capable of being used much more widely.

15.3.3 The implementation stage

The terminology used to describe this activity is apt to be misleading. The major task of this phase is to determine how the still relatively abstract model of the solution that

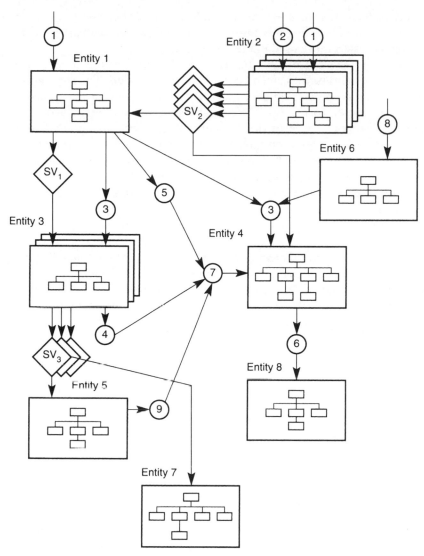

Figure 15.15 The JSD model at the end of the information function step (elaboration phase of the network stage).

has been developed in terms of long-running model processes can be mapped onto a physical system. It is therefore a physical design step, rather than 'implementation' in the normal sense of writing program code.

This phase is therefore concerned with determining, among other things, the forms that may best be used to realize the components of the design model, such as state vectors and processes (in the latter case, some might be realized as physical processes, while others could become subprograms); and, in turn, how the physical processes are to be mapped onto one or more processors. This phase is also constrained by the decisions about scheduling that were made during the network phase, since these may help to determine some of the choices about such features as hierarchy, and how this may influence process scheduling.

It is in this phase that most use can be made of the JSD heuristics that are described in the next section. (There are only three of these, and two of them are generally recognizable as parallels to those used in the JSP model.)

An important element of this step is to determine how the state vectors of the model processes are to be implemented in the physical design. The form adopted will, of course, depend on how the model processes are themselves to be realized, as well as the implementation forms available. As an example, where concurrent threads of execution in a program are provided by 'lightweight processes', and where these are contained in a single compilation unit, they can have shared access to data, types and constants, and so can be used to model the state vector mechanism quite closely. However, if the model processes are mapped onto (say) Unix processes, then each will occupy its own virtual address space, and there is no mechanism that permits direct access to the address space of another process. So in such a physical implementation form, a quite separate mechanism needs to be provided for the state vector form of communication.

Figure 15.16 shows the Transformation Diagram for the complete JSD design process (as always, this omits any of the revisions or iterations that will normally occur during the design process). One feature of this that is particularly worth highlighting is the more comprehensive nature of the final design model when compared with those produced from JSP or SSA/SD. The JSD physical design model has elements of the constructional, functional and behavioural viewpoints, captured through the ESDs, SSDs and physical mappings of the data transfer mechanisms that together make up the physical design model.

As a final comment, the parallels with JSP should not be drawn too far (as the previous paragraph demonstrates). While, like JSP, this method seeks to preserve in the structure of the solution the form of the basic structure that was developed for the model, the mapping is much less prescriptive than it is in JSP. By way of compensation, JSD is a method that is intended for use in developing much larger systems than would be possible with JSP.

15.3.4 The JSD design process

Our D-matrix description of the JSD design process is again based upon the three-stage model of Figure 15.16, and the individual phases that occur within this.

Entity analysis

We can regard the actions of this stage as being to identify a set of n design elements (at this point, all of the elements are also entities) and to model both their behaviour and also a small amount of information about related data (the attributes). So this first step can be described as follows:

$$
\begin{pmatrix} R^b \\ R^f \\ \varnothing^d \\ \varnothing^c \end{pmatrix} \quad E^1 \rightarrow \quad \begin{pmatrix} D_1^b & D_2^b & \dots & D_n^b \\ \varnothing_1^f & \varnothing_2^f & \dots & \varnothing_n^f \\ d_1^d & d_2^d & \dots & d_n^d \\ \varnothing_1^c & \varnothing_2^c & \dots & \varnothing_n^c \end{pmatrix}
$$

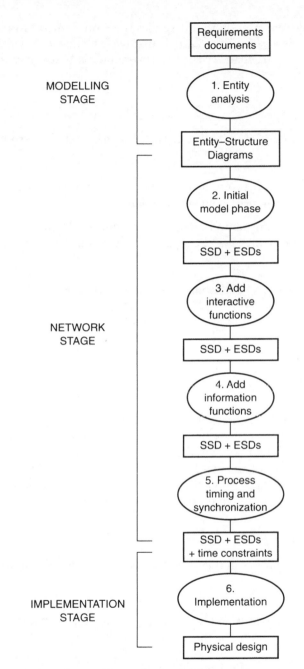

Figure 15.16 The complete JSD transformation model.

Again, the use of the lower case *d* for the data modelling viewpoint is to emphasize that this is largely supplementary information.

Here we are using the matrix in a more abstract manner than when describing JSP, so that each column now represents an entity model (in the form of an ESD together with supporting documentation that describes the entity's attributes). Indeed, one of the useful characteristics of the D-matrix is that we can choose to define the individual matrix elements to be at whatever level of abstraction is best suited to describing the processes involved.

Initial model phase

This corresponds to the start of the network stage, and the resulting model now includes:

- additional information about the behaviour of the elements, corresponding largely to decisions that have been made about connectivity;

- some 'functional' information relating to exchange of information across a particular connection (which may be organized through either a data stream or a state vector).

The resulting matrix model describing this is shown below:

$$
\begin{pmatrix}
D_1^b & D_2^b & \dots & D_n^b \\
\varnothing_1^f & \varnothing_2^f & \dots & \varnothing_n^f \\
d_1^d & d_2^d & \dots & d_n^d \\
\varnothing_1^c & \varnothing_2^c & \dots & \varnothing_n^c
\end{pmatrix}
E^2 \rightarrow
\begin{pmatrix}
D_1'^b & D_2'^b & \dots & D_n'^b \\
d_1^f & d_2^f & \dots & d_n^f \\
d_1^d & d_2^d & \dots & d_n^d \\
\varnothing_1^c & \varnothing_2^c & \dots & \varnothing_n^c
\end{pmatrix}
$$

In this the 'prime' symbol denotes that the information relating to the given viewpoint (in this case, the behavioural viewpoint) has been modified in this step.

One point here is that we can already see two contrasts with the matrix transformation models used for the preceding two design methods. One is the use of more viewpoints at an early stage, while the second is that individual design steps may well explicitly modify information in more than one viewpoint.

Interactive function step

The addition of new entities in this step means that our model will now have:

- more columns;

- revisions to the behaviour and functionality of existing elements, corresponding to the new network connections that are required by the extended model.

This results in the matrix model shown below:

$$
\begin{pmatrix}
D_1^b & D_2^b & \dots & D_n^b \\
d_1^f & d_2^f & \dots & d_n^f \\
d_1^d & d_2^d & \dots & d_n^d \\
\varnothing_1^c & \varnothing_2^c & \dots & \varnothing_n^c
\end{pmatrix}
E^3 \rightarrow
\begin{pmatrix}
D_1'^b & D_2'^b & \dots & D_m'^b \\
d_1'^f & d_2'^f & \dots & d_m'^f \\
d_1^d & d_2^d & \dots & d_m^d \\
\varnothing_1^c & \varnothing_2^c & \dots & \varnothing_m^c
\end{pmatrix}
$$

Information function step

From a transformational viewpoint (which is what the D-matrix effectively provides), this step is very similar to the preceding one and so is modelled by a further transformation of the form shown above.

System timing step

This step resolves issues of synchronization between the (potentially concurrent) system elements, chiefly through the assignment of priority to each model process. We can regard this as additional functional information that completes the information available for this viewpoint:

$$
\begin{pmatrix}
D_1^b & D_2^b \dots D_n^b \\
d_1^f & d_2^f \dots d_n^f \\
d_1^d & d_2^d \dots d_n^d \\
\varnothing_1^c & \varnothing_2^c \dots \varnothing_n^c
\end{pmatrix}
\quad E^5 \rightarrow \quad
\begin{pmatrix}
D_1^b & D_2^b \dots D_n^b \\
D_1^f & D_2^f \dots D_n^f \\
d_1^d & d_2^d \dots d_n^d \\
\varnothing_1^c & \varnothing_2^c \dots \varnothing_n^c
\end{pmatrix}
$$

Implementation

In this final stage the designer adds information about how the system is to be constructed (in terms of mapping model processes on to physical ones). To reflect the point that this does not encompass detailed constructional information, we therefore employ a lower case *d* symbol here for the constructional viewpoint. One of the other consequences of this stage is that the number of design elements will be reviewed and possibly modified (although not necessarily reduced), so that the final transformation described in our model becomes as follows:

$$
\begin{pmatrix}
D_1^b & D_2^b \dots D_n^b \\
D_1^f & D_2^f \dots D_n^f \\
d_1^d & d_2^d \dots d_n^d \\
\varnothing_1^c & \varnothing_2^c \dots \varnothing_n^c
\end{pmatrix}
\quad E^6 \rightarrow \quad
\begin{pmatrix}
D_1^b & D_2^b \dots D_m^b \\
D_1^f & D_2^f \dots D_m^f \\
d_1^d & d_2^d \dots d_m^d \\
d_1^c & d_2^c \dots d_m^c
\end{pmatrix}
$$

We can also conclude that the above D-matrix analysis does provide some degree of support for two of the assertions that are made about JSD.

1. It can reasonably claim to be a 'second generation' design method, in the sense that the transformations involve multi-viewpoint changes, and the final design model does incorporate elements of all viewpoints.

2. The transformations involved are solely elaboration steps (again, this is something of a characteristic of second generation methods), which does broadly endorse Michael Jackson's assertion that the JSD process is essentially one of refining a specification (model) and involves no major transformations of viewpoint.

(The latter point does require a somewhat wider interpretation of 'refinement' than is commonly the case, although it is by no means an unreasonable use of the term!)

15.4 JSD heuristics

As might be expected, the principal heuristics in JSD are largely (but not entirely) used for tasks analogous to those supported by the heuristics of JSP, although, of course, the scale of application is somewhat larger. This section very briefly reviews the roles of the following three forms of heuristic:

- program inversion

- state vector separation

- backtracking

Two of these are 'borrowed' from JSP, while the third is specific to JSD.

15.4.1 Program inversion

This technique is used much as in JSP, and provides a means of transforming a model process into a routine (or, more correctly, a coroutine), which can then be invoked by another process. As before, inversion can be organized with respect to either input or output, but the most common form is probably that in which it occurs around an input data stream, with the inverted process normally being suspended to wait for input from that stream.

One point in which the JSD model differs somewhat from that used in JSP is that it is possible for a JSD process to have both data-stream inputs and state vector inputs. The use of inversion is really only appropriate for data-stream inputs, which are deterministic and well-formed, whereas state vector inputs are essentially non-deterministic (the value obtained will depend upon exactly when the state vector was last updated) and so do not fit well into the inversion mechanism.

Program inversion is essentially a technique used during the implementation stage, when the designer begins to consider the detailed organization of a solution. Prior to that, the design activities are based on a more abstract model and are less concerned with the actual details of physical program organization.

15.4.2 State vector separation

This heuristic is specific to the multiple-process nature of the JSD model, and has no real analogy in JSP. It is used to improve efficiency where a JSD model has many processes of a given type. For example, in the ATC problem there might be many instances of the 'aircraft' process; and in a banking system there might be many instances of the 'customer' process. All the instances of a particular process can use the same code to describe its structure, but each will require to store different values for the local variables that define its state.

The situation is analogous to that which often obtains in multi-tasking operating systems, where one solution adopted to improve memory utilization is 're-entrancy'. This involves the system in maintaining copies of the data areas used by each process, but storing only one copy of the code. (The data area for a process includes the value for its program counter, used to determine which parts of the code are to be executed when it resumes.)

The method used to handle multiple instances of a process in JSD is to adopt a more abstract version of the above, and the design task involved is concerned with organizing the details of the re-entrant structures. The term used for this is 'state vector separation'. Since this is a task that is very much concerned with the physical mapping of the solution, it is normally performed during the final implementation stage.

15.4.3 Backtracking

Once again, the basic concepts involved in this heuristic have been derived from the experience of JSP. However, unlike the previous two heuristics, this one is normally used during the initial analysis tasks, rather than in the later stages of the design activity.

Backtracking helps handle the unexpected events that might occur in an entity's life history, such as its premature end. Once again, the purpose of this heuristic is to restructure any untidy nested tests and selections, and to handle those iterations whose completion may be uncertain. The details are largely similar to those of the technique used in JSP and we will not go into any further detail here.

Overall, the principal JSD heuristics are as prescriptive as might be expected for such a method, and compare not unfavourably with those used in the much less ambitious JSP. Perhaps the main point to make, though, is the relative lack of any heuristics that can be used with the (more rigorous) early stages of modelling – which is where it would be useful to be provided with some means of utilizing the experience of others.

Summary

The JSD method provides a very different set of abstractions for use by the designer from those described in the preceding chapters. And, as will be evident from the material of this chapter, JSD is a relatively extensive design method that does not readily lend itself to being used in any form of subset. Indeed, there are good arguments why we should not use JSD on small systems, since the activities involved in following the full JSD procedures are apt to be lengthy, and hence out of proportion to the benefits that are likely to be obtained from its use (Floyd, 1986). That is not an argument for not using JSD at all, simply one for using it only where appropriate. (To complain that a tractor does not have the acceleration of a sports car is to miss the point of its purpose and effectiveness in much the same manner.)

The larger scale of application of JSD means that it is less prescriptive than JSP, while sharing much of the basic philosophy about design. However, it is the later stages of JSD that are less prescriptive (particularly the information function step and the system timing step), while the initial analysis and model-building are much more highly structured.

The role of the implementation stage is also important, for it is in this transformation to a physical design that it is possible to undo many of the benefits of a good structure. Again, the JSD guidelines for this task are rather less extensive than might be hoped, but as we have continually observed throughout this book, this is in the nature of the act of designing itself, and there are definite bounds upon the degree of rigorous guidance that we can expect.

Overall, though, the argument that JSD as a compositional method is more systematic than the decompositional approach illustrated in Chapter 13 seems to be justified. The early analysis steps are relatively rigorous, and the 'creative' activities are deferred until a fairly sound model has been constructed. However, as we have also observed in the earlier parts of this book, any attempts to draw comparisons between design methods are apt to be two-edged, and we should particularly beware of drawing comparisons about the design strategy when it is considered apart from a particular problem or problem domain.

There is a quite solid base of experience with the use of JSD in the development process. In particular, there is some support available in terms of introductory textbooks, and particularly in terms of good case-study material – Cameron (1988a) and Sutcliffe (1988) contain quite extensive case-study material. As a method, it may still be capable of further development, and it has certainly exercised a wide influence on design thinking.

Further reading

The range of textbooks is relatively limited, although the existing ones complement each other quite well in terms of approach and style. Some major ones are as follows.

Cameron J. (1988). *JSP and JSD: The Jackson Approach to Software Development*. 2nd edn. IEEE Computer Society Press

The author has been one of the codevelopers of JSD, and has published quite widely on its application. Somewhat more than half of the book is dedicated to JSD, and while, like all IEEE tutorials, it is largely composed of reprinted papers, it has a much stronger tutorial element than is usual. A major source-book, but not so well suited to providing an initial introduction.

Sutcliffe A. (1988). *Jackson System Development*. Prentice-Hall

A compact book, written with a clear style, and providing two useful case studies in its appendices. It is not extensive enough to act as a complete practitioner's guide, but would provide a good introduction to the techniques of the method.

Ingevaldsson L. (1990). *Software Engineering Fundamentals: The Jackson Approach*. Chartwell-Bratt

A short text that is constructed around a running example. It has a rather strong DP flavour, and the author makes excellent use of annotated diagrams to help make his points.

15.1 Construct an ESD that describes:

(a) the 'customer' of a public lending library;
(b) the operational cycle of an automatic washing machine;
(c) the 'customer' of a car-hire firm.

15.2 Where a process has two data streams, there is a choice between receiving data from these separately and combining the data flow using rough merge. Discuss the benefits and disadvantages of each scheme, and for each one suggest an instance in which it would be appropriate to use such a form.

15.3 For the lending library of Exercise 15.1(a) above, consider what operations of a library records and issues system will need to be modelled by using:

(a) interaction function processes;
(b) information function processes.

Designing with Objects

16.1 The 'object concept'

16.2 Design practices for the object-oriented paradigm

16.3 Object-Oriented frameworks

16.4 Object-based design

16.5 Object-Oriented design

Objects with a capital 'O' have occupied a position centre-stage in software development since the early 1980s. The word 'object' appears in many conference titles. The literature on most aspects of their form, development and use is voluminous, with the possible, and rather significant, exception of empirical studies. In addition, almost all programming languages developed since 1990 have had object-oriented features, and such features have also been retro-fitted to some older programming languages! Indeed, object-oriented programming is widely accepted as an important and powerful way of creating software systems.

Despite all of this, the task of designing with objects remains a significant problem. Analysis and design methods have proliferated and been unified; the pattern concept described in Chapter 10 has been devised to help address the problem; and further mechanisms such as frameworks have been introduced. However, useful as all of these have been, designing with objects remains a complex cognitive task.

This chapter addresses the challenging question of how we can design systems with objects using design methods. It examines the concept of the object; reviews the conceptual issues it raises for design activities; and then describes some of the approaches to designing with objects that have been developed.

16.1 The 'object concept'

The concept of the **object** has already been encountered in various places in this book: as the basis for an architectural style; as the subject of design patterns; and by a number of the visual representations that were described in Chapter 7. For each of these topics we have employed only those elements of the object concept that were considered to be particularly relevant to the issue at hand. In this chapter we now study the object as a design element in its own right, and describe some of the procedural design methods that are employed for designing with objects.

There are good reasons for deferring the study of objects and object-oriented design until this relatively late stage. One of these concerns the nature of the object itself. Such studies as exist of how novice and expert designers grapple cognitively with objects (and there are surprisingly few of them), indicate that there are many conceptual issues involved (Vessey and Conger, 1994; Sheetz and Tegarden, 1996, Détienne, 2002). In addition, the design methods themselves employ relatively complex processes, that have also continued to evolve throughout the 1990s and into the 2000s. So, despite the relative longevity of the object concept itself, designing with objects is an activity that is by no means either well understood, easy to teach, or necessarily easy to practice, once taught!

This should not be considered as being an argument against the usefulness of the object concept itself, only as a rationale for deferring its detailed study until now. Object-orientation undoubtedly constitutes a valuable and powerful implementation paradigm, albeit one that is apt to be oversold on occasion. However, as we will see, claims for its 'naturalness' as an abstraction are not as convincing (at least for design) as some advocates would have us believe.

This chapter is therefore a large one. We begin by reviewing the concept itself in the rest of this section, go on to consider some of the implications of its characteristics for design, and then examine some examples of the procedural design practices that are employed when designing with objects.

16.1.1 The scope of the problem

In this chapter we address what must be the most complex design strategies that are described in this book. To some degree this has been compounded by the extent to which the term 'object-oriented' has been interpreted to mean so many, slightly different, things and, indeed, two distinct interpretations of this term will be examined in this chapter. (To help distinguish between the general and the specific, the term 'object-oriented', in lower case, will be used when referring to the general paradigm; upper-case leading letters will be used for the specific methods that are based on this strategy.)

The development of 'object-oriented' systems (regardless for the moment of the exact interpretation of the term) received much attention in the 1980s and through the 1990s. While there is now greater consensus about the meaning of the relevant concepts, we still lack any very prescriptive design methods based on them. Indeed, the words used by Tim Rentsch (1982) now seem to have been truly prophetic:

'My guess is that object-oriented programming will be in the 1980s what structured programming was in the 1970s. Everyone will be in favour of it. Every manufacturer

will promote his products as supporting it. Every manager will pay lip service to it. Every programmer will practice it (differently). And no one will know just what it is.'

The shift of conceptual viewpoint that the object-oriented paradigm involves is one that reflects the development of the imperative programming languages used to implement so many systems. Early programming languages such as FORTRAN and COBOL provided powerful structures for expressing actions, but had only relatively primitive forms for modelling the relationships that could exist between the data elements of a program. In the evolution that has led to the more recent imperative programming languages, such as Ada, Java, C++ and Eiffel, and through the influences of Pascal and Smalltalk especially, there has been a gradually changing emphasis, with increasing support within a language for implementing and using abstract data types.

Designing an abstract data type, normally involves seeking to establish the properties of the type elements, and identifying the operations that are performed upon them. In doing so, it is good practice to avoid making any implementation-specific assumptions and decisions. Given that information-hiding practices are now better supported by modern programming languages, it is not surprising that there has been a corresponding interest in developing and constructing systems based on the concept of the abstract data type (ADT), and much of this can be grouped under the heading 'object-oriented'.

Unfortunately, the relative success of the development of ways of implementing object-oriented structures (frequently termed 'object-oriented programming' or OOP) has not been matched by the same degree of success in designing around these concepts. Design methods have themselves evolved through the 1990s and into the 2000s. Drawing initially from the experiences of 'structured design', they have gradually evolved their own characteristic forms. Overall though, they are still less prescriptive in form than the methods that were examined in the previous three chapters. (Indeed, the problems encountered in devising suitable procedural practices for designing with objects may well be one of the motivations for devising 'alternative' mechanisms such as design patterns.) However, both patterns and methods provide access to much useful knowledge for the designer and, in the same way that studying patterns helps to extend our knowledge about object-oriented design, so does study of methods.

Before studying the methods though, we first need to enlarge a little on our picture of the 'object model' and its principal characteristics.

16.1.2 A brief history

The full history of the 'object concept' is quite long and complex; one of the best reviews of the whole object-oriented paradigm is given in Booch (1994), which includes a survey of historical issues. In contrast, Taivalsaari (1993) uses an interestingly different framework, and examines the 'notion' of an object from five 'viewpoints': conceptual modelling; philosophical; software engineering or data abstraction; implementation; and formal. For our purposes however, a much briefer outline covering a number of salient points should suffice.

The digital computer is basically an *action-oriented* device: its primitive operations (instructions) are concerned with performing actions (arithmetical operations,

Designing with objects

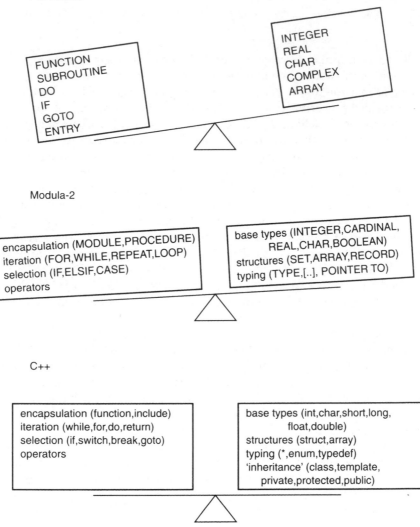

Figure 16.1 The evolution of programming language features between actions and data-modelling.

logical operations, copying of data, transfer of control, and so on). So it is not surprising that the early programming tools were themselves action-oriented in nature. Assembler code and early high-level languages such as FORTRAN have forms that are almost entirely concerned with describing the structure of actions, and provide little in the way of facilities for modelling *data structures*. Figure 16.1 shows the way in which the balance between these has evolved with programming language development.

So it is hardly surprising that the longer-established software design methods have generally provided an action-oriented emphasis in their approach to the construction of a model for a solution, with functional decomposition providing a rather extreme example of such a design strategy. Only in later forms, such as that of JSD, do we see a more even balance occurring between the elements of the model that are concerned with the actions and those concerned with the data. Even then, the design steps themselves are still directed towards developing the model by considering action-oriented features of a problem.

However, quite early on in the development of programming tools, the idea of modelling the structure of a problem around the concept of 'passive' objects of some form began to be explored. Simula in particular is generally considered a significant forerunner of the development of the object-oriented paradigm, not least for its introduction of the 'class', a concept which will be considered later in this section. (Such an approach to modelling a problem could perhaps be considered as 'noun-oriented' rather than 'verb-oriented'.) The Smalltalk system extended this model still further and introduced these concepts to a much wider audience.

In a relatively early and highly influential paper, David Parnas (1972) had already identified the benefits that could be gained through designing around the principle of information-hiding, which, as will be seen in the next subsection, is one of the characteristics of an object-oriented system. However, Parnas recognized that, while the principle was valuable, it was difficult to find any procedural form of design action that could be used for generating designs in such a way as to ensure they would possess the necessary properties. Unfortunately, as we will see, it appears that the efforts of the next three decades have failed to improve upon this position to any significant degree.

Over a period of time, these influences began to come together in the idea of the 'object model', characterized by implementations that:

- are organized around data (nouns) rather than actions (verbs);

- apply strict control of scope (visibility), so that data and operations within an object are not normally available for use by other objects except through the external mechanisms provided by the object;

- make use of little or no 'global' data (i.e. any data used in the system is stored within objects and only directly accessible to that object).

Some of these issues relating to scope and access were described in Parnas (1979).

As these ideas emerged, various efforts were made to maintain consistency of concepts and terminology. A useful contribution was made by a working group, whose conclusions are reported in Snyder (1993). A little later, the Unified Modeling Language (UML) has also played an important role in this, even though motivated, at least in part, by rather more commercial reasons.

The key outcome for our purpose here is that the essential properties of an object are now generally well agreed. Equally, the terminology, if not always agreed, is at least used fairly consistently. (These points probably apply chiefly to object-oriented analysis and design, rather than to implementation, since language designers appear to have delighted in finding new terms to use as well as different ways of using the same terms and keywords!)

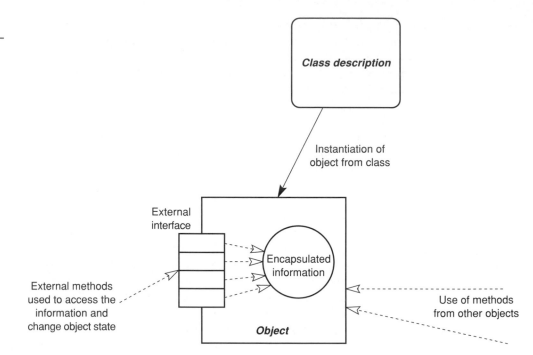

Figure 16.2 A simple illustration of the 'object concept'.

16.1.3 The properties that distinguish an object

For our purposes, we can regard an object as some form of entity that performs computations and has some kind of local state that may be modified by the computations. On this basis, an object possesses a *state*, exhibits *behaviour*, and has some form of distinct *identity*, as illustrated in Figure 16.2, which shows a model that we encountered in Chapter 10. (In many ways, this is very close to the concept of an abstract data type, although perhaps we would not usually consider that an ADT 'performs computations'.)

While this is hardly a rigorous definition, it is sufficient for us to be able to identify the prime characteristic of an object, which is the unification of algorithmic components and data abstraction. This combination of two different aspects that need to be described through the use of all four of the major viewpoints (function, behaviour, structure, data modelling) in turn creates two of the main characteristics of a design that has been developed using object-oriented principles: that it will possess

- relatively little global data; and

- a structure that is a network, rather than a tree.

This can be compared to the form of design produced by a process such as Structured Design, as described in Chapter 13. Here, the description of the resulting solution can be represented as a Structure Chart, which is of course treelike in form; and as the method provides no direct guidelines for creating local data structures, any data structures in the solution are likely to be global in scope.

An object-oriented model adds a framework to this basic concept of an object, in order to make what Booch terms the 'object model'. Booch considers that this model has four major elements:

- abstraction
- encapsulation
- modularity
- hierarchy

and these are briefly reviewed below. (We should note here that some authors merge modularity with encapsulation.)

Abstraction

Abstraction has already been identified as playing a major role in the design process in general. It is concerned with describing the external view of an object (that is, the 'essential features'). It provides a concise description of that object, which can then be used to reason about its behaviour, and about its relationships with other objects, without a need to possess any knowledge about its internal details.

It is an essential property for any form of design object that its characteristics should be capable of being identified in an abstract manner. For the 'object-oriented' forms of design process, abstraction performs an important role in modelling the objects in a system, and indeed object-oriented design is largely about how to select the 'correct' set of abstractions for use in modelling a problem.

Encapsulation

This is basically a term used to describe a realization of the concept of information-hiding, whereby we seek to conceal those features of an object that are not essential to its abstraction. By concealing the implementation details of an object, it is then much easier to make changes to them without creating side-effects for the system as a whole. Encapsulation is a very important issue for detailed design and implementation. At a more abstract level, the key issue is *what* to conceal. Obviously, the concepts of abstraction and encapsulation are largely complementary, and some authors would not separate them in this list of properties.

Modularity

Again, this concept is one that we have already encountered in a number of different forms. Basically it is concerned with partitioning the model of a system into individual components (often termed 'separation of concerns'), and an important criterion in evaluating any choice of components is the complexity of the interfaces between the resulting modules.

For many action-oriented design strategies, the basic level of modularity is the sub-program, and the interconnection mechanism is a combination of the subprogram-calling mechanism (invocation) and the parametrization of the subprogram interface.

For the object-oriented strategies, this concept takes on a somewhat wider connotation, and the form of the corresponding interface may be more complex in nature.

The 'correct' choice of modules is in many ways as critical for the success of any design process as the choice of abstractions. However, it is also a more implementation-based decision, and one that may need to take into account the features of the programming language that is to be used to realize the design, as well as the configuration of the hardware components of the final system.

Hierarchy

Hierarchy is mainly concerned with establishing some form of ranking for the abstractions that make up the system model. In the case of Structured Design, the abstractions will usually be realized as subprograms, and so the appropriate form of hierarchy to consider is that of subprogram invocation. For the object-oriented paradigm we need to consider two further hierarchies, which are based on:

■ class structure

■ interdependency of objects (the uses relationship)

Class hierarchy　The hierarchy based on class structure leads us to consider the concept of **inheritance**, by which the properties of an object can be derived from the properties of other objects (or, more correctly, of other classes). The question of the relative importance of inheritance for object-oriented design comes close to being a theological issue. Indeed, it introduces an issue that we will return to later, as to whether the 'right' design abstraction is the **object** or the **class**. So this forms a good point at which to discuss the class/object relationship more fully.

The concept of a class can be considered as a natural development of the concept of a *type* as used in a programming language. While the concept of type is normally applied to data objects (including the data elements of ADTs), the class notion is much more general, and a class can be considered an abstraction of an object, with an object forming an **instance** of a class. We can therefore expect that a class specification will describe behavioural features as well as data structures and that, further, these features may be made *visible* to other objects or kept *private* to the class.

Viewed in terms of the eventual implementation roles, a class specification can therefore be regarded as a form of *template*, used to create objects. The class defines the state and behaviour attributes of an object and, when an object is created (instantiated) from a class, it also acquires a unique identity.

This concept is not unique to software. A common example of the class concept that we use in everyday life is that of the *car* (which is itself a subclass of *vehicle*). The act of passing a driving test is intended to demonstrate that a person has the basic knowledge needed to handle the state and behaviour model associated with the class *car*. (Ignoring for the moment any differences of make and model, the concept of a car provides common ideas of behaviour, such as what happens when the brake is pressed, the steering wheel is turned, etc.) However, to be of practical use, this knowledge then needs to be employed with a particular instance of a car, which itself will have a unique identity (registration number, age, registered owner, model, maker, etc.), while still exhibiting the behaviour-state model of the class *car*. Because the ability to drive involves using knowledge that pertains to the whole class, the act of driving a different instance should then only involve making any necessary parametric adjustments to allow for its particular features (width, length, engine size, etc.).

While such an analogy should not be taken too far (the instantiation processes are clearly very different), it does demonstrate the usefulness of a class concept in providing a generalization that can capture behaviour-state interactions that will then apply to any instance.

In a programming language it is possible to construct new types from existing types, typically by compounding them in some way (records, sets, arrays), or by defining a subrange type. We can do much the same sort of thing with classes, but the associated inheritance mechanism used to create subclasses is much more complex than that needed for creating dependent types, since it needs to incorporate not just static data relationships but also behavioural qualities.

The subclasses of a class will share common structures and common features of behaviour. For example, a bank may provide customers with many different forms of account, which may have different rules about how interest is paid, how charges will be applied, the minimum balance required, withdrawal notice, and so on. However, all these forms are clearly recognizable as subclasses of the 'parent' class of bank account, and share some common information structures, such as:

- current balance

- identity of owner

- date of creation.

as well as some common operations, such as:

- creation of a new account

- addition of interest

- withdrawal of part of the balance

For this example, therefore, the class of 'bank account' provides a description of these common properties and behaviour, while the detailed form of a particular type of account will depend on the rules applying to that subclass. (For example, some accounts may pay no interest, others may pay interest annually, quarterly or monthly, and so on.) The behaviour of the eventual implementation objects (*my* bank account) will, of course, also depend on the values assigned to the data structures (the *amount* of my current balance). For design purposes, however, the designer is only concerned with the abstractions involved in the class (bank account), and the subclasses (three-year account, current account, high-interest deposit account, and so on). Figure 16.3 illustrates these points concerning the class concept.

Inheritance is the mechanism by which subclasses acquire the general properties of their parent class(es). (It is this relationship that forms the hierarchy associated with inheritance.) In our example, any specific form of bank account will inherit the

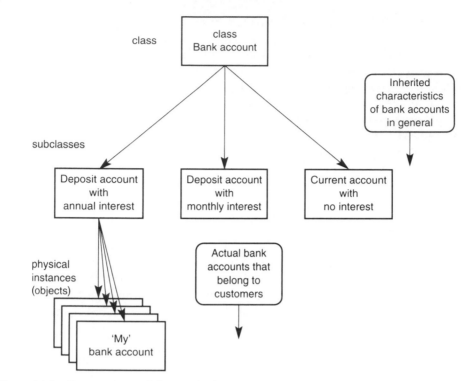

Figure 16.3 The concepts of class and inheritance.

properties of bank accounts in general, but may have some features that apply only to that subclass (minimum balance, interest period, and so on), while some of its operations may contain algorithms that apply only to that particular type of account. So inheritance is an important constructional concept (hence its rapid assimilation into programming languages).

In the above example of bank accounts, we have only considered the use of **single inheritance** (this is where a subclass inherits the properties of one superclass). However, it is also possible to employ **multiple inheritance**, through which a subclass will inherit the properties of two or more superclasses. Obviously this adds considerably to the complexity of the inheritance process (for example, what happens when the superclasses have conflicting property definitions?) and, indeed, for this reason some object-oriented programming languages, most notably Java, will only permit the use of single inheritance. From the design viewpoint, multiple inheritance certainly increases the scale of the cognitive tasks that the designer is expected to manage, with potential problems for future maintenance (Wood *et al.*, 1999).

Inheritance also (indirectly) leads to an issue that we have briefly touched upon already and that we will return to later in this chapter. This issue can be summarized through the question: 'Does object-oriented design involve designing with objects or with classes?' In other words, do we seek to identify candidate classes first, and consider specific objects later, or do we concentrate on modelling objects and then abstract from these to identify the classes? Of course, in practice, since both strategies are quite viable ones, our question then becomes more one of deciding which of them should be employed in any given context.

Uses hierarchy The form of dependency involved in an object structure hierarchy essentially corresponds to the uses relationship (Parnas, 1979) and it describes a hierarchy that exists among modules in terms of the services that they provide. While inheritance is concerned with identifying how the properties of objects are derived from those of their parents, the uses hierarchy, as shown in Figure 16.4, identifies the extent to which the operations of one object (module) depend upon the availability of the services provided by other objects (modules).

While there are those who consider the concept of inheritance as being central to the object-oriented paradigm, some 'object-oriented' design practices are only concerned with developing a design model by considering the first three properties of the 'object model', and with constructing a module hierarchy that is based largely on the

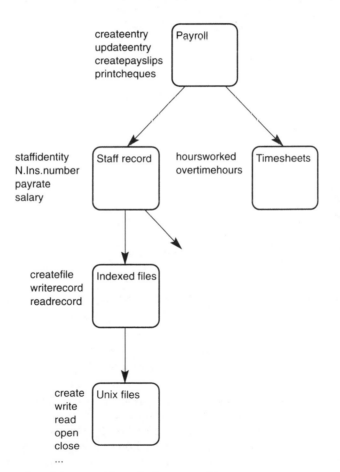

Figure 16.4 Examples of the uses hierarchy between objects.

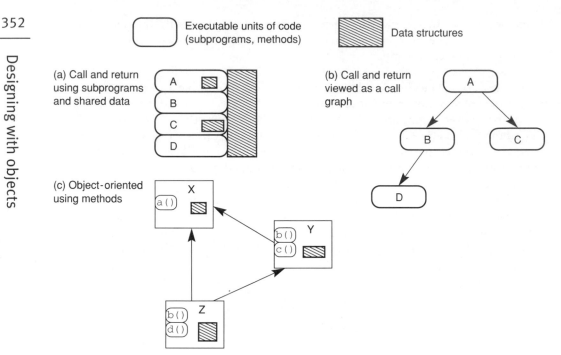

Figure 16.5 Comparison of static call and return construction with dynamic OO forms.

uses relationship. It is now common to describe such forms as being *object-based*, in order to make clear that they do not attempt to include decisions about inheritance, and this terminology will be used in the rest of this chapter and wherever this distinction requires to be made.

While these four elements are generally accepted as forming the major constituents of the object model, they are not the only ones. One other issue that we need to consider from the design perspective is that of **typing**, since the associated concept of **polymorphism** introduces an important constructional issue which we need to consider here.

Figure 16.5 illustrates schematically a key difference between 'conventional' program forms, based upon using subprograms in a *call-and-return* architectural style, and the form of an object-oriented solution. (From an implementational viewpoint, this distinction is sometimes further confused by the way that object-oriented programming languages such as Java can be used to construct both types of solution, admittedly at the price of some distortion.)

In Figure 16.5(a) we show a program that is constructed from four subprograms, A, B, C and D, rather as it might be mapped on to a computer's memory through the processes of compilation and link-editing. Figure 16.5(b) shows the corresponding call graph (equivalent to a Structure Chart) that shows how the subprograms are connected at run time. The data components are either 'global' to the program as a whole, or contained as local data within the subprograms. Linkages and connections between the subprogram and the data within such a program are effectively determined at the time when it is compiled and linked, and hence can be regarded as being *static* in nature.

The object-oriented equivalent is shown in Figure 16.5(c). Since this is purely a schematic illustration, we need not concern ourselves here with how the functionality is redistributed between the three objects X, Y and Z (which we will also assume are created from different classes). Each object provides a set of **methods** that provide access to its encapsulated data. (In many object-oriented programming languages, methods use a restricted form of the procedure/subprogram constructs.) So now, if object X wishes to access data held in object Y, it might do so by using the methods Y.b() or Y.c() for this purpose. (It is a common convention to give the full reference to a method as *object-identifier.method-identifier*.)

However, we might also note that object Z also provides a method b(). Since this can be referenced from X (or Y), as Z.b(), no confusion need arise. More usefully though, in an object-oriented system, whenever object X makes a reference to a method b(), we can expect that the context of that reference will be used to determine whether the appropriate method to use is Y.b() or Z.b(), with the appropriate choice being made automatically and at *run-time*. (The mechanism for determining which one is used will depend upon implementation detail.) Because in Figure 16.5(c) the bindings between the objects are created dynamically when the system runs, the decision about which method to use can be made at run-time. In contrast, in the statically-bound structure of Figure 16.5(a), the equivalent bindings are determined at time of compilation and cannot thereafter be modified.

It is this ability to select the appropriate method from a number of methods with the same name (or identifier), but originating in different classes, that is termed **polymorphism**. (Strictly, although our example is couched in terms of objects, the methods themselves are defined in the parent classes.) To return for a moment to the earlier example of the Bank Account and its subclasses, we might expect that all classes will provide a withdraw() method, but that the detailed form of the withdraw() operation will differ according to the type of account involved. So when this operation is used with any given account, the form used will depend upon the class of that account. We can therefore regard methods as being typed by the class that contains them, as well as by any data values that they return.

What is important here though is not the mechanism of polymorphism itself, but rather the way in which it highlights and illustrates the idea that the eventual system is one that is bound together at *run-time*, and that methods belong to the objects, rather than being a static element of the system. It is this characteristic that forms a key constructional distinction between object-oriented forms and other technologies, and also highlights the close link between the actions and the data that occurs in such systems. From a design perspective, it is also this characteristic that creates such a radically different conceptual model.

A valuable contribution to capturing the essentials of the 'abstract object model' is provided in Snyder (1993), which summarizes an attempt to draw up a list of 'core concepts' for such a model, with the aim of avoiding the confusions caused by variations in terminology. For this model, an object is considered to be

> 'an identifiable entity that plays a visible role in providing a service that a client (user or program) can request.'

A summary of the core concepts of the proposed model is given below: it seems to summarize the issues of the object-oriented paradigm very well.

- *Objects embody an abstraction* that is meaningful to their clients.

- *Objects provide services* characterizing the abstraction that is embodied in an object, where such a service may access or modify data within an object and may affect other objects.

- *Clients issue requests* for the services that are provided by objects.

- *Objects are encapsulated* so that clients cannot directly access or manipulate data associated with objects.

- *Requests identify operations* in terms of the service that an object is required to provide.

- *Requests can identify objects*, so that in issuing a request a client can identify the object that should service it.

- *New objects can be created* to support parallel operations and the time-varying behaviour of a system.

- *Operations can be generic* in that a service can have different implementations for different objects.

- *Objects can be classified in terms of their services* through the interface that they present to clients.

- *Objects can have a common implementation* so that objects may share code, although generally they do not share data, making for efficiency of implementation where multiple instances of objects exist in a system.

- *Objects can share partial implementations* so that not all elements of the behaviour of objects need be shared where the objects are sharing an implementation.

Having now reviewed the main characteristics of the object model, since this is a book about design, it is appropriate to conclude this introductory section by briefly considering some evidence concerning the conceptual issues that the object model raises when designing. In particular, we consider the difficulties that these can present for the novice designer.

16.1.4 Some conceptual issues presented by the object model

In order to design software that can be realized in a given architectural style, the designer needs to possess not only a good conceptualization of that style, but also some clear cognitive mappings that link design ideas (expressed as some form of abstract model) to the implementation constructs employed by that style. For the *call-and-return* style, the abstract model is one that is described in terms of statically-linked subprograms, with these having well-defined functional roles. For the call-and-return style, the control and data topologies are also more or less the same, so that mapping a design model on to a given procedural language is a relatively straightforward process. Likewise, the *pipe-and-filter* style employs fairly simple architectural elements and, again, both control and data topologies are closely linked, so that mapping a design in this form on to (say) Unix processes can be a relatively direct operation.

When employing the *object-oriented* style, the basic concepts used, both for formulating the abstract model, and for mapping it on to some implementation language, turn both of these into more complex tasks. To take a simple example, we noted in an earlier chapter that observational studies of designers showed that they often 'mentally executed' their design models to ensure that they behaved as intended. While it is possible to perform such mental execution with an object-oriented solution, the differing control and data topologies, together with the run-time binding of methods, make this a much more complex task than when using styles such as *call and return* and *pipe and filter*.

One of the arguments that is apt to be made in favour of the object-oriented style is that it is more 'natural' than (say) *pipe and filter* or *call and return*. The basis for this argument is that the object-oriented style is one that more closely reflects 'real world' structures, whereas these other styles are based upon 'artificial' computing constructs. Hence (so the argument quite reasonably continues), the process of analysis should be able to identify the objects in the problem domain, and then use the resulting model to help formulate a set of corresponding 'solution objects'. However, in practice this approach has not proved to be a particularly effective strategy, and as Détienne (2002) observes:

> 'early books on OO emphasised how easy it was to identify objects while later ones, often by the same authors, emphasise the difficulty of identifying them'

which rather undermines the case for 'naturalness'.

That said, Détienne also notes that comparative studies have shown that:

- object-oriented design tends to be faster and easier than procedural (structured) design;

- different designers will produce solutions that are more similar when using an object-oriented approach than when using other approaches;

suggesting that once the necessary levels of knowledge have been acquired by the designer, the object-oriented architectural style does have some substantive benefits to offer.

A key issue here would appear to be the steep learning curve involved in *learning* about object-oriented design. Studies by Fichman and Kemerer (1997), Vessey and Conger (1994) and Sheetz and Tegarden (1996) have all recognized that novice designers struggle to acquire and deploy the concepts. Learning to design with objects would seem to take longer than for 'traditional' structure approaches (Vessey and Conger); and existing (non-transferable) experience with such structured approaches can actually be a hindrance to acquiring object-oriented concepts (Fichman and Kemerer). In the study by Sheetz and Tegarden, they specifically identified the following object-centred design issues as being among the problems or sources of confusion for the novice designer:

- organizing the distribution of the functionality of the 'problem space' across a number of objects;

- using the existing class hierarchy;

- designing classes (including making use of inheritance);

- use of polymorphism, where the semantics of methods with the same name may differ;

- evaluating solutions;

- communication among objects;

- designing methods (the mechanism used to provide services).

Some of this complexity is structural, but some also arises from the cognitive load imposed by the need to comprehend and model so many issues at each step in design. This latter aspect will become more evident when we come to analyse some of the object-oriented design methods using the D-matrix. This reveals not only that the resulting model is highly complex even at early stages of developing a solution, but also that the design decisions at each step are apt to affect many aspects of it. This is in contrast to more traditional methods where each step tends to focus upon a single design attribute or viewpoint (although, even with these, more than one viewpoint may be affected).

While much more can be (and has been) said about the object concept, we are now in a position to examine some of the consequences for design practices. In the next section we extend the above discussion a little further and identify some of the ways in which object-oriented design practices have needed to extend and diverge from the thinking and models that were used by the previous generation of design methods. We briefly review something of the way in which object-oriented design practices have evolved, and then in the remaining sections we review some of these design practices in more detail.

16.2 Design practices for the object-oriented paradigm

In the preceding section, it was remarked that, in identifying the benefits that could be obtained through using the principle of information hiding, Parnas (1972) also recognized that it was difficult to produce such structures by following any well-formed set of procedures. By the time the object-oriented philosophy began to coalesce in the late 1970s, it was obvious that this difficulty with providing any form of design process that incorporated encapsulation still remained a significant problem, and, indeed, that the problems were increased further by the nature of the object-oriented model being so very different from the forms previously experienced.

A further spur to finding a design process that could encompass object-oriented principles came from the development of the Ada programming language, which became an ANSI standard in 1983. While the 1983 form of Ada is not strictly an object-oriented programming language, it can be considered to be object-based in its form, since its structures support the use of:

- *abstraction*, both in terms of data typing and through the `generic` mechanism, with the latter allowing for some abstraction in the description of the algorithmic part;

- *encapsulation*, since the scope of data instances can be controlled via the `private/public` mechanism;

- *modularity*, through the use of the `package` construct (and arguably by using the `task` and the `procedure` mechanisms).

However, although the `generic` mechanism of Ada-83 can be used to support a definition of an ADT that is not bound to any specific base types, this is really a form of 'template', rather than a means of providing inheritance (which was finally added to Ada in the 1995 revision).

Abbott (1983) proposed a strategy that could be employed to develop a design around the 'object-oriented' concepts in such a way that it could be implemented using the main features of Ada-83. His approach was based upon identifying the objects present within a textual narrative that described the intended solution. This was developed further and extended by Grady Booch in the first edition of his book *Software Engineering with Ada* (Booch, 1983). Booch also added a diagrammatical notation to assist with describing the final structure of a design. The main steps in this design strategy are:

- produce a written description of a 'rough' design solution;

- analyse this description in terms of the nouns and the verbs, using the former to help with identifying the design objects and the latter to help with identifying the operations (methods) associated with the objects;

- refine the descriptions of the objects to help produce a more complete solution.

We will examine how this strategy can be employed more fully in a later section, and so will not pursue it further at this point, other than to observe that, while this technique can undoubtedly be made to work successfully, it does not readily scale up for use with larger systems. Its use also requires the designer to possess some initial degree of intuitive understanding of how a design solution might be formed, in order to help with generating the initial rough design. These points were recognized by Booch, and in the second edition of *Software Engineering with Ada* he moved away from a dependence upon this technique (Booch, 1987), and also developed further the notation that he used for describing the form of the design solution.

The late 1980s and early 1990s produced a veritable flood of methods for object-oriented analysis and design. Trying to review and analyse all of these in any detail here would not be profitable, not least because as Iivari (1995) commented in a review of six analysis methods that we will return to shortly:

'Books introducing new OOA&D methods are being published at an accelerating pace, but most of the methods they describe are quite immature both theoretically and empirically.'

A rather larger survey by Wieringa (1998) provides outline descriptions of the main features of 18 object-oriented methods in its appendix, all of which are described in books, rather than just papers at conferences or in journals. Since this is by no means a complete total of object-oriented methods, it is therefore, even more, a figure which should be sufficient to indicate something of the 'method morass' that has tended to be associated with the object-oriented paradigm!

Rather than trying to analyse and describe a selection of methods, we will review two of them in some detail in later sections, and in the rest of this section we seek to review and summarize the outcomes from several surveys of object-oriented analysis and design methods. Each of these was conducted using rather different criteria and 'method sets'; nevertheless, taken collectively, they illustrate something of the evolution of thinking that has occurred and highlight some issues connected with the methods themselves.

Any attempt at making comparisons between design practices will encounter some obvious methodological problems. One of these is the difficulty of finding a suitable framework for conducting the comparative element of the study, given that methods use such different mixes of practices and notations. Indeed, examining the frameworks used in the surveys we review here is probably as, if not more, informative than their findings! Another problem is the rather ephemeral and loosely-structured nature of analysis and design methods themselves. ('Ah yes, that feature wasn't included in version 3.22 of the method, but it has now been added, and so if you look at the current version (3.41), you will find it there . . .') An effective way of constraining this problem is to adopt the criterion employed by Wieringa that, in order to be included, a method has to have been published in book form. This can then be regarded as providing a reasonably definitive baseline description of that particular method, which in turn can be used for making any comparisons.

For rather obvious and practical reasons, most comparisons of methods also tend to focus upon the structures of the method processes and their representation parts, rather than upon such factors as ease of learning, ease of use or the type of design structure that a given method tends to produce. Indeed, one of the more noticeable features of the whole 'object-oriented landscape' is the relative lack of empirical studies of any kind, whether concerned with processes or resulting structures. Although a number of empirical studies are reviewed in Détienne (2002), they are really disproportionately few when compared to the many papers about different aspects of using objects. (In fairness, at the time of writing, this situation is slowly beginning to change, but much more empirically-based study of the different aspect of the object-oriented paradigm is badly needed.)

In the rest of this section, therefore, we begin by reviewing four surveys of analysis and design methods: describing each in turn in terms of the way that it was conducted; the framework that was used for making comparisons; and any significant observations the authors may have made that are relevant to our theme. (As an additional overview, the methods included in the different surveys, and frameworks used by each one, are listed in Tables 16.1 and 16.2.) Following this, we also examine the questions of how large classes and objects should be, and of how effectively object-orientation really supports the idea of software reuse, since both of these are topics that are related to the object-oriented practices being reviewed.

Table 16.1 Analysis and design methods included in the four survey papers

Method	Date	Fichman & Kemerer 1992	Iivari 1995	Wieringa 1998	Johnson & Hardgrave 1999
Bailin OO req specification	1989	*			
Coad & Yourdon	1991	*	*	*	*
Shlaer & Mellor	1992	*	*	*	*
Wasserman *et al.*	1989	*			
Booch OOD	1989	*			
Wirfs-Brock	1990	*	*		
Jacobson *et al.*	1992		*	*	*
OOSE	1995			*	
Martin & Odell	1992		*	*	*
	1995			*	
Rumbaugh *et al.* (OMT)	1991		*	*	
Booch	1994			*	*
Embley	1992			*	
De Champeaux	1993			*	
Firesmith	1993			*	
FUSION	1994			*	*
Octopus	1996			*	
SOMA	1994			*	
ROOM	1994			*	
MOSES	1994			*	
Syntropy	1994			*	
OMT	1995			*	*
Mainstream Objects	1995			*	
BON	1995			*	
OOram	1995			*	

Table 16.2 Frameworks used for comparison in the four survey papers

Paper	Year published	Framework
Fichman & Kemerer	1992	11 modelling dimensions for analysis, and 10 modelling dimensions for design. For each method surveyed, considered both the presence of a dimension and its form.
Iivari	1995	2 × 3 grid: on one axis looking at 'individual object' versus 'object community', and on the other looking at structure, function and behaviour.
Wieringa	1998	Seven properties: system functions system behaviour system communication conceptual decomposition component functions component behaviour component communication
Johnson and Hardgrave	1999	Used a self-administered survey that identified method preferences for both expert and trainee designers.

16.2.1 Survey 1: Fichman and Kemerer, 1992

This paper provides one of the earliest comparative studies of object-oriented methods. It also takes a slightly different approach to the others reviewed here; it is more business-oriented rather than technology-oriented in its goals in the sense that, when assessing the choice of a method, the authors consider the act of making this choice as being primarily a business investment.

Writing at what was still a relatively early stage of object-oriented method development, they were also interested in comparing object-oriented techniques with the more established 'conventional' design methods. Indeed, part of the purpose of their comparison was to examine the evidence to see what support it provided for either of the following two interpretations of object-orientation (Yourdon, 1989) as:

- *revolutionary* – regarding the object-oriented paradigm to be fundamentally different from 'traditional' structured design approaches, rendering existing ways of thinking about design obsolete; or

- *synthesis* – considering the object-oriented paradigm to be an elaboration of 'structured' thinking, involving the addition of further engineering principles to existing design ideas and methods.

For their survey they selected six analysis methods and five design methods from both the 'structured' and object-oriented categories. For inclusion, a method had to be both 'well-documented' and also 'broadly representative'. (Table 16.1 lists only the object-oriented methods involved in their survey.)

Comparison framework

The analysis methods were compared using 11 modelling 'dimensions' that represented the superset of all the modelling techniques employed in the six methods. These dimensions included such headings as: *identification/classification of entities*; *top-down decomposition of functions*; and *states and transitions*. The comparison was not only concerned with whether a modelling technique was employed in a method, but also how it was used. (The list of dimensions is clearly rather mixed, reflecting the inclusion of both structured and object-oriented practices.)

The design methods were compared on a similar basis, using ten design-centred dimensions (here the distinction between structured and object-oriented methods also becomes more marked). Headings used included: *hierarchy of modules (physical design)*; *object states and transitions*; and *assignment of operations/services to classes*. As with analysis methods, the comparison included a description of how a particular technique was used within a method.

Key observations

Fichman and Kemerer noted a number of issues that have consequences for some of our later topics, and which also reflect some earlier ones. The ones of particular interest here are as follows.

- Object-oriented analysis methods represented radical change when they were compared with the function-centred structured methods, but only an incremental change over the data-centred structured methods. (We have already seen that object-oriented class diagrams have a considerable resemblance to ERDs, and will return to the intermediate role of JSD later.)

- Object-oriented design methods represented a radical change from the practices employed in *both* function-centred and data-centred structured methods, as they modelled 'several important dimensions of a target system not addressed by conventional methods'.

- There were three areas that were seen as needing further development work, with these being:

  - *system partitioning/object clustering* (identifying classes);

  - *end-to-end process modelling* (modelling global processes that might involve many objects);

  - *harvesting reuse* (how to achieve this).

Of these three areas, the last is probably the most interesting in the present context, and we will return to it later in this section.

Perhaps the key issue they identified at this quite critical stage in method development was that adoption of object-oriented practices did represent a radical change for an organization. (This theme is one that the same authors have studied further, with their findings being described in Fichman and Kemerer (1997).)

16.2.2 Survey 2: Iivari, 1995

This survey is actually concerned with object-oriented analysis rather than design. However, as we have recognized throughout this book, analysis and design activities are rarely cleanly separated, and so a description of this survey is still quite relevant to any review of how object-oriented design practices have evolved. In addition, as can be seen from Table 16.1, there is also some overlap with the methods examined in Fichman and Kemerer's study described above.

Comparison framework

Iivari looked at a series of previous comparative analyses and comparisons (including the one described above), and made the observation that these tended to 'use a broad brush to analyse and compare the object-oriented approaches'. To make the process more rigorous, he chose to employ a two-dimensional framework to aid the processes of analysis and comparison. This framework is shown in Figure 16.6 in the form of a 2×3 grid. (One square of this was actually not populated in the study, since the chosen analysis methods did not address the functionality of an object community.) It is also interesting to note the similarities between the elements in the vertical axis and the elements of the viewpoints model that was introduced in Chapter 5.

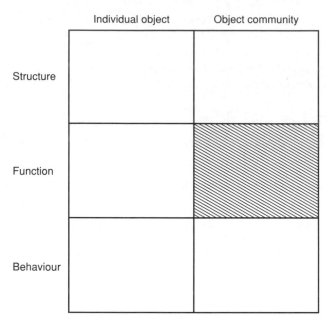

Figure 16.6 Iivari's analytical framework for method comparison.

Key observations

The main outcomes from this survey were to highlight the strengths and weaknesses of the individual methods for each element in the framework (or, at least, for five of the elements.) We might also observe that the lists of weaknesses were mostly longer than the lists of strengths, although that could be regarded as a consequence of the methodological approach employed! Obviously the weakness already noted of the lack of means for modelling the aggregated system functionality was another issue identified in the survey.

For our immediate purposes, Iivari's study is more valuable in terms of its methodology than its outcomes. The framework for analysis that he used, shown in Figure 16.6, helped to place the comparison of techniques on a more 'formal' basis, and especially helped with identifying where there were 'gaps' in the support for analysis or design that was provided in a method.

16.2.3 Survey 3: Wieringa, 1998

This was conducted on a rather larger scale than the other surveys discussed in this section. Indeed, Appendix B of this paper provides a very comprehensive survey of the features of over 18 object-oriented methods. As mentioned previously, the criterion used for including a method was that it had to be described in a book. (An interesting side-note is that Wieringa suggests that JSD occupies an intermediate position between the structured and the object-oriented methods. This also partly reinforces the observation by Fichman and Kemerer of an affinity between the data-centred structured methods and the object-oriented methods.) Also, like Fichman and Kemerer, this paper does review a number of structured methods although, again, we will not consider them here.

Comparison framework

Although not strictly a part of the comparison framework used in the study, Wieringa expected a method to provide at least the following elements.

- *Techniques* for representing properties of software, such as diagrams.

- *Interpretation rules* for the techniques. Essentially this is the semantic element of diagrams, concerned with their meaning.

- *Interconnection rules* that describe how the different techniques inter-relate and combine into a 'coherent specification of software'.

- *Heuristics* for the use of the techniques.

This model is quite similar to the viewpoint and process models used in this book, although it places more emphasis upon the structuring of the representation parts of the methods and less upon the processes (which may well be appropriate in an object-oriented context!).

The framework used for the actual comparisons is not unlike that employed by Iivari, although structured rather differently. This framework, and the rationale for its use, is discussed in some detail in the paper. In summary, the properties assessed for each method consist of its ability to describe:

- *system functions* (what the system provides);

- *system behaviour* (how the system as a whole behaves over time);

- *system communication* (how the system interacts with external entities);

- *conceptual decomposition* (how the system is composed);

- *component functions* (what each component class provides);

- *component behaviour* (how component classes behave over time);

- *component communication* (how each class interacts with other classes).

While also recognizing the need to model the non-functional properties of a design model, Wieringa observes that none of the methods reviewed in his survey offer techniques for doing so, and so omits this aspect from his comparison (as other authors have also done).

Key observations

One of the problems inherent in conducting such a large-scale survey is how to emerge with anything coherent at the end. However, this survey does emerge with some interesting observations and comments, largely because, as noted above, it looks quite closely at the representation parts of the methods surveyed. The conclusions of imme-diate interest are as follows.

- *Use of DFDs.* Wieringa observes that the use of DFDs (and of any 'close relatives') is incompatible with object-oriented structuring because of the enforced separation of data storage from the data processing that is implicit in the DFD model. As was observed in the previous section, the encapsulation of data and related operations forms a core element of the object model.

- *Use of Finite State Diagrams.* These are seen as being the form that is most suited for use in object-oriented modelling because they allow 'the specification of local state, state transitions, and behaviour'.

- *Conceptual system decomposition.* Despite the variety of approaches to this found among the methods in this survey, Wieringa observes 'overwhelming agreement that the decomposition must be represented by a class diagram, component beha-viour by a statechart, and component communications by sequence or collabor-ation diagrams'. However, he also observes that there are quite extensive syntactic (and interpretative) variations in the use of these forms by different methods.

Wieringa goes on to discuss the consequences of this last point in terms of notational needs of methods and, indeed, identifies this as forming part of the rationale for devel-opment of the UML.

16.2.4 Survey 4: Johnson and Hardgrave, 1999

The form adopted for this fourth study differs quite substantially from those employed for the previous three studies we have reviewed. One key difference is that it was per-formed using a survey technique employing two separate groups of subjects: experi-enced developers and trainees. Also, the focus was upon the respondents' attitudes and preferences with regard to object-oriented methods and tools, rather than upon the forms of the specific methods.

Comparison framework

Separate survey forms were used for each of the two groups and a total of 160 subjects took part in the survey (102 experienced developers and 58 trainees). Since the survey was conducted on-line, there are some methodological questions about sampling and representativeness, as indeed the authors acknowledge.

The authors also observed that the degree of comparison that could be achieved was limited. This was chiefly because 'a theory explaining attitudes and behaviour toward, and use of OOAD methods does not currently exist', and hence they argued that the survey offered an inductive approach that would 'use facts to develop general conclusions' and lay some of the groundwork for the development of such a theory.

In terms of its comparative element, this survey was chiefly concerned with the degree of training provided for developers, their familiarity with and preference between, object-oriented methods, and their attitudes towards them.

The entry for this study in Table 16.1 indicates the set of methods that were most familiar to the respondents. (The three most familiar with experienced developers were those of Booch, Rumbaugh and Jacobson, which have subsequently been brought together in the *Unified Process* that we examine in Section 16.5.)

If we again select those observations most relevant to our themes, these include the following.

■ The relatively large proportion of time spent on analysis and design of objects relative to the time spent on coding/testing when compared to 'normal' expectations for software development. It was thought that this might be because creating the design for an object is more time-consuming than the equivalent task for other architectural styles.

■ The steep learning curve required for object-oriented methods (although the respondents did view them as useful once the knowledge had been acquired). This is consistent with the findings from the earlier study on learning different forms of analysis and design methods described in Vessey and Conger (1994).

■ The limited expectations about code reuse. Here the authors observe that 'one of the most advertised benefits of OO is reuse, yet developers rated this lower than trainees'. Their conclusion was that 'this is perhaps a case of trainees believing the hype about reuse and developers actually realising the difficulty in creating reusable code'.

Overall, the study found high levels of satisfaction with object-oriented methods, both for analysis and design. However, as the authors caution, this may be partly an artifact caused by the self-selection of subjects, since developers and trainees who have a positive view of object-orientation may well be more likely to have responded to a survey of this type.

Having looked briefly at these four surveys, we now address two other issues related to object-oriented design practices. The first (size of objects) was not an issue that specifically arose from these surveys, although it is of importance for object-oriented design practices. The second (reuse) did get mentioned in two of the surveys, and raised an equally important set of issues in terms of design practice.

16.2.5 How large should an object be?

This question is one that has been discussed quite extensively in terms of object-oriented development practices. Obviously, when viewed from a constructional aspect, objects can be as small or as large as the developer wishes. What, however, is at issue here, is the question of *quality*, and of whether this is more readily achieved through the use of many smaller, but simple, objects, or fewer larger, but more complex, ones.

When considered in terms of the cognitive aspects of understanding and managing the design of objects, then clearly we might reasonably expect that larger objects are likely to be more difficult to develop and deploy (and to reuse). On the other hand, the aggregated behaviour of many small objects may also be difficult to model and deploy effectively.

An empirical study by El Emam *et al.* (2002) has examined the theory of 'optimal size' for objects. This theory, arising from a number of sources, suggests that there is a U-shaped curve that relates the number (or density) of defects likely to occur in an object to its size, and hence deduces that the 'optimal' size for an object will be at the base of the 'U'. On this basis, objects that are too large or too small are likely to be more error prone and, for a given implementation form, there will be a size of object that is 'just right'. However, their findings do not support this hypothesis, and show that there is a simple continuous relation between the size of a class and the number of faults it is likely to contain.

So what then does this imply for design? The first thing is that there is no magic 'right size' for objects. This is an important finding in its own right, since if the existence of such a 'right size' were to be the case, it would constitute an additional constraint for a designer to have to incorporate into their design solutions. Secondly, there is the degree to which larger objects are likely to contain more faults (and hence, design errors). This is also a factor to be considered, and it does suggest that the use of very large and complex objects is likely to be undesirable.

However, what we can conclude from this study is that what constitutes the 'right' size for any given object should be a consequence of the needs of the problem, and not be influenced by any implementation-related magic numbers.

16.2.6 The case for reuse

The idea of reusing software is an attractive one, and has been so since the earliest days of computing. Given that software is difficult to develop and debug, reusing tried and tested units of software provides one way in which developers can hope to improve development time while maintaining or even improving quality. Indeed, at a relatively low level of abstraction, in the form of the **library** (usually of subprograms), reuse has proved to be a very effective and widely used mechanism.

Unfortunately it has proved difficult to progress from this level of reuse to achieve reuse of larger units of software. Some of the reasons for this are technical ones. Using libraries is largely a constructional practice, and so reuse at this level has little effect upon the design process itself. In contrast, seeking to achieve reuse above that level can become a significant influence upon a designer's decisions. Also, given that software is so pliable (or at least, appears to be), designers are likely to be less willing to accept the constraints imposed by reuse than is the case in other domains, where fabrication is a more complex process. However, expecting that a unit should be modified as necessary in turn removes much of the benefit of reusing tried and tested code. There is also a tendency to design 'made to measure' solutions with software and, indeed, design methods almost always assume that this is so, making little provision for explicitly seeking to reuse existing previously developed part-designs. Equally, few methods (or designers) pay serious attention to the idea of 'designing for reuse' by explicitly seeking to design objects that will be reusable in other systems.

(There are also organizational considerations that may encourage or inhibit reuse (Lynex and Layzell, 1998). While we do not have space to review these issues here, it is important to be aware that reuse is an *organizational* issue, not just a goal for the individual designer or design team. Indeed, many of the serious barriers to reuse are likely to be organizational rather than technical.)

One of the potential benefits from the use of object-oriented development is that it has scope to encourage reuse. This arises chiefly from technological factors, not least that object-orientation promotes reuse through both the uses relationship and also through *inheritance*.

Unfortunately, this does not seem to be evident in practice, as was observed in both the study by Fichman and Kemerer and that of Johnson and Hardgrave. From these, and also from the subsequent study undertaken by Fichman and Kemerer (1997), it would appear that reuse is only likely to occur as the consequence of separate and specific initiatives within an organization, reinforcing the arguments of Lynex and Layzell that organizational barriers are significant and that 'reuse requires the whole organisation and funding of development to be revised'.

There may also be cognitive reasons why inheritance in particular has not proved to be a particularly strong vehicle for supporting reuse. Détienne (2002) suggests that the study of **categorization behaviour** recognizes that when hierarchies are used for classification, users (designers) will assign a special cognitive status for certain 'basic level' objects in a hierarchy, and that these 'stand at an intermediate level of abstraction and form an anchor point for classification and reasoning'.* However, in contrast to this, the use of inheritance in object-orientation requires the anchor points containing the major attributes to be assigned to the top of the abstraction hierarchy. Indeed, from a design perspective, most designers are probably happier using wide shallow inheritance trees rather than deep ones.

Reuse remains an important objective, and is a theme that we will be discussing in both the next section and the following chapter. At this point therefore we confine ourselves to noting that, while object-orientation provides support for reuse, this is not sufficient in itself to make reuse practical.

This section has covered a wide range of issues and, taken together with the material of the preceding section, it provides a quite extensive context for the remaining sections of this chapter. In these, we examine some of the procedural approaches that are used to develop object-oriented systems in rather more detail.

16.3 Object-Oriented frameworks

At the end of the preceding section, we examined some of the reasons why the *inheritance* mechanism has proved to be a less universal solution to the problem of software reuse than might have been hoped. However, the intrinsic uses and *inheritance* mechanisms are not the only ways in which object-oriented design solutions can be reused, in whole or in part. Another example is the *design pattern* mechanism described in Chapter 10, which provides a more conceptual mechanism that can be employed to encourage reuse of design solutions.

The **object-oriented application framework** offers yet another reuse mechanism, but this time one that is based upon reusing 'physical' objects. Less abstract than the design pattern (which itself can be used to describe frameworks), the key characteristic

---

* Détienne offers the example of the hierarchy: living thing; animal; mammal; bear; polar bear, and observes that the basic level object that most humans would use in assigning distinctive classification attributes would be bear.

of a framework is its domain-centred nature. Since frameworks are much more closely related to implementation than to design (and in many ways, to the well-established concept of the 'library'), this section is confined to providing a description of the characteristics of a framework, and then examining some of the ways in which the use of frameworks might influence the design process.

(Much as for the concept of a design pattern, there is really no overwhelming reason why the use of application frameworks should be confined to the object-oriented architectural style. However, as we noted when describing the design pattern concept, the sheer complexity of the object-oriented paradigm – amply demonstrated in the preceding two sections – does lead to procedural design practices that are either less well-defined or, alternatively, more complex than their 'structured design' equivalents. Hence the attraction of seeking other, more tightly focused, ways of achieving the transfer of design knowledge.)

16.3.1 Characteristics of object-oriented frameworks

A good review of the framework concept is provided in the set of papers making up a special issue of *Communications of the ACM*, and especially in the introductory paper by Fayad and Schmidt (1997). In terms of their definitions, some of the chief characteristics of the framework concept are summarized below.

- *Reuse through modularity.* Rather than using hierarchy as the basis for reuse, object-oriented frameworks employ the concept of 'separation of concerns' through *modularity*. (As a reminder, in Section 16.1 we identified abstraction, encapsulation, modularity and hierarchy as being the major elements of the object model.)

- *Definition of generic components.* At a higher level, this is an extension of the 'library' concept. In the case of sub-program libraries, the key to success is identifying well-defined functional operations that can be parameterized and hence easily reused. The same criteria can be used for frameworks although, clearly, achieving successful parameterization of a much larger system unit is a rather more difficult objective.

- *Inversion of control.* This is a run-time architectural characteristic that enables the customization of event handling within a framework. When a given event occurs, the framework's event dispatcher first invokes 'hook methods' supplied by the application to perform application-specific operations. This 'inversion' then 'allows the framework (rather than each application) to determine which set of application-specific methods to invoke in response to external events').

This emphasis upon reuse of actual code means that the framework concept, like that of the library, is only really likely to be effective where elements of a system perform tasks that are likely to be needed by a range of different applications. So frameworks have tended to be particularly useful for performing well-defined roles. One of these is the graphical user interface (GUI) where some of the earliest frameworks evolved (notably *MacApp* and *Interviews*). Another is that of communication 'middleware' providing a layer of operations to link (potentially) remote objects through such

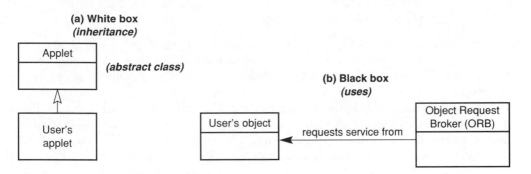

Figure 16.7 Examples of white box and black box frameworks.

mechanisms as the **Object Request Broker** (ORB), with CORBA probably being one of the best known examples of this form.

Fayad and Schmidt also classify frameworks as being 'white box' or 'black box' in form, using these terms much as we have done throughout this book. Figure 16.7 illustrates examples of these categories, which can be described as follows.

- *White box frameworks* employ object-oriented mechanisms such as inheritance and polymorphism as the means of configuration. Such frameworks clearly need to make the structure of the parent classes 'visible', and are apt to be language-specific in their form. A good example of such a white box framework is Java's *Applet* structure, illustrated in Figure 16.7(a). The abstract class *Applet* defines the operations that individual applets can perform (and provides empty methods for these), with an actual applet then providing over-riding methods to replace these as necessary. As a result, all applets conform to a given structure, which is why their operations can be called from any browser which knows about the form of that framework.

- *Black box frameworks* define interfaces that enable other elements to be 'plugged in' to the framework code. However, while this makes it unnecessary for a user to know any details of the inner workings of the framework, the development of such frameworks is made correspondingly more difficult, since the framework designer needs to anticipate all of the ways in which the framework is likely to be employed. In exchange, though, there is also more scope to make such a framework independent of specific programming languages (such as occurs with CORBA), although other forms such as Java's AWT (Abstract Window Toolkit) are still essentially language-specific. (In contrast again, the Tk window toolkit is not language-specific, being usable from both the tcl and perl scripting languages.)

While this is a fairly simplistic classification (needless to say, some frameworks end up being classified as a **grey box** model), it does identify an important distinction that needs to be considered by anyone seeking to design around a framework.

One other term also used when speaking about frameworks is the concept of the **hot spot**. The hot spot is best defined as being that part of the framework that needs to be customized for a particular application.

16.3.2 Designing applications using frameworks

The literature on frameworks, rather akin to that on design patterns, is apt to be much more concerned with providing guidance on how to develop frameworks than on how to use the end product! (There are some overlaps with the pattern concept and, indeed, Johnson (1997) argues that both are *reuse* mechanisms. There are also overlaps with the *component* concept that will be addressed in Chapter 17, although Johnson also argues that frameworks are different from components as they are more customizable and also have more complex interfaces. On that basis, he suggests that a better view of a framework is as a mechanism that can help with developing new components.)

Frameworks can certainly be viewed as being as much design reuse as 'physical' reuse (Johnson). However, this then begs the question of *how* they can be reused systematically. One immediate issue we can identify is that the answer to that question is likely to be very specific to a given framework! Designing an application that will use (say) Java's AWT is a task that, at least in detail, is highly influenced by the form of the AWT and the mechanisms that it provides.

So our conclusion from this is that mechanisms such as design patterns are probably more suited for designing applications that use frameworks than procedural methods. A pattern provides a stylistic guide that can be more readily adapted to the needs of a specific framework than is likely to be possible for a method. Fayad and Schmidt (1997) identify behavioural patterns such as **Template Method** for use with white box frameworks (this pattern 'defines the skeleton of an algorithm in an operation, deferring some steps to subclasses'); and **Strategy** for black box frameworks (this 'defines a family of algorithms, encapsulates each one, and makes them interchangeable'). Both of these patterns are described in Gamma *et al.* (1995).

Whether such behavioural patterns are sufficient for detailed design tasks is a moot point. They make a useful contribution in terms of overall system architecture, but offer little guidance on how to partition the concerns of a system, to use one particular example.

Since frameworks are most successful when addressing quite specific roles in a system, any large-scale attempt at incorporating reuse in a design can be expected to require the use of multiple frameworks, much as we often use multiple libraries to provide different aspects of system functionality. However, since the elements of libraries are usually subprograms in some form, their use rarely imposes any significant architectural constraints, which is not really the case for frameworks.

Mattsson *et al.* (1999) have examined some of the design issues involved in integrating multiple frameworks in a design solution. In doing so, they also provide a useful introduction to a number of aspects of framework use. Their analysis identifies six common problems, which they further classify into architectural and detailed design categories as follows.

■ **Architectural design issues** (which partly anticipate some of the issues that we will consider in Chapter 17, when we come to look at the broader, but related, concept of the *component*) are:

   ■ *inversion of control*, by which, as described above, the framework code calls the application code as needed, can lead to problems when two or more frameworks assume ownership of the application's main event loop and try to call this simultaneously;

- *integration with legacy systems*, which can create problems where the 'expectations' of the framework and the existing code differ in any way;
- *framework gap*, that occurs when the use of two or more frameworks does not cover all of the application's needs, requiring the addition of further mediating software;
- *architectural mismatch*, reflecting a wider 'component issue' (Garlan *et al.*, 1995), but which may occur even when both frameworks have been developed using object-oriented principles, but different object-oriented techniques or implementations.

- **Detailed design issues** are more concerned with the content of the frameworks involved, and these are described as:

  - *overlapping of framework components*, where real-world components may be used by different frameworks (such as a sensor), but with each framework making use of different representations of the data or even of different data from that component;
  - *integrating functionality from different frameworks*, which can arise within layered systems that use different frameworks to provide the layers.

Space does not permit us to go into further detail about their analysis of the causes of these problems, nor of the possible solutions that they review and assess, including the use of wrappers, design patterns and mediating software. However, their paper docs provide a very good review of some of the practical issues affecting the use of frameworks, as well as of how these can be addressed.

We can conclude this section by observing that the development of ideas about both object-oriented frameworks and design patterns saw an immense and exciting flurry of activity in the mid-1990s, tailing off in the latter part of the decade. While both of these concepts are now well established in the object-oriented repertoire, both are still rather lacking in terms of the availability of guidelines which would enable their effective use for design. So far, most of the available guidance about their deployment has been concerned largely with more detailed design and constructional issues, something which may well change as they mature and become more widely employed.

Having examined the physical reuse of objects in design, in the next two sections we go on to look at the forms of procedural object-oriented design practice that have also emerged through the 1980s and 1990s.

16.4 Object-based design

Although the concepts of inheritance and polymorphism were core elements of the object model from an early point in its development, they had less influence upon the evolution of imperative 'object-oriented' programming languages than modularity, encapsulation and the uses relationship. So, while object-based languages such as Ada-83 and Modula-2 incorporated these latter features, they did not include an inheritance mechanism, and this only came into wide practical acceptance with the development of the C++ language, and then later with Java.

Early thinking about designing with objects was also strongly influenced by the development of the Ada programming language in 1983. As a major project of the US

Department of Defense, this language was intended to support and rationalize the engineering of large complex systems, and hence it was recognized that object-based design practices needed to be developed in order to map these needs on to the features that it provided.* Many of these systems were also expected to be real-time in nature, providing an extra challenge for the method developers.

While in one sense this section can be considered as describing 'object history' (especially now that Ada itself has evolved to include full object-oriented features), it still has some relevance. In the first place, designing with objects does not necessarily mean that inheritance *has* to be used, so that, for some applications, an object-based strategy may be quite adequate. In the second, the less complicated design processes provide a rather gentler introduction to the processes of designing with objects.

16.4.1 The choice of HOOD

Since one of the motivations for developing object-based design strategies was to provide a means of designing for Ada, it is appropriate to select one of the Ada-oriented methods as an example of such a strategy. HOOD forms a good basis for this section, since it is fairly well documented, and, while targeted at Ada, there seems no reason why it should not be used with other object-oriented languages. However, being an object-based method according to our earlier definition, it provides no real guidelines on developing effective ways of using the inheritance property provided through the class mechanisms of C++ and Java.

The HOOD (Hierarchical Object-Oriented Design) method was developed for the European Space Agency by CISI–INGENIERE, CRI and MATRA, and it is the third version that we describe here (ESA, 1989; Robinson, 1992). The process part is based heavily on the form used in Booch's earlier work (Booch, 1983; 1986), together with some input from MATRA's 'abstract machines' approach.

The same general format will be used in this section that was adopted for describing the design methods in previous chapters. A description of the representation forms is followed by an outline description of the process part, and finally comes a review of the available heuristics.

16.4.2 HOOD representation forms

The difficulty of identifying and modelling both problem and solution 'objects' using diagrammatical forms means that, as one of the earliest methods, HOOD leans heavily on the use of written text to describe the abstract design models. It does, however, have a diagrammatical representation, although this essentially provides only a constructional viewpoint of the design model, and so is used mainly to represent the outcome of design rather than to support the individual development steps. There are no specific forms used for capturing behavioural, functional or data-modelling aspects of the object model.

---

* Whether this was recognized by the DoD is a debatable point. Although it invested large sums of money in developing Ada compilers and development environments, the task of creating the design practices needed to exploit its features was largely left to others.

In order to explain the form of the diagrams, two further HOOD concepts must be described.

■ HOOD recognizes the existence of both 'passive' and 'active' objects in a system. A **passive** object essentially provides a service, in that it provides a set of operations and associated abstract data types. The operations of a passive object can be activated only when control is passed to them directly, as occurs during the invocation (calling) of a method. An **active** object can provide a parallel thread of execution that can respond to synchronous and asynchronous 'events' (or timeouts) needed for handling real-time features. Active objects may interact with both passive and active objects, but passive objects may make use only of other passive objects, and so cannot be used to activate active objects.

■ The hierarchy described in a HOOD diagram can also take two forms. The first is a uses hierarchy, of the form described by Parnas (1979). Such a hierarchy shows the dependence of one object on the services provided by other objects, as shown earlier in Figure 16.4. For this relationship, the above rules governing interaction between active and passive objects will apply, with the added constraint that passive objects may not use one another in a cyclic manner. The second form of hierarchy is based on **functional composition**, whereby an object may be internally composed from child objects. The child objects provide the functionality of the enveloping object.

We will examine these concepts further in looking at how the representation form can be utilized. The relationships with the Ada task, package and procedure structures should be fairly obvious.

The basic form of representation used to denote a passive object is that shown in Figure 16.8. The outer bounds of the object are indicated by a box with rounded corners. An object has an 'object identifier' at the top of the box, and a 'boundary box' on

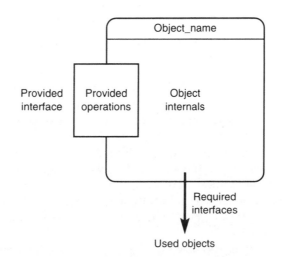

Figure 16.8 The HOOD graphical representation of a passive object.

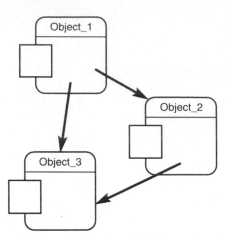

Figure 16.9 An example of the uses relationship between several passive objects.

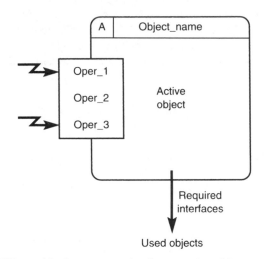

Figure 16.10 The HOOD graphical representation for an active object.

its perimeter, which lists the 'provided operations' that are visible for this object. The uses relationship is then represented by a broad arrow drawn between object boxes, as can be seen in Figure 16.9, which shows such relationships between a number of passive objects.

An active object is described by essentially the same form, but an additional zig-zag arrow is also drawn next to the 'provided operations' box to denote the use of an external trigger, in order to show that the associated 'provided operation' is invoked in response to an event, rather than by a fully synchronous procedure call. (This aspect of the notation seems rather clumsy.) Figure 16.10 shows an example of the representation of an active object.

The parent–child composition hierarchy is shown by drawing the child objects inside the parent object, as shown in Figure 16.11. The provided operations of the

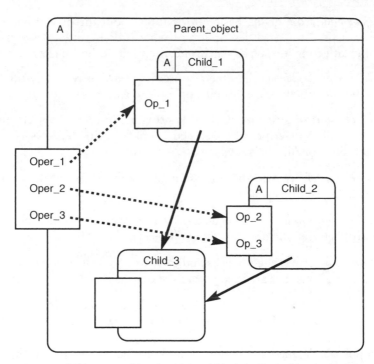

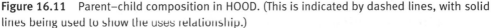

Figure 16.11 Parent–child composition in HOOD. (This is indicated by dashed lines, with solid lines being used to show the uses relationship.)

parent object are also linked to those of the child objects, to indicate which child object will be responsible for implementing each operation. In Figure 16.11, the objects Child_1 and Child_2 supply the provided operations of the parent object. Data-flow arrows can also be used to show the flow of data between child objects.

Where an active object is composed in this way, there is the added possibility of composing it from a mix of active and passive child objects. An example of this is also shown in Figure 16.11, where Child_3 is a passive object.

There is not much else that can usefully be said about the HOOD diagrammatical notation at this point, other than to remark that it can be extended to include descriptions of exception-handling, and also that it includes a form of class object that relates fairly closely to the Ada-83 generics mechanism. A HOOD class object, however, only provides a form of object 'template', rather than capturing all of the properties of a true object-oriented class mechanism, and inheritance in particular.

Before concluding our description of the HOOD representation forms, we need to include a brief description of the textual notation that is used to form an intermediary between the diagrammatical forms and the Ada language. (It does not really play any part in the development of the object model, only in its eventual refinement.) The **Object Description Skeleton**, or ODS, is a structured textual description of an object which refines and extends the information provided in the diagrammatical notation.

In version 3.1 of HOOD (Robinson, 1992), an ODS contains seven main sections, which provide structured descriptions of the following object features.

1. *The object definition*, giving basic information about the object: name, whether passive or active, a textual description of what it does, and a description of any constraints affecting it, such as synchronization with other objects or events.

2. *The provided interface* specifies the resources that are provided by this object for use by other objects (types, constants, operations (methods), exceptions).

3. *The Object Control Structure (OBCS)* is provided for active objects only, and is itself a structured description, concerned primarily with object synchronization details (in terms of Ada-83's *rendez-vous* mechanism).

4. *The required interface* describes the use made by the object of the resources that are provided from other objects.

5. *Data and exception flows* is a heading concerned with describing the flow of data and control between the object and other objects.

6. *The internals* describes child objects and their use, as well as any types, constants, data and operations that are used within the object.

7. *The Operation Control Structure (OPCS)* is a structured description of a provided operation, with an OPCS being specified for each operation provided by the object.

The ODS supplies a detailed description of an object, and its relative formality acts as a 'checklist' for the detailed design processes. In some ways, the form of the ODS has some similarities with the structures used in the Z notation we examine in Chapter 18 and, indeed, a number of authors have explored this relationship more closely, as described in Zheng *et al.* (1998) and Huang (1998).

16.4.3 The HOOD process

The descriptions of the preceding subsection may already have made it clear that the constructional viewpoint provided by the HOOD diagrammatical form is really only well suited to describing the final outcome of the design process. So the process itself remains largely based on manipulating textual descriptions of the design model – a form that is inherently unsuited for use with large systems.

The overall strategy used in HOOD is described as 'globally top-down' in form, and it consists of a sequence of refinements to an object-based model of the problem. The basic process can be summarized as a sequence of four transformations, termed design 'steps'. These are:

1. definition and analysis of the problem

2. elaboration of an informal strategy

3. formalization of the strategy

4. formalization of the solution

and for each step the HOOD design process identifies:

- the activities the designer should perform;
- the input 'documents' required;
- the output 'documents' to be generated;
- any validation procedures to be used.

An outline description of the main transformations involved in the HOOD design process is shown in Figure 16.12. As elsewhere, this section will not attempt to

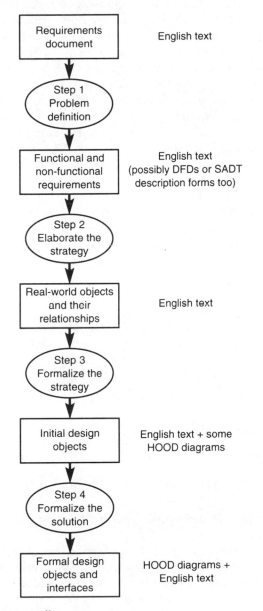

Figure 16.12 HOOD process diagram.

describe all the details of this process, and of the documentation issues in particular for which the reader is referred to ESA (1989) or Robinson (1992). We will mainly focus our attention on outlining the first two steps, since the key design decisions are made within them and the later ones largely elaborate upon these choices.

The first activity of the design process in step 1 requires the designer to perform an initial analysis of the problem. This is really a major task, and ideally would itself be undertaken in an object-oriented fashion, so that the analysis of the problem in terms of its constituent objects could be used to provide guidance to the designer in the next task, which is to identify suitable candidates for solution (design) objects.

In the absence of suitable analysis techniques, Booch originally recommended the use of Structured Systems Analysis for this task, while the HOOD developers have suggested that SADT provides a good alternative form (Marca and McGowan, 1988). Both of these analysis techniques are, of course, based on the use of functional decomposition rather than on a true object-oriented strategy, and indeed, as we observed in Section 16.2, the enforced separation of date storage and data processing is incompatible with the object model (Wieringa, 1998).

The unsatisfactory form of step 1 (in terms of building an object-oriented model from the beginning) leads to the difficulties of step 2. This step essentially requires the designer to 'rough out' an initial architectural solution to the problem, which can then be analysed to provide a more detailed object-based design model.

Step 2 therefore has to act as a 'bridge' between the (possibly function-oriented) model produced by the analysis of step 1, and the object-centred needs of the succeeding steps. Without doubt this remains an inelegant and poorly structured transformation, and one that has probably most inhibited the further development of HOOD.

16.4.4 HOOD heuristics

The relatively weak structure of the HOOD design process might reasonably lead to the interpretation that this effectively consists almost entirely of heuristics. However, even then, as Buxton and McDermid (1992) have observed 'the published heuristics seem a little vague'!

These authors observe too that HOOD 'identifies several classes of object, only one of which corresponds to a "real-world" entity', and summarize these as being:

- *entities* from the problem domain;

- *actions*, often expressed through active objects;

- *virtual machines* that group operations that are all used at some 'superior level';

although they consider the distinction between the first two forms to be rather artificial.

Despite these limitations though, HOOD (and its notation) has continued to be used for a variety of applications and to attract some interest from researchers. However, there has not been enough of either to have led to any significant further evolution or developments in terms of the method itself.

In many ways HOOD has proved to be something of an evolutionary 'dead-end'. HOOD is very much aimed at designing systems that are to be implemented in Ada-83, and as such it is able to identify successfully some ways of using the major Ada structures (such as the package and the task) in a real-time context.

Perhaps the main reservations about its 'integrity' as a design method can be summarized in the following observations.

- The design model should ideally capture the behavioural, functional, constructional and data-modelling viewpoints in a balanced manner. However, the emphasis in textual analysis is on building a description that contains a mixture of the behavioural, functional and data-modelling aspects, and the process of extracting the constructional viewpoint of the model from this is far from being well-structured.

- The diagrammatical representation is not really used in the design process, and does not aid the design procedures in any way. So these only employ the (rather loosely structured) description provided through the use of natural language in order to capture the design model and refine it to produce an ODS for each object.

- It is not clear that the process itself scales up well (although it is likely that it can be scaled up for those problems where it is at least possible to identify a clear parent–child hierarchy).

HOOD extends the basic object model in a number of ways: adding parent–child composition, including the real-time concept of active objects in the design model, and providing a diagrammatical form that is able to encompass these (although not in a particularly elegant way). However, it confines itself solely to the object characteristics of modularity, encapsulation and abstraction, together with a uses hierarchy and makes no attempt to capture the concept of the class hierarchy.

16.5 Object-Oriented design

Both the review of the four survey papers provided in Section 16.2 and the summary of the methods that they surveyed shown in Table 16.1 demonstrate that there has been no dearth of (often immature) procedural methods available for the would-be designer of object-oriented systems. A full list, could it be compiled and were it worth the effort to do so, would be much longer still!

Keeping to the 'mainstream' though, we can very loosely group the development of object-oriented design methods into three eras as follows.

- *First generation methods* that tended to be evolutionary rather than revolutionary, at least for their analysis elements. Most of the methods developed in the late 1970s and early 1980s fall into this category and, in some ways, the HOOD method described in the previous section is a fairly typical example of a method of this generation, inasmuch as any method can be regarded as 'typical' of so varied a set of approaches to design. Methods of this generation tend to be characterized by limited forms of diagrammatical notation and weak processes, as method developers struggled to adapt procedural forms and familiar notations to this radically different architectural style.

■ *Second generation methods* that evolved from these first generation practices around the mid-1990s, drawing heavily upon experiences with their use and limitations. By this stage, the evolutionary element was essentially discarded and all methods could be considered as revolutionary. While some methods of this generation evolved directly from specific first generation methods, others, such as the Fusion method described in Section 16.5.1, drew more widely for their inspiration.

■ *The Unified Process* that emerged through the late 1990s as a result of bringing together the ideas and approaches employed by Booch, Jacobson and Rumbaugh (the last survey reviewed in Section 16.2 noted that these were the approaches most popular with developers). Related closely to the parallel development of the UML, this can perhaps be regarded as a 'third generation' method (or, at least, as being at generation 2.5), and we will also study this method in this section.

One problem with this process of evolution is that the complexity of the object-oriented paradigm has tended to mean that methods have, in part at least, tended to advance through a process of aggregation, with obvious consequences in terms of the complexity of the processes and the variety of notations.

Since this is a book about designing software, rather than about the use of specific methods, there is limited scope to provide other than limited descriptions of the two methods included in this section. However, for both Fusion and the Unified Process, we will use the same descriptive framework as previously, beginning by examining the representations used and the design processes involved, to help contrast their forms with those of the methods examined in earlier chapters.

16.5.1 The Fusion method

This was developed at HP Laboratories in the UK (Coleman *et al.*, 1994) and, as implied by the name 'Fusion', the aim of the development team was to integrate and extend the most successful elements of existing practices. Hence Fusion can be considered as a second generation object-oriented analysis and design method. Wieringa (1998) notes that there have been some subsequent developments to the method but, as these are not readily accessible, this section has been confined to describing the 1994 version. From a historical point of view at least, this is perhaps right, since Fusion was certainly one of the earliest examples of the second generation category of methods.

The Fusion representation forms

The analysis and design steps of Fusion employ a set of notations that are derived from a variety of sources, some of which are rather similar to those already described in Chapter 7. So the description in this section has been kept relatively brief, and it is chiefly concerned with identifying how the different viewpoints are described. Like

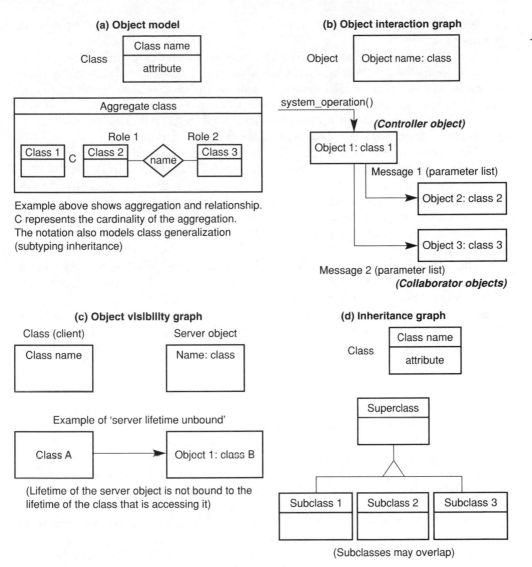

(a) Object model

Class

Class name
attribute

Aggregate class

Class 1 C | Class 2 | Role 1 ⟨name⟩ Role 2 | Class 3 |

Example above shows aggregation and relationship.
C represents the cardinality of the aggregation.
The notation also models class generalization
(subtyping inheritance)

(b) Object interaction graph

Object | Object name: class |

system_operation()

(Controller object)

| Object 1: class 1 |

Message 1 (parameter list)

| Object 2: class 2 |

| Object 3: class 3 |

Message 2 (parameter list)
(Collaborator objects)

(c) Object visibility graph

Class (client)

| Class name |

Server object

| Name: class |

Example of 'server lifetime unbound'

| Class A | ⟶ | Object 1: class B |

(Lifetime of the server object is not bound to the
lifetime of the class that is accessing it)

(d) Inheritance graph

Class

Class name
attribute

| Superclass |

| Subclass 1 | Subclass 2 | Subclass 3 |

(Subclasses may overlap)

Figure 16.13 Examples of the Fusion diagrammatical forms.

HOOD, Fusion employs a mix of text and diagrams, although the proportion of diagrams is much greater, and it is this latter form that we will concentrate on in this description. The basic forms of diagram are outlined in Figure 16.13, although this does not show all of the variations.

Like many object-oriented methods and like the UML, Fusion employs a class diagram (termed the **object model**) that is strongly related to the ERD notation described in Section 7.2.2. This is essentially concerned with providing a constructional viewpoint, and an example of its form is shown in Figure 16.13(a).

Modelling of the class behaviour makes use of textual descriptions. Informally, in Coleman *et al.* there are examples that use a form similar to the UML *message sequence diagram* to describe scenarios, but this is not a formal part of the Fusion set of notations.

At a more detailed level of model description (for design), functionality is described in terms of collaboration between objects through the medium of the **object interaction graph,** with graphs being constructed for each system operation. Figure 16.13(b) shows an example of this notation. In many ways, this form is quite unlike most of the diagrammatical forms that we have used so far, reflecting the need to find new ways of describing the characteristics of object-oriented models.

The second form of notation that can perhaps be considered as specific to Fusion is the **object visibility graph,** a simple example of which is shown in Figure 16.13(c). This is used to define the 'reference structure of classes in the system', identifying the objects that class instances need to access and the forms that these references should take (including the permanency or otherwise of such references). In effect, this notation aims to describe encapsulation, and hence can be regarded as providing a data-modelling viewpoint.

The last form used in Fusion is the **inheritance graph,** which is a fairly conventional constructional form that we need not describe further here, other than to note that a simple example of this is provided in Figure 16.13(d).

Overall, the Fusion notations can be considered as fairly typical of second generation methods. Remaining rather constructional in emphasis, while using a greater variety of diagrammatical forms than a first generation method such as HOOD, but still employing structured text for some purposes.

The Fusion process

Reflecting, at least partly, earlier comments about the increased complexity of second generation methods, the Fusion process has no fewer than eight distinct steps. Four of these are classified as *analysis* (i.e. black box modelling), while the remaining four are white box design steps. Figure 16.14 summarizes the overall design process.

An important element in providing continuity links through the Fusion process is the use of a *data dictionary*, which act as 'a central repository of definitions of terms and concepts' (Coleman *et al.*). Arguably this is the one element that is most evidently (and sensibly) carried over from earlier structured design practices.

Returning to Figure 16.14, we can describe the steps of the process as follows.

Step 1 (analysis): Develop the object model One of the tasks of this first step is to identify a set of candidate classes, relationships and attributes to place in the data dictionary.

Fusion does not identify a specific means of carrying out the first step, only what the outcomes from this should be. These outcomes can be summarized as being entries in the data dictionary, plus a set of diagrams making up the initial object model for the system as a whole, together with its environment. Techniques such as brainstorming and noun–verb analysis are suggested for this step.

In addition to identifying candidate classes, relationships and attributes, this process should also identify any *invariants* and include these in the data dictionary. For our purposes, we can consider an invariant as being a constraint upon the overall state of the system.

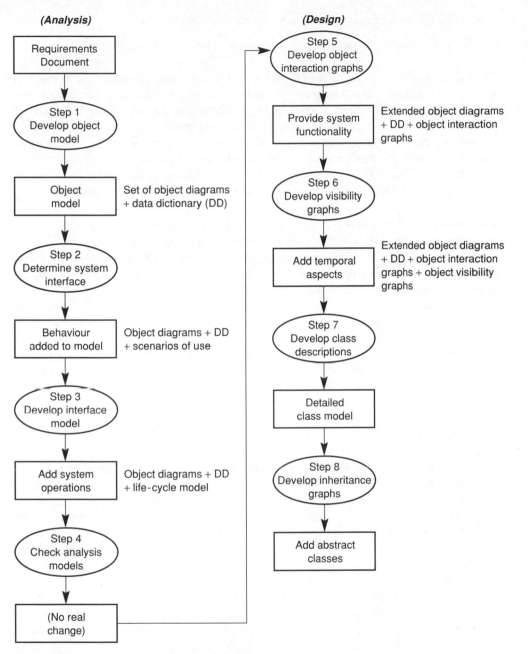

Figure 16.14 The Fusion analysis and design process.

Step 2 (analysis): Determine the system interface This step extends the (essentially) static model developed in the first step to describe the dynamic behaviour of the system as a whole. In so doing, it also clarifies the system bounds by determining what is or is not included in the system itself. The designer is therefore encouraged to consider:

■ how is the system to respond to external input events?

■ what events are the system to generate when inputs are processed?

The process suggested for this is to identify a set of scenarios of system use (these can be depicted using *timeline diagrams*). The concept of the scenario is an important one, which we touched upon in Section 7.2.6 when discussing the role of use cases within UML. Each timeline diagram (similar in form to message sequence diagrams) can only be used to represent a single scenario so, where there are optional paths through a use case, these need to be described by using a set of such diagrams.

A further effect of this step is to extend the data dictionary to include descriptions of both *events* (and the agents which instigate them) and also system operations.

Step 3 (analysis): Development of the interface model   There are two elements to this step, with one providing assistance with the development of the second.

The first element involves constructing a 'life-cycle' model containing what are effectively use cases that generalize the scenarios produced in the previous step. (In Fusion these are termed *life-cycle expressions*.)

The second element is the 'operation model' that defines the semantics (meaning) for each system operation in terms of informal pre-condition and post-condition specifications, and hence can be considered as providing a functional description of the system. These can (in part at least) be created by considering the effect of the life-cycle model upon the system. The outcome from this is of course a new set of entries in the data dictionary that describe the operations and their contexts.

Step 4 (analysis): Check the analysis models   The purpose of this step is to ensure completeness and consistency in the analysis model, rather than to extend the model in any way, preliminary to beginning the white box design tasks.

An assessment of *completeness* is largely a matter of cross-referencing with the requirements specification, to determine whether there are any aspects of this that have not been covered by the black box model produced from the previous three steps. (Since requirements specifications are not necessarily complete in themselves, the comparisons may of course identify gaps either in the specification or in the analysis model.) The primary concerns here are to check the completeness of the set of scenarios (life-cycles) and operations, and to ensure that all invariants have been recognized and included.

Assessing *consistency* is really a process of ensuring that the different viewpoint models developed in the previous three steps form projections from the same overall design model. The constructional, behavioural and functional models (and the invariants) need to be checked against each other. Techniques that can be used include using scenarios to aid tracing of event paths through objects.

As always in designing, there will be iterations of the above steps, but one role of this fourth step is to try to ensure that these are performed on a reasonably systematic basis.

Step 5 (design): Develop object interaction graphs   These are used to describe the designer's intentions concerning how the objects will interact at run-time in order to provide the required functionality, and so this forms the first step in developing a white box model of the system. The step involves creating an *object interaction graph* for each system operation and, in doing this, making any related decisions about message passing between objects and resulting state changes to these. The sequences of messages passing between the design objects then determines the combined functional behaviour of these objects. One of the elements also clarified in this step is just when objects should be created from the classes. (Although the descriptions tend to be couched in terms of *objects*, since these are the executable elements of the eventual system, the model itself is really described in terms of *classes*, while recognizing that many classes will only lead to the creation of a single instance or object.)

One question that arises here is whether the set of objects is essentially the same one that was created in Step 1? The answer to this is 'yes', as the objects in an object interaction graph are defined as being design objects that are derived from the analysis objects. So these are still relatively high-level elements that may later need to be expanded or refined.

Each object interaction graph has a single *controller object* which has a message entering from outside the particular set of objects involved in the operation, and also one or more *collaborator objects* which make up the rest of the set. Identification of the controller is an important design decision, and may well involve comparing several candidate object interaction graphs. In addition, new objects (classes) may need to be introduced in order to provide some of the required functionality.

Step 6 (design): Develop visibility graphs As described above, these diagrams are used to describe the other classes that a given class needs to reference, together with the forms of reference to be used and their lifetimes (i.e. whether the knowledge involved is persistent through the life of the system, or more transitory).

This temporal aspect is an important (and distinctive) element of this Fusion step. However, the role of time here is chiefly in terms of its influence on constructional aspects, rather than on any behavioural or functional ones.

Step 7 (design): Develop class descriptions This step involves a degree of drawing together of the original object model with the outcome of the previous two steps in order to provide (textual) class descriptions for each class in the system, where these specify the following:

- the methods and their parameters (derived from the object interaction graphs and the object visibility graphs);
- the data attributes (largely determined from the object model and the data dictionary);
- the object attributes (extracted largely from the object visibility graph for the relevant class);
- the inheritance dependencies.

This last element is the first time inheritance structures have been mentioned during the design steps, although we should note that the method makes provision for identifying subclasses and superclasses when creating the original object model in Step 1. In this step, it is those analysis-related structures that form the basis of the inheritance dependencies for a class.

Step 8 (design): Develop inheritance graphs   While the previous step involved the designer in consolidating and codifying ideas about specialization through inheritance obtained from the original domain-centred model, this step considers inheritance as a design construct. The designer is encouraged to look at the relationships between the classes, as codified in Step 7, and to identify common abstractions. This step is therefore chiefly concerned with identifying new abstract superclasses that can generalize sets of the classes identified in the model. As such, this then provides an important input to the following task of implementation.

Obviously, there is much about the Fusion design process that we cannot describe in so brief an outline as this, but the above description provides an interesting contrast with that of the HOOD method that was the subject of the preceding section. While some elements of Fusion are still relatively loosely structured (the model building in Step 1 provides an obvious example), there is considerable scope to refine and revise the object model in the subsequent steps (both analysis and design), and Fusion certainly makes much more extensive use of diagrammatical notations both to develop the behavioural and functional viewpoints that are only weakly modelled in HOOD, and also to ensure consistency between the different viewpoints.

To provide a slightly more formal analysis of the Fusion process, we next show a short description of the eight steps, as modelled using the D-matrix notation that illustrates how the state of the design model evolves.

A D-Matrix model of the Fusion process

Step 1: Develop the object model   The main contribution of this step is in creating the initial object model, largely described in terms of constructional relationships. However, a minor data-modelling element is included in our D-matrix representation, describing the data abstractions that are implicit in the classes themselves. (The data dictionary is more a representation of the design model and, indeed, we could usefully regard the D-matrix as providing an abstract visual description that combines the information in the data dictionary and the set of diagrams at the end of each step.)

$$\begin{pmatrix} R^b \\ R^f \\ \emptyset^d \\ \emptyset^c \end{pmatrix} \quad E^1 \rightarrow \quad \begin{pmatrix} \emptyset_1^b & \emptyset_2^b \dots \emptyset_n^b \\ \emptyset_1^f & \emptyset_2^f \dots \emptyset_n^f \\ d_1^d & d_2^d \dots d_n^d \\ D_1^c & D_2^c \dots D_n^c \end{pmatrix}$$

Step 2: Determine the system interface   This step adds an event-centred behavioural viewpoint description to the model (arguably this incorporates a small functional element too, but this is not the main purpose of the step). One effect of this step, which draws a clearer boundary around the system itself, is that the set of system objects may change, with some of the objects that were identified in Step 1 being placed outside the system boundary, and hence excluded from the revised design model.

$$\begin{pmatrix} \varnothing_1^b & \varnothing_2^b \dots \varnothing_n^b \\ \varnothing_1^f & \varnothing_2^f \dots \varnothing_n^f \\ d_1^d & d_2^d \dots d_n^d \\ D_1^c & D_2^c \dots D_n^c \end{pmatrix} \quad E^2 \rightarrow \quad \begin{pmatrix} D_1^b & D_2^b \dots D_m^b \\ \varnothing_1^f & \varnothing_2^f \dots \varnothing_m^f \\ d_1^d & d_2^d \dots d_m^d \\ D_1^c & D_2^c \dots D_m^c \end{pmatrix}$$

Step 3: Development of the interface model This step addresses the semantics of each system operation and so adds a functional element to the model of the system (note that we are still largely concerned with a black box model, and so the D-matrix cannot fully represent the groupings of system objects that may be involved in a given operation).

$$\begin{pmatrix} D_1^b & D_2^b \dots D_n^b \\ \varnothing_1^f & \varnothing_2^f \dots \varnothing_n^f \\ d_1^d & d_2^d \dots d_n^d \\ D_1^c & D_2^c \dots D_n^c \end{pmatrix} \quad E^3 \rightarrow \quad \begin{pmatrix} D_1^b & D_2^b \dots D_n^b \\ D_1^f & D_2^f \dots D_n^f \\ d_1^d & d_2^d \dots d_n^d \\ D_1^c & D_2^c \dots D_n^c \end{pmatrix}$$

Step 4: Check the analysis models This step is more concerned with local adjustments to the model than with any systematic elaboration of it, and so is adequately described in terms of local changes to the elements of the D-matrix.

$$\begin{pmatrix} D_1^b & D_2^b \dots D_n^b \\ D_1^f & D_2^f \dots D_n^f \\ d_1^d & d_2^d \dots d_n^d \\ D_1^c & D_2^c \dots D_n^c \end{pmatrix} \quad E^4 \rightarrow \quad \begin{pmatrix} D_1'^b & D_2'^b \dots D_n'^b \\ D_1'^f & D_2'^f \dots D_n'^f \\ d_1^d & d_2^d \dots d_n^d \\ D_1^c & D_2^c \dots D_n^c \end{pmatrix}$$

Step 5: Develop object interaction graphs The main outcome of this step is that the detailed provision of functionality is elaborated. Since the 'object set' may also change slightly, we also include this in our model.

$$\begin{pmatrix} D_1^b & D_2^b \dots D_n^b \\ D_1^f & D_2^f \dots D_n^f \\ d_1^d & d_2^d \dots d_n^d \\ D_1^c & D_2^c \dots D_n^c \end{pmatrix} \quad E^5 \rightarrow \quad \begin{pmatrix} D_1^b & D_2^b \dots D_m^b \\ D_1'^f & D_2'^f \dots D_m'^f \\ d_1^d & d_2^d \dots d_m^d \\ D_1^c & D_2^c \dots D_m^c \end{pmatrix}$$

Step 6: Develop visibility graphs This step can simply be regarded as a refinement of the constructional elements of the design model.

$$\begin{pmatrix} D_1^b & D_2^b \dots D_n^b \\ D_1^f & D_2^f \dots D_n^f \\ d_1^d & d_2^d \dots d_n^d \\ D_1^c & D_2^c \dots D_n^c \end{pmatrix} \quad E^6 \rightarrow \quad \begin{pmatrix} D_1^b & D_2^b \dots D_n^b \\ D_1^f & D_2^f \dots D_n^f \\ d_1^d & d_2^d \dots d_n^d \\ D_1'^c & D_2'^c \dots D_n'^c \end{pmatrix}$$

Step 7: Develop class descriptions   The effect of this step upon the overall model is very similar to that of the previous step (being a further refinement of constructional aspects), with the added element that the data modelling is completed, which we show by changing the 'd' to 'D' for the data-modelling elements.

$$
\begin{pmatrix}
D_1^b & D_2^b & \dots & D_n^b \\
D_1^f & D_2^f & \dots & D_n^f \\
d_1^d & d_2^d & \dots & d_n^d \\
D_1^c & D_2^c & \dots & D_n^c
\end{pmatrix}
E^7 \rightarrow
\begin{pmatrix}
D_1^b & D_2^b & \dots & D_n^b \\
D_1^f & D_2^f & \dots & D_n^f \\
D_1^d & D_2^d & \dots & D_n^d \\
D_1'^c & D_2'^c & \dots & D_n'^c
\end{pmatrix}
$$

Step 8: Develop inheritance graphs   Again, this largely refines the constructional description of the model. Since it may involve adding some (abstract) classes, we also need to take account of possible changes in the number of elements.

$$
\begin{pmatrix}
D_1^b & D_2^b & \dots & D_n^b \\
D_1^f & D_2^f & \dots & D_n^f \\
D_1^d & D_2^d & \dots & D_n^d \\
D_1^c & D_2^c & \dots & D_n^c
\end{pmatrix}
E^8 \rightarrow
\begin{pmatrix}
D_1^b & D_2^b & \dots & D_m^b \\
D_1^f & D_2^f & \dots & D_m^f \\
D_1^d & D_2^d & \dots & D_m^d \\
D_1'^c & D_2'^c & \dots & D_m'^c
\end{pmatrix}
$$

(We might note that the class/object distinction of the object-oriented paradigm is not easily represented in the D-matrix, which is probably best interpreted, as here, in terms of modelling class descriptions. However, as discussed further below, the whole issue of class and object can be rather confusing when studying such a method as Fusion.)

Fusion – some observations

This description of Fusion, brief as it is, should be sufficient to allow us to make a number of observations about its features as an object-oriented design method. These in turn arise from three different analyses that we can make: comparison with the practices and forms used by 'structured' design methods; comparison with HOOD as an example of a first generation object-oriented design method; and assessment against the features of the object model itself. We therefore conclude our review of Fusion by looking at each of these in turn.

A comparison with the processes used in the methods that were studied in the earlier chapters on design methods, and especially with the structured analysis and structured design method described in Chapter 13, leads to the following observations.

1. Fusion leads to the development of a much more complex four-viewpoint model at a relatively early stage in the analysis and design process. In contrast, structured methods tend to have single- or double-viewpoint models in their early stages.

2. The process throughout is much more one of refinement and elaboration (closer to that of JSD), rather than of transformation, which in turn leads into the next point.

3. The basic set of candidate objects (a major design decision) is determined right at the start of the process. A benefit of this is that the design options are thereby

constrained from an early point, while a disadvantage is that it becomes more critical to get the right model established right at the very start. While iteration between steps is always part of designing, this still faces the inexperienced designer with making key decisions at the start.

4. The characteristics described by the constructional viewpoint play a much more 'up front' role in analysis, rather than emerging at a relatively late stage in design.

If we then proceed to make a comparison with HOOD, we find that, while some of the above observations are still appropriate, the following ones are added.

■ Fusion offers a much better use of the different viewpoints across the design process (implying a more balanced basis for decision-making). Although the constructional viewpoint is still important, it plays a less dominant role than in HOOD.

■ Fusion makes more extensive use of diagrammatical notations to assist with the modelling process. Although text is still used to record many of the outcomes of design steps, it plays a much smaller role in the decision-making processes themselves.

■ The concept of inheritance is more effectively integrated into Fusion, although interestingly, it appears either very early (seeking to recognize domain-based opportunities to use inheritance), or at the end (looking for more constructionally-based opportunities to use inheritance).

■ The initial analysis processes, leading to the choice of objects, remains less well-supported by either techniques or notations.

Finally, we need to consider how well Fusion addresses the major features of the object model itself. Very briefly.

■ *Abstraction* is quite well supported, both in terms of the notations used and also the design processes. Fusion has a quite good black box to white box process model that encourages the designer to think at the appropriate levels at each step.

■ *Modularity* is similarly addressed quite effectively through the classes, and through some other aspects of these that we have not explored in this brief description. The object interaction graphs and object visibility graphs also provide support for this.

■ *Encapsulation* is likewise reasonably well encouraged within the process, and again the object visibility graphs play a role here.

■ *Hierarchy*, from the viewpoint of inheritance and uses, is supported well.

The remaining question here is how well Fusion handles the often quite difficult distinction between the class and the object during the design process. As we have already remarked, this one can pose problems for the designer if not kept clear. When considering static and abstract issues, and specifying general characteristics, then the *class* is the better abstraction to employ. However, when tackling questions about system behaviour, and about temporal and dynamic features of a system, then the *object* is probably the right abstraction to employ. Fusion, in general, does manage to keep these concepts distinct, as well as identifying where either one is the 'right' abstraction to employ.

Overall, we can conclude that Fusion, taken as an example of a second generation object-oriented design method, represents a quite substantial advance over the previous generation of methods. It is able to address the 'object' issues well, and also offers a reasonably well-defined process, supported by a set of analysis and design techniques. However, it is a requirement of Fusion that decisions about the choice of objects are made at an early stage. This is critical to the form of the eventual design and is also not particularly well supported by the process.

16.5.2 The Unified Process

The Unified Process (UP) stems from the work of the 'three amigos': Grady Booch, James Rumbaugh and Ivar Jacobson. In particular, it draws upon early work by Jacobson at Ericsson, and his later development of the *Objectory* (*Object* Fac*tory*) method. The UP also exists in various commercially extended forms, such as the Rational Unified Process (RUP), but in this section we are concerned only with the form described in the open literature.

The authoritative text on the UP is Jacobson *et al.* (1999), although there are many other texts available, two of which are referenced at the end of this chapter. In this section, the main purpose is to examine the structure of the UP and to consider how the various elements are supported by the UML (or, at least, by those elements of the UML that are of particular interest in this book).

While, like Fusion, the UP represents a merging of ideas from many sources, it differs from Fusion in two significant ways.

1. The sources for the UP have been some of the most popular of the available methods and notations, as identified in Johnson and Hardgrave (1999).

2. The resulting process structure has a much less sequential form than is employed in Fusion and the other methods that we have been examining. In many ways, the process is closer in philosophy, and sometimes in form, to that of the DSDM method described in Chapter 12.

The consequence of the first of these differences is that its associated UML has therefore been, at least in part, more familiar to users. The consequence of the second is that its structure is much less easily presented in the forms we have used so far and, equally, less easily presented in a sequential form such as a book, or part of a book. To some extent this reinforces our earlier argument that this method is at least at generation 2.5, if not a third generation of object-oriented methods.

A useful way of describing the form of the UP is as a two-dimensional grid (there are even arguments for making this three-dimensional!). This then presents textbook authors with the dilemma of deciding whether to develop their theme on a column-first or row-first or entwined basis! A grid-based overview of the UP is presented in Figure 16.15, and Figure 16.16 shows the interactions between its elements.

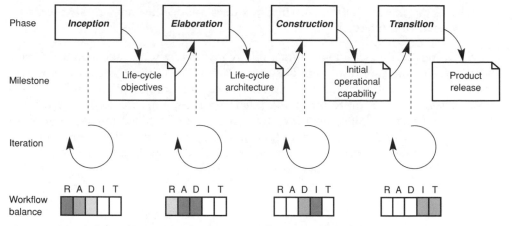

Figure 16.15 The structure of the Unified Process.

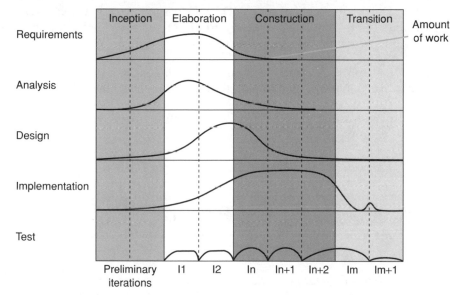

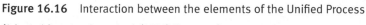

Figure 16.16 Interaction between the elements of the Unified Process

(Adapted from Jacobson *et al.* (1999) Figure 1.5)

From this we can see that the processes of the UP comprise the following.

■ Four project-based *phases* of development (Inception, Elaboration, Construction, Transition) that each complete a major milestone in a project.

■ Each phase consists of a set of one or more *iterations* or 'mini-projects'.

■ Each iteration cycle contains elements from five technically-focused *workflows* (Requirements, Analysis, Design, Implementation, Test), where the degree of effort allocated to a workflow will depend upon the phase. (In Figure 16.15 this has been indicated using shades of grey to interpret the curves of Figure 16.16 in order to indicate the degree of effort. A white box does not denote complete absence, only a low level of emphasis.)

So for this section we adopt a rather different structure to the one used to describe most of the methods in this book. First, we examine the purpose and nature of each phase, and then we look at the five workflows, keeping throughout an emphasis upon those issues most relevant to this book. (Hence, for example, we do not discuss any details about testing.) Since iterations form part of the detailed implementation of phases, and are also specific to particular projects, we do not discuss the iteration cycles either. Finally, we draw some comparisons with some of the other design methods that we have examined in this and earlier chapters.

The UP phases

The phases are very project-driven, and create a framework that emphasizes the strong user links and iterative practices that characterize the UP (both of which are rather reminiscent of DSDM although, of course, DSDM does not provide any equivalents to the workflows). The descriptions are kept fairly brief and are chiefly focused on the more technical issues rather than project-centred ones.

1. Inception This phase is primarily concerned with getting a project 'under way', and so most of its goals are related to planning activities. These include:

- establishing the feasibility of the project (possibly with the aid of one or more exploratory prototypes);

- developing a business case that relates the outcomes of the project to the organization's needs;

- eliciting the essential core functional and non-functional requirements for the system and agreeing these with the stakeholders;

- identifying the critical risk factors, and determining how these will be addressed in the project.

The milestone for this phase, *Life Cycle Objectives*, can be quantified in terms of a set of deliverables (documents, models, prototypes) that encompasses those goals, and which includes a *candidate architecture* (initial architectural design) for the system.

As shown in Figure 16.16, this phase largely employs the workflow techniques of Requirements Elicitation and Analysis (the latter largely for the purpose of establishing an initial set of use cases). The Design workflow has a relatively small, but critical, role in this phase, chiefly concerned with establishing the high-level architectural form of the system.

In terms of the models produced as part of the milestone documents, this phase should result in:

- an initial domain-based class model

- a set of domain-based use cases

- initial analysis and design models

Although iteration of the workflow tasks is implicit in the UP, this phase is one where a single cycle is normally expected to suffice.

2. Elaboration   Viewed from a design perspective, this phase is more significant. Its purpose is to create the *architectural baseline* (the top-level design) for further development. Hence its goals include the following:

- providing the architectural baseline model that describes the system from all aspects, albeit at a high level of abstraction;

- developing further use cases;

- addressing questions about quality factors, including any that describe performance requirements.

The milestone for this phase, the *Life Cycle Architecture*, is a partial working system. (The UP stresses that this is not a prototype although, as we have seen, this term is used quite loosely. The Life Cycle Architecture is not an exploratory prototype, but one could make the case that it is fairly close to being an evolutionary prototype.)

In terms of the five workflows, this phase completes any tasks concerned with requirements elicitation, performs the bulk of the analysis tasks, and undertakes substantial design work in order to progress from conceptual analysis models to physical design models. The resulting set of models will include the following:

- static domain-based class models;

- a fuller set of use cases;

- analysis models (both static and dynamic);

- static and dynamic architectural design models.

The emphasis upon model-building, and the need to ensure that these are consistent, means that some degree of iteration may well be needed during this phase.

3. Construction   Despite the name, this phase still involves some design work. (Within the model, of course, all phases tend to have some element of almost every workflow.) The milestone for this phase is one of *Initial Operational Capability*, which corresponds to the delivery of a beta version of the system. Hence its goals include:

- completion of any requirements elicitation or analysis tasks

- completion of models

and, clearly, the detailed physical design tasks are essential elements of this.

4. Transition   This phase should involve little or no design activity, unless structural problems were revealed in testing the beta version produced in the Construction phase. Its purpose is to lead to the final milestone of *Product Release*, and so the workflows involved in this phase are mainly those of Implementation and Testing.

One thing that should now be obvious is that many terms such as 'implementation' or 'construction' do get used quite differently within the context of different design methods. We noted this when looking at JSD and, in the same way, the UP implementation workflow does involve a certain amount of design activity.

For this reason, we will look at all five workflows, although not in equal detail. For each one, we will examine its main features, and then consider how it contributes to the overall task of design.

1. The requirements workflow   From the stance of a technical description, this workflow relies extensively on use case modelling (one advantage of the use case is that it can record both functional and non-functional elements). The UML use case diagram is primarily concerned with identifying the boundaries of a use case, as shown in the example of Figure 16.17. The detailed specification of a use case is not part of the UML specification, and usually designers employ some form of text-based template, although other forms can also be used to model these (Ratcliffe and Budgen, 2001). There is a good introduction to use case modelling in Arlow and Neustadt (2002) and, indeed, most books on the UML discuss this even though it is not part of the modelling notations.

One of the attractions of employing use cases is that they provide a good mechanism for verification of a design model against requirements. 'Executing' a design with a scenario from a use case provides a walk-through mechanism that forms a direct link

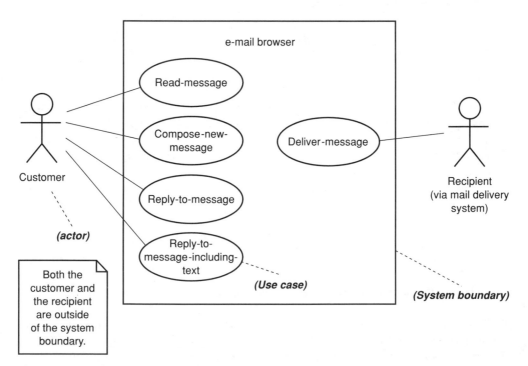

Figure 16.17   The UML use case diagram: a simple example.

between these two stages of development. Use cases also provide a framework for the analysis workflow.

2. The analysis workflow   The UP interprets analysis in the conventional black box sense of producing a model of *what* the system is to do, but not *how* it will be done. The actual UP process is conducted at a range of levels, and inevitably some of the many activities are ones that might equally well be classed as design. (We have observed before that the distinction between analysis and design is convenient, but not always clear-cut.) Indeed, this is not entirely surprising, given the phase-based nature of the UP.

The objectives of the analysis workflow are to:

- identify *analysis classes* that model elements in the problem domain;

- produce *use case realisations* that show how the analysis classes interact to create the system behaviour required for a given use case.

As always, identifying analysis classes remains a difficult problem. The UP provides a useful framework for structuring this in the shape of the use case, as each use case can be separately analysed to identify both the analysis classes and the way that they collaborate, so providing both a convenient partitioning of the analysis task and a means of cross-checking. However, the actual problem of identifying classes still remains, and relatively long-established techniques such as noun–verb analysis and CRC brainstorming (class, responsibility, collaborators) are among those suggested.

The output from this workflow can be expressed using a range of UML notations:

- static properties of the system are modelled using *class diagrams* to capture such relationships as *uses* and *inheritance*;

- dynamic properties are typically shown in terms of *collaboration diagrams* and *message sequence diagrams*.

Collaboration diagrams (an example is shown in Figure 16.18) model the structural form of interactions (describing *which* elements are involved, and *how*), rather than the *when* aspects that are captured through message sequence diagrams. Collaboration diagrams can be used to model class collaborations (the *descriptor* form) and object collaborations (the *instance* form), with each form recording slightly different capabilities.

Analysis classes and use case realizations can also be grouped as *analysis packages* (which can be represented using the UML *package* notation, as shown in Figure 16.19). A package is one of the UML 'management' elements, and can be considered as a container for the modelling elements and diagrams. Since packages can also contain other packages, the analysis model can itself be considered as a package. A key role for this notation is to help keep track of the analysis elements, and the overall analysis architecture can be considered as being defined by the high-level analysis packages.

3. The design workflow   This is a major element of both the Elaboration and Construction phases. As usual, the design workflow is intended to provide the white box

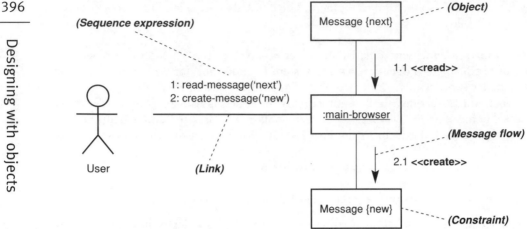

Figure 16.18 The UML collaboration diagram: a simple example (instance form).

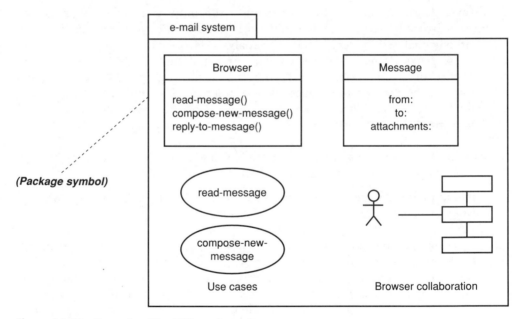

Figure 16.19 Example of the UML package diagram.

description of *how* the black box model produced from the analysis workflow is to be achieved.

While some of the tasks are familiar enough (such as how to identify design objects), other aspects are specific to the nature of the object-oriented model, and the UP, like Fusion, has to address these during the design process. One such issue is what can be considered as part of the 'mechanics' of object-orientation, namely when to create the actual executable objects from the static classes. A second, related, issue is that of the persistence or lifetime of an object, and when and how objects should be discarded. (Some of this may also be related to the form of implementation to be employed.) A third such issue is the more structural one of how to employ the inheritance mechanism, and whether reuse can play any part in this.

The UML architectural design model can be described using the package notation again, much as for the analysis architecture, with the exception that the term *subsystem* is now used in place of *package* to indicate the greater degree of detail provided.

The UP design process reasonably expects that design classes will be fairly closely based upon analysis classes (although not necessarily matched on a one-to-one basis), and also aims to provide fuller descriptions not only of the classes, but also of the interactions between them. Again, the use case provides the linking thread between analysis and design, much as it did between requirements and analysis. Also, rather as occurred when creating analysis use cases, we can expect that the use case descriptions will themselves need to be elaborated for the design steps.

The UML design workflow therefore addresses many detailed issues concerned with developing the design classes and their interfaces. Many of these reflect the design principles that have been explored throughout this book, while others are specific to the object model, or form object-oriented interpretations of more general issues. Perhaps the main change in the model, apart from elaboration of detail, is the development of the *behavioural* viewpoint (largely through the use of UML statecharts), which also assists with addressing the issues of object creation and persistence that were identified above.

As with Fusion, the white box design tasks of the UP are largely concerned with elaborating detail (and, as a corollary, ensuring consistency between the different parts of the design model), rather than with developing new interpretations. Most of the key architectural decisions are made as part of the analysis workflow although, as always, these may be subject to revision as part of the design workflow. So, viewed from the standpoint of a methodological analysis, the design workflow does not introduce many new elements into the development process. Indeed, as we observed for Fusion, object-oriented design processes do seem to require fairly key structural decisions to be made at an early stage, and the UP is no exception to this.

4. The implementation workflow   Rather conventionally, this workflow is concerned chiefly with producing executable code. As always, there is likely to be some element of design activity in doing so, since the translation from the design model to the implementational form will involve some degree of interpretation. Again too, issues such as object persistence and creation may need to be resolved within this particular implementation framework. However, the UP implementation workflow does not actively form a part of the design development process that is of particular interest to us.

5. The test workflow   Although this workflow forms a part of all but the Inception phase, it has little relevance to our theme, and hence is not discussed further here.

The UP: a comparative view

The UP design process is part of a much more complex development process structure than has been the case for the other methods that we have looked at. Indeed, the overview provided in this section has not attempted to describe the interweaving of the development phases and the workflows, so graphically described in Figure 16.16.

Similarly, because of the iterative nature of the development process, together with the distributed nature of the workflow tasks, we have not attempted to model the UP using the D-matrix form.

A key element of the UP is the role of the *use case*. While the detailed modelling of use cases themselves is not a particularly well-developed aspect of the UML, the concept itself provides a valuable framework that provides manageable-sized analysis tasks; a thread through requirements, analysis and design; and a mechanism that not only partitions the tasks of these workflows, but also gives scope for cross-checking for verification and consistency. Indeed, the matrix form of the UP would probably be impractical without the unifying theme of the use case.

When the processes of the UP are compared with those of Fusion, we can observe both similarities and also signs of greater evolution. Many of the same modelling issues are evident (class relationships, interfaces, persistence), but the UP makes much better use of diagrammatical forms of modelling, with little dependence upon textual descriptions (except for the use case descriptions, which are strictly not part of the model anyway). And, as noted in the preceding paragraph, the UP's use case mechanism is also much more fully integrated as a unifying thread.

A key question is whether so complex a process model is practical and, also, whether it can be adequately simplified and adapted for small projects. There is little to no systematic empirical evidence to offer any firm answers to these questions at the time of writing, but we should note that the form adopted for the UP draws heavily upon a relatively lengthy period of experience with the use of Jacobson's *Objectory* method and its predecessors.

Summary

This has been a long, complex and wide-ranging chapter although, even so, it has not been the only one concerned with designing for the object-oriented architectural style!

Our initial review of the 'object model' revealed the relative complexity of this, both structurally, through the interactions between its elements, and also in terms of the challenges that this complexity then poses for the software designer. Not the least of these challenges is the need to employ a diversity of viewpoint interpretations from an early stage of model development – a consequence that should perhaps not be too surprising, but which does limit the extent to which procedural design practices have been able to follow an evolutionary path and build upon the ideas of 'structured design'.

In the first edition of this book, written when object-oriented design practices were still evolving rapidly, the argument was put forward that 'since the object-oriented model potentially involves all of the four major viewpoints, and imposes no order of precedence on their use, this may effectively render it impossible to devise any design practices that use a procedural form'. This has certainly not proved to be wholly true, inasmuch as Fusion does use a procedural form; however, the matrix structure of the UP is certainly not procedural in the conventional sense.

Indeed, despite the relative simplicity and elegance of the basic ideas making up the object-oriented model, and its dominance in terms of implementation mechanisms, it continues to provide a major challenge to the designer and for the transfer of design knowledge between designers. Design patterns, frameworks and methods all have a contribution to make and, indeed, the would-be designer of object-oriented systems really requires some degree of familiarity with all three!

A question sometimes raised is whether, after three decades of object-orientation, this paradigm has really delivered what was promised? In some areas there are certainly questions that remain. Reuse has not proved to be as easily achieved as was once claimed, and some of the powerful implementation mechanisms of object-orientation, such as inheritance, have not proved easy to use well. On the other hand, there are also those domains such as the design of distributed systems, an important topic even if one not explicitly pursued in this book, where the object-oriented architectural style has found wide acceptance. The pragmatic view must be one that recognizes that, while object-orientation has not delivered all that was originally hoped for (and we might well ask what software architectures have ever done this), it is now a major implementational paradigm, and so one for which we need to be able to develop design models as effectively as possible.

Further reading

Snyder A. (1993). The essence of objects: Concepts and terms. *IEEE Software*, January, 31–42

A very well-written and carefully produced summary of both the object concept and the ideas that go with it. The author writes on behalf of a 'task force' that has tried to provide a set of terms to help with understanding of the concepts and with communication between those who may be using those concepts. The paper defines a set of terms, and provides a taxonomy for their meanings, and probably represents one of the clearest summaries of key issues available.

Booch G. (1994). *Object-Oriented Analysis and Design with Applications.* Second Edition. Benjamin-Cummings

Grady Booch is one of the most elegant and informative writers about the object concept, and this book provides an excellent introduction to these issues. Since it pre-dates the UML, the notations are now little used, but that does not detract from the fact that this book provides a very informative and useful introduction to the object model and also to many of the issues about designing with objects.

Coleman D., Arnold P, Bodoff S., Dollin C., Gilchrist H., Hayes F. and Jeremes P. (1994). *Object-Oriented Development: The Fusion Method.* Prentice Hall

A very readable text on this method, and one that introduces many of the issues through a case study approach that greatly assists with following the key points. The dominance of the UP in current literature should not be allowed to conceal the fact that methods such as Fusion are simpler in form, whilst also addressing most of the same development issues.

Arlow J. and Neustadt I. (2002). *UML and the Unified Process: Practical Object-Oriented Analysis and Design.* Addison-Wesley

This is a very clear introduction to the Unified Process which uses a workflow-first approach and gives a very clear view of the key design and analysis elements.

www.omg.org

This is the website for the *Object Management Group* (OMG), the non-commercial body that 'owns' the UML. It offers a wide set of useful links to many object topics in addition to the UML, including providing information about tools, courses and OMG standardization activities.

Exercises

16.1 In a simple banking system, one candidate for the role of an 'object' might be a customer account. Consider how each of the four major viewpoints might be used in modelling the operation of a bank account, and suggest forms that might be suitable for each viewpoint. (There is scope for using inheritance here, too, in that the bank may provide different forms of account, and although each will provide certain standard methods, the details of these might vary with the type of account involved.)

16.2 An issue records system for use in a public lending library is required (such as that modelled in Exercise 15.1 of Chapter 15). Suggest a set of suitable candidates for 'objects' in this system, and for each of these identify the major attributes and provided operations.

16.3 Consider the simple filling station that was used as an example in Chapter 14. Think how you might model the working of this in an object-oriented manner, and sketch a HOOD diagram to represent your ideas.

16.4 Apply the D-matrix notation to each of the phases of the UP, using Figure 16.16 as your outline guide to the weighting that should be placed on each of the elements. Can you identify better ways of modelling the UP process?

16.5 Compare and contrast the general set of notations used for Fusion with those of the UML that have been described in this book. Where is each of these at any form of advantage or disadvantage? (Suggestion, consider how well the processes of Fusion could be supported by the UML, and vice versa, how the UP could be supported by the Fusion notations.)

Component-Based Design

In discussing the use of objects, we noted that, despite initial hopes and promises, these did not readily deliver software *reuse* without undertaking a separate programme of effort towards this. The concept of the software *component*, as developed during the 1990s, has been very much driven by the goal of software reuse although, again, achieving any form of software 'plug and play' development has been apt to prove a more elusive goal than expected, at least for unconstrained forms of component reuse.

In this chapter we review some ideas about how the concept of a component can be interpreted in a software context. We also consider both how systems can be developed with components and how the components themselves might be developed. Finally, we examine the nature of the most constrained form of component, the *Commercial Off The Shelf* (COTS) component.

Ideas about components are as yet much less mature and less well established than those about objects. However, the study of component-based design introduces some new concepts, and reminds us of a number of issues touched on previously.

17.1 The component concept

Although the goal of reusing elements of one system in other systems has long been associated with the object-oriented paradigm, it really has a much longer history, as we observed in the previous chapter. As we also noted, actual reuse through object-orientation would appear to be quite difficult to achieve. At the 'system facilities' level there are some successful examples such as Java's *Abstract Windowing Toolkit* (AWT). For this type of example, reuse is motivated both by the need to avoid rewriting major low-level elements of software, and also by the influence of human factors, since users generally like to see a consistent presentational style for the images on a screen, regardless of the application producing them. In general though, the practical extent to which software can be reused has been limited by the factors that we discussed when looking at the use of frameworks in Section 16.3.

For other domains in which design is an important process, the idea of component reuse is fairly well established, although systematic practices to support such reuse are relatively informal. One motivation for reuse of components is that it reduces the manufacturing costs of the final product, something which of course does not have any parallel for software development and distribution. Indeed, although the concept of 'product lines' appears to have become established by the early 1900s,* the adoption of manufacturing (and hence design) reuse on a really large scale would appear to have been largely motivated by the need to increase manufacturing volume drastically during the Second World War.

Perhaps one of the most visible examples of designing around reusable components that can be encountered in the current era is that of the motor car. While a given manufacturer's models may differ substantially in appearance, many elements such as switches, instruments, starter motors etc. will be common across these.† Manufacturing and design reuse is also (if less visibly) used very successfully in such domains as electronics, as well as in the building industry (for example, through the standardization of dimensions for windows, doors, pipes), and in many other domains. The motivation may well be ease of both manufacturing and maintenance. While the former is more relevant to software, the latter may also be a significant factor when viewed across the often long lifetimes of software products, even if maintenance of these is interpreted in a rather different way.

While such reuse may often be centred upon quite small elements, larger – possibly composite – ones are reused too (car engines provide a good example). However, there are two important characteristics of such reuse that we need to note here.

- The first is that it is commonly based upon well-defined *functionality*. Most physical components have very well-defined roles (starter motor, pump, switch, etc.),

---

* One of the earliest examples of a product line is probably when Sir Marc Brunel (father of Isambard) established his block-making machinery in Portsmouth dockyard around 1806 and so introduced an important element of standardization in the fitting out of sailing ships. However, there is no evidence that this had any impact upon ship design practices! (Also see page 14.)

† The author had direct experience of this while maintaining an aging car when a penurious postgraduate student. Visits to the local scrap-yards could well find an exact match for some sought-for item such as a cylinder-head under the bonnet of a car that was very different in style and size to mine.

making it easy for the designer to identify the appropriate manufacturer's catalogues and then search them in order to view what is available to them.

- The second is that the elements themselves have well-defined *interfaces*. Indeed, an important corollary of this is that there may also be several manufacturers who are able to provide a given component ('second sourcing'). Substitution may be an exact functional and non-functional match (as tends to occur for integrated circuits), or may differ slightly in terms of non-functional characteristics, while still conforming to the specified interface.

These are not accidental properties but, rather, ones that are driven by several economic factors. These include the need to minimize the cost of manufacturing an item, pressure to maintain a marketplace position, and the user's need to protect their supply chain (here the 'user' is another manufacturer who makes use of a given component for integration into their own product). Sometimes the standards necessary to enable this emerge from marketplace factors, leading to the acceptance of one manufacturer's format as a standard for all; at other times an industry may set up a standards body to undertake the role of agreeing standards. Whatever the route leading to the standards, there is significant pressure on manufacturers to conform to them.

For the engineering designer, as mentioned above, catalogues of components are now readily available in many domains, with examples ranging across electronic and electrical, mechanical and civil engineering. However, the *ways* in which these catalogues are used during the design process appear to be a rather more elusive concept. A good example of this is given in Pugh (1991), who provides the following quotation from Cooke (1984):

> 'The designer of electronic-based products has available an enormous range of basic building blocks of high or still increasing complexity. What he often does not have is either training or well-established conceptual tools for working out levels of sophistication.'

A situation which still seems largely unchanged! Similarly, in Pahl and Beitz (1996), widely cited as a repository of engineering design knowledge, the discussion of 'design catalogues' is almost entirely confined to consideration of how such a catalogue should be *constructed*. The authors suggest that component classification should be based upon function, since the assumption is that the catalogue will be searched for components that will meet specific subfunctions of the conceptual design. Indeed, their view of component reuse is very much that this is a subsidiary element of the design process.

Turning to software, the above characteristics take very different forms (or have done so to date). Functionality is apt to be blurred, and can be extended or modified with relative ease (whereas no-one would even think of (say) modifying the design of a car's starter motor so that it can also be used to power the engine's cooling fan). It is easy to generate variants of a software unit, and hence there are few catalogues of software components, only of the end products. Interfaces are rarely standardized to any great degree and producers are much less motivated to conform to such standards as may exist. Likewise, although standards bodies may exist, they are likely to be less effective than their manufacturing counterparts. Second sourcing of components from more than one supplier in order to protect a supply chain exists only in a limited form, although the motivations for adopting this practice may not be so different.

All of this is important when we come to examine the ways in which the component concept has been mapped on to the software domain. In the rest of this section we examine how the concept has been interpreted, identify the characteristics of a software component, and consider how business models may have to be modified to cope with these characteristics. The following sections then examine more design-centred ideas about how to design with components and how to design components for reuse, as well as considering the effects of the 'proprietary factor'.

17.1.1 The software component

The *component* concept in software is broader and much less architecture-specific than that of the object (although objects can of course be components, providing that they conform to the wider definitions that we discuss below). However, on occasion it is hard not to feel that the quotation from Tim Rentsch (1982) that we used at the beginning of the previous chapter could quite easily and accurately be rephrased for components rather than objects! Indeed, Brown and Wallnau (1998) use very similar sentiments when they observe, in writing an introduction to a special section on Component Based Software Engineering (CBSE) in *IEEE Software*, that:

> 'CBSE is coherent engineering practice, but we still haven't fully identified just what it is.'

An early and concise definition from Brown and Short (1997) describes a component as:

> 'an independently deliverable set of reusable services'

(Note that there is no concept of a specific architectural style being necessary, so a component could be an object, but could equally well be a framework, a process or even an operating system.) The emphasis here is upon *reuse* (needing a clear specification of interface) and upon *independent delivery*. This second aspect is important since it implies that a component should not be aware of its context, especially in terms of any embedded dependencies or expectation of the presence of some external shared resource. Associated with this is the implication that a component needs to be integrated with other components in order to provide the overall system functionality. In other words, it is a part, rather than a whole.

In the first book to address the component theme exclusively, Szyperski (1998) defines the characteristic properties of a component as:

> 'a unit of composition with contractually specified interfaces and explicit context dependencies only. A software component can be deployed independently and is subject to third-party composition.'

This definition particularly adds the concept of *black box* reuse to the more abstract definition provided by Brown and Short. In order for a component to be reusable by third parties, it is essential that it should be completely 'plug and play' in form.

A slightly more evolved definition still is that provided in Heineman and Councill (2001), where they define a software component as:

'a software element that conforms to a component model and can be independently deployed and composed without modification according to a composition standard.'

This definition is interesting because it separates out two further supporting concepts, which are those of:

- the *component model* that incorporates 'specific interaction and composition standards'; and

- the *composition standard*, that 'defines how components can be composed to create a larger structure'.

Both of these are important concepts in terms of considering how we can design with components, and also how components themselves should be designed in order to be reusable. They also raise, indirectly, a further issue about component reuse, which is the question of architectural style, and the extent to which the process of composition may need the range of component architectural styles to be constrained to those that conform to the 'standard' being used.

None of these definitions is really contradictory in any way. Rather, they differ, if anything, in the level of abstraction used to express the ideas, and in terms of the emphasis that they place upon particular characteristics of a component. However, apart from these technical characteristics, there are also business factors that influence the component model and its acceptance (Brereton and Budgen, 2000). Indeed, a more business-centred view of CBSE is presented in Brown (2000), but for this chapter we will generally continue to focus the discussion upon those technical aspects that have implications for the CBSE design process.

17.1.2 Reusability

When looking at the preceding definitions of software components, the concept of reuse makes an explicit appearance in the definition provided by Brown and Short, and implicit appearances in the others. Strictly, of course, reuse is not an essential characteristic for a component, only a desirable one. If a large system contains one or two uniquely crafted components among a set of reused ones, then this can be considered as a quite pragmatic design decision that reduces the detailed design problem to that of designing only a few components, rather than a whole system. (We should remind ourselves too of the earlier observation that, while hardware systems are typically scaled up through the inclusion of many instances of a possibly small set of components, large-scale software systems tend to require a large number of individual component forms.)

At the start of this chapter we observed that, in the wider context, reuse of components (of any form) required:

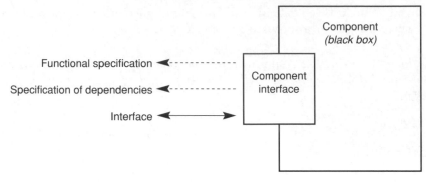

Figure 17.1 Characteristics of a software component.

- well-defined functionality
- well-defined interfaces

To this, we can now add a further characteristic for software components which is needed over and above these two. This is the characteristic of *independence*, by which a component should not have any context-specific dependencies. What dependencies do exist should also be fully specified. This set of characteristics is summarized in Figure 17.1. (We should note here that the UML component diagram is a very specific interpretation of the concept and of little use in CBSE. Indeed, perhaps because the component concept lacks an association with any one specific architectural style, there are really no diagrammatical forms that are widely used in developing CBSE systems.)

To some extent, many other forms of component do have context-specific dependencies too. For example, the starter motor for a car will require an electrical supply with a specific voltage and power rating. However, software dependencies can be much more subtle (types, ranges of value, state). There is therefore a need to ensure that a software component can be treated as a black box as far as is reasonably possible, with any such dependencies being made explicit in the interface specification. (This latter is an essential. As an example of the need for this, and of the difficulty of ensuring that it is fully achieved, see the analysis of the $500 million failure of Ariane 5 in 1996 that is provided in Jézéquel and Meyer (1997).)

Again, we are concerned here chiefly with the technical criteria that make reuse possible. The organizational issues identified in Lynex and Layzell (1998) still need to be considered if a CBSE strategy is to be used within a business. So we complete this introductory section by examining some particular aspects of the business context.

17.1.3 The business context

A component-based approach to software development clearly needs more than simply a set of technological criteria. Indeed, even more than an object-oriented approach, this needs clarification of the various roles of the different **stakeholders** involved, and to be supported by some form of **component marketplace**, whether internal to an organization or open.

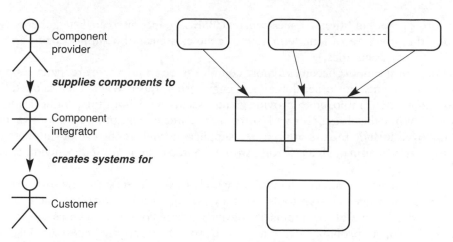

Figure 17.2 The key roles in CBSE development.

Culturally, designers in other disciplines expect to turn to specialist suppliers for those components that perform specialized functions, such as pumps, integrated circuits etc., rather than fabricate them for themselves. Since software creation, while a speciality in itself, is also independent of specialist (and possibly very expensive) manufacturing facilities, and the functional boundaries are less well-defined, the idea of the specialist component producer is not yet a fully-developed part of the software development culture, except in a few instances.

Within such a culture of greater specialism, we can identify three types of stakeholder roles, as shown in Figure 17.2, although any one person or organization may well undertake more than one of these roles. Indeed, for the reasons identified above, many often do undertake multiple roles (Brereton and Budgen, 2000). These stakeholder roles are as follows.

1. *Component providers.* Suppliers of components are needed in order to create a component marketplace. Such marketplaces do exist within large organizations, and outside of these, albeit in a more rudimentary form than in other domains (Traas and van Hillegersberg, 2000). Providers of components need to be able to index and describe their products; to meet any certification standards; and to maintain these in the sense of adapting them to new technologies and platforms as well as extending their functionality as necessary.

2. *Component integrators.* The integration role is where the major technical challenges are likely to occur and, indeed, much of the discussion of this chapter is centred around this.

3. *Customers.* The role of the customer is (as usual) one of identifying the needs and acting as the end-user. While in principle there should be no reason why customers should be concerned about, or even aware of, whether or not a product is component-based, there are some relevant business issues that are discussed below.

The customer for component-based systems may need to take account of a number of factors. Most of these are relevant to any software acquisition process, but also need to address some additional issues where CBSE is concerned. In brief, these issues include the provision of long-term support; the existence of a supply chain; and the management of upgrades.

Long-term support becomes a more complex issue where there are many suppliers of system elements. For other domains of engineering, this is where the use of 'second sourcing' is often employed to provide greater security for both the producer and the end user. While this does occur with software to some extent, other solutions that can be employed include the use of preferred suppliers as well as the use of suppliers that employ a mechanism such as *escrow*, storing source code in an independent, trusted and secure repository.

The existence of a supply chain is not wholly novel either, since few software suppliers also construct the basic tools that they use for creating software, such as compilers. (Indeed, some of the popularity of open source compilers such as gcc among system developers probably stems at least in part from an awareness of this.) The major problem that this provides for the customer is one of assigning responsibility for any problems that may arise in use. The role of the integrator, and their relationship with the customer, is likely to be a key element in this.

Lastly, the question of upgrades needs to be considered. Since individual suppliers may upgrade components independently, there are possible consequences for the management of overall system maintenance, and for the scheduling of upgrades. The distributed nature of this process may make it more difficult to manage and, while the technical responsibilities may lie chiefly with the integrator, the customer does need to be aware of this issue when planning their own risk-avoidance strategies and system upgrades.

17.2 Designing with components

Having discussed the nature of the basic design elements used in CBSE design, we now address the question of how to design systems using software components. The diverse nature of components, the variety of architectural styles used for their construction, and the relative immaturity of the concept means that no well-established practices have yet evolved. Indeed, to use the terms we introduced in the previous chapter, the development of systematic design procedures for CBSE is more likely to be a revolutionary process than one of synthesis.

However, there are a number of issues that we can consider, including possible design strategies, as well as the activities that support them. So in this section we look at these inasmuch as the limited experiences available will permit, and then briefly consider the question of how knowledge and experience of component-based design ideas might be most effectively shared and transferred.

17.2.1 Finding components

Assuming that the design task is not limited to using locally-developed components, then a key task for the designer is when and how to search for any components that they need.

Despite the existence of a fairly extensive and growing literature on CBSE, and on the subject of component characteristics, there is very little guidance available about

Horizontal integration to
provide system functionality
from a set of components

409

Designing with components

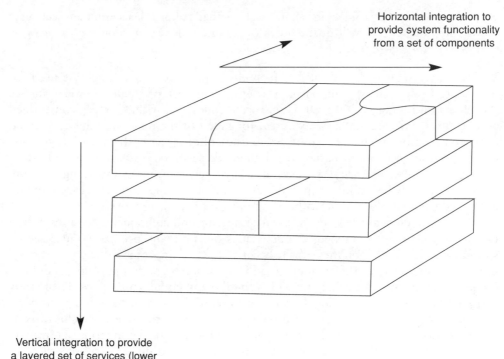

Vertical integration to provide
a layered set of services (lower
levels are likely to be monolithic
rather than component-based)

Figure 17.3 Horizontal and vertical integration of components.

how to develop a design by using components, even for a well-established architectural style (for example, JavaBeans). This is further complicated by the way that components can be used to perform *horizontal* roles in a system (distributing the overall system functionality between them) and also *vertical* roles (providing 'layers' of services through mechanisms such as CORBA or .NET). This is illustrated in Figure 17.3, and in interpreting this we should also recognize that components might be used in providing the structure for both directions, or for either one by itself. Decisions about vertical structuring choices can be thought of as forming the architectural design element, whereas the horizontal structuring can be thought of as being the detailed design element, not least because they only make sense in that order. In this chapter we are primarily concerned with how horizontal design choices are made, although we do need to recognize that these choices are made within a context which is influenced by the vertical design choices, and that it is therefore possible that the designer may need to address both forms.

When seeking components that will make up the given functionality of a system therefore, two possible strategies that might be employed within a wider component marketplace are as follows:

■ to identify the general needs of the problem, and then to search for a set of components that collectively match that functionality, finally bringing these together to form a system (we have termed this *element first*);

- to decompose the problem into fairly well-defined subproblems and then seek a set of components that will fit the needs of the individual subproblems (this can be termed *framework first*).

We have investigated the extent to which either of these two strategies is used for 'horizontal' selection of components through a number of small empirical studies (Pohthong and Budgen, 2000; 2001) that were conducted within a fairly constrained architectural style. As might be expected, for much of the time our subjects worked opportunistically, mixing the strategies as the solution evolved. However, for less experienced subjects (in the design sense), there did seem to be a fairly clear indication that pursuing an *element-first* strategy was more likely to result in a working solution. This may possibly be because identifying the available components can assist with creating a conceptual model of how the system might be made to work.

At a more tactical level, the question of how to find components requires both a means of specifying component characteristics (an on-going problem) and a search strategy that is based upon these. A fairly early study of this topic is the one described in Frakes and Pole (1994). This study used Unix processes as components (as did our own), since these provide a large set with a suitably unhelpful name-space. Their study explored the effects of searching this space using four different ways to index the components (attribute-value, enumerated, faceted and keyword). Their conclusion was that there were no significant differences between these strategies in terms of effectiveness, but that the different strategies did also tend to find different subsets of components. From this, the authors suggested that:

- a component set should be represented in as many ways as possible;
- free-text keyword searches offered the best cost–benefit since there was no need for any human indexing effort;
- none of the methods adequately supported acquiring an understanding of the components.

(To reinforce this last point, in Pohthong and Budgen (2000) we provided subjects with a range of searching mechanisms of the forms they suggested, and also observed that our subjects made extensive use of supporting documentation during the searching process.)

More recent work has focused on the idea of using *component brokers* to perform this service and to help provide a uniform 'search space' for the integrator. This separates out the question of *where* to look for components (which may be constrained by company policy or completely unconstrained) and provides a third party role that can also assist through such means as independent certification and possibly even an escrow mechanism.

17.2.2 Fitting components together

In composing a system from a set of components, the designer needs to be able to model and predict their aggregate behaviour and functionality and, in so doing, to identify the potential for the occurrence of any of the problems shown schematically in Figure 17.4. These problems can be classified as follows.

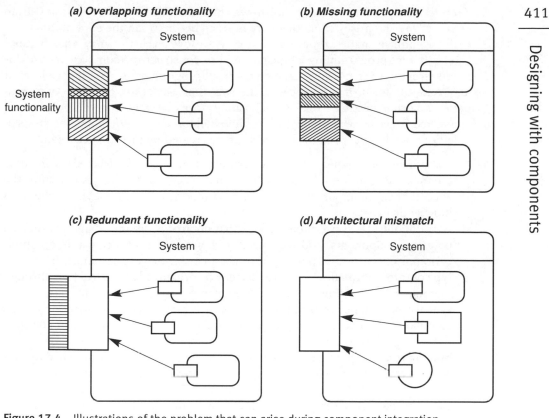

Figure 17.4 Illustrations of the problem that can arise during component integration.

1. *Overlapping functionality.* This occurs where two or more components are able to provide a particular system function. The designer's task is to determine which one should perform the task, and how to ensure that it is only performed by the chosen component. From a design point of view, it is particularly undesirable to have the same function being provided by different elements (possibly with different ranges and limits), and this also creates a problem for system maintenance and upgrading.

2. *Missing functionality.* The problem arises when the total functionality available from the system is less than that required. The solution to this is fairly simple (find another component or, possibly, create one). So the problem is chiefly a short-term one of identification.

3. *Redundant functionality.* Components may well provide services over and above those that are the basis for choosing those components. The designer's choice is then either to incorporate this added functionality (with possible adverse consequences should this lead to overlapping functionality at a higher level of integration), or to find some way to isolate and disable the unwanted functions. The latter strategy is likely to be the sounder one, but may be quite difficult to achieve.

4. *Architectural mismatch.* This problem was first identified and described in Garlan *et al.* (1995) and arises when there are mismatches between the expectations that each component makes about its context. At a low level, this may arise because (say) different programming languages used to construct the components use different structures for passing parameters on subprogram calls. At a higher level, it may take the form of differences in the way that events are handled (two components both expecting to have responsibility), or the way that components are connected in terms of topology. In Yakimovitch *et al.* (1999), examples are provided of how architectural mismatches can be created by inconsistencies in:

■ **component packaging** – where components may be constructed as *linkable* components (objects, libraries, etc.) that need to be integrated into the executable system, or as *independent* components, that may be scheduled independently;

■ **type of control** – concerning the way that control is organized and transferred between components, and whether this is managed centrally within an application or concurrently (possibly through an event-driven mechanism);

■ **type of information flow** – where this may be organized as control flow through method calls, data flow through shared memory, or in a mixed format;

■ **synchronization between components** – concerning whether or not components can 'block' the execution of other components (synchronous) or can continue to run regardless (asynchronous);

■ **binding time** – depending on the time at which components are attached to connectors, possibly during compilation, link-editing, execution, etc.

Perhaps the one significant conclusion that we can draw from all of this is that, while component-based development has potential to bring together components from a variety of sources and in a range of forms, using components with a consistent architectural style is probably the wisest strategy to adopt. This does not prevent the occurrence of the first three problems shown in Figure 17.4, but these are likely to be much more tractable than the fourth form of problem (architectural mismatch). Since architectural styles can themselves be supplemented in different ways, even this is not guaranteed by such a choice!

17.2.3 Predicting system behaviour

A system that is created by assembling a set of components can be expected to have properties that are in some way an *aggregation* of the properties of the individual elements. Sometimes the form of aggregation concerned is simply additive, as for:

■ the weight of a mechanical system, which will simply be the sum of the weights of its constituent parts;

■ the memory size required for a software system, which again will be the sum of the sizes of the individual elements (assuming no shared parts).

Unfortunately, while these are useful, the properties likely to be of principal interest to the designer are also the ones that are apt to be predicted only through the use of more complex aggregation rules. For software, we can include functionality and behaviour as examples of these, as well as any performance measures.

Once again, the use of a single architectural style for components is likely to help with this, since it does provide a single set of rules for aggregation, even if these are not necessarily simple in themselves. As a topic, this has formed one of the research themes for the Software Engineering Institute at Carnegie Mellon University in the USA, and a number of their Technical Reports address different aspects of aggregation. While it is too detailed an issue to pursue further here, the interested reader should consult the website referenced at the end of the chapter.

17.2.4 Is there a model for a component-based design process?

The immediate answer to the above question has to be 'no'. None of the forms used for transferring design knowledge that we have examined in this book have as yet been successfully adapted for component-based design. Indeed, it seems questionable whether the processes involved could ever be embodied in any form of procedural method, although there would seem to be scope for developing some form of 'agile method', along the lines described in Chapter 12. However, at the time of writing, no such method would appear to exist.

We can identify several reasons why CBSE design practices have so far largely been left uncodified. One of these is the nature of component-based design itself. The design process is strongly driven by the availability of existing components (and by any policies which define the set of acceptable components), and as such is strongly opportunistic in its form. It is also heavily influenced by the descriptions available to the designer, by past experience of use, and by feedback from prototypes. None of these maps readily on to procedural forms or even to a mechanism such as design patterns. A second possible reason is that the variety of component forms leads to a lack of consistent representations, necessary to support any systematic description of design knowledge. A third may just be sheer complexity. The design processes described in the last section of the preceding chapter may well represent the realistic limits to what can be done with procedural forms, with CBSE requiring additional support beyond what can be achieved using such forms.

Another question that this raises is whether the process of design is entirely centred upon reuse? One option for the designer of a component-based system is to design their own components where necessary. There may be good reasons to do this, especially if the required elements address specialist needs of the problem or domain, for which reusable components are unlikely to be available. However, there are some obvious pitfalls to this route, among them the risk that arises of constructing components that will complicate the maintenance process, and of misusing this option to construct components that are really little different from those already available. So, overall, while this may be possible, it does need to be justified with some care and, indeed, this is another reason why a more risk-driven approach such as that used in the DSDM method may be a useful one to adopt.

Overall though, we can conclude that, as yet, component-based design practices are neither well understood nor in a state to be able to provide any form of structured knowledge transfer.

17.3 Designing components

As might be expected, the guidelines for designing components can themselves be divided into those that deal with general properties of a component and those that are specific to the needs of a particular architectural style. In other words, there are characteristics that are common to all components, and those that are needed by a particular architectural style. In addition, the characteristics that are common to all may still need to be interpreted according to the chosen architectural style.

The general guidelines applying to component characteristics were discussed at the start of the chapter. We can summarize these as requiring that a component:

- possesses well-defined functionality;

- provides a set of well-defined interfaces;

- clearly specifies any explicit dependencies.

Achieving the first of these is very much a general design task, although the other two may be influenced by the choice of architectural style, possibly assisted or even enforced by tools such as compilers. As an example of the second, the interface form required for a JavaBean is very well defined, down to the form of identifiers to be used for the externally-visible methods. In contrast to this, although a Unix process may use the standard input and standard output mechanisms, there is no specific expectation about how this should be organized within the component itself, nor about any other dependencies that may be created.

Returning to the question of functionality, designing components for reuse does also imply that the designer should strive to make a component as general as is reasonably possible. The criteria of *coupling* and *cohesion* are probably still the most useful aids that can be used to assist with thinking about what constitutes an acceptable form and degree of generality relating to functionality. Some particularly good examples of clear-cut definitions of component functionality are found in GUI-based mechanisms such as Java's AWT.

Our conclusion must be largely the same as in the preceding section when it comes to providing any more specific guidelines. However, the concept of the design pattern is adaptable for use with architectural styles other than just that of objects, and it does have the potential to provide rather more support for designing components than is likely to be obtained from procedural forms.

In Crnkovic and Larsson (2002), which provides one of the few published case studies on component use, the authors examine the evolution of two components within the system being studied (a control system package used for industrial systems). While not specifically concerned with component development, this still looks at key component characteristics, and how they affect the two particular aspects that were studied: evolution of the components across platforms and the replacement of proprietary components with industry-standard ones. Also, although in the 'vertical' sense the two components are relatively low-level (one can be considered as middleware, while the other is a class library), the general experiences seem relevant to components as a whole.

Some of the particular issues that the case study identifies from the viewpoint of individual component design are as follows:

- the benefits of large components that are easy to reuse in preference to smaller ones that could be developed in-house;

- the high cost of maintaining backward compatibility with early installations (this arises largely because the system studied was a 'product line' rather than a single system);

- the need to separate out those features of a component that depend upon platform interactions in order to assist with ease of change (implementational differences when using different C++ compilers created some particular problems).

Overall, this case study emphasizes the need for thorough planning (including design planning) and control when developing and maintaining components. Such systems have many sources of additional costs (the authors comment on the estimate in Szyperski (1998) that developing a reusable component requires 3–4 times the resources needed for a 'non-component' implementation, but provide no estimates of additional effort required for this particular case study). In particular, not all of these additional costs are easily predicted, since they may arise partly through external factors such as platform changes that are not under the developer's control.

One aspect of component development that has not received the attention it is probably due is the *domain* aspect. A survey by Frakes and Fox (1995) observed that there were 'significant differences in the reuse of lifecycle objects between different industries' (domains), although the reasons for this were not identified. In Roschelle *et al.* (1999) a number of component developers identified the lessons learned from developing educational software components in collaboration with educators, and specifically identified the influence of the domain as an important factor in determining component granularity.

There is of course a potential tension here. The commercial supplier of components wants the largest possible marketplace for their products (unless these are produced to the end-user's specification and for their use alone). Also, the relative immaturity of CBSE means that few domains are likely to have developed widely used 'standard components'. However, it may well be that the future success of CBSE will depend upon the successful adoption of a more domain-centred approach to component development.

17.4 At the extremity – COTS

Those components generally considered as being in the form of COTS can be regarded as representing an extreme, in the sense that the end user or integrator has no control whatever over their form and properties and no knowledge about their workings. So a COTS component is one that is quite expressly black box in its nature.

(Actually, this view is itself probably something of an extreme position! As Carney and Long (2000) point out, COTS software spans something of a range of forms, and

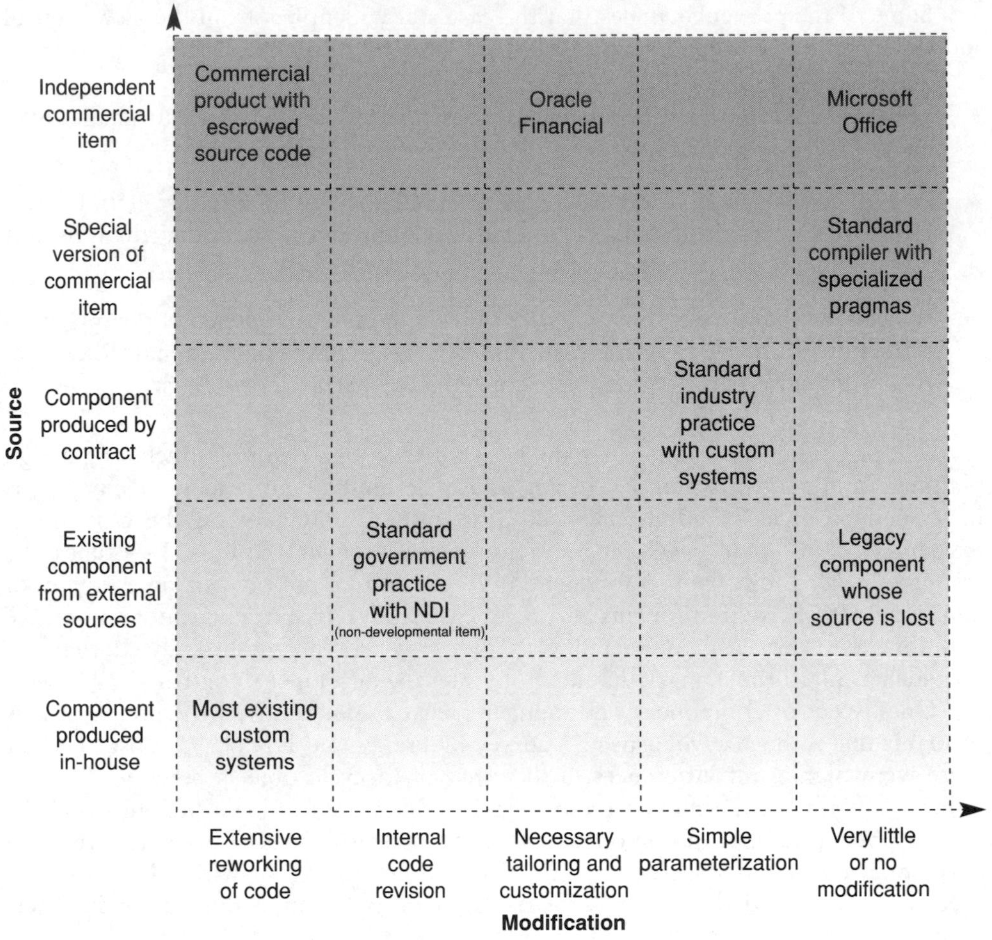

Figure 17.5 Source and modification axes for component classification.

(Taken from Carney and Long (2000) © IEEE 2000)

some of these are capable of varying degrees of parameterization, with the degree of modification possible often depending upon the financial and political 'clout' of the customer. To help resolve this, they propose the use of a 5 × 5 grid that relates the sourcing of a component to the degree of modification that can be accommodated, as shown in Figure 17.5 which also contains some examples of such components. As a result, they argue against the use of such terms as COTS, on the basis that these are too simplistic in their categorization.)

Many other authors make little distinction between using COTS components and any other forms, as, for example, in the study described in Yakimovitch *et al.* (1999). Indeed, from the viewpoint of their use in the design process this is not unreasonable, since the main characteristic that distinguishes COTS components is a business one. However, this black box property does also constrain the designer's options when seeking to integrate COTS elements in a system, especially since COTS elements may well incorporate redundant functionality and may have particular expectations about context.

One of the key factors to consider for COTS is the 'shelf-life'. The effect of commercial and business pressures makes it likely that the supplier of any COTS component will cause it to be upgraded reasonably frequently. (Obvious examples on a large scale include components such as operating systems and web browsers.) Since the development of such components is strongly market-driven, the individual end-user probably has little or no influence upon any changes that may occur between versions. If the customer's business is operating in a rapidly-changing and 'emergent' context then this may not form a particular disadvantage, and it may be more than off-set by the benefits of rapid development. In contrast, there needs to be more doubt about employing COTS where an application may need to be used over a longer period.

So far, there would appear to be relatively little published research into the use of COTS. This is perhaps not surprising, given its relative volatility, but it does mean that there are few guidelines available to the designer.

Summary

Component-based software development is still at a relatively immature stage, and hence there has so far been limited opportunity to consolidate experiences and develop recommended practices. For the designer, the problem of accumulating and codifying the experiences of CBSE design is further compounded by the multiplicity of architectural styles that can be employed. That this is a characteristic of CBSE rather than a passing state does not help!

Many of the issues in this chapter have resonances with the issues that we discussed in Chapter 12. This should not be surprising since one of the motivations for using CBSE practices is to speed up system development. Indeed, the concept of the agile method may be one of the more useful ones for the longer-term goal of providing guidance on CBSE practices.

Further reading

Garlan D., Allen R. and Ockerbloom J. (1995). Architectural mismatch: why reuse is so hard. *IEEE Software*, **12**(6), 17–26

An interesting paper that was really written primarily as a discussion of the effects of architectural style, but which *en route* identifies the importance of this for CBSE. It provides some examples of particular problems encountered in a case study.

Heineman G.T. and Councill W.T. (2001). *Component-Based Software Engineering: Putting the Pieces Together*. Addison-Wesley.

This book is really a collection of papers on components, many of which have been written to fit around the definitions provided by the principal authors and editors. Well-organized, it provides a useful baseline for learning about CBSE, even if the quality of the individual papers is rather mixed. The main shortcoming is that it is somewhat light on case studies.

www.sei.edu

The Software Engineering Institute (SEI) at Carnegie Mellon University has had a group working in the area of CBSE for some time and there are some very useful Technical Reports available from this website on various aspects of components and of COTS.

Exercises

17.1 Identify a non-software domain where components are extensively employed as a means of achieving reuse across different design solutions. What characteristics do these components have that particularly aid reuse, and how can these characteristics be interpreted in a software context?

17.2 JavaBeans are a form of software component that employs a very well-defined form of interface. Find out about this, and identify how well the JavaBean model matches the criteria that were identified as assisting with component reuse. How might this reuse be improved or extended?

17.3 Component-based systems usually use some form of 'glue' to link components together (for example, when using Unix processes as components, the glue is likely to be a shell script). Identify other forms of glue used with different forms of component, and how this varies when the components are:

(a) executing on the same machine;
(b) executing in a distributed environment.

A Formal Approach to Design

The design representations and methods that have so far been described in this book have largely been *systematic* in nature, lacking formal mathematical underpinnings (the main exception has been the Statechart). While the informal syntax and semantics of systematic forms of notation can assist the designer with exploring and developing ideas about a design, their lack of rigour can sometimes create difficulties for such tasks as those involved in verifying a design, or communicating ideas about it to the implementors.

The topic of the so-called 'formal methods' is a very large one, and can only be treated fairly briefly in this text. This chapter therefore concentrates on examining how the mathematical underpinnings provided by such techniques can help to address such problems as those described above.

18.1 The case for rigour

The role of so-called 'formal methods' in the software development process is a large topic, and one that is still developing and evolving. This chapter will chiefly be concerned with describing the forms of notation and the procedures that they employ, and with considering how their application fits within the framework for the software design process that was developed in Chapter 9. Taken together, these will allow us to make some comparisons with the properties of the systematic methods that were described in the previous chapters.

The systematic software design methods, such as those described and analysed in the preceding chapters, all make use of graphical representation forms, supported to varying degrees by structured text and free text. One problem with these notations is that they generally lack any rigorous syntactic and semantic foundations, and so it is difficult to reason about them in any 'formal' manner. In particular, to understand the meaning of any diagram we may well need to resolve ambiguities of interpretation by consulting the textual components. (This is not to say that *all* diagrams have no well-defined syntax and semantics. Jackson's Structure Diagram form has a very well-defined syntax, together with some semantic content, while the Statechart described in Chapter 7 can certainly be regarded as more rigorous, since it is based on mathematical formalisms and therefore unambiguous in nature.)

The problems caused by this lack of a firm syntax and well-defined semantics for many of the diagrammatical notations used in systematic design practices can easily be seen when we consider issues such as design verification. In many of the forms considered so far, it is virtually impossible to perform any kind of verification operation to make a comparison between the eventual design and the initial requirement. This is because the design transformations have so changed the forms of description (or their interpretation), that there is little or no scope to perform such checks in a rigorous manner, or to reason analytically about the properties of the design itself. As a result of these transformations, the design virtual machine that is used in the early stages of the design process is unlikely to be compatible with that which is used in a later stage.

Formal methods seek to overcome this problem through the use of formal specification languages, based on mathematical structures. The use of such forms permits the application of mathematical techniques in reasoning about a design and its properties. In return, there is of course a corresponding reduction in terms of the powers of abstraction that are offered by such notations when compared with the systematic forms of diagram. In seeking to remove ambiguity, the penalty incurred is to reduce abstraction and enforce a greater attention to detail than may always be desirable in terms of the needs of the design process.

The role of formal methods can therefore be summarized as being to provide mathematically based techniques that can be used for describing system properties – remembering, though, that the notations can still be diagrammatical in form, as in the example of the Statechart.

In terms of the framework for describing a 'method' used in this book, the formal methods are skewed in a very different manner to the systematic methods, in that they have:

- fairly simple process parts;
- relatively few well-established design heuristics;
- but (in compensation) very powerful representation parts.

For this reason they are often termed 'Formal Description Techniques' (or 'FDTs' for short) and, where appropriate, this term will be preferred in the descriptions of this chapter.

While FDTs can be used almost anywhere in the software development process and life-cycle, the roles for which they are best suited are:

- specifying system properties during requirements specification (black box);
- specifying the detailed form of a solution in the detailed design stages (white box).

Both of these tasks are enhanced by the FDTs' power of detailed notation. In contrast, the operations involved in making what we might term the *architectural* design decisions (concerned with such issues as the choice of modules and the division of function between them), in which the designer needs to manipulate relatively abstract concepts, are much less well suited to such forms. Figure 18.1 suggests how FDTs

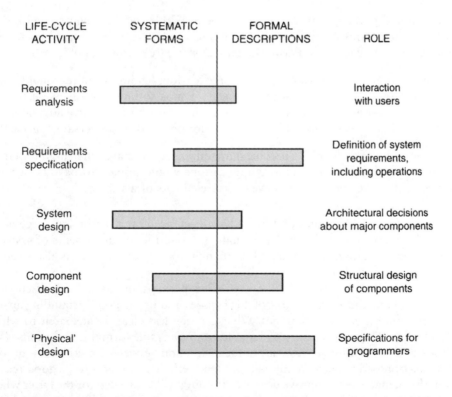

Figure 18.1 Roles of formal and systematic description techniques and notations in the software development life-cycle activities.

might be employed for the main activities of the software life-cycle introduced earlier, in Chapter 3.

Although a number of FDTs are very well developed, their industrial use has so far been limited, although it is undoubtedly growing, as is the scale of problem for which they have been used (Hall, 1990). Some of the reasons for the relatively slow adoption have been identified by authors such as Sommerville (2001) and Hall, and these include:

- The conservative approach of many project managers (like most software engineering techniques, FDTs require long-term 'up-front' investment in training and in project development time). The same problem may also affect the expectations of customers, who may have a reluctance to adopt 'unfamiliar' techniques and notations.

- The use of FDTs requires some familiarity with logic and with discrete mathematics (Gibbins, 1988).

- The existing forms are not suited for use with all problems. Such aspects as Human–Computer Interaction (HCI), some features of parallelism, the non-functional elements of real-time systems, all present difficulties for these forms of description.

- Only limited tool support has tended to be available (perhaps aggravated by the rather varied forms of mathematical symbols used, presenting difficulties for the simple word processor, and also by a lack of standardization of notation).

- There has been a degree of overselling on occasion, leading to unreasonably high expectations and subsequent disillusionment. (This is nothing new of course: the history of software engineering has many examples of genuine technical advances that have been unfairly criticized when they did not prove to be universal panaceas!)

- The limitation of scale. FDTs become more difficult to manage when used for larger problems, and the most successful applications would appear to have been those where FDTs have been used to develop key elements of a system.

Despite this, Hall (1990) notes that FDTs have been used on a reasonably large number of real projects, especially for key (usually safety-critical) components of systems. The increased trend towards making FDTs mandatory for certain tasks is also likely to increase interest in their use.

The second of the points in the above list perhaps merits a brief discussion. Without a doubt, the effective *use* of FDTs does require a good grounding in the appropriate mathematical techniques. What is much less clear is the extent to which this level of training is necessary to be able to *understand* formal descriptions. (We have previously encountered this issue of the distinction between the skill levels needed to *create* as opposed to those required to *understand*.) There seems to be good reason to think that a much less extensive degree of training will be needed for the latter where FDTs are concerned. The staff on a project who need the higher skill levels are likely to be considerably fewer than those who need only enough knowledge to understand formal specifications, and it may well be that the 'formal methods community' have unwittingly created a barrier to wider acceptance by failing to make this distinction clearer.

The more general issues involved in the use of FDTs have been well reviewed in a paper by Gerhart (1990), in which she addresses such topics as the factors affecting the wider adoption of these techniques. In particular, Gerhart points out that there are cultural differences between Europe and the USA, which can be summarized as:

■ developments in Europe have been based on exploiting the powers of formal specification, using languages such as the Vienna Development Method (VDM) and Z (pronounced 'zed') to reason about the properties and behaviour of the end-system, and making only limited use of tools;

■ in North America the focus has been much more on program-proving techniques, aimed at verifying a solution against a requirement and supported by software tools.

So while both approaches seek to use mathematical forms and techniques to specify behavioural and structural properties of a system, the two communities are working from quite different starting points.

It has been observed that a formal specification language provides the following features (Wing, 1990):

■ a notation (the 'syntactic domain');

■ a universe of objects (the 'semantic domain');

■ a rule stating which objects satisfy each specification.

The formal techniques that are in current use can also be grouped into two principal categories:

(1) The *model-based* forms, in which the specifier defines the behaviour of a system by constructing a 'model' of the system using structures such as sets, functions, tuples and sequences. Notable examples of these forms are VDM and Z.

(2) The *property-based* forms, in which the specifier defines the behaviour of a system indirectly, by stating a set of properties that it must satisfy. There are two further subcategories of these:

  (a) *Axiomatic* forms use *procedural* abstractions based on first-order predicate logic. Examples of these are OBJ, Anna and Larch.
  (b) *Algebraic* forms model *data* abstractions using axioms in the form of equations. Examples of such forms include Clear and Act One.

This division is summarized in Figure 18.2.

This general classification of form provides the basis for the structure that has been adopted for this chapter. This introduction is followed by two major sections that respectively examine the nature of the model-oriented and property-oriented forms.

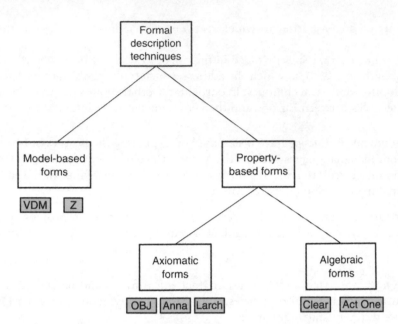

Figure 18.2 General categorization of formal methods.

Two further classifications that can be applied to FDTs, and which extend beyond these, while being related to them, are as follows:

■ *Visual languages* use graphical forms for their syntactic content. Statecharts and Petri Nets provide two examples of such forms.

■ *Executable forms* use specifications that can be 'executed' via an interpreter. The requirement that their functions must be computable restricts the scope of these to a greater degree than the non-executable forms, and their role and scope have been subjects of debate (Hayes and Jones, 1989). Examples include Prolog and PAISley (Zave, 1984).

The form and application of formal methods are very wide subjects, and it is well beyond the scope of this book to attempt to describe any of these methods in detail. One obvious question is why they have made less of an impact in the 1990s than might have been expected, given the growing level of interest through the 1980s? Some of the debates about the role of FDTs that occurred during the late 1980s are reviewed in Shapiro (1997), and further analysed in Glass (2002). Glass views this debate as partly a clash of diverse academic and industrial cultures, with the 1990s then being a period of moving from extreme positions to a shared one, on the one hand abandoning the 'silver bullet' claims, and on the other overcoming a reluctance to accept formality in software development. An example of a more balanced and less proselytizing approach is presented in *Ten Commandments of Formal Methods* (Bowen and Hinchey, 1995), which examines some of the misconceptions about the roles that FDTs can play in system development.

A slightly different, but not wholly incompatible, explanation is offered by Sommerville (2001), who argues that the key change has been that of the marketplace for software. He argues that growing demands throughout the 1990s, and continuing unabated into the 2000s, to achieve more rapid time to market, together with a willingness by users to accept software with some faults in order to obtain earlier delivery, have been generally incompatible with the use of FDTs. Indeed, for emergent organizations, the overheads implied by the use of FDTs are simply not acceptable for all but the most critical areas.

The collection of papers in Gehani and McGettrick (1986) are mostly 'classical' in nature, and provide a useful introduction to the subject of specification forms and the thinking behind them. Good reviews of strengths and weaknesses are provided in both Gibbins (1988) and Hall (1990), with the latter citing some useful examples of application. Fraser *et al.* (1994) provides one of the few papers that examines how FDTs can be incorporated into existing software development practices, and particularly addresses the problem of how to scale their use up from addressing small subproblems to meeting large-scale needs. Finally, Saiedian (1996) draws together a forum which includes some of the leading FDT researchers, as well as others, to examine why FDTs have made less progress in terms of general acceptance than might have been expected.

This chapter is concerned less with the detailed nature of the forms used in a given category of method than with the question of how to describe them within our present model of the design process. As observed earlier, formal methods generally combine very strong representation parts with quite weak process parts, with the latter usually involving some form of stepwise refinement. (The use of the term 'specification' in describing these forms places a not inappropriate emphasis on representation as against procedural content.) As such, therefore, the creative design component is apt to get pushed to a very early stage (usually the development of the basic model). Also, the roles and uses of design heuristics are harder to identify; this point will be examined a little more in each of the next two sections.

One question that is raised by the use of such forms is whether formal methods are essentially domain-specific, in that some problems lend themselves more readily to the use of this type of design model. This is a rather wide question, but it will be examined a little further when specific forms are considered.

18.2 Model-based strategies

In the previous section, model-based specification forms were described as those in which the specifier uses various mathematical forms to construct a 'model' of the system, and then uses this as the basis for reasoning about the properties and behaviour of the system. We begin a rather more detailed discussion of these design strategies by examining one of the methods using such an approach. It has features that will be readily recognizable to anyone with experience of imperative programming forms (although the analogy should be treated with due caution). It is also closer than the property-based forms to the approach used in the systematic methods described in the preceding chapters, in both its philosophy and its features; since the property-based forms concentrate more on describing the external features of a system than on the mechanisms that are used to produce these features.

A formal approach to design

18.2.1 The Z language

Most users would probably classify the Z FDT as being more of a 'language' than a method. Indeed, the process elements are probably less developed than in some comparable formalisms such as VDM. Z was created by J-R Abrial in the Programming Research Group at the University of Oxford, underwent major development through the 1980s, and became established through the 1990s. The text by Spivey (1992) is widely regarded as being the authoritative definition, but there are now many texts on Z, assuming various levels of mathematical sophistication on the part of the reader. For example, the introductory text by Currie (1999) provides a fairly gentle introduction, without getting into some of the deeper waters of Z.

Formalisms rarely constrain design strategy, and Z is no exception. Specifications can be developed on a top-down (decompositional) or bottom-up (compositional) basis, although the former is probably the easier to employ if the choice is available. The development process begins with the creation of a model of a system using discrete mathematical structures (primarily sets), together with predicate logic that is used to specify the relationships between the structures. Logic is then used to describe precisely how the model will be changed for each operation that the system can perform, expressed in terms of *what* changes should occur, rather than *how* they should come about. This process is repeated to gradually refine the specification until it reaches a level that is suitable for being interpreted through the medium of a programming language.

Such a process is fairly typical of the formal methods in general. Iteration of refinement tends to be the dominant strategy, and there is little of the interplay between viewpoints that we observed for many of the systematic design methods. Each step has the form of an elaboration step; there are no transformations in this type of method.

18.2.2 The Z formalism

Perhaps one of the greatest inconveniences of using Z is its enthusiastic use of a very wide range of (mathematical) symbols. While presenting no problem when using a whiteboard, it does tend to become something of a strain for the word processor! We should note too that while *proof* is an important element of Z, it is not an essential one, and in this section we will only discuss the role of Z for *specification*.

It is therefore useful to begin by reviewing the basic *vocabulary* of Z. There are three elements of this: sets, set operations and logic, each with their own notational features.

Sets

A *set* is a collection of elements (or set members), in which no sense of ordering of elements is involved. In Z there are some pre-defined set types such as:

$\mathbb{Z}$ – the set of all integers; and
$\mathbb{N}$ – the set of all natural numbers (positive integers and zero).

In addition, the user may specify their own set types (and, for many problems, is likely to want to do so of course). The convention is to employ all upper case italic letters for the identifier of a set type, and the elements of the set may be described using plain text, as in:

[*AIRCRAFT*] the set of all aircraft in a given airspace

or by enumerating the set elements, as in:

RUNWAY ::= *main* | *north* | *west*

where the airport has three runways, distinguished by their direction.

Variables of these types may be declared, and are given identifiers which are mainly in lower case and italics, and which begin with a lower case letter, as in:

stacked : *AIRCRAFT*
availableRunways : *RUNWAY*

which identify the variable *stacked* as being of the set type *AIRCRAFT* (clearly it may contain several aircraft that are waiting to land), and the variable *availableRunways* as likewise being a set of those runways that are currently free for use. Obviously, both can be assigned the value of the empty set (denoted by {}).

Sets may also be described using a subset formalism, as in:

gateNumbers == {1..31}

which indicates that an airport gate may have an identifier number in the series 1 to 31.

Set operations

The most obvious operation to employ with sets is that of **membership,** used to test whether or not an object is a member of a set (and therefore returning a boolean value). For example, all of the following would be true:

$3 \in \mathbb{Z}$
main $\in$ *RUNWAY*
$40 \notin$ *gateNumbers*

where $\in$ is the **set membership operator** and $\notin$ is the complementary operator that is used to test for non-membership of a set.

The number of elements in a set is termed the **cardinality** of the set, and is denoted by prefixing the set identifier with the character #, as in:

$\#RUNWAY = 3$

The operations upon sets that are used in Z are all fairly standard, and include those that are shown in Table 18.1.

Table 18.1 Set operations used in Z

Operation	Denoted by	Comment
Equality	$=$	Both sets contain the same members
Subset	$\subseteq$	One set is entirely contained within the other (its elements are all members of both sets)
Powerset	$\mathbb{P}s$	The powerset is the set of all subsets of s
Union	$\cup$	The resulting set contains all elements of the two 'input' sets
Intersection	$\cap$	The set of elements that are members of both sets
Difference	$\setminus$	The set of elements that are only members of one of the sets

Table 18.2 Logic operations used in Z

Symbol	Description
$\neg$	Not
$\wedge$	And
$\vee$	Or
$\Rightarrow$	Implies
$\leftrightarrow$	Equivalence (if and only if)
$\forall$	For all (universal quantifier)
$\exists$	There exists (existential quantifier)
$\exists_1$	There exists exactly one
$\bullet$	It is true that
$\mid$	Such that

Logic

In Z, the operations and relations in a system specification are usually expressed by using the standard operators of predicate logic. The set of symbols used for this in Z include those shown in Table 18.2.

The logical operators can then be combined with the set elements and used to describe characteristic rules affecting a set, usually in the general form of

$$declaration \mid predicate \bullet expression$$

where the

declaration introduces the variables of concern to the rule
predicate constraints their values
expression describes the resulting set of values

As an example, we might identify a subset of terminal gates that can be used for some particular operation, using the rule

$$\{\, n : gateNumber \mid n > 10 \bullet n \,\}$$

which identifies a set of gate numbers, where the values are greater than 10, but also, since it is of the set type *gateNumber*, the value must also be 31 or lower, according to our previous definition.

The role of the **schema** in Z is to describe a system operation, and this is usually drawn as an open box. A schema has three key elements:

- the schema *name*;

- the *signature* that introduces any variables and assigns them to set theoretic types;

- the *predicates* that form the *state invariants*, describing how the elements of the signature are related and constrain the operation, and that are described in terms of preconditions and postconditions.

A very basic example is shown below, based upon a simplified airline (or train, coach, etc.) reservation system.

$$
\boxed{
\begin{array}{l}
\underline{\quad ReserveSeat \quad} \\[4pt]
passengers,\ passenger': \mathbb{P}\ PERSON \\
p? : PERSON \\
\hline
\#passengers < aircraftCapacity \\
p? \notin passengers \\
passengers' = passengers \cup \{p?\} \\
\#passengers' \le aircraftCapacity
\end{array}
}
$$

Here:

- the *schema name* is *ReserveSeat*;

- the *signature* describes the 'before' and 'after' states of the set of passenger (elements in the powerset of *PERSON*), with the convention that the primed identifier denotes the state of the set after the operation;

- the *predicate* describes the invariants required to reserve a seat, which are as follows:

  - firstly the number of existing passengers should be fewer than the capacity of the aircraft (precondition 1);
  - the new passenger should not already have a reservation (and hence not a member of the initial set of passengers) (precondition 2);
  - the new passenger list will consist of the original set of elements and also the passenger added in the operation (postcondition 1);
  - the number of passengers after the operation must now be either less than the aircraft capacity or equal to it (postcondition 2).

The use of the '?' character in the identifier *p?* indicates that this is an *input* that is required for the operation. (An output identifier would end with '!' instead.)

Clearly this is not a complete specification (for example, we have not specified a value for the capacity of the aircraft, or that the passenger should have a ticket for the journey), but it should be sufficient to show the general style of a Z schema. Here our objective is to show how the state of an aircraft booking list is to be modified by the *ReserveSeat* schema. Note also that this type of specification is not an executable one that could be used as a prototype, although obviously it could be used as the basis for producing one.

The Z schema is clearly something that very much specifies individual black box operations, and as such could be used to refine both analysis and design activities. Deriving the actual operations might then involve performing an analysis of any use cases for the system, or using more 'traditional' forms of system analysis.

The schema mechanism provides scope to use other schemas in 'layers' of abstraction. Continuing with our example, we can use two schemas to describe the state of the reservation system before and after the operation. These are shown below and, again, employ the prime notation to indicate the new state.

```
┌───────── ResSyst ─────────
│ passengers : ℙ PERSON
├───────────────────────────
│ #passengers < aircraftCapacity
└───────────────────────────
```

```
┌───────── ResSyst' ─────────
│ passengers' : ℙ PERSON
├───────────────────────────
│ #passengers' ≤ aircraftCapacity
└───────────────────────────
```

which then allows us to rewrite the original schema as

```
┌───────── ReserveSeat ─────────
│ ResSyst
│ ResSyst'
│ p? : PERSON
├───────────────────────────────
│ p? ∉ passengers
│ passengers' = passengers ∪ {p?}
└───────────────────────────────
```

We can also identify 'inspection' operations that do not cause any change to the state of the system, as in the operation *PassengerCount* below, which returns the number of passengers with reservations, but makes no change to the state of the reservation list.

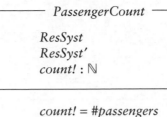

$$
\begin{array}{|l}
\hline
\quad PassengerCount \\
\hline
ResSyst \\
ResSyst' \\
count! : \mathbb{N} \\
\hline
count! = \#passengers \\
\hline
\end{array}
$$

(Here we see that *count* is an output variable by means of the '!' suffix.)

Two further conventions that we ought to note in this very brief review of the main specification features of Z are the **delta** and the **xi** (denoted by Δ and Ξ symbols). The Δ convention is used to represent a change of state, and combines the before and after states in one otherwise empty schema. For our reservation example we get:

$$
\begin{array}{|l}
\hline
\quad \Delta\ ResSyst \\
\hline
ResSyst \\
ResSyst' \\
\hline
\end{array}
$$

and we can then write the *ReserveSeat* operation in yet another (still more concise and explicit) form as:

$$
\begin{array}{|l}
\hline
\quad ReserveSeat \\
\hline
\Delta ResSyst \\
p? : PERSON \\
\hline
p? \notin passengers \\
passengers' = passengers \cup \{p?\} \\
\hline
\end{array}
$$

The Ξ operator is used where no change of state occurs, so that the *PassengerCount* operation can also be rewritten in a more concise form as:

$$
\begin{array}{|l}
\hline
\quad PassengerCount \\
\hline
\Xi ResSyst \\
count! : \mathbb{N} \\
\hline
count! = \#passengers \\
\hline
\end{array}
$$

(Implicitly adding the constraint that the number of passengers is not altered by this operation.)

One last element in a specification is to specify what the initial state of the system should be. We can describe this using the following initialization operation.

$$
\begin{array}{|l}
\hline
\quad\text{\textit{InitResSyst}} \quad\text{—}\\
\textit{ResSyst}'\\
\hline
\textit{passengers}' = \{\,\}\\
\hline
\end{array}
$$

(This should also set a value for *aircraftCapacity*, based on the type of plane allocated to the flight, but we will omit this detail here.)

The schema mechanism forms the building block for constructing more complex specifications in Z. (For example, we can create new operations by using logic to combine other operations.) So the general form of a full Z specification for a system will include at least the following elements.

1. Specifications of the given sets (types), user-defined sets, and global definitions required for the system.

2. Specification of the abstract states of the system, followed by the Δ state and Ξ state specifications.

3. Specification of the initial state, to assert that at least one state exists.

4. Specifications for all of the operations, identifying successful results and also the error cases.

Indeed, not only is this a structure that can be used for a specification, but it can also be regarded as the outline for a development process (and, of course, like any such process, will be likely to involve iteration between the steps). Again, an analysis process such as use case analysis will be needed to identify the operations.

There is much more to specifying systems with Z than has been described here. However, from these descriptions of the basic elements, we can begin to recognize the type of model that will be produced through the use of Z. This is basically a combination of the behavioural and functional viewpoints, with an element of the data modelling viewpoint included. At no point does a Z specification create a constructional viewpoint of the model (nor does any other formal method of course).

18.3 Property-based strategies

18.3.1 Overview

The model-based specification form of FDT that was described in the previous section is concerned with specifying *how* a system is to operate in terms of how the model states are changed by the operations. The property-based approach that is described in this section is more concerned with identifying the external properties of a system, and hence with codifying *what* the system is to do.

It could therefore be argued that the model-based strategy comes somewhat closer to supporting the white box-centred activities of *design*, while the property-based strategy is closer to meeting the black box needs of *requirements specification*. While this view is undoubtedly over-simplified, it does emphasize the difference between these strategies: one emphasizes how the properties of the system are changed, whereas the other focuses on its external responses. For that reason, we should not expect the property-based forms to use an explicit model of system state, such as was used in the model-based example of Z.

In this section the general characteristics of algebraic specification will be examined, as being sufficiently representative of the property-based approach for our needs.

In this context, algebraic specification can be regarded as a technique whereby an object class or type is specified in terms of the relationships between the operations defined on that type. For purposes of illustration, it is most easily demonstrated using abstract data types for the objects, but it should be recognized that the technique is not restricted to this form alone. Once again it can be seen that some elements of the general 'object model' are reflected in this form of description. Even though the concept of state might be absent, an algebraic specification is able to capture many of the external properties of an object, including the uses relationship, the inheritance hierarchy, and the provision of operations for use by other objects.

As in the previous section, most description and discussion will be centred on examining the form and properties of the representation part used for algebraic specification. Again, this emphasis is really a reflection of the major strengths of the formal techniques in this area.

18.3.2 Algebraic specification: representation part

One of the less attractive features of the formal techniques is the relative complexity of their notations! In this section a relatively simplified form will be adopted, based closely on that employed in Sommerville (2001) for the same purpose of describing the general approach used with these forms. An alternative example of a fairly simple form is used in Bradley (1989).

A term that is widely used in algebraic specification is **sort**. An entity (or object) is regarded as being an instance of a sort, and so this is a concept that is essentially related to the idea of a type or class. Strictly speaking, a sort is a set of objects, but we will not be exploring this aspect particularly closely in this section.

An algebraic specification usually consists of the following four main parts (these are shown schematically in the example of Figure 18.3).

■ *Introduction*. This specifies the entity being defined, together with its sort and the names of any other specifications that are needed for its description.

■ *Informal description*. This is an English-language description of the entity and of the operations performed upon it.

■ *Signature*. This defines the names of the operations, and provides the details of any parameters that they require.

■ *Axioms*. This part actually defines the operations and the relations that exist between them.

Each of these will now be described a little more fully, using the specification of a simple structure. This is the 'aircraft table' used in an Air Traffic Control system to

OBJECT	
Introduction	External features, details of the **uses** relations
Informal description	English text description
Signature	Operations **provided** by this object
Axioms	Definitions of the operations

Figure 18.3 Schematic of an algebraic specification.

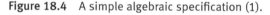

AIRCRAFT_TABLE(AIRCRAFT_DETAILS)	
Introduction	**sort** aircraft_table **imports** integer, aircraft_track, aircraft_details

Figure 18.4 A simple algebraic specification (1).

maintain a run-time record of aircraft in the airspace or on the ground. (For those who like to have a more concrete picture of the behaviour of this abstract data type, it will essentially correspond to that of a hash table.)

The introduction

The heading of the introduction identifies the 'entity' (or 'object' according to preference) that is to be described. The exact syntax for this varies according to the preferred method. Figure 18.4 shows the heading parametrized by a set of elements, where the type of the elements is specified externally. So specific a parameterization is not essential, since we are only describing the external behaviour of an object, and could use a more general parameter (such as Elem) to emphasize this. (That is, we can describe a generic form that will eventually need to be 'instantiated' for a specific type.)

The sort of the entity is also described in this introduction; in this case it is simply 'aircraft_table'.

The third part of the introduction is used to identify both the other object sorts or types that are used in the definition and the way in which they are used. Broadly speaking, there are two ways in which a specification can make use of other types/sorts.

■ *Importing* a sort and its operations brings them into the scope of the new specification, so that they can be used within it, but do not become a part of it. (This roughly corresponds to the **import** directive sometimes used in programming languages, in order to identify a **uses** relationship. In the same way that an operation

	AIRCRAFT_TABLE(AIRCRAFT_DETAILS)
Introduction	**sort** aircraft_table
	imports integer, aircraft_track, aircraft_details
Informal description	The aircraft_table is used in an Air Traffic Control system to record the details of sets of aircraft within the airspace controlled by the system. (These aircraft may be in flight or on the ground.) The size of an aircraft_table has an upper bound (discovered by operation last), and individual elements are accessed via their 'track number' (which may actually be a combination of letters and digits).
	The operation **create** takes the size of the new table as its parameter, and initializes the value of the table to *Undefined*. The operation **insert** creates a new table where the selected element has been assigned a value, and **eval** reveals the value of a specified entry in the table. The operation **remove** creates a new table where the entry for the specified element has been reassigned to a value of *Undefined*.

Figure 18.5   A simple algebraic specification (2).

in such a programming language may need to be prefixed (qualified) with the object type, so the identifier for an operation may need to be qualified with its sort, in order to make clear the particular instance of the operation that is required.) The specification of Figure 18.4 uses 'aircraft_track' (which may eventually be of type integer, but not necessarily so), and also 'aircraft_details'.

■ *Enrichment* allows a new sort to be defined that inherits the operations and axioms of another specification. (In some cases, new operations may be defined that will in effect overwrite some of these.) This concept is obviously closely related to the inheritance mechanism used in object-oriented programming.

The present example is too simple to make use of enrichment, but it does import the sort integer, since this is required in the later definitions.

The informal description

The previous section illustrated the need for, and the importance of, textual comments used to explain the mathematical formalism and to relate this to the real-world entities where appropriate. The same purpose is performed by this section of the specification in the case of the property-oriented forms. In Figure 18.5 this is added to the introduction provided in Figure 18.4.

The signature

The purpose of the signature is to define the external 'appearance' of an object, by describing its basic properties using a set of operations. These operations usually fall into two groups:

	AIRCRAFT_TABLE(AIRCRAFT_DETAILS)
Introduction	**sort** aircraft_table
	imports integer, aircraft_track, aircraft_details
Informal description	The aircraft_table is used in an Air Traffic Control system to record the details of sets of aircraft within the airspace controlled by the system. (These aircraft may be in flight or on the ground.) The size of an aircraft_table has an upper bound (discovered by operation last), and individual elements are accessed via their 'track number' (which may actually be a combination of letters and digits).
	The operation **create** takes the size of the new table as its parameter, and initializes the value of the table to *Undefined*. The operation **insert** creates a new table where the selected element has been assigned a value, and **eval** reveals the value of a specified entry in the table. The operation **remove** creates a new table where the entry for the specified element has been reassigned to a value of *Undefined*.
Signature	create(integer) --> aircraft_table insert(aircraft_table, aircraft_track, aircraft_details) --> aircraft_table remove(aircraft_table, aircraft_track) --> aircraft_table last(aircraft_table) --> integer eval(aircraft_table, aircraft_track) --> aircraft_details

Figure 18.6   A simple algebraic specification (3).

- *Constructor* operations are used to create and modify entities of the defined sort. These will typically have identifiers such as **create, update, add**.

- *Inspection* operations are used to evaluate the attributes of the entity's sort.

(In the case of our example, we now see why it was necessary to import the sort integer, since this is needed to provide an upper bound to the size of the table.)

While the constructor operations are fairly standard, regardless of the sort of the entity, the inspection operations are obviously very sort-specific. Figure 18.6 shows the example extended to include the signature. The operations **create, insert** and **remove** are obviously constructor operations, while **last** and **eval** are inspection operations.

The axioms

It is here that we get into the use of mathematical notation. Basically, this section provides the definition of the inspection operations in terms of the constructor operations. Indeed, the construction of these definitions can be regarded as the main technical problem of developing an algebraic specification, and is discussed further in the next section. Essentially, though, a set of equations is developed that gives mathematical expressions defining these relationships. These are shown for our example in Figure 18.7, which now provides a fully expanded definition for the aircraft_table, using this simplified form of algebraic notation.

	AIRCRAFT_TABLE(AIRCRAFT_DETAILS)
Introduction	**sort** aircraft_table **imports** integer, aircraft_track, aircraft_details
Informal description	The aircraft_table is used in an air traffic control system to record the details of sets of aircraft within the airspace controlled by the system. (These aircraft may be in flight or on the ground.) The size of an aircraft_table has an upper bound (discovered by operation last), and individual elements are accessed via their 'track number' (which may actually be a combination of letters and digits). The operation **create** takes the size of the new table as its parameter, and initializes the value of the table to *Undefined*. The operation **insert** creates a new table where the selected element has been assigned a value, and **eval** reveals the value of a specified entry in the table. The operation **remove** creates a new table where the entry for the specified element has been reassigned to a value of *Undefined*.
Signature	create(integer) --> aircraft_table insert(aircraft_table, aircraft track, aircraft details) --> aircraft_table remove(aircraft_table, aircraft_track) --> aircraft_table last(aircraft_table) --> integer eval(aircraft_table, aircraft_track) --> aircraft_details

Axioms	last(create(x)) = x
	last(insert(x, n, y)) = last(x)
	last(remove(x, y)) = last(x)
	eval(create(x, y), n) = undefined
	eval(insert(x, n, y), m) = **if** m > last(x) **then**
	                    undefined
	        else
	            if m = n **then** y **else** eval(x,m)
	eval(remove(x, n), m) = **if** m > last(x) **then**
	                    undefined
	        else
	            if m = n **then** undefined **else** eval(x, m)

Figure 18.7   A complete algebraic specification.

In the example of the aircraft_table, each of the inspection operations can be related to each of the constructor operations. So, for example, the inspection operation **last** is first related to the operation **create**, by stating that **last** will return a value that corresponds to the upper bound used in the **create** operation. **last** is then related to the **insert** and **remove** operations using a recursive form of definition.

The **eval** operation can also be related to each of the constructor operations. The axiom used to relate it to **create** can be interpreted as meaning: 'inspecting any element in a newly defined table will result in an undefined result'. This makes sense, since no values will have been inserted into the table at the point of its creation, and so attempting to read from it will have undefined effects.

This (and the next relation between **eval** and **insert**) should make the interpretation of these axioms somewhat clearer. The axioms define the effect of performing the operation on the object when the object is in a particular state. However, rather than using an explicit model to define the state (as would be used in Z), it is defined in terms of the constructor operations. So each axiom relates the effect of one of the inspection operations on the aircraft_table after it has been modified by a constructor operation.

The axiom used to relate **eval** and **insert** therefore first tells us that if the aircraft_track value is greater than the size of the table (however these are defined), the result will not be specified by these relationships. It then goes on to show that if a particular value of aircraft_details has been inserted for the chosen track, then the details of this will be retrieved by **eval**. Failing such a correspondence, the rule will need to be applied to another element.

The relationships between **eval** and **remove** are similar. Again, the second of these observes that if a particular aircraft_track has been deleted from the table, then attempting to read this will produce an undefined result.

Having examined, therefore, something of the general form of such a specification, we now need to consider briefly how this might be developed.

18.3.3 Algebraic specification: process part

Once again, the algebraic formal description technique really lacks any 'process part' of the form that is provided by the systematic design methods, and most of the literature is more concerned with describing the form of a specification than its derivation. As with the object-oriented strategies, the form of the specification makes it equally well suited for use with a top-down or bottom-up development strategy. Features such as the uses mechanism also aid the designer in the task of partitioning the functionality of a system.

In the absence of any overall strategic guidelines on how a system should be structured, there are various guidelines for the more detailed task of constructing the specification of an object, or a set of objects. The techniques for ensuring that the set of axioms is complete and correct are also well established, and to the practising engineer they have the particular attraction of using more familiar mathematical forms and techniques (algebra). An added useful side-effect is that the task of generating the axioms also effectively generates a set of guidelines for testing the eventual implementation (Bradley, 1989).

The strategy for developing algebraic specifications, like that used for Z specifications, readily encompasses both the top-down and bottom-up strategies. But it is probably more difficult to construct this form of specification for a very large system without very extensive experience of its use.

18.3.4 Heuristics for property-based specification

One thing that the algebraic form currently lacks is a good tutorial textbook along the lines of those now available for Z. Partly as a result of this, there are no well-documented heuristics for algebraic forms, although this is not to imply that none have been developed by the practitioners.

Summary

This chapter has only skimmed the surface of a large and technically complex topic, and one that is still an area for research. However, it should have provided sufficient detail to give the reader an appreciation of why some familiarity with the strengths and limitations of formal methods is an important part of the software designer's repertoire. There are times when a more rigorous approach to specification of behaviour, or of component structures, is needed, and it is important to appreciate that there are techniques that can provide support when this arises.

What does emerge from the material covered in this chapter is that formal descriptions can provide a very powerful aid to developing a design, especially when issues such as consistency and verification are considered. However, the *design* techniques needed for the derivation of a formal specification (as opposed to the *mathematical* techniques) are much less well developed. This leaves open the question of when to make use of these techniques and on what scale. There is relatively little documented use of formal methods for the development of very large systems and, indeed, this may not be the best way of making use of their strengths. There is evidence of increasing use for the development of high-integrity systems – or at least, of those parts of a large system that may require high integrity (including those often termed 'safety-critical'). It is here that we may well find that these techniques can make their largest contribution.

Further reading

Hall A. (1990). Seven myths of formal methods. *IEEE Software*, 7(5), 11–19

A highly-acclaimed paper written by an industrial practitioner and providing a refreshingly unbiased appraisal of what such approaches can provide, and where their limitations lie.

Bowen J.P. and Hinchey M.G. (1995). Ten commandments of formal methods. *IEEE Computer*, **28**(4), 56–63

A very practical set of guidelines for the successful use of formal methods in practical projects, distilled from observations of their use in projects.

Currie E. (1999). *The Essence of Z*. Prentice Hall

A slim and readable volume on the basics of Z, beginning with a helpful tutorial on the mathematical underpinnings. The emphasis of the book is on the use of Z for specification and modelling of systems.

Exercises

18.1 For the example of the simple reservation system used in Section 18.2.1, create specifications for the following operations:

   (a) *CancelSeat* (the opposite action to *ReserveSeat*)
   (b) *AvailableSeats* (an operation which returns the number of unreserved seats)

18.2 Write simple Z specifications that describe some of the top-level operations of a bank autoteller machine, including the operations:

(a) *RequestBalance* to enquire about the user's current bank balance

(b) *WithdrawCash* to make a cash withdrawal from the machine (note that the conditions for this to succeed are that the amount to be withdrawn is within the user's daily limit, is available in their account, and is also available as cash from the hoppers in the machine)

18.3 For the example algebraic specification provided in Figure 18.4, add an operation that updates the aircraft details for a given track, so that the signature will now include:

update (aircraft_table, aircraft_track, aircraft_details) → aircraft_table

Whither Software Design?

In drawing together the ideas of the preceding chapters, this final chapter seeks to 'stand back' a little, and to consider how software design practices might evolve in the future. We begin by considering how far the changes in the form of software that have occurred through the 1990s and 2000s, and particularly the emergence of distributed networked systems, require corresponding changes to our thinking about design. Our main conclusion is that this is probably more a matter of embracing an extended *interpretation* of system structures than one that requires radical changes. We then review the ways in which design knowledge is currently codified for use and transfer, and consider how much further present forms might be able to evolve, and where particular limitations are becoming evident. Finally, we consider the longer-term needs of the future, and try to identify how we might improve our ability to capture, share and disseminate software design knowledge.

19.1 What is software now?

When the cheap and widely available microprocessor revolution changed the face of computing in the late 1970s and early 1980s, causing many new users to begin writing their own programs, there were those who regarded the effect as being to set back the growing acceptance of software engineering ideas and well-structured development practices. It is difficult to refute this view in its entirety since, at that time, the widening of the programming community did lead to much reinvention of the wheel and to some poorly structured systems. However, from a less narrowly technical viewpoint, there were also longer-term benefits, not least because of the increasingly greater economic importance and impact of software, coupled with the growing dependence of many businesses upon the support provided by their software systems.

The same can probably be argued for the developments of the 1990s, as the availability of cheap and powerful computers, of growing communications bandwidth, the structures of the web, and scripting forms coupled to HTML have caused yet another wave of new settlers to arrive on the computing prairies! Many of them untutored, like their predecessors, they have nevertheless created new markets, new opportunities and the demand for new tools and techniques. (Oh, and some awful websites too, although not all of these can be laid at the doors of the inexperienced.)

The economic consequences of these developments are also far-reaching and continue to evolve rapidly. In particular, they have created enormous pressure upon developers to provide rapid delivery of new 'software' (in whatever form). Indeed, speed of production has been an increasingly important factor, requiring developers to adapt their practices and seek new ways of improving delivery time.

The point about form is important. Software is no longer simply code written in a language such as C, Ada or (even) Java. It is increasingly likely to involve a complex mix of forms, including HTML, XML, scripting languages such as perl, PHP and Javascript, as well as building upon quite powerful and complex infrastructures such as .NET, Enterprise JavaBeans and Websphere.

Indeed, some of us would argue that the logical longer-term outcome will be to divorce the use of software from possession and ownership, and that with continually increasing bandwidth, the task of the designer will become more one of combining different *services* to provide instantly reconfigurable responses to a user's needs (Brereton *et al.*, 1999; Bennett *et al.*, 2001). For the moment though, the designer still has to contend with the need to bring together a variety of software elements in order to meet user demand.

19.1.1 The effect upon design thinking

If we stand back a little, examine the frenetic announcements of yet more (new) software technologies, and ask ourselves what impact these have had upon design thinking, then the answer is likely to be relatively little. This is not wholly unreasonable, given that developing ideas about designing in almost any form is by its nature a process of accumulating and distilling experience. When the experiences come thick and fast, exhibit constant change, and involve new (often inexperienced) participants, then any thinking about design practices is almost bound to lag well behind.

When reading the design literature of the 1990s, one noticeable feature is the degree of emphasis upon 'conventional' programming as the means for realizing a design as a system. Although 'agile methods' were emerging during this period, in part-response to the demand for faster delivery (Boehm, 2002), much of the remaining design thinking has largely been geared to an expectation of eventual implementation via more traditional programming paradigms, at least implicitly if not explicitly.

In many ways this should not matter. In many cases, a good design should be one that can be realized using a variety of technologies. Using the UML (say) to model a solution need not assume an eventual implementation using Java or C++, but the evidence, unsystematic as it is, does suggest that this is what is often assumed and, of course, the eventual form of implementation does create some constraints for the designer, especially where issues such as optimization and reuse are concerned.

The previous 18 chapters have reviewed our knowledge and understanding of how to design software-based systems. That knowledge may be incomplete, it may sometimes be difficult to interpret or codify, it may be equally difficult to express it in a clear manner, *but* it does exist. The question for this last chapter is therefore how this knowledge can be most effectively employed and interpreted in the ever widening context of 'software'.

The further questions that this then raises are how well existing design knowledge can be employed with the new and emerging forms, how it can be most effectively represented and codified, and how it can be made accessible to others? The rest of this section briefly addresses the first of these, while the others are discussed further in the following two sections.

19.1.2 Applying design ideas

As demonstrated in Chapter 16, constructing software around a new and radically different architectural style is apt to require *revolutionary* rather than evolutionary changes to the design process in order to cope with the new features that the architectural style introduces. However, few of the developments of the 1990s and 2000s can really be considered to have led to major changes in terms of architectural style. Forms such as HTML and XML have roles that are primarily descriptive (respectively concerned with visual layout and syntactic form), while mechanisms such as CORBA and .NET are essentially object-oriented in nature. Their influence upon the design process may well be more in the nature of placing additional *constraints* upon the form of a design solution than in introducing anything that requires new procedures.

That said, one of the observations about component-based design that we made in Chapter 17 was to the effect that there were both 'horizontal' and 'vertical' strands of design choice that needed to be made for CBSE solutions. As Figure 19.1 illustrates, this can be seen as part of the transition from monolithic implementation forms to distributed ones. The vertical layer may be constrained in scope and form, *but* it is nonetheless a part of the design task to address this, although most design practices do not really achieve this particularly well. Overall though, this forms an additional (complicating) element to the design task, rather than adding something that is radically new or different.

So for many of these developments, the task of design can be addressed by using existing mechanisms such as object-oriented design methods and design patterns, as

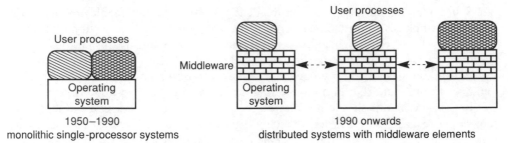

Figure 19.1 Evolution of vertical architectural elements.

well as the agile methods. Design patterns in particular do offer the ability to distil experience fairly rapidly about structures that work (it is certainly a quicker process to write a new pattern, once recognized, than to develop a new design method).

The same can be considered to apply to descriptive forms too. We have no shortage of notations that can describe the properties embodied in the basic four viewpoints (function, behaviour, data modelling and construction). What may be needed, however, is some adaptation of the *interpretation* of these forms when being used other than with procedural code. Indeed, the question of which elements of a web-based system need to be modelled is more the key issue than the choice of forms to use.

For a typical web-based client–server system, neither the server structure nor the browser form are of major interest to the application designer (although they may constrain the options of course). Instead it is 'pages, hyperlinks and dynamic content on the client and server' that need to be modelled (Conallen, 1999). Much of this can be quite adequately achieved by using and adapting existing forms.

What is less clear perhaps is how extensively such systems are developed by using any form of systematic design practice, whether methods or patterns. Indeed, the processes of design for such systems are probably very informal (and for smaller systems at least, this may well be quite adequate).

Overall, therefore, we would appear to have the means of coping with designing systems around most of the variations in the form of software, even if this may require some adaptation at times. In the next section we briefly review how well we can capture and codify design knowledge, and ask whether the existing forms and practices are likely to evolve further and, if so, by what means this might occur.

19.2 Codifying design knowledge

Since design knowledge takes many forms and can encompass many 'levels' of abstraction, the problems of codifying such knowledge are not confined to the software domain! However, as we have recognized in the early chapters, the unique characteristics of software do present the designer with additional challenges and opportunities.

In this section we begin by briefly considering knowledge about the *form* of a system, and then knowledge about the *processes* that might be used to create it.

Probably one of the most curious aspects of software design as a topic is the way that the main underpinning ideas about quality have changed so little since they were first put forward in the early 1970s. The concepts of *information hiding*, *coupling* and *cohesion* are still widely employed in the design of software, despite all the subsequent developments in the form of software itself, and in the processes involved in its development. We might also add *separation of concerns* to this list, even though one can argue that this has some overlap with coupling and cohesion, since both are concerned with how a system is to be composed from separate modules.

Maybe part of their durability as ideas lies in their very independence from the specific forms of any method or manner of implementation. All four are relatively abstract concepts, and all still elude any simple means of quantification.

At a more detailed level, the concepts of the *architectural pattern* and the *design pattern* have provided useful means of codifying experience of implementation structures that work, and which also possess characteristics that make it possible to adapt and change them as needed. There seems to be scope to widen the use of patterns to cope with emerging technologies, although the latter probably need to become more stable and established before this can occur on any useful scale (not least because the pattern development process is really one that depends upon the emergence of a community of experienced developers who are able to pool and share their experiences).

Much is still needed here, especially to support the emerging area of CBSE, for which there are few usable notations, and little in the way of well-documented experience of a type that might be reused. Perhaps the major underpinning need is to find better ways of representing architectural styles in a suitable abstract manner.

Indeed, the whole area of *notations* is one that desperately needs further study and, especially, systematic investigation of its cognitive aspects. Diagrammatical forms such as the UML are based upon a mix of experience and compromise, but the usefulness of particular forms has not been evaluated empirically, nor do many of them have solid theoretical underpinnings of any sort. As this book shows, there is an extensive range of notations (and variants) in use, yet no over-arching theoretical model that describes them, nor empirical investigations that might help us to understand when and how to use particular forms.

19.2.2 Codifying knowledge about processes

The three key elements in codifying this form of knowledge (illustrated in Figure 19.2) are:

- *architectural style* as a framework for design activities;
- *design methods* to provide procedural practices that provide a structure for the design process itself;
- *design patterns* to provide abstract templates describing 'part-solutions' that can be reused.

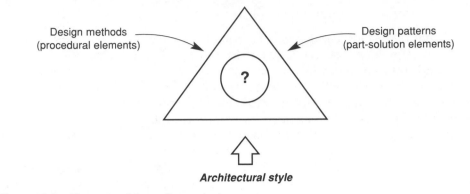

Figure 19.2 Elements of the software design process.

Strictly speaking, the notion of architectural style does not directly influence the structure of a design process. However, indirectly, the choice of style, and the options that such a choice then provides, mean that it has an important influence upon how a design is developed. Indeed, we could argue that the development of ideas about architectural style forms one of the most important contributions in the evolution of thinking about software design, and continues to have a growing influence upon this.

Design methods, in contrast, may well be a declining element of the designer's repertoire. Many methods quite strongly embody assumptions about a waterfall life-cycle of development; their procedural forms are ill-suited to accommodating reuse; and, as we saw in Chapter 16, the procedural approach is barely able to cope with complex architectural styles such as object-orientation. This is not to suggest that design methods no longer have a value to the designer, but it may well be that their role now needs to evolve, possibly to being used for well-defined parts of the overall design task. Indeed, to meet the 'strategy' needs of agile methods, we might yet see the emergence of 'micro-methods', that are intended to assist with designing particular, specialist elements of a system. (Indeed, JSP already performs such a role for the larger and more elaborate SSADM method.)

So in terms of further potential, the design pattern probably offers much greater scope for further development and evolution, including extending its scope to address forms other than the object-oriented architectural style. However, as we have already observed, the need here is to improve procedures for their use. Certainly patterns do seem to offer the best way to meet the needs of agile methods, which themselves place an emphasis upon reuse.

Forecasting future developments in technology is always a risky business. History reveals many famous examples of failure to anticipate new developments, technological steps, or uses. Certainly our present knowledge, and the mechanisms that we use to pass it on to others, could well benefit from new forms and ideas. However, we do need to avoid expectations of 'silver bullets' (Brooks, 1987). Design problems are very much *wicked* problems, and the characteristics of software (including its invisibility and complexity) further compound the problems facing the software designer.

CASE tools (Computer Assisted Software Engineering) formed one of the 'silver bullets' of the 1980s, but somehow never quite achieved the impact that was hoped for. There are probably many reasons for this, but a major one must be their relative rigidity and lack of flexibility, coupled with steep learning curves (Budgen *et al.*, 1993). Certainly, tools are useful for recording the form of a design, but of questionable use for the creative elements of its development. Even where such a tool contains analytical elements to help check a design for consistency and completeness, these can only address syntactic aspects, while the key need is for assessing a design against the requirements of the problem that it is intended to address.

CASE tools are also constrained by the notations that they use. Even if we consider our diagrams to be 'projections' from a single abstract design model, it is quite difficult to record that in a systematic and usable manner (Reeves *et al.*, 1995).

Another class of tool that may offer some real help with developing design solutions is the 'broker' that we mentioned when discussing CBSE developments. A broker can help with locating patterns, frameworks and components and has the potential to form a 'design catalogue' if provided with suitable forms of interface. Indeed, if a broker could be combined with a suitable flexible form of CASE tool of the 'traditional' type, then this might greatly extend the scope of tools in terms of being able to provide really useful support for designers.

19.3 Improving knowledge transfer

A key theme that we keep returning to throughout this book is the idea of transferring knowledge about how to design software and, indeed, all of the chapters deal with some aspect of this task. However, as befits an academic text, the focus has been largely on those practices that are in reasonably widespread use. In this final section though, we briefly consider what other techniques might have the potential to provide new ways of transferring knowledge.

We have already discussed one of the possible ways forward at the end of the preceding section, namely making fuller use of tools to assist the process. As we recognized there, while tools are limited in what they can do because of the strongly creative aspects of the design process, there may well be scope for them to do more. However, such developments may need a better understanding of notations as well as of how software design models can be described.

In terms of techniques rather than tools, one possible route is to seek ideas from other branches of computing. One of the more promising of these is that of Case-Based Reasoning (CBR), as discussed in Grupe *et al.* (1998). CBR has long been used in the artificial intelligence domain, and is part predicated upon the premise that software objects and components embody reusable experience, since a CBR system needs to be built around a variety of previously successful design solutions. However, while this may prove a valuable concept for future use (and is not wholly unrelated to the idea of a design pattern), its development needs a much richer basis of established and well-documented design examples than is currently available.

Another idea, and one that has been mentioned in an earlier chapter, is that of the *design studio* (Tomayko, 1996). This has been used successfully on a limited scale, and there is probably scope to extend and develop this approach. Its main limitations are probably the need for a supply of experienced designers, and its rather labour-intensive form.

Moving still further from technology, there is the question of how existing techniques can be deployed more widely and effectively. In the case of patterns, we have identified the *broker* concept as having the potential to improve their effectiveness. Similarly for methods, we have raised the question as to whether procedures that address part-solutions might be a useful addition.

All of these have some potential to improve our understanding of how software might be designed. However, to realize that potential, they do need to become accepted by the technical community, as well as by project managers and others. Indeed, as studies of *diffusion of innovation* across a range of domains have shown, successful acceptance is not merely a matter of technical excellence (Rogers, 1995). Indeed, technical excellence is by no means a pre-requisite for success.

According to Rogers, successful acceptance of change (diffusion of ideas) is commonly seen as a social process, possibly spread over a relatively long timescale, and characterized by its (sequential) acceptance by the following five groups.

1. *Innovators*. These are people who actively seek information about new ideas; have a wide network of contacts; and can cope with a high degree of uncertainty about the likely success of adopting a given technology.

2. *Early Adopters*. This group are often opinion leaders within their particular community and, as part of this, are expected to deliver a subjective evaluation of new ideas to others.

3. *Early Majority*. The group who adopt a new process or product just before the average, demonstrating a 'deliberate' approach to acceptance of change.

4. *Late Majority*. The members of this group tend to be cautious, and indeed their acceptance may be as much due to economic pressure to keep up as with anything else.

5. *Laggards*. This group tend to be suspicious of innovation; the members are often isolated, and hence hesitate longest to accept a change, possibly also because of limited resources.

A number of researchers have begun to examine the factors that influence such processes of diffusion within the 'software community' (Fichman and Kemerer, 1999; Pfleeger, 1999; Pfleeger and Menezes, 2000). While we do not have scope to explore their findings here, the very existence of these studies is itself significant, as it reflects a recognition that adoption of technology is not merely a technical matter, but involves a social dimension too.

Perhaps one group that really stands out as key from the above list is the *Early Adopters*. Their role in forming opinions and influencing others is key to wider acceptance (although not a guarantee of this, the processes are much too complicated for so simplistic a model).

So, in terms of the question that is implicit in the heading of this section, we need to recognize that improving knowledge transfer is more than just a matter of devising new forms. Indeed, providing evidence about what works and when it works, that will be acceptable to such groups as the early adopters, is in many ways as important as, if not more important than, polishing and refining technologies.

However, as we observed at the end of the first edition of this book, software design will remain one of the most creative and exciting forms of design activity, and the search for ways of improving our techniques will continue to be a vital part of it.

Summary

Software design knowledge remains elusive, in terms of knowledge about products, and also about the processes used to develop them. This chapter has examined some possible vehicles for improving these, and has also looked at the extent to which their acceptance is a social process.

Further reading

Rogers E.M. (1995) *Diffusion of Innovations*. 4th edn. Simon and Schuster

This book offers an insight into the social processes by which innovative ideas (usually technical, but not wholly) either succeed or fail to become established. As well as defining and analysing the categories of adopter described briefly in the last section, it provides a range of case studies drawn from a variety of domains.

Sharp H., Robinson H. and Woodman M. (2000). Software engineering: community and culture. *IEEE Software*, **17**(1), 40–47

An interesting paper in which three software engineers report on studies of the software engineering community, conducted using techniques drawn from ethnographical sociology and discursive psychology. Some characteristics of specific specialist communities are examined, with results that some may find surprising.

Bibliography

Abbott R.J. (1983). Program design by informal English descriptions. *Comm. ACM*, **26**(11), 882–894

Adelson B. and Soloway E. (1985). The role of domain experience in software design. *IEEE Trans. Software Eng.*, **SE-11**(11), 1351–60

Akin O. (1990). Necessary conditions for design expertise and creativity. *Design Studies*, **11**(2), 107–13

Alexander C., Ishikawa S., Silverstein M., Jacobson M., Fiksdahl-King I. and Angel S. (1977). *A Pattern Language*. Oxford University Press

Arlow J. and Neustadt I. (2002). *UML and the Unified Process: Practical Object-Oriented Analysis and Design*. Addison-Wesley

Avison D.E. and Fitzgerald G. (1995). *Information Systems Development: Methodologies, Techniques and Tools*, 2nd edn. McGraw-Hill

Baker F.T. (1972). Chief programmer team management of production programming. *IBM Systems J.*, **11**(1), 56–73

Barrow P.D.M. and Mayhew P.J. (2000). Investigating principles of stakeholder evaluation in a modern IS development approach. *Journal of Systems & Software*, **52**(2/3), 95–103

Batini C., Ceri S. and Navathe S.B. (1992). *Conceptual Database Design*. Benjamin/Cummings

Bennett K.H., Munro M., Gold N.E., Layzell P.J., Budgen D. and Brereton O.P. (2001). An architectural model for service-based software with ultra rapid evolution. In *Proceedings of ICSM'01*, Florence, pp. 292–300. Los Alamitos, California: IEEE Computer Society Press

Bieman J.M. and Kang B-K. (1998). Measuring design-level cohesion. *IEEE Trans. Software Eng.*, **24**(2), 111–24

Birrell N.D. and Ould M.A. (1985). *A Practical Handbook for Software Development*. Cambridge University Press

Blackburn J.D., Scudder G.D. and Van Wassenhove L.N. (1996). Improving speed and productivity of software development: A global survey of software developers. *IEEE Trans. Software Eng.*, **22**(12), 875–84

Boehm B.W. (1981). *Software Engineering Economics*. Prentice-Hall

Boehm B.W. (1988). A spiral model of software development and enhancement. *IEEE Computer*, **21**(5), 61–72

Boehm B.W. (2002). Get ready for Agile Methods, with Care. *IEEE Computer*, **35**(1), 64–9

Booch G.R. (1983). *Software Engineering with Ada*, 1st edn. Benjamin/Cummings

Booch G.R. (1986). Object-oriented development. *IEEE Trans. Software Eng.*, **SE-12**(2), 211–21

Booch G.R. (1987). *Software Engineering with Ada*, 2nd edn. Benjamin/Cummings

Booch G.R. (1991). *Object-Oriented Design with Applications*. Benjamin/Cummings

Booch G.R. (1994) *Object-Oriented Analysis and Design with Applications*, 2nd edn. Benjamin/ Cummings

Bowen J.P. and Hinchey M.G. (1995). Ten commandments of formal methods. *IEEE Computer*, **28**(4), 56–63

Bowman I.T., Holt R.C. and Brewster N.V. (1999). Linux as a case study: Its extracted software architecture. In *Proceedings 21st International Conference on Software Engineering*, Los Angeles, CA, pp. 555–63. Los Alamitos, California: IEEE Computer Society Press

Bradley I.M. (1989). Notes on algebraic specifications. *Information & Software Technology*, **31**(7), 357–65

Branscomb L.W. and Thomas J.C. (1984). Ease of use: A system design challenge. *IBM Systems J.*, **23**(3), 224–35

Brereton P., Budgen D. and Hamilton G. (1998). Hypertext: the next maintenance mountain? *IEEE Computer*, **31**(12), 49–55

Brereton P., Budgen D., Bennett K.H., Munro M., Layzell P.J., Macaulay L., Griffiths D. and Stannett C. (1999). The future of software. *Comm. ACM*, **42**(12), 78–84

Brereton P. and Budgen D. (2000). Component-based systems: a classification of issues. *IEEE Computer*, **33**(11), 54–62

Briand L.C., Wüst J., Daly J.W., and Porter D.V. (2000). Exploring the relationships between design measures and software quality in object-oriented systems. *J. Systems & Software*, **51**(3), 245–73

Brooks F.P. Jr (1975). *The Mythical Man-Month*. Addison-Wesley

Brooks F.P. Jr (1987). No silver bullet: essence and accidents of software engineering. *IEEE Computer*, **20**(4), 10–19

Brooks F.P. Jr (1988). Grasping reality through illusion – interactive graphics serving science. In *Proceedings of the ACM SIGCHI Human Factors in Computer Systems Conference*, May 1988, 1–11

Brough M. (1992). Methods for CASE: A generic framework. In *Advanced Information Systems Engineering* (Loucopoulos P., ed.), Lecture Notes in Computer Science No. 593, 524–45. Springer-Verlag

Brown A.W. and Short K. (1997). On components and objects: the foundations of component-based development. In *Proceedings of 5th International Symposium on Assessment of Software Tools and Technologies*, Pittsburgh, PA, pp. 112–21, ed. E. Nahouraii. Los Alamitos, California: IEEE Computer Society Press

Brown A.W. and Wallnau K.C. (1998). The current state of CBSE. *IEEE Software*, **15**(5), 37–46

Brown A.W. (2000) *Large-Scale Component-Based Development*. Prentice-Hall

Brown W.J., Malveau R.C., McCormick H.W. III and Mowbray T.J. (1998). *AntiPatterns: Refactoring Software, Architectures, and Projects in Crisis*. Wiley

Budgen D. (1995). 'Design models' from software design methods. *Design Studies*, **16**(3), 293–325

Budgen D. (1999). Software design methods: life belt or leg iron? *IEEE Software*, **16**(5), 133–6

Budgen D. and Friel G. (1992). Augmenting the design process: transformations from abstract design representations. In *Advanced Information Systems Engineering* (Loucopoulos P., ed.), Lecture Notes in Computer Science No. 593, 378–93. Springer-Verlag

Budgen D. and Marashi M.M. (1988). Knowledge-based techniques applied to software design assessment. *Knowledge-Based Systems*, **1**(4), 235–9

Budgen D., Marashi M. and Reeves A.C. (1993). CASE tools: masters or servants? In *Proceedings of 1993 Software Engineering Environments Conference*, University of Reading, UK, pp. 156–65. Los Alamitos, California: IEEE Computer Society Press

Buschmann F., Meunier R., Rohnert H., Sommerlad P. and Stal M. (1996). *Pattern-Oriented Software Architecture: A System of Patterns*. Wiley

Buxton J. and McDermid J. (1992). HOOD (Hierarchical Object Oriented Design). In *Software Engineering: A European Perspective* (R.H. Thayer and A.D. McGettrick, eds), IEEE Computer Society Press, 222–5

Cameron J.R. (1986). An overview of JSD. *IEEE Trans. Software Eng.*, **SE-12**(2), 222–40. Reprinted in Cameron (1988a).

Cameron J.R. (1988a). *JSP and JSD: The Jackson Approach to Software Development*, 2nd edn. IEEE Computer Society Press

Cameron J.R. (1988b). The modelling phase of JSD. *Information & Software Technology*, 30(6), 373–83. Reprinted in Cameron (1988a).

Carney D. and Long F. (2000). What do you mean by COTS? Finally a useful answer. *IEEE Software*, **17**(2), 83–6

Chen P.P. (1976). The entity-relationship model: toward a unified view of data. *ACM Trans. Database Systems*, **1**(1), 9–37

Chidamber S.R. and Kemerer C.F. (1994). A metrics suite for object-oriented design. *IEEE Trans. Software Eng.*, **20**(6), 476–93

Coleman D., Arnold P., Bodoff S., Dollin C., Gilchrist H., Hayes F. and Jeremes P. (1994). *Object-Oriented Development: The Fusion Method*. Prentice-Hall

Conallen J. (1999). Modelling web application architectures with UML. *Comm. ACM*, **42**(10), 63–70

Connor D. (1985). *Information System Specification and Design Road Map*. Prentice-Hall

Conte S.D., Dunsmore H.E. and Shen V.Y. (1986). *Software Engineering Metrics and Models*. Benjamin/Cummings

Cooke P. (1984). Electronic design warning. *Engineering Design*, **9**(6), 8

Coplien J.O. (1997). Idioms and patterns as architectural literature. *IEEE Software*, **14**(1), 36–42

Cross N. (ed) (1984). *Developments in Design Methodology*. Wiley

Crnkovic I. and Larsson M. (2002). Challenges of component-based development. *J. of Systems & Software*, **61**(3), 201–12

Currie E. (1999). *The Essence of Z*. Prentice-Hall

Curtis B. and Walz D. (1990). The psychology of programming in the large: team and organizational behaviour. In *Psychology of Programming* (Hoc J.-M., Green T.R.G., Samurçay R. and Gilmore D.J., eds), 253–70. Academic Press

Curtis B., Krasner H. and Iscoe N. (1988). A field study of the software design process for large systems. *Comm. ACM*, **31**(11), 1268–87

Cusumano M.A. and Selby R.W. (1997). How Microsoft builds software. *Comm. ACM*, **40**(6), 53–61

Davis A.M., Bersoff E.H. and Comer E.R. (1988). A strategy for comparing alternative software development life-cycle models. *IEEE Trans. Software Eng.*, **SE-14**(10), 1453–60

De Marco T. (1978). *Structured Analysis and System Specification*. Yourdon Inc.

Denning P.J., Comer D.E., Gries D., Mulder M.C., Tucker A., Turner A.J. and Young P.R. (1989). Computing as a discipline. *Comm. ACM*, **32**(1), 9–23

Détienne F. (2002). *Software Design – Cognitive Aspects*. Springer Practitioner Series

DSDM Consortium (1999). *Dynamic Systems Development Method (Version 3)* (Stapleton J., ed.). Tesseract Publishing

El Emam K., Benlarbi S., Goel N., Melo W., Lounis H. and Rai S.N. (2002). The optimal class size for Object-Oriented software. *IEEE Trans. Software Eng.*, **28**(5), 494–509

ESA (1989). *HOOD Reference Manual* Issue 3.0. European Space Agency

Fayad M.E. and Schmidt D.E. (1997). Object-oriented application frameworks. *Comm. ACM*, **40**(10), 32–8

Fenton N.E. and Pfleeger S.L. (1997). *Software Metrics: A Rigorous & Practical Approach*, 2nd edn. PWS Publishing Co

Fichman R.G. and Kemerer C.F. (1992). Object-oriented and conventional analysis and design methodologies. *IEEE Computer*, **25**(10), 22–39

Fichman R.G. and Kemerer C.F. (1997). Object technology and reuse: lessons from early adopters. *IEEE Computer*, **30**(10), 47–59

Fichman R.G. and Kemerer C.F. (1999). The illusory diffusion of innovation: an examination of assimilation gaps. *Information Systems Research*, **10**(3), 255–75

Finkelstein A., Kramer J., Nuseibeh B., Finkelstein L. and Goedicke M. (1992). Viewpoints: a framework for integrating multiple perspectives in system development. *Int. J. of Software Eng. and Knowledge Eng.*, **2**(1), 31–57

Floyd C. (1984). A systematic look at prototyping. In *Approaches to Prototyping* (Budde R., Kuhlenkamp K., Mathiassen L. and Zullighoven H., eds) 1–18. Springer-Verlag

Floyd C. (1986). A comparative evaluation of system development methods. In *Information Systems Design Methodologies: Improving the Practice* (Verrijn-Stuart A.A., Olle T.W. and Sol H.G., eds), 19–54. North-Holland

Frakes W.B. and Fox C.J. (1995). Sixteen questions about software reuse. *Comm. ACM*, **38**(6), 75–87

Frakes W.B. and Pole T.P. (1994). An empirical study of representation methods for reusable software components. *IEEE Trans. on Softw. Eng.*, **20**(8), 617–30

Fraser M.D., Kumar K. and Vaishnavi V.K. (1994). Strategies for incorporating formal specifications in software development. *Comm. ACM*, **37**(10), 74–86

Friel G. and Budgen D. (1997). Design transformation and prototyping using multiple viewpoints. *Information & Software Technology*, **39**(2), 91–105

Gamma E., Helm R., Johnson R. and Vlissides J. (1995). *Design Patterns – Elements of Reusable Object-Oriented Software*. Addison-Wesley

Gane C. and Sarsen T. (1979). *Structured Systems Analysis: Tools and Techniques*. Prentice-Hall

Garlan D., Allen R. and Ockerbloom J. (1995). Architectural mismatch: why reuse is so hard. *IEEE Software*, **12**(6), 17–26

Garlan D. and Perry D.E. (1995). Introduction to the special issue on software architecture, *IEEE Trans. on Softw. Eng.*, **21**(4), 269–74

Gehani N. and McGettrick A.D. (1986). *Software Specification Techniques*. Addison-Wesley

Gerhart S. (1990). Applications of formal methods: developing virtuoso software. *IEEE Software*, **7**(5), 7–10

Gero J.S. (1990). Design prototypes: a knowledge representation scheme for design. *AI Magazine*, **11**(4), 26–36

Gibbins P.F. (1988). What are formal methods? *Information & Software Technology*, **30**(3), 131–7

Gladden G.R. (1982). Stop the life-cycle, I want to get off. *ACM Software Engineering Notes*, **7**(2), 35–9

Glass R.L. (1999). Inspections – some surprising findings. *Comm. ACM*, **42**(4), 17–19

Glass R.L. (2002). The proof of correctness wars. *Comm. ACM*, **45**(8), 19–21

Gomaa H. (1986). Software development of real-time systems. *Comm. ACM*, **29**(7), 657–63

Gomaa H. (1989). Structuring criteria for real-time system design. In *11th International Conference on Software Engineering*, pp. 290–301. Los Alamitos, California: IEEE Computer Society

Green T.R.G. (1989). Cognitive dimensions of notations. In *People and Computers V* (Sutcliffe A. and Macaulay L., eds) 443–60. Cambridge University Press

Green T.R.G. and Petre M. (1996). Usability analysis of visual programming environments: a 'cognitive dimensions' framework. *J. Visual Languages and Computing*, **7**, 131–74

Grupe F.H., Urwiler R., Ramarapu N.K. and Owrang M. (1998). The application of case-based reasoning to the software development process. *Information & Software Technology*, **40**, 493–9

Guindon R. (1990). Designing the design process: exploiting opportunistic thoughts. *Human–Computer Interaction*, **5**, 305–44

Guindon R. and Curtis B. (1988). Control of cognitive processes during software design: What tools are needed? In *Proceedings of CHI'88*, 263–8. ACM Press

Hall N.R. and Preiser S. (1984). Combined network complexity measures. *IBM J. Research and Development*, **28**(1), 15–27

Hall A. (1990). Seven myths of formal methods. *IEEE Software*, **7**(5), 11–19

Halstead M.H. (1977). *Elements of Software Science*. North-Holland

Hardy C.J., Thompson J.B. and Edwards H.M. (1995). The use, limitations and customization of structured systems development methods in the United Kingdom. *Information & Software Technology*, **37**(9), 467–77

Harel D. (1987). Statecharts: a visual formalism for complex systems. *Science of Computer Programming*, **8**, 231–74

Harel D. (1988). On visual formalisms. *Comm. ACM*, **31**(5), 514–30

Harel D. (1992). Biting the silver bullet: toward a brighter future for system development. *IEEE Computer*, **25**(1), 8–20

Harel D., Lachover H., Naamad A., Pnueli A., Politi M., Sherman R., Shtull-Trauring A. and Trakhtenbrot M. (1990). STATEMATE: a working environment for the development of complex reactive systems. *IEEE Trans. Software Eng.*, **SE-16**(4), 403–13

Harel D. and Gery E. (1997). Executable object modeling with Statecharts. *IEEE Computer*, **30**(7), 31–42

Hatley D.J. and Pirbhai I. (1988). *Strategies for Real-Time System Specification*. Dorset House

Hayes I.J. and Jones C.B. (1989). Specifications are not (necessarily) executable. *Software Engineering J.*, **4**(6), 330–38

Heineman G.T. and Councill W.T. (2001). *Component-Based Software Engineering: Putting the Pieces Together*. Addison-Wesley

Henderson-Sellers B. and Constantine L.L. (1991). Object-oriented development and functional decomposition. *J. Object-Oriented Programming*, **3**(5), 11–17

Henderson-Sellers B. and Edwards J.M. (1990). The object-oriented systems life-cycle. *Comm. ACM*, **33**(9), 142–59

Henry S. and Kafura D. (1984). The evaluation of software systems' structure using quantitative software metrics. *Software Practice and Experience*, **14**, 561–73

Hoare C.A.R. (1978). Communicating sequential processes. *Comm. ACM*, **21**(8), 666–7

Huang R. (1998). Formalizing hierarchical object-oriented design method. *ACM Software Eng. Notes*, **23**(5), 82–8

Humphrey W.S. (1991). *Managing the Software Process*. Addison-Wesley

Iivari J. (1995). Object-orientation as structural, functional and behavioural modelling: a comparison of six methods for object-oriented analysis. *Information & Software Technology*, **37**(3), 155–63

Jackson M.A. (1975). *Principles of Program Design*. Academic Press

Jackson M.A. (1983). *System Development*. Prentice-Hall

Jacobson I., Christerson M., Jonsson P. and Overgaard G. (1992). *Object-Oriented Software Engineering: A Use Case Driven Approach*. Addison-Wesley

Jacobson I., Booch G. and Rumbaugh J. (1999). *The Unified Software Development Process*. Addison-Wesley

Jézéquel J-M. and Meyer B. (1997). Design by contract: the lessons of Ariane. *IEEE Computer*, **30**(1), 129–30

Johnson R.E. (1997). Frameworks = (Components + Patterns). *Comm. ACM*, **40**(10), 39–42

Johnson R.A. and Hardgrave W.C. (1999). Object-oriented methods: current practices and attitudes. *J. Systems & Software*, **48**(1), 5–12

Jones J.C. (1970). *Design Methods: Seeds of Human Futures*. (Revised edn 1981) Wiley-Interscience

Kitchenham B., Pickard L.M. and Linkman S.J. (1990). An evaluation of some design metrics. *Software Eng. J.*, 5(1), 50–8

Koepke D.J. (1990). The evolution of software design ideas. In 'Anecdotes' (Tomayko J.E., ed.), *Annals of the History of Computing*, 12(4), 269–76

Kruchten P.B. (1994). The 4+1 view model of architecture. *IEEE Software*, 12(6), 42–50

Lee J. (1991). Extending the Potts and Bruns model for recording design rationale. In *Proceedings of the 13th International Conference on Software Engineering*, Austin, TX, pp. 114–25. Los Alamitos, California: IEEE Computer Society

Lehman M.M., Stenning V. and Turski W.M. (1984). Another look at software design methodology. *ACM Software Engineering Notes*, 9(2), 38–53

Lehman M.M. and Ramil J.F. (2002). Software evolution and software evolution processes. *Annals of Software Engineering*, 11(1), 15–44

Lientz B.P. and Swanson E.B. (1980). *Software Maintenance Management*. Addison-Wesley

Littman D.C., Pinto J., Letovsky S. and Soloway E. (1987). Mental models and software maintenance. *J. Systems & Software*, 7, 351–5

Long J. (2001). Software reuse antipatterns. *ACM Software Engineering Notes*, 26(4), July, 68–76

Longworth G. (1992). *Introducing SSADM Version 4*. Blackwell

Lynex A. and Layzell P.J. (1998). Organisational considerations for software reuse. *Annals of Software Eng.*, 5, 105–24

Marca D.A. and McGowan C.L. (1988). *SADT: Structured Analysis and Design Technique*. McGraw-Hill

Mattsson M., Bosch J. and Fayad M.E. (1999). Framework integration: problems, causes, solutions. *Comm. ACM*, 42(10), 81–7

McCabe T.J. (1976). A complexity measure. *IEEE Trans. Software Eng.*, SE-2(4), 308–20

McCracken D.D. and Jackson M.A. (1982). Life-cycle concept considered harmful. *ACM Software Engineering Notes*, 7(2), 29–32

Mellor S.J. and Johnson R. (1997). Why explore object methods, patterns, and architectures? *IEEE Software*, 14(1), 27–30

Miller G.A. (1957). The magical number 7 plus or minus 2: some limits on our capacity for processing information. *Psychological Review*, 63, 81–97

Monroe R.T., Kompanek A., Melton R. and Garlan D. (1997). Architectural styles, design patterns, and objects. *IEEE Software*, 14(1), 43–52

Myers G.J. (1973). Characteristics of composite design, *Datamation*, 19(9), 100–102

PAC (1999). Committee of Public Accounts first report: *Improving the Delivery of Government IT Projects*. HMSO

Page-Jones M. (1988). *The Practical Guide to Structured Systems Design*, 2nd edn. Prentice-Hall

Pahl G. and Beitz W. (1996). *Engineering Design: A Systematic Approach*, 2nd edn. Springer-Verlag

Parnas D.L. (1972). On the criteria to be used in decomposing systems into modules. *Comm. ACM*, 15(12), 1053–8

Parnas D.L. (1979). Designing software for ease of extension and contraction. *IEEE Trans. Software Eng.*, SE-5(2), 128–37

Parnas D.L. (1999). ACM fellow profile. *ACM Software Eng. Notes*, 24(3), 10–14

Parnas D.L. and Clements P.C. (1986). A rational design process: how and why to fake it. *IEEE Trans. Software Eng.*, SE-12(2), 251–7

Parnas D.L. and Weiss D.M. (1987). Active design reviews: principles and practices. *J. Systems & Software*, 7, 259–65

Perry D.E. and Wolf A.L. (1992). Foundations for the study of software architecture, *ACM Software Eng. Notes*, **17**(4), 40–52

Peters L.J. and Tripp L.L. (1976). Is software design 'wicked'? *Datamation*, **22**(5), 127

Pfleeger S.L. (1999). Understanding and improving technology transfer in software engineering. *J. of Systems & Software*, **47**, 111–24

Pfleeger S.L. and Menezes W. (2000). Marketing technology to software practitioners. *IEEE Software*, **17**(1), 27–33

Pfleeger S.L. (2001). *Software Engineering Theory and Practice*, 2nd edn. Prentice-Hall

Pohthong A. and Budgen D. (2000). Accessing software component documents during design: An observational study. In *Proceedings of 7th Asia-Pacific Software Engineering Conference*, Singapore, pp. 196–203. Los Alamitos, California: IEEE Computer Society Press

Pohthong A. and Budgen D. (2001). Reuse strategies in software development: an empirical study. *Information & Software Technology*, **43**(9), 561–75

Potts C. (1989). A generic model for representing design methods. In *Proceedings of the 11th International Conference on Software Engineering*, Pittsburgh, PA, pp. 217–26. Los Alamitos, California: IEEE Computer Society Press

Potts C. and Bruns G. (1988). Recording the reasons for design decisions. In *Proceedings of the 10th International Conference on Software Engineering*, Singapore, pp. 418–27. Los Alamitos, California: IEEE Computer Society Press

Prechelt L., Unger B., Tichy W.F., Brössler P. and Votta L.G. (2001). A controlled experiment in maintenance comparing design patterns to simpler solutions. *IEEE Trans. on Softw. Eng.*, **27**(12), 1134–44

Preece J., Roger Y. and Sharp H. (2002). *Interaction Design: beyond human–computer interaction*. Wiley

Pressman R.S. (2000). *Software Engineering: A Practitioner's Approach*, 5th edn. McGraw-Hill

Pugh S. (1991). *Total Design: Integrated Methods for Successful Product Engineering*. Addison-Wesley

Rajlich V.T. and Bennett K.H. (2000). A staged model for the software life cycle. *IEEE Computer*, **33**(7), 66–71

Ratcliffe M. and Budgen D. (2001). The application of use case definitions in system design specification. *Information & Software Technology*, **43**(6), 365–86

Reeves A.C., Marashi M. and Budgen D. (1995). A software design framework or how to support *real* designers. *Software Eng. J.*, **10**(4), 141–55

Rentsch T. (1982). Object oriented programming. *ACM Sigplan*, **17**(9), 51–7

Rising L.S. and Callis F.W. (1994). An information-hiding metric. *J. Systems & Software*, **26**(3), 211–20

Rittel H.J. and Webber M.M. (1984). Planning problems are wicked problems. In *Developments in Design Methodology* (Cross N., ed.), 135–44. Wiley

Robinson P.J. (1992). *Hierarchical Object-Oriented Design*. Prentice-Hall

Rogers E.M. (1995). *Diffusion of Innovations*, 4th edn. Simon and Schuster.

Rolt L.T.C. (1970). *Isambard Kingdom Brunel*. Penguin Books

Roschelle J., DiGiano C., Koutlis M., Repenning A., Phillips J., Jackiw N. and Suthers D. (1999). Developing educational software components. *IEEE Computer*, **32**(9), 50–58

Royce W.W. (1970). Managing the development of large software systems: concepts and techniques. In *Proc. Wescon*. (Also available in *Proceedings of ICSE 9*. Los Alamitos, California: IEEE Computer Society Press.)

Rumbaugh J., Jacobson I. and Booch G. (1999). *The Unified Modeling Language Reference Manual*. Addison-Wesley

Saiedian H. (1996). An invitation to formal methods. *IEEE Computer*, **29**(4), 16–30

Sanden B. (1985). Systems programming with JSP: example – a VDU controller. *Comm. ACM*, **28**(10), 1059–67

Shapiro S. (1997). Splitting the difference: the historical necessity of synthesis in Software Engineering. *IEEE Annals of the History of Computing*, **19**(1), January–March, 20–54

Sharp H., Robinson H. and Woodman M. (2000). Software engineering: community and culture. *IEEE Software*, **17**(1), 40–47

Shaw M. and Clements P. (1997). A field guide to boxology: preliminary classification of architectural styles for software systems. *Proceedings COMPSAC'97, 21st International Computer Software and Applications Conference*, August 1997, Washington, DC, pp. 6–13. Los Alamitos, California: IEEE Computer Society Press

Shaw M. and Garlan D. (1996). *Software Architecture: Perspectives on an Emerging Discipline*. Prentice-Hall

Sheetz S.D. and Tegarden D.P. (1996). Perceptual complexity of object oriented systems: a student view. *Object Oriented Systems*, **3**(4), 165–95

Shepperd M. and Ince D. (1993). *Derivation and Validation of Software Metrics*. Clarendon Press

Simon H.A. (1984). The structure of ill-structured problems. In *Developments in Design Methodology* (Cross N., ed.), 145–66. Wiley

Simpson H.R. and Jackson K. (1979). Process synchronisation in MASCOT. *Computer J.*, **22**(4), 332–45

Snyder A. (1993). The essence of objects: concepts and terms. *IEEE Software*, **11**(1), 31–42

Sommerville I. (2001). *Software Engineering*, 6th edn. Addison-Wesley

Spivey M.J. (1992). *The Z Notation: A Reference Manual*, 2nd edn. Prentice-Hall

Stevens P. and Pooley R. (2000). *Using UML: Software Engineering with Objects and Components*. Addison-Wesley

Stevens W.P. (1991). *Software Design: Concepts and Methods*. Prentice-Hall

Stevens W.P., Myers G.J. and Constantine L.L. (1974). Structured design. *IBM Systems J.*, **13**, 115–39

Sutcliffe A. (1988). *Jackson System Development*. Prentice-Hall

Swartz A. J. (1996). Airport 95: Automated baggage system? *ACM Software Engineering Notes*, **21**(2), 79–83

Szyperski C. (1998). *Component Software: Beyond Object-Oriented Programming*. Addison-Wesley

Taivalsaari A. (1993). On the notion of object. *J. Systems & Software*, **21**(1), 3–16

Tomayko J.E. (1996). Carnegie Mellon's Software Development Studio: A Five Year Retrospective. In *Proceedings 9th Conference on Software Engineering Education*, Daytona, FL, 119–29. Los Alamitos, California: IEEE Computer Society Press.

Traas V. and van Hillegersberg J. (2000). The software component market on the internet: Current status and conditions for growth. *ACM Softw. Eng. Notes*, **25**(1), 114–17

Troy D.A. and Zweben S.H. (1981). Measuring the quality of structured designs. *J. Systems and Software*, **2**, 113–20

Truex D., Baskerville R. and Klein H. (1999). Growing systems in emergent organisations. *Comm. ACM*, **42**(8), 117–23

Van Vliet H. (2000) *Software Engineering Principles and Practice*, 2nd edn. Wiley

Vessey I. and Conger S.A. (1994). Requirements specification: learning object, process and data methodologies. *Comm. ACM*, **37**(5), 102–13

Visser W. (1987). Strategies in programming programmable controllers: a field study on a professional programmer. In *Empirical Studies of Programmers: Second Workshop* (Olsen G.M., Sheppard S. and Soloway E., eds.), 217–30. Ablex

Visser W. and Hoc J.-M. (1990). Expert software design strategies. In *Psychology of Programming* (Hoc J.-M., Green T.R.G., Samurçay R. and Gilmore D.J., eds), 235–49. Academic Press

Ward P.T. (1986). The transformation schema: an extension of the data-flow diagram to represent control and timing. *IEEE Trans. Software Eng.*, **SE-12**(2), 198–210

Ward P.T. and Mellor S.J. (1985). *Structured Development for Real-Time Systems*, Vols 1–3. Yourdon Press

Warnier J.D. (1980). *Logical Construction of Programs*. Van Nostrand

Webster D.E. (1988). Mapping the design information representation terrain. *IEEE Computer*, 21(12), 8–23

Weinberg G.M. (1971). *The Psychology of Computer Programming*. Van Nostrand Reinhold

Weinberg G.M. and Freedman D.P. (1984). Reviews, walkthroughs and inspections. *IEEE Trans. Software Eng.*, **SE-10**(1), 68–72

Wieringa R. (1998). A survey of structured and object-oriented software specification methods and techniques. *ACM Computing Surveys*, 30(4), 459–527

Wing J.M. (1990), A specifier's introduction to formal methods. *IEEE Computer*, 23(9), 8–24

Wirth N. (1971). Program development by stepwise refinement. *Comm. ACM*, 14(4), 221–7

Wood M., Daly J., Miller J. and Roper M. (1999). Multi-method research: an empirical investigation of object-oriented technology. *J. of Systems & Software*, 48, 13–26

Wu M.-W. and Lin Y.-D. (2001). Open source software development: an overview. *IEEE Computer*, 34(6), 33–8

Yakimovitch D., Bieman J.M. and Basili V.R. (1999). Software architecture classification for estimating the cost of COTS integration. In *Proceedings of 21st International Conference on Software Engineering*, Los Angeles, CA, pp. 296–302. Los Alamitos, California: IEEE Computer Society Press

Yourdon E. (1979). *Structured Walkthroughs*. Yourdon Press

Yourdon E. and Constantine L.L. (1979). *Structured Design*. Prentice-Hall

Yourdon E. (1989). Object-oriented observations. *Am. Programmer*, 2(7/8), 3–7

Zahniser R.A. (1988). The perils of top-down design. *ACM Software Engineering Notes*, 13(2), April, 22–4

Zave P. (1984). The operational versus the conventional approach to software development. *Comm. ACM*, 27(2), 104–18

Zheng M., Zhang J. and Wang Y. (1998). Integrating a formal specification notation with HOOD. *ACM Software Eng. Notes*, 23(5), 57–61

Index